## THE CLASSICS OF GOLF

original edition

# THE GREAT WOMEN GOLFERS

compiled and edited
by

## Robert S. Macdonald

and

## Herbert Warren Wind

Foreword by Herbert Warren Wind
Afterword by Peggy Kirk Bell

# Acknowledgements

*Our special thanks to Marlene Korim of* Sports Illustrated *and to Robert Sommers, Karen Bednarski, Nancy Stulak, and Rand Jarris of the United States Golf Association. Our thanks to Rhonda Glenn, who showed the way with her superior "The Illustrated History of Women's Golf",* Golf Digest, Golf *magazine,* The New York Times, Golf for Women, The New Yorker, Golf week, *Scribner's Publishing, and many other publications. And what would a researcher do without the New York Public Library?*

*Undoubtedly, we have failed to track down every permission. If any reader finds an error or an omission, please write The Classics of Golf, 67 Irving Place, ninth floor, New York, New York 10003.*

Robert S. Macdonald

# Foreword

*In 1983, when The Classics of Golf brought out its first book—Bobby Jones's "Down the Fairway", which originally appeared in 1927—the goal that Robert Macdonald, the publisher, and I, the editor, set for ourselves was to make available first-class new editions of some of the outstanding golf books of all time. With few exceptions, these books were no longer accessible except in the outstanding public libraries and private collections.*

*Along the way, since there appeared to be a need for them, The Classics of Golf decided to publish some "new" books as well. For example, there was no book available that dealt with the advanced method of shotmaking and the lengthy career of Harry Vardon, the first great British champion, who came to the front shortly before the turn of the twentieth century. The Classics of Golf's book, "Vardon on Golf," was made up of extended excerpts taken from four books by Vardon that were published in 1905, 1912, 1920, and 1933.*

*In 1992 The Classics of Golf faced a tough problem. By that time we had settled on the book that would be the thirty-sixth and final selection, but we were having trouble finding a superior book for the thirty-fifth spot. When we came up with it, we knew instantly how fortunate we were. That book—which you have in your hands—is devoted to the best writing by and about the outstanding women players: Lady Margaret Scott, the winner of the first British Ladies' championship in 1893, Margaret Curtis, Joyce Wethered, Glenna Collett, and Virginia Van Wie; Patty Berg, Babe Didrikson Zaharias, and Louise Suggs; Mickey Wright, Anne Quast Sander, JoAnne Gunderson Carner, Catherine Lacoste De Prado, and Kathy Whitworth; Nancy Lopez, Pat Bradley, Juli Inkster, Patty Sheehan, and two young women with bright futures, Brandie Burton and Vicki Goetze.*

*It should be mentioned that what gives this anthology an extra dimension is the job Robert Macdonald did in tracking down the striking photographs that help to bring these wonderful golfers and personalities vividly to life.*

*Herbert Warren Wind*

v

# Table of Contents

## Long Ago
### 1867–1936

# Mid-Century
## 1941–1971

## Recent Times
### 1973–1993

# The Early Years

## Enid Wilson

"A History of Golf in Britain"        Cassell and Co., Ltd., 1952

The origins of golf being shrouded in antiquity, it is not surprising that the first women players are unknown to us. We do know, however, that Mary Queen of Scots was playing golf and pell-mell in the fields at Seton shortly after the death of her husband, Darnley. Also, in old prints and paintings of the Dutch 'kolven' we see young ladies disporting themselves at what is generally considered to be one of the earliest sources of golf, and if this is so we may assume that women have enjoyed the game from the time it began.

It is in the records of one of the oldest golf clubs that we find the first mention of a competition arranged by the menfolk for the women to play for prizes, the Minutes of the Musselburgh Club on December 14, 1810, being enlivened by the following:

> The Club resolve to present by Subscription a new Creel and Shawl to the best female golfer who plays on the annual occasion on 1st Jan. next, old style (12th Jan. new), to be intimated to the Fish Ladies by the Officer of the Club.
>
> Two of the best Barcelona silk handkerchiefs to be added to the above premium of the Creel.
>
> Alex. G. Hunter. C.

Unfortunately, the name of the winner and the manner in which she accomplished her victory are lost to posterity, and a further fifty years elapse before we come to any consistent records of women's golf.

Some of the earliest of these are provided by the *St. Andrews Gazette and Fifeshire News*, which by August 31, 1872, considered the activities of the ladies on the links of sufficient interest to form the subject of a second leader, from which the following is a brief extract:

> ... The Ladies' Golf Club is an institution that was born in the soil of St. Andrews links and made its struggle for existence there a few

*St. Andrews at the time of the formation of the first Ladies' Golf Club in 1867.*

years ago. . . . Its remarkable success has led to the introduction and culture of golf as a female recreation in England and elsewhere. . . . Of course, the yielding of the club assumes a mild form under the sway of the gentler sex and has never as yet extended beyond the simple stroke of the putting green. . . .

They evidently received every encouragement at St. Andrews, as in addition to the reports of their regular monthly and annual meetings, we find frequent accounts of competitions for prizes presented by members of the men's club. On these occasions it seems that everyone set out to enjoy themselves, and on one of them we find the 'gentler sex' embarking on a sort of golf marathon: 'All players who scored above 52 in the first round were thrown out. Those under this continued to play; and round after round was played, the number of competitors becoming less every round until the players became equal to the number of prizes. A final round was then played for a decision.' From this ordeal, six of the forty-two starters emerged triumphant to receive their prizes from a Dr. Macdonald, who was one of those who took a great interest in the club from its inauguration and for many years gave prizes annually for competitions.

The Ladies' Golf Club at St. Andrews was formed in 1867, and by 1886 there were five hundred members. By 1872, the St. Andrews La-

*The semi-finalists in the first Ladies, championship*
*at Lytham and St. Anne's in 1893. Miss Isette*
*Pearson, on the left, was instrumental in the*
*establishment of the Ladies Golf Union in 1893.*
*She had the misfortune of meeting Lady Margaret*
*Scott, on the right, in the first three Ladies'*
*championships and losing each time.*

dies' Spring and Autumn Meetings were regular events, at which they competed for a gold medal and the Douglas Prize; by 1879, a silver cross had been added as second prize. During the early days of these meetings, the most persistent and regular winners were Miss F. Hume M'Leod, Miss A. Boothby, Miss Mary and Miss May Lamb, and Miss Douglas.

At about the same time that the women in Scotland were forming their club at St. Andrews, there was a similar move afoot in the southwest of England at Westward Ho! Five years later, there were women's clubs at Musselburgh and Wimbledon. Carnoustie, Bath and Yarmouth had their lady pioneers, too, and the remoteness of these places from one another suggests that the urge for women to play golf was pretty general throughout Scotland and England.

Whether it was that the Scots were more severe in keeping women off their links, or that the Englishwomen had greater powers of persistence than their cousins in the north, we do not know; but all the records suggest that once the game was known south of the Border, the women went ahead rapidly, and Englishwomen were the prime movers in the formation of what is now the premier women's golfing organization in the world.

In 1893, Miss Isette Pearson, who would have been a pioneer and outstanding leader in any field to which she turned her hand, with the aid of Mr. Laidlaw Purves and other members of the Wimbledon Club, was instrumental in calling a meeting in London on April 19, which was really the beginning of the Ladies' Golf Union. Wimbledon was supported by Ashdown Forest, Barnes, East Sheen, Great Harrowden, Great Yarmouth, Lytham and St. Anne's, Minchinhampton, North Berwick, North Warwickshire, Portrush, Belfast, St. Andrews, Southdown and Brighton. The meeting decided that an annual golf championship should be held, the winner to receive a gold medal and to be styled Lady champion for the year. Lytham and St. Anne's had already thought of something on these lines and had advertised a challenge cup valued at £50 for competition annually over their links. This was amicably settled by the Ladies' Golf Union agreeing to hold the first championship over the Lytham and St. Anne's course. Subscribers towards the championship cup were forthcoming from the clubs who were in at the birth of the Ladies' Golf Union. All entries for the initial championship were subjected to the approval of the Lytham and St. Anne's Club, and any disputes were to be settled by the Council of that Club. On June 13, 1893, thirty-eight ladies were vying for the cup, and after three days' golf, the winner was Lady Margaret Scott. The play was over the Ladies' Course of nine holes, and the winner was a model of steadiness because her scores were always between 40 and 42. There were entries from Ireland and France, but none, unfortunately, from Scotland.

Lady Margaret Scott defeated Miss Isette Pearson in the final, and thus came together two women whose names will be legendary as long as women play golf. They met again in the final the following year, 1894, at Littlestone, and although Miss Pearson was the honorary secretary and backbone of the newly formed Ladies' Golf Union, she had found time to improve her game—not sufficiently, however, to prevent any change in the ultimate result, as Lady Margaret Scott was again the winner from a field of sixty-three. This second championship marked a venture, which was the employment of the men's course, though from shortened tees.

Meanwhile, there were stirrings across the sea, and the Irish women launched their native championship at Carnalea, Miss Mulligan being the winner. This probably had something to do with the migration of the Ladies' Golf Union, who visited the Royal Portrush Club for their championship meeting in 1895. There was an auction selling sweep before the championship began and Lady Margaret Scott, the hot favourite, went for £30. Her purchaser must have felt rather rash when she was four down at the turn in the semi-finals to Mrs. Ryder Rich-

*Lady Margaret Scott was the first great woman golfer. She easily won the first three Ladies' Golf championships in 1893, 1894, and 1895. She did not play in the championship again.*

ardson; but the holder of the championship won six holes of the homeward half, and the next day she went on to win for the third year in succession. After the final, there was an informal international match between England and Ireland with six players a side, the scoring being by holes, and England the winner by thirty-four holes to nil.

The championship at Portrush was remarkable for the début of two of the Hezlet sisters and Miss Rhona Adair, who watched Lady Margaret Scott with astonishment, interest and determination. So, with the passing of one giantess, three others were born. Portrush was the last appearance in competitive golf of Lady Margaret Scott, who retired unbeaten and never again took part in any serious contest. She was, by the unanimous consent of all the critics of those days, the most graceful swinger of her time. Lady Margaret must have been exceptionally supple, because we have pictures of her swinging with the club almost past the ball at the top of her backswing—a horrible sight to modern teachers. On this tremendous backswing, her left heel hardly moved from the ground, and this is all the more remarkable when we consider the fashions of the '90s, which demanded tight lacing and wasp waists.

Before going any further, it might be interesting to pause for a moment or two and consider the fashions that were prevalent when women first began to play golf. The dress was formal and distinctive, and the leading ladies were strictly conventional in observing the correct turnout. Red coats, with the club facings, and buttons of gilt bearing the club crest were popular, and each course had a uniform. Those which did not approve of the conspicuous red had jackets of a more sombre hue, which were embellished by multi-coloured pipings to denote their origin. Medals were worn on the left breast of the jacket in military style. Deep starched collars formed plinths, around the bases of which club ties were correctly draped. Also popular with the ladies were broad webbing or leather belts with monstrous buckles, which bore the club insignia or their owners' monograms. Voluminous cloth or tweed skirts draped the

*Mabel Stringer was one of the fine early golfers, an assistant Secretary of the Ladies Golf Union for many years, and the first woman golf journalist. She wrote of the early fashions: "How on earth any of us managed to hit a ball, in the outrageous garments which fashion decreed we should wear, is one of the great unsolved mysteries. I wore all grades of the stiff collar, first the plain stand up, then the double collar, highly glazed and as deep as possible. Often one got a raw sore neck all round the left side after playing in these monstrosities. Every self-respecting woman had to have a waist, and the more wasplike the more it was admired. This was a terrible drawback for golf. The skirts had stiff petersham belts, too, which were uncomfortable, and we wore two petticoats, which came down nearly to the bottom of the skirt and were heavy and cumbrous."*

first women golfers from their waists downwards, and remained the accepted fashion until the game was interrupted at the outbreak of the 1914–1918 war. Thick boots with a few metal tackets in them were concealed beneath the draperies. On their heads, the ladies wore what must have been the most unmanageable portion of their dress, stiff boaters, with braids of club colours around the crowns. How they were kept in position was a secret known only to those who wore them.

In England, golf became fashionable, and there were soon reports of it in the society journals. The earlier meetings—and, for that matter, the championships, during their first few years, until the large entries removed the intimacy—were run on the lines of a large house or garden party. After the day's golf, it was the custom to entertain and be entertained with musical evenings in which everybody took part.

To revert to actual play: 1895 was the first year that a Scottish entry, that of Miss Sybil Wigham, was received for the Ladies' championship, and she returned the lowest score in the Open Meeting held by the Royal Portrush Club prior to the commencement of the championship. During this same year, Ranelagh was revisited by the ladies, and Miss Pearson presented a trophy for inter-club competition which has since become one of the most famous golfing cups.

Also in 1895 the Ladies' Golf Union published the first of a long line of annual handbooks, and contained within the pages of this volume was a system of handicapping which was not given a serious trial for many months. Such was the beginning of a world-wide system for which the Ladies' Golf Union is famed and envied.

The most remarkable aspect of the Ladies' championship in 1897 was the unfurling of the Ladies' Golf Union flag in Scottish air for the first time. Gullane was the venue, and it attracted over one hundred entrants. The final was distinguished by a match between two sisters, Miss E. C. Orr defeating a younger sister; and a third member of this family reached the last eight. This was the only time the Orrs left North Berwick, and was their first and last venture in big golf. At this meeting, it was possible for the serious-minded to make a comparison between English and Scottish swings, and the opinion was that Scottish swings were quicker and shorter.

On we go, to the second visit of the Ladies' Golf Union to Ireland, Newcastle, Co. Down, in 1899. The Irish ladies held their championship over the same course during the week before the Ladies' Golf Union held their event, and at 17 years of age Miss May Hezlet achieved the double, winning the Irish and the Ladies' championship within a space of eight days. This was the commencement of a tremendous career which gave her three wins in the Ladies' championships and five in the Irish by 1908, and so ensured her immortal fame in the record book. Fifty-one years after her initial success in the Ladies' championship, she returned to watch this event held over the Newcastle course, but regrettably few of the competitors were aware of their distinguished spectator, although they must all have been familiar with her wonderful record.

To continue the story of women's golf, we must return to Newcastle, Co. Down, in 1899, and observe that a second 'informal' international took place there between England and Ireland with ten players a side,

*May Hezlet won the Ladies' championship
three times and the Irish Ladies'
championship five times. She also wrote
extensively about the game.*

the result being counted by holes. England won by thirty-seven holes to eighteen.

The Ladies' Golf Union took their championship to Wales—their first visit to the principality—in 1901, and at Aberdovey, England and Ireland renewed their friendly rivalry with another informal international, which was decided by matches instead of holes. Ireland won this time, and the direct result of this contest was a gift from Mr. T. H. Miller, who presented the Ladies' Golf Union with a beautiful shield, which is now competed for by England, Scotland, Ireland and Wales. The 'Home Internationals' then became the prelude to every British championship.

The Scottish Ladies' Golfing Association was formed in 1903, and the Welsh Ladies' Golf Union in 1905, both mainly for the purpose of holding their native championships and fostering their players until such time as they could hold their own with all comers in the British.

By this time we had achieved all the major events and meetings, and they are run on much the same lines today, with slight modifications brought about by the intervals caused by the two wars.

A match which has great historical interest took place at Cromer in 1905, when the British championship had gone there and attracted an entry of American women who were a sufficiently large party to make up a team. They met an English side—though why it achieved this caption, with an Irish and Scottish content larger than the home representation, it would not be wise to inquire. The galaxy of women stars who took part in this friendly contest make it worth while recording the results in full:

| AMERICA | | ENGLAND | |
|---|---|---|---|
| Miss Georgiana Bishop | 1 | Miss Lottie Dod | 0 |
| Miss Margaret Curtis | 0 | Miss May Hezlet | 1 |
| Miss M. B. Adams | 0 | Miss Molly Graham | 1 |
| Miss Harriot Curtis | 0 | Miss Elinor Nevile | 1 |
| Miss Lockwood | 0 | Miss F. Hezlet | 1 |
| Miss Frances Griscom | 0 | Miss Alexa Glover | 1 |
| Mrs. Martin | 0 | Miss Dorothy Campbell | 1 |
| | 1 | | 6 |

It would be foolish for anyone who did not experience the atmosphere of those early golfing days to be anything other than factual when discussing them. The leisurely *tempo* of an age when road transport depended on the horse, and there were husbands who would not allow their wives to go to golf fixtures if doing so necessitated travelling by train, seems to belong to another world. Nor can we understand the ordeal which each advancement and expansion into the sporting world cost and meant to the women who dared to venture. They did this with bold spirit, asking in return only that the quality of their golf might improve and that the numbers who could join in might multiply.

Some mention must now be made of the equipment which the early women golfers used. During the period which we have been examining in detail, there was one radical change: this was in the evolution of the construction of the ball from the solid rubber 'gutty' to the 'rubber-core'. The rubber-cored ball was much nicer to hit and travelled better, but although the effect of this was profound, it came gradually. When it was first on the market in 1902, it was expensive and easily damaged, and although the ladies preferred it to the solid 'gutty', they did not change over to it immediately because they could not afford such a luxury. No doubt, when the early difficulties had been overcome and the ball was more serviceable, it did make the game more attractive to women. But there was no question of the revolution being instantaneous and complete; it came over a matter of several years, during which time the leading lady golfers used both types of ball.

# Women's Golf Spreads around the World

## Henry Cotton

"A History of Golf Illustrated"          J.B. Lippincott Co., 1975

We know that Mary Queen of Scots was playing some form of golf in the fields beside Seton in 1567, but it is not until the eighteenth century that we have any further reference to women playing, this time at Musselburgh, where the fisherwomen appear to have relaxed by chipping and putting.

The first ladies' golf club was founded in 1867 at St. Andrew's, Scotland. The Westward Ho! Ladies' Club in England was formed the next year, and then followed a string of new clubs as the popularity of the game spread among the ladies. In France, the home of many fine women players, Pau was founded in 1874. In the early days of these clubs it is almost certain that only the putting greens were used and the only club wielded was the putter. But in June, 1893, the first British Ladies' championship was held over nine holes of the Lytham and St. Anne's Club, on the Lancashire coast. Ladies' courses were then separate from the men's and remained so for a very long time. The holes were short and by modern standards easy. The card for that first championship at Lytham and St. Anne's shows lengths of 244, 221, 328, 182, 207, 337, 120, 272 and 221 yards. The quality of play was poor and, surprisingly, not one Scot was competing. By far the greatest of those who did compete was Lady Margaret Scott, the winner, who beat Miss Isette Pearson by 7 and 5, but her total of 41 strokes for the first nine holes (the championship was played over two rounds of the course) was not very remarkable. (Her brother, the Hon. Michael Scott, won the British Amateur in 1933 at the age of fifty-five, the oldest man ever to win the trophy.)

However, the ladies were on the golfing map and the biggest spur to their ambitions was the formation, shortly before that first British Ladies' championship, of the Ladies' Golf Union on 19 April 1893. The driving force behind it was Miss Isette Pearson, and other members of the Royal Wimbledon Club, ably assisted by Dr. W. Laidlaw Purves, of

*The first Ladies' Golf Championship in 1893 at Royal Lytham and St. Anne's.*

*Back Row:*
Miss Welch
FORMBY
Mrs. Brown
ST. ANNE'S
Miss Starkie Bench
EASTBOURNE
Mrs. E. Catterall
ST. ANNE'S
Mrs. Ainsworth
FORMBY
Mrs. Ryder Richardson
EASTBOURNE
Miss E. Wrigley
FORMBY
Miss M. Lythgoe
ST. ANNE'S

Miss B. Welch
FORMBY
Miss Terry
ST. ANNE'S
Mrs. Smith Turbeville
KENILWORTH
Hiss Helen Cox
PORTRUSH
Lady Margaret Scott
COTSWOLD
Mrs. Hermon
ST. ANNE'S
Miss Florence Carr
FORMBY
*Middle Row:*
Miss K. Moeller
ILKLEY

Miss Newall
PAU
Miss O. Hoare
EASTBOURNE
Miss Drake
EASTBOURNE
Miss Lythgoe
ST. ANNE'S
Miss Mugliston
ST. ANNE'S
Mrs. Davies
MINCHINHAMPTON
Mrs. Müller
ST. ANNE'S
Mrs. Eason
ST. ANNE'S
Miss A. Welch
FORMBY

*Front Row:*
Mrs. Wilson Hoare
MINCHINHAMPTON
Miss Pearson
WIMBLEDON
Miss Lena Thompson
WIMBLEDON
Miss Mary Cunliffe
ST. ANNE'S
Miss M. Newall
PAU
Mrs. Stewart
ASHDOWN FOREST
Miss M. Mugliston
ST. ANNE'S

The great Lady Margaret Scott as Lady Margaret Hamilton Russell playing the Samaden links, Switzerland. Lady Russell won the Swiss championship three years in a row.

Cecil Leitch resting during the French Ladies' championship at Le Touquet, which she won in 1912, 1914, 1920, 1921, and 1924.

Early days on the Knokke links, Belgium.

*Beatrix Hoyt was the first great American woman
golfer. In 1896 at the age of sixteen, she won the
first of three consecutive national Amateur
championships.*

the same club. The aims of the Union were simple: to promote the
interests of the game; to obtain uniformity of rules; to establish uniform
handicapping; to act as arbitrators over points of uncertainty; to arrange the Annual championship competition and to obtain the necessary funds. Lady Margaret Scott was to win the first three Ladies'
championships, but then gave up competitive golf. Others, later,
showed that the ladies' game was as good, if not as long, as the men's.
Today the LGU performs the same function as well as arranging international matches.

In the United States the first Women's championship took place in
November, 1895, at the Meadowbrook Club, Hempstead, New York. It
was decided by stroke play and the winner was Mrs. Charles S. Brown.
No one could possibly say that the score was impressive. The last six

holes of her first nine were 4, 5, 7, 9, 14 and 6. However, the breakthrough for women had been made, and although it was some time
before professionalism crept in, the early women players had made
another inroad into the spheres traditionally preserved for men. The
liberation of the sporting woman had advanced a step.

The year after Mrs. Brown's victory, the U.S. Ladies' championship
was won by a teenager, Beatrix Hoyt, only sixteen years old. She, like
Lady Margaret, won for three successive years, and then in 1900 gave
up tournament golf. At about the same time, two sisters, Harriot and
Margaret Curtis were making their names. 'Peggy' Curtis was a superb
brassie player, who could hit the ball with this club further than many
men. She was the runner-up in the U.S. Ladies' championship in 1900
and 1905 and won it in 1907 (defeating Harriot), in 1911 and 1912. Her
last championship was in 1949, when she was sixty-nine. Her sister
Harriot, who was two years older, won the championship in 1906. For
women's golf the Curtis sisters were all-important. They had come to
Britain for the British Ladies' championship in 1905, when it was held
at Cromer in Norfolk, and an unofficial match was played between the
ladies of the two countries. Much later, in 1930, an unofficial match
between the American and the British ladies at Sunningdale, in Berkshire, created such interest that the sisters donated a trophy, and in
1932 the first Curtis Cup match took place. The setting was Wentworth
in Surrey, and the British, though they fielded a team which included
Joyce Wethered, Enid Wilson, Wanda Morgan, and Molly Gourlay,
were far too casual. The Americans won by five matches to three. In
those early days the match consisted of three 36-hole foursomes and six
36-hole singles, but in 1964 the formula was changed to three 18-hole
foursomes and six 18-hole singles. Since the first match, the Curtis Cup
has been competed for every other year, except for the war years. It was
resumed in 1948. Britain at last won its first Curtis Cup match at
Muirfield in 1952.

In her own Ladies' championships, Britain was supreme at home
until 1927, when a great French golfer Mademoiselle Simone Thion de
la Chaume, wrested the title from its native isles. Later she married
René Lacoste, the tennis player, and their daughter, Catherine, became
a golfing champion. The British Ladies' championship was won by another French golfer, Mlle. Manette Le Blan, but not until the amazing
'Babe' Zaharias captured it at Gullane in East Lothian, Scotland, in
1947, was it won by an American. The British Ladies' has always been
a match-play championship, and since 1913 it has been played over
thirty-six holes. It is, of course, a purely amateur tournament.

In the early years of the twentieth century the standards of women's golf rapidly improved. Dorothy Campbell won both the British and the U.S. Ladies' championships in 1909, and she went on to win the British again in 1911 and the U.S. in 1910 and 1924. She had been born a Scot but later married an American named Hurd. In 1910, one of Britain's greatest lady golfers, Cecilia (Cecil) Leitch, defeated Harold Hilton in a 72-hole handicap match at Walton Heath and Sunningdale in England. Receiving 9 strokes a round, she won by 2 and 1. Cecil Leitch had first attracted notice when the LGU visited St. Andrews in 1908. She was seventeen years old, and Enid Wilson has written that she 'struck the ball with a crispness and ferocity that was a revelation to all who saw her reach the semi-final in her first appearance in the British. Her iron shots were particularly powerful. She became the British Ladies' champion in 1914, and after the First World War she went on to win it again in 1920, 1921 and 1926. She was twice runner-up (in 1922 and 1925), both times to Joyce Wethered. The United States had an equally impressive player in Alexa Stirling, Bob Jones's lifelong friend, who won the U.S. Ladies' championship in 1916, 1919 and 1920 and was runner-up in 1921, 1923, and 1925. But the real excitement of the 1920s was the competition between Cecil Leitch and Joyce Wethered. Miss Leitch was playing in the English Ladies' championship in 1920 at Sheringham, in Norfolk. She reached the final easily, and there seemed no reason why she should not win. Her opponent happened to be a tall, pale young lady from Surrey, in southern England, Joyce Wethered. By the third hole of the second round, Miss Leitch was 6 up with 16 to play, and her position, as was to be expected, seemed impregnable. Miss Wethered, inexperienced though she was, produced a run of threes and went on to win 2 and 1. So started the career of a golfer of whom Bob Jones said: 'I have not played golf with anyone, man or woman, amateur or professional, who made me feel so utterly outclassed.'

These two players were very different in style and temperament—Miss Leitch, with a flat, ungraceful swing and a vital outgoing personality, and Miss Wethered with a fluid swing, a frailer physique, and retiring personality. Their rivalry in the 1920s did a great deal for women's golf and was watched with increasing fascination. Joyce Wethered won the British Ladies' championship in 1922, 1924, 1925 and 1929. She was the English Ladies' champion from 1920 to 1925. One more informal event that she made famous was the Worplesdon Mixed Foursomes. It is played annually on a pleasant heathy course in Surrey. It started in 1921, when Joyce Wethered and her brother Roger were defeated, but after that Miss Wethered won no fewer than eight times, making her last appearance, with her husband, in 1948, when they were beaten in the final.

*Harold Hilton, who as an amateur had twice won the British Open championship, played a match against Cecil Leitch in 1910. He gave her nine strokes a round (one on every other hole). She won 2 and 1, and her victory was celebrated by women everywhere, especially by the sufferagettes.*

In America, Miss Glenna Collett had annihilated most opponents in 1924 and crossed the Atlantic in the spring of 1925 to challenge Miss Wethered. The British golfer proved too good for her on that occasion, but the American's play alerted Britain to the new transatlantic threat. Miss Collett, later Mrs. Edwin H. Vare, never captured the British Ladies' championship, but she was twice runner-up (in 1929 and 1930), beaten by Joyce Wethered and then Diana Fishwick, but she won the U.S. Women's a record six times—in 1922, 1925, 1928, 1929, 1930 and 1935.

# The First Power Player: Cecil Leitch

## Enid Wilson

"A History of Golf in Britain"          Cassell and Co., Ltd., 1952

The British Ladies' championship was held on the Old Course at St. Andrews in 1908, a momentous breakthrough for women's golf. If there was any awe shown by the competitors at the grandeur of the occasion, none was shown by a very young lady making her debut in the championship: seventeen-year-old Miss Cecil Leitch. She proceeded to strike the ball with a ferocity and a crispness that heretofore had been the hallmark of the male golfer, and she slashed her way to the semi-finals. The impact of her game and her tremendous personality have had a more far-reaching effect on women's golf than those of any other player. In the early summer of 1914, the British, English native, and French Open championships fell into her hand like over-ripe cherries; but, alas, the achievement, and the enjoyment that it merited, were swept away by the Great War.

When hostilities ceased in Europe, the women soon set about restoring their golfing calendar to its former shape. Everything was ready for the British to be resumed in 1919, at Burnham in Somerset, but a strike of the railwaymen upset this, and it was not until the following year that Miss Leitch was called upon to defend the title. In the meantime, she had met Mrs. Temple Dobell, *née* Ravenscroft, in the final of the English at St. Anne's and beaten her in no uncertain manner. The pre-war queen had no intention of being usurped; she was clearly the best player of her own generation, and the likelihood of anyone new and inexperienced beating her was unthinkable.

Miss Leitch was a natural leader, who took command of the game of golf on the first tee as instinctively as she drew breath. Her swing was not pretty to watch; it was incredibly flat compared with modern teaching. She used the palm grip with her right hand very much under the shaft. This and her straight left arm, always stiff like a ramrod, gave her exceptional control and power over her iron shots. This style was her own instinctive method of attacking a golf ball from early childhood

17

*Seventeen-year-old Cecil Leitch at
St. Andrews in 1908.*

on. She and her sisters learned their golf at Silloth, where their father
had laid out a nine-hole course, and for a long time an old cleek and a
gutty ball were her only equipment. Lured from obscurity by the thrill
of playing in the British championship at St. Andrews in 1908, Cecil
and her sister Edith, daughters of a Fifeshire man, inside a week had
become national figures. The limelight never dimmed from that début.
Most of it was Cecil's, but her sister Edith, when she had become Mrs.
Guedalla, won the English championship nineteen years later, and so
achieved her own right to fame. Cecil captivated the sporting world
because of the downright and forceful manner in which she hit the ball.
Miss May Hezlet and Miss Rhona Adair had commenced their successes
at an equally early age; but although they must have hit hard to have
gone as far as they did, the power of their strokes was concealed in full
and flowing swings, and they did not use their iron clubs with the same
crispness as the Silloth girl. Miss Leitch revealed to her sex that there
were distinct possibilities of their being able to reproduce the artistry of
the irons, which had hitherto been the prerogative of the best men
golfers. This, then, was her gift to the game, which in turn rewarded
her with the highest honours.

# The Emergence of Joyce Wethered

## Enid Wilson

"A History of Golf in Britain"     Cassell and Co., Ltd., 1952

Miss Leitch was never in danger of relinquishing her hold on the Ladies championship in 1920, and only a month later she was at Sheringham with every prospect of winning the English native (or home) championship for the third time in succession. The prelude to the English was a qualifying round, 18-hole medal, and no one took any heed of the occupant of 25th place. As the week wore on, Miss Leitch made her way to the final, only once being in any danger at all, and extracting herself with fireworks when cornered. Her opponent in the final was the young lady who had occupied 25th place in the qualifying test: a tall, pallid, Surrey player who had come to Sheringham for the purpose of acting as companion to Miss Molly Griffiths and with certainly no thoughts of setting Sheringham and the whole of the golfing world on fire.

Thus, modestly, arrived Miss Joyce Wethered. As she progressed, she left in her wake a series of opponents who were full of praise for her golf—praise that was very quickly turned to awe. Miss Leitch dominated the first round of the final and went into lunch with a comfortable lead of four holes, which was increased to six by Miss Wethered's mistakes at the first two holes in the afternoon. Six up and sixteen to play in Miss Leitch's favour was the sort of thing that her followers hoped for and expected; and she herself had every reason to believe that she was virtually home against a player with no championship experience other than that acquired during the week. Then Miss Wethered, playing with the utmost calmness, as though she was oblivious of the state of the game and the stake that depended upon it, delivered a volley of threes—invincible stuff, which must have taken Miss Leitch by surprise. The champion found herself one down with four holes to play; and it was Miss Wethered who won by two and one.

Referring to this match after she had retired, Miss Wethered suggested that she would not have won at Sheringham had the ground not

*Joyce Wethered at nineteen, the year after she won
the 1920 Ladies' championship. She learned her
golf from playing with her brother, Roger, and his
friends on the Oxford golf team. In the 1921
British Open, Roger Wethered tied for first with
Jock Hutchison but lost in the play off.*

been baked to brick-like consistency. This shortened the course so much
that Miss Leitch found her most telling shot, the punch with an iron to
the holeside, denied her. Another observation of Miss Wethered's about
her first championship was that she found herself launched in championship golf before she had even thought about it. Those who were not
at Sheringham could not be blamed for thinking that perhaps Miss
Leitch had been toppled by a flash-in-the-pan sort of golfer.

In the meantime, American eyes were being cast on our British
championship, and the cream of their players came over to Turnberry
in 1921: Miss Alexa Stirling, thrice holder of the U.S. championship;
Miss Hollins, who won the championship from Alexa later on that year;
Miss E. Cummings, Miss Elkins, and Miss Fownes. With them came
Miss Ada Mackenzie, the Canadian. By the third round they had dis-

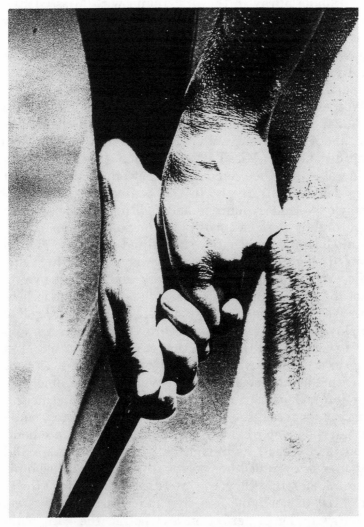

*Joyce Wethered's grip was the foundation of her "perfection of style and a hitherto unknown degree of accuracy."*

appeared. Miss Leitch saw to the going of the two most redoubtable—Miss Alexa Stirling in the first round, and Miss Hollins in the next. The Leitch-Stirling encounter was the last match in the first round, and any hopes that the American's supporters may have had were extinguished by vile weather which drenched the players and buffeted Miss Stirling's swing to pieces.

Miss Leitch's opponent in the final was Miss Joyce Wethered, who had come through the other half with little difficulty apart from a desperate 19-hole affray in the first round with Miss Gladys Bastin. Here was proof that more than luck had given Miss Wethered the English title at Sheringham; but she was not yet ready to relieve Miss Leitch of the British crown. At Turnberry, Miss Leitch won the title for the third time in succession. She was seven up at the half-way stage of the final, and eventually triumphed by four and three.

Miss Wethered stalked unmolested through the English champion-ship in 1924, improving enormously with every championship she played in, and it was patently obvious by now that, so far as British golf was concerned, she and Miss Leitch were in a class alone. Both of them were vulnerable, but they could call on powers of recovery and strokes that were denied their rivals. In the quality of greatness both had liberal portions—and in courage and fighting ability, too. But in ev-erything else they were as opposite as the poles are apart.

Miss Leitch, immensely vital, strong and energetic and physically tough, was distinguished-looking in any company in which she chose to walk. Miss Wethered, tall and thin, shy and unobtrusive, became a student of the game largely because of the enthusiasm of her brother, Mr. Roger Wethered. When he was captain of the Oxford golf team, she met and played with his friends, was drawn into their arguments, and must have theorized on the perfection of style and the composition of the swing in a manner which no other woman had ever done before. Playing with the leading amateurs developed her game quickly and made her impervious to superior power. From a quiet house or a se-cluded part of an hotel, she would come to the first tee, smile charm-ingly at her opponent when they met at the commencement of their game, and then, almost as though in a trance, become a golfing ma-chine. She never obtruded her personality, and those who played her had the impression that they, the crowd, and the state of the game had ceased to exist in her mind and that her entire faculties were being focused on swinging to perfection and holing the ball in the fewest number of strokes. The match concluded, Miss Wethered would vanish and be seen no more until the starter called her name for the next round. Her seeming remoteness from all the stress and strain that troubles ordinary people who go to championship meetings bewildered her opponents; her indifference to what they did became positively nightmarish to them, and made her task very much easier. This cloak of inhumanity was not created to frighten the enemy; it served to con-ceal an intense concentration, and to conserve its owner's physical strength. Miss Wethered was fragile in appearance, and there was nothing of the Amazon about her. Strength and stamina she must have had to withstand the physical and mental effort of a week's championship golf; but perhaps, knowing that her resources were not over-abundant, she evolved the most economical method to suit her physique and by shutting out everything of an extraneous nature avoided the strain which others found so sapping and destructive, although this strain was not unknown to her in the later stages of her more memorable battles with Miss Leitch and Miss Collett. Miss Leitch brought power into women's golf; Miss Wethered brought power combined with perfection of style and a hitherto unknown degree of accuracy. After the first surprise encounter at Sheringham, any meeting between these two players became an event of national importance, and the publicity which was accorded to it naturally caught and held the attention of an ever-increasing number of women golfers.

The inevitable came to pass in 1922: Miss Leitch and Miss Wethered were in opposite halves of the British championship held at Prince's, Sandwich, and once again they met in the final. On this occasion the roles were reversed, Miss Wethered remaining inflexible and Miss Leitch recovering brilliantly, and the younger player had the lead at lunch-time—only one hole, but a hole of the value of diamonds in a match of that calibre. In the second round Miss Leitch's powers of recovery were still needed—and they deserted her. So Miss Wethered won easily.

To mention that Miss Wethered annexed the English for the third time in succession that year is, by comparison, almost prosaic; and we will dwell for a moment on the fact that she entered for the English each year between 1920 and 1924, and was never beaten.

# "What Train?"

## Bernard Darwin

"Golf Between Two Wars"          Chatto & Windus, 1944

Miss Cecil Leitch's adversary in the finals of the 1920 English championship at Sheringham was a young lady who had qualified with two strictly moderate scores. She was chiefly known, as far as she was known at all, as Roger Wethered's sister, but she had played very well in this tournament and beaten some strong opponents. I do not suppose that the young lady herself or anyone else thought she had much chance. They thought so less when she was four down at lunch, less still when she played the first two holes in the afternoon very badly and lost them both. Then in the desperate situation of six down with sixteen to play, she unmasked her batteries. Holes seldom melt away "like snow off a dyke" unless the leader does something to help them, and I have no doubt—I was not there—that Miss Leitch made mistakes, but Miss Wethered not only took advantage of them, but put in some fierce thrusts on her own account, such as three threes in a row. The holes changed hands so quickly that Miss Wethered was one up with four to play. Miss Leitch rallied to win the fifteenth, but her opponent placidly ran through a bunker at the next and rubbed it in by holing a putt. She likewise won the seventeenth and with it an astonishing match by two up and one to play.

By the way, it was near the seventeenth green that there first appeared the traditional railway train which puffed and snorted loudly as Miss Wethered putted and of which she was so entirely unaware that, on being congratulated on her imperturbability, she is alleged to have asked, "What train?" This story has appeared several times since in various versions at various courses, and I myself incline to place it at Troon. Miss Wethered herself could naturally not give evidence. Miss Leitch assigns it to Sheringham, and she ought to know. It may be a ghost train that haunts all the links on which the champion played, but let Sheringham at least have its due!

# Dr. Stirling's Daughter: 1916, Belmont Springs

## Bunker Hill

The American Golfer                                      November, 1916

Nothing, if not dutiful, is this nineteen-year-old from Atlanta, Georgia—Alexa Stirling. Ten years ago, her father, Dr. Stirling, decided that she should win the Women's National championship, and so she did, and she won it on a fine course: the Belmont Springs Country Club course in Waverly, Massachusetts, designed in 1912 by Donald Ross. Normally, an exceedingly demanding test of golf, the course played easier than usual during the week of October 2nd because the fairways had been baked hard by the recent drought, and the wind which normally rakes the course was entirely benign.

Not only did Miss Stirling reveal a new proficiency in hitting iron shots, she ended a virtual "Boston" monopoly over the championship that had persisted for some dozen years. The South has risen. Earlier in the year, another Atlantan, a playmate of Alexa's, who matriculated at the same East Lake course just outside of Atlanta, had nearly dethroned the defending U.S. Amateur champion, Robert Gardner, in the championship at Merion. The young man's name is Bobby Jones, and he is only fourteen-years-old. There can be little doubt that he will be following in Alexa's footsteps. He won his first junior tournament at East Lake when he was only six, but he always claimed that it was Alexa who really won and deserved to have the little silver trophy.

Both youngsters learned their golf by watching the long, flowing swing of Carnoustie-born Stewart Maiden, the East Lake professional. Under Maiden, tomboyish Alexa developed an attacking manner in executing her iron shots through aggressive hand-action unlike the method taught to most women golfers.

In the championship at Belmont, Miss Stirling started slowly, and her prowess in iron play wasn't revealed until her match with the formidable Miss Elaine Rosenthal in the quarter-finals. Then her talent burst forth, and iron shot after iron shot was hit with sharpness and accuracy. She beat Miss Rosenthal 2 and 1, and she beat Boston's Miss

*Stewart Maiden, a Scot from Carnoustie, with three of his pupils at
the East Lake Golf Club outside Atlanta: Alexa Stirling, Bobby Jones,
and Perry Adair.*

Auchincloss on the last hole in the semi-finals, largely because of a
brilliant 39 on the first nine. In the final, Miss Mildred Caverly played
as well as she could especially with her wooden clubs, but Miss
Stirling's iron play and strong putting carried the day, 2 and 1. Those
three matches with strong opponents attest to the young Atlantan's
nerves as well as to the boldness of her game, a boldness new to wom-
en's golf in this country. Miss Stirling will undoubtedly begin to post
scores in the 70s, and other women golfers will follow her.

# Alexa Stirling Renews Her Claim

The American Golfer                                    October, 1920

Through a drift of Indian summer days, Alexa Stirling of Atlanta, again proved her right to wear the queen's crown on this side of the Atlantic. Cecil Leitch, of Great Britain, alone remains to challenge her supremacy.

Miss Sterling won the Women's championship of the U.S.G.A. for the third time in succession by making her way through a brilliant field at the Mayfield Country Club, in Cleveland, not only a championship course but one of the best in the world. The test was extreme and yet Miss Stirling, in her last two rounds against Mrs. C. H. Vanderbeck and Mrs. Dorothy Campbell Hurd, romped around at an 80 clip. The champion's exhibition of skill astonished the big galleries day after day. She was straight down the fairway from two hundred to two hundred and twenty yards on one hole after another, and her iron play was crisp and firm—the same as Stewart Maiden's other renowned pupil, Bobby Jones. Her firm hand-action allowed little room for error, and her timing throughout was unusually good. Miss Stirling has a knack of bending in her right knee while addressing the ball, and one of the main features of her play is her ability to time her hitting action without hurrying the stroke.

This championship was played in early October. The Mayfield course winds its way through valleys bordered by oaks and maples with their myriad autumn tints, a beauty that few courses in our country can match. There are many hills and ravines along with a drifting brook loafing its way back and forth. Through the care of Bertie Way, the Mayfield professional, the battleground was in perfect shape. It is easy to see why Vardon and Ray were so enthusiastic over this course, for there are none prettier and few harder in the country.

Mrs. Vanderbeck, of Philadelphia, was Miss Stirling's main opponent, and when they met in the semi-finals the issue was not decided until the seventeenth green. The Philadelphian hung on courageously, and, with a wonderful display of putting, she kept the battle going to the end. The Atlanta star had to be at her best to win. She was out in

*Alexa Stirling*

39 and back in 41, and the wonder is that Mrs. Vanderbeck could stay with this stiff pace. One example of Miss Stirling's play came at the 460-yard third hole. Much comment had been aroused the week before the championship when Ted Ray had reached the uphill green in two shots. Nevertheless, after driving close to 240 yards, Miss Stirling was only a few yards short of the green with her second, and her chip left her a short putt for her 4. She seems to have the knack of lengthening her drive ten or twenty yards whenever distance is required.

In her match in the final against Mrs. Hurd, a previous winner of both the British and American championships, Miss Stirling again showed her ability. On the second hole, which calls for a carry over a high hill, the approach requires a well-placed pitch to an elevated green surrounded by traps. The pitch must be hit with backspin in order to hold the small green. In the final, Miss Stirling sliced her tee shot into the rough. She was left with a full iron, an almost impossible shot to that type of green, and yet she not only reached the bunkered plateau safely but stopped her ball a few yards from the pin. Exhibitions of this sort under pressure accounted for Miss Stirling's third victory against one of the best fields that ever battled for our women's title.

The first outstanding feature of this tournament developed in the qualifying round when Miss Marion Hollins, the former Metropolitan champion, shattered the women's course record. The New York star sped around the difficult course in 82 strokes, and this included a seven on both the outbound and incoming nines. At the 515-yard sixth and again at the 525-yard eleventh, her efforts to gain extra distance caused Miss Hollins to miss the fairway, and this was costly. Both holes cost her seven strokes.

# A New Crop of American Golfers: Alexa Stirling, Marion Hollins, Edith Cummings, Glenna Collett

## Grantland Rice

The American Golfer                    March, 1922

While the average male champion is eight or nine strokes better than the leading women players from the same tee markers, the latter are capable of surprising results when affairs begin to break in the right direction. The men's golf world was badly jolted early this spring by the scores posted in Florida where Miss Glenna Collett and Edith Cummings were busy giving par the battle of his young life.

On two occasions over the narrow, twisting No. 2 course at Belleair, Miss Collett was around in 76 while Miss Cummings had a 78. A 76 over this course is rarely beaten by first-class male golfers, as there are at least eight holes from four hundred to five hundred and forty yards in length.

Even more astonishing, Miss Cummings played the difficult No. 1 course in 77 strokes on a day when roistering fresh gales blew in from the gulf which borders the course. A 77 over this course is substantially better than the average 5-handicap male golfer can do. Both distance and direction are called for, and, in one of the last big men's tournaments held there with a fine field entered, only two men turned in lower scores.

It is no longer a sensation when the best of the women players work their way down into the 70's. Miss Leitch, over good courses, has been as low as 73. At Fontainebleau last summer in the final round of the French championship, she had a 39-35 for a 74, with conditions far from ideal. There is no amateur who would care to go out and make a point of beating this score. He could do it, but there would be no certainty attached.

Two years ago over the six-thousand, four-hundred-yard Hamilton course in the Canadian championship, Miss Stirling was around in 75. A 75 over this long, well-trapped course is no soft undertaking for any man to face.

*Marion Hollins and Glenna Collett were the two longest hitters of the emerging American women golf stars, and Glenna was the dominant player. Marion, who won the national championship in 1921, had other talents. She founded both the Cypress Point Golf Club and the Pasatiempo resort in California, and she arranged for Dr. Alister MacKenzie to design both courses. The grand opening of Pasatiempo in 1929 featured an exhibition match, pictured above. From the left: Cyril Tolley, the British Amateur champion, Marion, Bobby Jones, and Glenna. Jones was so impressed with MacKenzie's work at Cypress Point and Pasatiempo that he asked him to co-design the Augusta National Golf Club.*

Last fall Miss Marion Hollins, the United States champion, played a 79 at the National, one of the hardest courses in the world. So you can see from this that the territory between 70 and 80 is no longer exclusive property of the male sex.

It is true that not many women golfers are capable of breaking 80. But among those who can be listed are the Misses Leitch, Hollins, Stirling, Collett, Cummings, Wethered and Jackson. They are capable of breaking 80, because they have broken 80 more than once.

And yet, why not? Miss Collett, for example, can drive around two hundred and thirty yards and play an iron from one hundred and seventy to one hundred and eighty yards. At Belleair, on the five hundred and sixty-five yard sixteenth hole, we saw her get home with a drive, brassie and mashie niblick and then sink her putt for a 4. On holes around four hundred and ten yards in length, we have seen her get home with a drive and an iron. Most of her drives are not only long— longer than the average male player—but usually straight.

Strangely enough when her scores run high, the lapse is due to faulty putting. And yet this is not strange, as the same defect attacks the scores of the high and low alike, the duffer and the star.

We should say the two longest drivers among the women in America are Miss Hollins and Miss Collett. Both have a range of well over two hundred yards. If the course is inclined to be a trifle fast, both can move up to two hundred and forty or even two hundred and fifty yards on occasions. They can hit the ball up with most men, and their long irons will take them home from one hundred and seventy to one hundred and eighty yards. Miss Stirling is a good, consistent driver, but the soundness of her iron play and the steadiness of her short game have helped her most.

There is now a list of younger girl golfers coming along who will soon be heard from. Some of them will come to the fore as suddenly as Miss Collett. In fact, we know of one instructor who is now teaching a fourteen-year-old girl golfer who will, he believes, outplay the field in a few seasons.

In the course of the next five years there will be at least eight or ten women golfers good enough to break 80 on occasion. On second thought, that estimate could easily be doubled.

Golf is taking hold swiftly among the youthful feminine contingent. For that matter, with two or three more years experience, there is no reason why Glenna Collett shouldn't occasionally wander down among the 72's and 73's. Not often, perhaps, but often enough to make more than a few ambitious males start gnashing their teeth.

You may think this an unreasonable projection. Why is it? If a girl around eighteen, or a young lady around eighteen, can turn out two 76s within ten days, why should a 72 or a 73 be an impossible score by the time she is twenty-one or twenty-two? Miss Collett has compactness, grace, and power in her very sound golf swing. And she isn't easily bothered or worried. So why shouldn't she, and others, give Par all the battle he can meet?

# My First National Championship

## Glenna Collett

"Ladies in the Rough"                              Alfred A. Knopf, 1928

As far back as I can remember, I was interested in some kind of sport. I could swim and dive at nine and drove an automobile at ten. My real interest, however, centered in baseball. I played with my brother Ned on his team on a field near our home in Providence, Rhode Island, until I was nearly fourteen. Then my mother suggested that I take up a game more becoming a young girl. I tried tennis and would have continued to play the game if I hadn't accompanied my father to the Metacomet Golf Club one afternoon.

Standing on the broad veranda, perched high on a Rhode Island hill, I watched Dad send a long, raking tee shot through the air. It landed far down the fairway. Tremendously impressed, I hurried out onto the course and asked permission to play along with him. With beginner's luck, my first tee shot went straight down the fairway. The length and accuracy of my initial drive stirred the enthusiasm of my father and several spectators. "The coming champion!" shouted one sun-browned veteran, who asked me to show them my swing. His comments were followed by lavish praise and warm encouragement by the other men as we moved from hole to hole. I had a natural golf swing, they said. With proper instruction, I could hit a golf ball as far, if not farther, than any of the woman golfers. Dad was elated. As I came off the course after that round, my destiny was settled. I would become a golfer.

It was, in retrospect, as simple as that. No bypaths, no hesitation, no doubts. No longer would mother have to worry about my ball-playing with my brother. No longer would I aspire to honors on the tennis court.

I was born in New Haven, Connecticut, on June 30, 1903, but I remember little or nothing of that city, because my family moved to Providence, Rhode Island, when I was six years old. We have lived there ever since. My school days in Providence and the period when I aspired to be a baseball player are easily summoned whenever I meet old friends from school or the neighborhood.

There was no golf tradition in our family. My father was known in his younger days as a bowler and a champion bicyclist. I know very little about the bicycling craze that swept the country thirty years ago other than that dad won the national amateur championship in 1899. My penchant for going abroad seeking golf honors can be explained as a trait inherited from dad, who toured Europe twice and raced against the best riders on the continent. By the way, in New Haven dad was well-known as a bowler. In 1904, he rolled a perfect 300. This is the equivalent of a hole-in-one in golf. He is very fond of golf. When I showed an aptitude for the game, he showed me all he knew and then turned me over to John Anderson, a local professional. My long hours of practice were sandwiched in between playing in local tournaments. You can picture me at the time, slim, shy, and very young, matching my game against matronly women and suffering from embarrassment when the gallery's interest centered on my game. I was regularly beaten in the second or third round.

Being young, impatient, and ambitious, I was terribly depressed by my slow progress. I was long off the tee, but my work with the brassie and putter in particular was pitifully weak. I never seemed to have the well-balanced game that would carry me to the top. There was at the Shennecossett Country Club in New London, Connecticut, a professional named Alex Smith who had emigrated from Scotland. He was linked with the success of Jerome D. Travers, the only man in this country who was able to win the National Amateur championship three times in the last twenty years. Dad arranged for me to receive instruction from Alex Smith twice a week over a three-year period, both at Shennecossett and at Belleair in Florida during the winter. Alex Smith was not only one of the pioneer Scottish professionals in this country, but he was and is a singular personality. A two-time United States Open champion, he brings to the game a vast native intelligence, and he has a deep-set impatience with lady-like hitters of the ball, either masculine or feminine. He taught me a sound philosophy as well as a better way of handling the mashie and the putter. He strengthened my driving to such a degree that when I was eighteen, five-feet-six inches tall, and weighed a hundred and twenty-eight pounds, I drove a ball a measured distance of three hundred and seven yards—thirty-six yards longer than the longest drive Babe Ruth ever belted and, at that time, the longest drive ever hit by a woman.

My first round of eighteen holes was something of an ordeal. I can't remember a more unpleasant afternoon. Struggling along, missing more shots than I made, getting into all sorts of hazards, and finishing with the embarrassing score of 150, I was ready to give up the game. The only thing that kept me interested was the thrill of hitting the ball far down the fairway. But what really renewed my interest in the game was the appearance of four youthful players at the Wannamoisett Club in Providence.

In 1916, Alexa Stirling (now Mrs. Fraser), Elaine Rosenthal (now Mrs. "Spider" Reinhardt of Chicago), Bobby Jones, and another young boy from Atlanta about fifteen, Perry Adair, toured the country in a series of exhibition matches for the Red Cross, the proceeds to go to war relief in Europe. This quartet of youngsters played at my home course, and I recall the excitement their splendid golf aroused. Miss Stirling had just won the National Women's championship, and she was regarded as the greatest woman player in the land. Bobby Jones in that same year, 1916, made a name for himself by qualifying for the match-play rounds in the National Amateur at Merion. He was only fourteen. Both Miss Rosenthal and Perry Adair had national reputations as youthful stars. Naturally I was curious to see these famous players and awaited their arrival impatiently. My interest in the game soared when

I saw how young they were—just one or two years older than I was. I fluttered around the club in a high pitch of excitement.

Except for the players, I was the busiest girl on the links that day. Bobby Jones attracted the most attention of the young players. With his head topped by a blazing red beret, he was a fiery figure, but I—and I guess most of the women—watched Alexa Stirling's every move. The first thing about Alexa that attracted my admiration was her wonderful poise, especially under fire. She was never flustered, she never hurried. I believe that she possessed the perfect temperament for a golfer. Elaine Rosenthal was also impressive. She was not as contained or as business-like as Alexa, but I remember the quality of her shots. She went around Wannamoisett in 80—the last word in women's golf at that time. I had never seen such players. What happened to my own game after watching these golfers was a common thing for an aspiring player. The next time I played, I was in an inspired mood. I didn't think of my stance, my hands, or my feet. All I tried to do was hit the ball, and I must say it was a decided improvement. I shot a 49 for nine holes—by far the best score I had ever made.

The first big tournament I entered was the Rhode Island Women's championship in the fall of 1918. Up to that time I had devoted my efforts to improving my game. I took lessons from the club professional and I tried desperately to break a hundred. My first appearance in a tournament of importance was anything but impressive. All the other players had gone out when I stood on the first tee. I didn't even have a playing partner. Two much older women followed me and kept score. I finished with a humiliating 132. The next day, when I looked in the newspaper, I saw my name at the bottom of the long list. However, I had experienced my baptism in tournament play.

The next season, 1919, proved to be a rather ambitious undertaking for a sixteen-year-old girl. It consisted of ten formal tournaments, starting in June and finishing in October. I managed to enjoy increasing success, although my début in the Women's Eastern championship at the Apawamis Club, near Rye, New York, almost crushed my aspirations then and there. Matched against a swift field that included such names as Mrs. Gavin, Miss Hollins, and Mrs. Vanderbeck assured me I was in fast company. The first day I was paired with Mrs. Caleb Fox, the oldest player in the tournament. (I was the youngest.) We became the target of a battery of cameramen who followed us from hole to hole. It was just a few weeks before my sixteenth birthday, and I suffered from a severe case of tournament nerves. My brassie refused to cooperate, and my putter was as stubborn as ever. I came in with a 107. That annoyed me. Although several of the topnotchers floundered terribly, that was no consolation for me, because I had been playing my own course consistently around a hundred. Then I suddenly realized that a hundred on your home course with a professional along to help you was a kind of golf not to be confused with the wear and tear of tournament play with an army of photographers clicking their black boxes.

Since that day my attitude towards crowds and championship play has altered. I've learned to steel myself against the little irritations and distractions one encounters in tournaments. Yet I cannot forget the mood of disgust that followed my poor golf in the Women's Eastern championship. This attitude was in turn followed by a feeling of impatience to get into another tournament and play the kind of golf I knew I was capable of. You see, I was infected with the golf disease that manifests itself in tournaments—a fever that still persists and keeps me chasing the little white ball over the fairways year in and year out. My score for the Eastern was 214 for thirty-six holes. Mrs. Gavin, who took about thirty-five strokes less, won the tournament.

Alex Smith came to Providence in 1919 and suggested that I take a few lessons before entering the National Women's championship at Shawnee-on-Delaware. Spurred on by the confidence Alex inspired, I went around in 93, my best score up to then. Alexa Stirling and Mrs. Gavin tied for qualifying honors with 87s. I finished eighth and felt pretty good about it. Then I was put out in the second round by Mrs. DuBois, but I didn't feel so discouraged. My touch of success did wonders for me.

I returned to school in the fall and forgot about golf at the suggestion of my French teacher, who kindly remarked that she wouldn't mind my absences if I showed any proficiency at the game. I was not a remarkable French pupil and my chances of passing the course went a glimmering when I traveled down to Pinehurst in the winter of 1920. I entered the Women's North and South championship. I was eliminated in the first round by Mrs. Ralph Hammer, and then returned north to continue my attempts to master French. When I returned to Pinehurst that spring, it was impossible to do justice to my school work. Whenever circumstances and weather permitted, I was out on the links. Up to this time I had not won anything. I wasn't concerned about it. My play improved under the tutelage of Alex Smith. I concentrated on hitting long drives and iron shots, and I also picked up a better understanding of the art of putting. Championship fever might have been delayed if I hadn't won the Shennecossett Country Club championship. After tying Mrs. Barlow in the qualifying round with an 86, I pushed through to the final. Matched against Elaine Rosenthal, I

*Glenna Collett at seventeen.*

went out with everything to gain and nothing to lose, played my best game, and won our match, 1 up.

Victory was sweet indeed. The desire to win was very strong. Mother accompanied me to Cleveland for the 1920 National Women's championship at the Mayfield Country Club. Alexa Stirling won it for the third time in five years. Encouraged by the laudatory words of the sportswriters, I had a 93 in the qualifying round. That was the same score I had the year before, but instead of being in eighth place, I was tied for eighteenth this time. In a single year, American women's golf had shown a marked improvement. In the qualifying round at Cleveland, for example, Marion Hollins posted an 82 and bettered by four strokes a record that had stood for seven years.

In the first round of the championship I met Elaine Rosenthal for the second time that summer, and, by way of proving that my earlier victory had been a flash in the plan, I was beaten 2 and 1. At that tournament I was helped by watching the play of Mrs. Quentin Feitner, the former Lillian Hyde, and Doreen Kavanaugh, now Mrs. Campbell from California. Mrs. Campbell had a graceful and orthodox style, similar to those of Miss Stirling and Mrs. Feitner, and she later won the California state championship by defeating Miss Mary K. Browne, the tennis star.

What helped me more than anything at this point in my career was a remark Alexa Stirling made to me one day on the first tee. She said that at the top of my swing with the driver—and, I presume, with all of my clubs—the face of the club was pointing upward. This had caused most of the unsteadiness in my driving. I immediately corrected this fault by keeping my left wrist under the shaft at the top of the swing. Another thing: I found that my backswing was almost as fast as my downswing. By slowing it down, I gained a great deal more control.

In 1921, I had high hopes when I went to the Hollywood Golf Club in Deal, New Jersey, to play in my third Women's National championship. The presence of Miss Cecil Leitch, then the British champion, her sister Edith, Mrs. Latham-Hall, and Miss Doris Chambers, all of England, added interest to the matches. The first time I saw Cecil Leitch, I was impressed by her extremely unorthodox swing which gave her tremendous distance off the tees. Little wonder she had won almost every championship honor at one time or another! Miss Leitch had begun to play golf near her home in Silloth, where wind, rain, and sleet were considered minor hazards compared to the heavy gorse and heather and the sand-blown fairways. It fell to my lot to be eliminated 3 and 2 by her sister Edith in the first round after I had tied for low medal at 85 with Mrs. Latham-Hall.

A week later, in the Berthellyn Cup matches at the Huntingdon Valley Country Club, near Philadelphia, I had the opportunity to play against Cecil Leitch in the first round. My only hope was to halve as many holes as possible. When I lost the first hole, I was almost beaten, but I rallied somehow to win the second hole and continued to hold my own the rest of the way. Cecil was not on her game, while I was in a trance. I concentrated on halving every hole and had the satisfaction of projecting after each one that I would be beaten by a smaller margin than I had expected. When we reached the sixteenth hole, I surprised myself by dropping a treacherous putt and went on to reach the eighteenth 1 up. I had a chance, a real chance, and I tried to arrest the nervousness that so often came over me.

On the eighteenth green I had to drop a ten-foot putt to win. I tapped the ball gently with my blade. It moved slowly over the green. It flirted with the lip of the cup and dropped in.

To anyone else, perhaps the fact that I had beaten Cecil Leitch was unimportant—an off-day for the champion. To me it was the beginning of a successful career. I had gained the confidence I needed so badly. My nerves became steadier, my shots bolder. No opponent held any terror for me now.

One thing more. I continued to play solid golf in that tournament, winning the final from Mrs. William A. Gavin.

When I headed for White Sulphur Springs, West Virginia, in the late summer of 1922 to compete in the Women's National championship, I believed that if I ever intended to win the title I had to do it that year.

I was nineteen. Four years had passed since my first appearance in Boston, when I had been referred to as the "coming champion" by the local sports writers. But the years had slipped away, the title went to other women, and the term "coming champion" became something of a burden. My newspaper reputation had outdistanced my development until the disparity between the two disturbed my peace of mind. But the golf writers were still singing my praises and predicting that I had more than a chance of winning the Women's National championship after I had come through in the North and South, at Pinehurst, and then had carried off the Eastern over the Westchester-Biltmore course in Rye, New York, with a total of 246 over three rounds, a record for the event.

In retrospect, it is a source of amusement to dwell on the determination I manifested in winning the Eastern. Aside from my personal satisfaction, there was Dad, my most enthusiastic supporter, who expected such extravagant things of me and had secretly hid his disap-

*An elated Glenna Collett defeats
Mrs. Gavin in the final and wins
her first national championship.*

pointments. Taking to heart all the things said about my game, I considered it necessary to live up to what was expected of me.

However, my aspirations wilted when I looked over the field that had gathered at the Greenbrier Golf Club in White Sulphur Springs, West Virginia, for the Women's National championship in late September, 1922. There was Marion Hollins, the defending champion; Edith Cummings, my most formidable rival in tournament play; Mrs. E. C. Letts, known as "The Giant Killer"; and Mrs. Gavin, that outstanding English player who was fresh from winning the Canadian championship. It was going to be mighty hard work.

My mood lightened somewhat and my confidence increased when I went around the Greenbrier course in 75 just two days before the championship started. I immediately tried to find out the secret of that 75 and finally settled on the premise that it had something to do with the food I was eating. I remembered having two lamb chops, creamed potatoes, and string beans for dinner the night before. I continued to eat the same thing every night during the championship. I also wore the same skirt, sweater and hat. This was ridiculous, but I needed something to cling to on the qualifying day when I joined the other one-hundred-and-thirty-three starters in the clubhouse and around the first tee. My qualifying round was played with Marion Hollins and resulted in my winning the medal with an 81 to her 83.

Then the long grind started. I have forgotten almost all the Shakespeare I ever knew, but the words "Tomorrow and tomorrow and tomorrow creeps in its petty pace from day to day" described my feeling on waking each day and realizing that it was going to be harder than yesterday. My first two matches were preliminaries to my match with Edith Cummings, who was playing her usual game. Edith was in a winning mood, playing very good golf. Today, in tournament play, I miss the friendly rivalry that spurred both of us on to our best game. Our spirited battles are among the high points of my golf career.

My match with Edith in the semi-final round of the 1922 United States Women's championship, was one of the hardest I've ever had in head-to-head play. I was out to win, and Edith's attitude is best explained by a newspaper clipping: "Miss Cummings was determined to win from Glenna Collett. She swaggered along as jauntily as a bullfighter, ready to pounce on any mistakes her opponent made. She was a striking, up-and-coming figure. No handsomer girl ever graced an athletic contest. She has Marilyn Miller and Julia Sanderson beaten a mile for sheer beauty. She looked like a bewitching blonde."

Edith started fast and was three up after the first nine holes of our match. I fought back and, standing on the seventeenth tee, we were all even. I hit a good drive but Edith's found the rough. I won the hole to go 1 up with the eighteenth to play. We both pitched boldly over the creek to the home green. My ball finished nearer the cup. I was tired. I remember pausing on the bridge over the stream on my walk to the green. Wearied by the hard match, I looked down enviously at the trout sunning on the rocks, happily oblivious of the two harassed girls laboring under the strain of a tight semi-final struggle. Edith laid me a partial stymie with her third shot, but I made the putt and won the match. Edith had an 83, and I had an 82.

In the final I met Mrs. Gavin. She had reached the final of our championship in 1915 but had lost to Mrs. C. H. Vanderbeck, one of the many fine golfers from the Philadelphia area. She made her way to the final a second time in 1919 at Shawnee-on-Delaware, but Alexa Stirling defeated her, 6 and 5. At White Sulphur Springs, Mrs. Gavin was in impressive form. In the third round she edged out Alexa, 1 up, and in the semi-finals she was headed for a 77 or 78 when she closed out Mrs. Katherine Harley Jackson, of Greenwich, 4 and 2. In our 36-hole final, I had a good morning round, my drives leaving Mrs. Gavin's twenty to fifty yards behind. I went to lunch six up. Mrs. Gavin had not been in her best form. She played much better in the afternoon, but the damage of the morning round was too much to overcome. The match ended on the fourteenth green.

Even when it was over and I had won the championship, I couldn't believe it. It meant something to win that title.

# The Dazzling Edith Cummings

## Grantland Rice

The American Golfer                                    October, 1923

There are occasions now and then when golf greatness runs strongly through the same clan. The Wethereds of England are notable examples. Roger Wethered won this year's (1923) British Amateur championship, and his even more famous sister, Joyce, won the Women's championship a year ago.

Last June, Dexter Cummings, the long-hitting Yale star from the Onwentsia Club in Lake Forest, on the edge of Chicago, won the Intercollegiate championship. Now his sister, Miss Edith Cummings, who is in the neighborhood of twenty-three, is the new Women's champion of the United States.

Miss Cummings has been playing fine golf for several years. Her home course, Onwentsia, has bred other notable golfers including Robert A. Gardner, who won the U.S. Amateur in 1910 and 1915, and it hosted the 1899 Amateur and 1906 Open championships. It pays to learn your golf on a good course. Just four years ago, Jim Barnes, the 1921 Open champion, saw Miss Cummings play three or four strokes and predicted then that within five years she would win the championship. "Here is a girl who has rhythm and power," remarked Barnes. "She has a fine swing, and she has the punch. That combination is certain to land in time."

In addition to rhythm and power, Miss Cummings proved over the long, arduous West Course of the Westchester-Biltmore, made up of numerous hills and valleys, trees and brooks, that she also has the heart of a champion.

Few of Miss Cummings' followers believed there was the slightest chance for the Chicago star to win the championship when she came to the seventeenth green in her semi-final match with Mrs. Clarence Vanderbeck, of Philadelphia. At this point, Mrs. Vanderbeck was two up and two to play. All she needed was to halve one hole. To cast an even thicker shadow over the scene, Mrs. Vanderbeck, by virtue of two solid wooden shots, was on the seventeenth green in two, and Miss

*The dazzling Edith Cummings*

Cummings was fifteen feet beyond the green, in the thick rough with a curling, downhill chip to play. Even if she were able to get her chip shot close, it seemed certain that Mrs. Vanderbeck, with her steady short game, would also get down in two putts for her 4.

Against these dark odds, Miss Cummings responded gallantly. She played a well-controlled chip shot to within three feet of the cup. Mrs. Vanderbeck, somewhat rattled, failed to get down in two from forty-five feet and lost the hole. Miss Cummings was far from being safely out of the jungle. On the eighteenth she was faced with holing a nine-foot putt over a sloping green to stay in the championship. She struck the ball firmly, and once more proved her courage. She had to go to the twentieth hole to win, which she did by playing the two extra holes in par.

For the first time in her career Miss Cummings had reached the final. Her opponent was one of the best match-players of the day, Alexa Stirling who had won three national titles and was in the final for her fifth time. The battle was fought out under difficult scoring conditions. A raw wind roistered over the course and made accurate play extremely difficult. On the eighteenth green Miss Cummings had a twenty-inch putt to become only one down. When she missed, the bulk of the gallery thought that the match was over. The shock of the tournament fol-

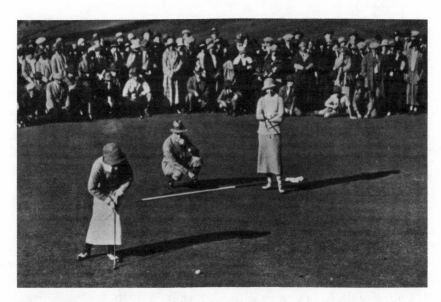

*Alexa Stirling putting on the fourth green of the morning round in the final
of the 1923 national championship against Edith Cummings.*

lowed. Miss Cummings, having dismissed all thought of the missed
short putt on the eighteenth green, suddenly took charge on the first
nine holes of the afternoon round. With the cold wind shifting back and
forth, the greens hard and fast, Miss Cummings began her attack in
this fashion: 4-3-5-4-5-4-4. This was more than Miss Stirling could handle. She lost five holes in a row. Instead of 2 being up, she was 3 down
going to the eighth. On the final nine, Miss Stirling counter-attacked.
On the thirteenth, a hard, long, par-5, she got home with two magnificent wooden shots, birdied the hole, and now she was only one down.
Miss Cummings then won the fourteenth with a stout-hearted pitch-
and-run from over a hundred yards to within ten feet of the pin. Miss
Stirling, apparently shaken, made two mistakes, and Miss Cummings
closed out the match on the sixteenth.

Edith Cumming's swing throughout the week, was well-timed and
powerful. Dexter Cummings is known for his long hitting, and his sister
goes after the ball in the same smashing style. There is no question,
however, that her greatest asset is her ability to meet any crisis with a
stout heart and a cool head.

The last four championships have been won by a dynamic young
group of ladies who believe in hard-hitting. They are Alexa Stirling,
Marion Hollins, Glenna Collett and Edith Cummings, and they are
changing the way women play golf.

# On First Meeting Albertine

## Marcel Proust

"Within a Budding Grove"                    Chatto & Windus, 1924
Translated by C. K. Scott Moncrieff

One would like always to remember a thing accurately, but at the time one's vision was clouded. And yet that Albertine and the girl whom I had seen were one and the same person was a practical certainty . . . the countless images that have been furnished me by that dark young golfer, however different they may have been from one another, have overlaid one another (because I now know that they all belong to her), and if I retrace the thread of my memories I can, under cover of their identity, and as though along a tunnelled passage, pass through all those images in turn without losing my consciousness of the same person behind them all . . . as she was to be staying (and I too) for a long time at Balbec, I had decided that the best thing was not to make my efforts to meet her too apparent, but to wait for an accidental encounter . . . "What weather!" she began. "Really the perpetual summer of Balbec is all stuff and nonsense. You don't go in for anything special here, do you? We don't ever see you playing golf, or dancing at the Casino. You must be bored stiff. You must have plenty of time on your hands. I can see you're not like me; I simply adore all sports". . . . Whenever I had gone for several days without seeing her, I would refresh my spirit by repeating to myself: "We don't ever see you playing golf", with the nasal intonation in which she had uttered the words, point blank, without moving a muscle of her face. And I thought then that there could be no one in the world as desirable.

# The Champion Who Cheated

## F. Scott Fitzgerald

"The Great Gatsby"                    Charles Scribner's Sons, 1925
(The Authorized Text)

For a while I lost sight of Jordan Baker, and then in midsummer I found her again. At first I was flattered to go places with her because she was a golf champion, and every one knew her name. Then it was something more. I wasn't actually in love, but I felt a sort of tender curiosity. The bored haughty face that she turned to the world concealed something—most affectations conceal something eventually, even though they don't in the beginning—and one day I found what it was. When we were on a houseparty together up in Warwick, she left a borrowed car out in the rain with the top down, and then lied about it—and suddenly I remembered the story about her that had eluded me that night at Daisy's. At her first big golf tournament there was a row that nearly reached the newspapers—a suggestion that she had moved her ball from a bad lie in the semi-final round. The thing approached the proportions of a scandal—then died away. A caddy retracted his statement, and the only other witness admitted that he might have been mistaken. The incident and the name had remained together in my mind.

Jordan Baker instinctively avoided clever shrewd men and now I saw that this was because she felt safer on a plane where any divergence from a code would be thought impossible. She was incurably dishonest. She wasn't able to endure being at a disadvantage and, given this unwillingness I suppose she had begun dealing in subterfuges when she was very young in order to keep that cool insolent smile turned to the world and yet satisfy the demands of her hard jaunty body.

It made no difference to me. Dishonesty in a woman is a thing you never blame deeply—I was casually sorry, and then I forgot. It was on that same house party that we had a curious conversation about driving a car. It started because she passed so close to some workmen that our fender flicked a button on one man's coat.

"You're a rotten driver," I protested. "Either you ought to be more careful, or you oughtn't to drive at all."

"I am careful."

"No, you're not."

"Well, other people are," she said lightly.

"What's that got to do with it?"

"They'll keep out of my way," she insisted. "It takes two to make an accident."

"Suppose you met somebody just as careless as yourself."

"I hope I never will," she answered. "I hate careless people. That's why I like you."

\*     \*     \*

There was one thing to be done before I left, an awkward, unpleasant thing that perhaps had better have been let alone. But I wanted to leave things in order and not just trust that obliging and indifferent sea to sweep my refuse away. I saw Jordan Baker and talked over and around what had happened to us together and what had happened afterward to me, and she lay perfectly still listening, in a big chair.

She was dressed to play golf and I remember thinking she looked like a good illustration, her chin raised a little, jauntily, her hair the color of an autumn leaf, her face the same brown tint as the fingerless glove on her knee. When I had finished she told me without comment that she was engaged to another man. I doubted that though there were several she could have married at a nod of her head but I pretended to be surprised. For just a minute I wondered if I wasn't making a mistake, then I thought it all over again quickly and got up to say goodby.

"Nevertheless you did throw me over," said Jordan suddenly. "You threw me over on the telephone. I don't give a damn about you now but it was a new experience for me and I felt a little dizzy for a while."

We shook hands.

"Oh, and do you remember"—she added—"a conversation we had once about driving a car?"

"Why—not exactly."

"You said a bad driver was only safe until she met another bad driver? Well, I met another bad driver, didn't I? I mean it was careless of me to make such a wrong guess. I thought you were rather an honest, straightforward person. I thought it was your secret pride."

"I'm thirty," I said. "I'm five years too old to lie to myself and call it honor."

She didn't answer. Angry, and half in love with her, and tremendously sorry, I turned away.

# Three Briggs Cartoons

## Clare Briggs

"The Duffer's Handbook of Golf"          The Macmillan Co., 1926

# How to Make a Correct Turn

## Glenna Collett

"Golf for Young Players"                     Little Brown and Co., 1926

I have been asked more questions about my pivot than I have been asked about any other part of my swing. I am not aware that it differs radically from the pivot or turning that other players make. I know that, again, it was through the influence of Alex Smith that I became accustomed to coming up so high with the left heel.

I have a little scheme of telling you how to gauge the feeling of the pivot. If you stand as you would in an ordinary manner and place both your hands easily on your hips, you will find nothing akin to the golf stroke in that; next, however, I want you to turn your head and look at an object directly behind you. Your hips have made a turn such as they will make in a full golf swing. If you return the head to the front without changing the position of the hips and look at the spot where the golf ball would have been if you were playing, then you will find the head and the hips in the correct place for a hit and, also, the correct bend to the left knee while the right leg has the proper straightness.

I think it is a good plan to try this in front of a mirror. The feeling of the bend to the knee, the shifting of the weight from the left leg to the right one, and the whole scheme of the balance, or equilibrium, are then felt and understood.

This is the first mention I have made of body balance, but it really is not so hard as some people would make it out to be. Balance means to me the keeping of myself from falling over. When I lift one foot from the sidewalk as I go along, I am not conscious of my one hundred and twenty-five pounds being on the other foot. When I go from left foot to right on the swing, I am still unconscious of the shifting weight. However, I have the weight on the right foot, where I want it. I want my weight to be in back of the ball, where I can make use of it in sending the ball on its journey.

To find out how far the hips can go around on the backswing without making the head move, I have met in my golfing travels this scheme,

51

and here is how I use it. If I place my forehead against a wall and bend at the waist as I would in addressing a golf ball on the tee, and if I then place my hands on the hips, I can feel the hips moving from left to right. As I pivot, I can find out how far the hips will naturally move for me and yet keep my head still and maintain a perfect balance.

One of the most helpful thoughts to good golf is the thought of hitting with the hips. I often try to see how far I can send the ball by taking the club back as I ordinarily would and, not paying any attention to a pivot, just propelling the club with the hip movements. It certainly is a surprise to see the distance you can get in that way. I think at times of pulling the right shoulder under on the swing-back and hitting through with the right hip. Not so strange as it sounds, if you can get what I mean.

It is not advisable to take too seriously all the different parts of the golf swing. The complete whole is a happy consummation, and it comes in due time to all who go after it willingly and with a desire for understanding. I have told you about the essentials, and I know they are easily followed and can be perfected by practice. The whole picture of the golf swing is put together bit by bit like the House that Jack Built. As in that story, you have the house, the malt, the rat, the cat gathered one at a time until all the friends of Noah's Ark have been accounted for, so, too, in my story, all the sections of the swing go to form a perfect whole.

> For there is a way to sole the club,
> And there is a stance to take,
> And there is a grip that holds the stick
> And a proper route to take.
> There are pivots and bends and also twists
> That move the knees and hips and wrists,
> And perhaps much more, if I made two lists
> Of the things one does in a golf stroke.

# Profile: Glenna Collett

## Niven Busch, Jr.

The New Yorker                                    September 17, 1927

Glenna Collett may not be able to play golf better than any other woman. Anyway, there's doubt enough about it to give some point to the tournament that is being played next week at Cherry Valley. But one thing is certain, and that is that no woman has been able to make golf seem as attractive as she does—attractive, I mean, as a game for a woman to play. Most women who spend a lot of time playing in tournaments get a kind of baked look. Well, Glenna Collett isn't like that. She is a very nice-looking girl.

She isn't quite as pretty as Helen Wills, but she dresses just as well; she is smaller, a little less muscular, a little more talkative than the tennis champion. The comparison may make sense, because in the last three years Helen Wills has been photographed more often and given more publicity than Glenna Collett. Everyone knows that Helen Wills is called "Little Poker Face." The same phrase, or one like it, would fit Glenna Collett. These two girls have the same quietness, the same poise, the same ability to hide what they're thinking about.

It's easy to see what has made Glenna Collett popular. "She's like Hagen," another golfer said, "she knows how to sell." He didn't mean that Glenna Collett lay awake at night to think up ways to advertise herself, but that she has, naturally, the knack of doing things. And not only in her large public efforts, but in her personal comings and goings. For instance, in Providence, where she lived from the time she was six years old until last year, she is a kind of local heroine. The townspeople, old and young, would wave when they saw her car—a little blue Mercer that some friends gave her after she won the National Women's championship in 1925. Sometimes it went by at seventy miles an hour; then there would be the splutter of another motor, and a Providence cop on a motorcycle would swing out after her. Later, standing still, with his foot on her running-board, the officer would plead with her.

*Glenna Collett was a tremendous athelete, and she didn't have that "baked look."*

"I've asked you and asked you, Miss Collett—just for the looks of it—stay under fifty when you pass the court house."

That may be just a story, but there is another speed story about her family that is a matter of record. It concerns her father, who is now in the insurance business. He used to be a professional bicycle rider.

That was a long time ago—before Glenna Collett was born—but the ideas and some of the physical and mental qualities that her father took with him when he left the bicycle-riding business he passed on to Glenna Collett, and those ideas and qualities have made her successful in golf. Her father started her playing. He had taken up the game to keep in condition and done pretty well. One day in Providence when Glenna Collett was fourteen, he took her out to the club, gave her a mashie, and put a ball down in front of her. She had strong wrists and shoulders even then, and he could see by the easy way she hit the ball that she would be a good player if she ever got to like it. Two years later she qualified eighth in her first national championship. And on June 20, 1925, she won the Women's championship of France at La Boulie.

Her father got the cable in Providence. It made him think about a lot of things . . . about June 20, 1903, and the crowd yelling at the velodrome in Paris. That was the day Glenna Collett was born. George Collett had a big race that day. He couldn't get out of it. That was the day he won the bicycle sprinting championship of Europe. . . . Now, with the cable in his hand, he went to the telephone to send an answer.

There was a long period of steady practice and fluctuating tournament luck between Glenna Collett's start and 1925—her big year. She didn't get far in her first national, in spite of her good qualifying score. It wasn't really until 1921 that Glenna Collett got noticed. Cecil Leitch, champion of Great Britain and Canada, called the greatest woman golfer in the world, came over that season to see if she could win a third championship, and Glenna Collett, eighteen, beat her at Philadelphia.

Later Glenna Collett took a beating, and one that was particularly hard to take. The championship was being played in her own town, in Providence, that year, and Mary K. Browne, who had just been runner-up in the national tennis championships, played against her in the semi-finals. The townspeople of Providence, the storekeepers her family traded with, the cops who wouldn't arrest her, the teachers who had known her when, with her hair down her back, she played prisoner's base in the yard of the Lincoln School, all came out to the course that day. Everyone was sure she was going to win, and it looked as if they were right, for Glenna Collett came to the eighteenth hole one up and hit a long, straight drive down the middle of the fairway. Mary K. Browne sliced her drive. The ball ended up far to the left, under an apple tree.

Only a small part of the gallery tramped through the long grass to see Miss Browne play her second shot. However, when she arrived at the apple tree, she saw that things were not as bad as they might have been. Her ball was teed up on some stubbly grass and she could see the white flag on the green and the crowd gathered on the far side. She took her brassie and hit the ball as hard as she could. It rolled dead fifteen feet from the pin. That squared the match. On the first extra-hole, both women were on the edge of the green in three. Glenna's approach putt finished two inches past the cup. Mary K. Browne, putting from a different angle, also played a good-looking putt. As it approached the cup, it kissed off Glenna's ball and went in.

Mary K. Browne is not a player Glenna Collett has any reason to be afraid of. There is only one woman in the world she fears and that is Joyce Wethered. At Troon, Miss Wethered beat her 4 and 3 in the British Ladies' championship. That was in 1925, just before Glenna Collett had won the French championship. Lately, Miss Wethered hasn't been playing much golf; she spends a large part of her time pulling red salmon out of the cold rivers of Scotland. If the two played again now, Collett would be an even choice, I think. Her game has gotten better; long hot days in January and February down at Bellaire, Florida, under the sharp eye of Alex Smith, have made her steadier with her irons and surer on the greens. She has always played her wood shots beautifully—a long, easy backswing, a pause, and then the downswing, the wrists and arms sending the ball away. There is none of the lunging hips and shoulders you see in so many women golfers, even good ones. Maureen Orcutt and Virginia Van Wie putt and approach just as well as Glenna does, but they don't drive as far as she does. She outdrives every woman except, again, Joyce Wethered.

Glenna Collett, as a rule, is serious on the golf course. Whether she misses a shot or gets a lucky break, her expression never changes. With her small, set, oval face, she stalked after her ball to win our national ladies championship twice (in 1922 and 1925), the Canadian twice, the North and South four times, as well as a great many lesser tournaments, invitations, and exhibition matches.

Now twenty-four, Glenna Collett earns her own living—or part of it—as an associate of Mr. Devereux Emmet, who builds golf courses. He is promising a new golf club exclusively for women—the Women's Westchester—near Greenwich; Glenna Collett is head of the membership committee. But Glenna Collett has plenty of time to go to parties. When urged, she does a solo Charleston or a Black Bottom, and people usually urge her because these dances are worth watching the way she does them, even if they aren't the rage any more. She rides well. She plays good bridge. In fact, she can do all the things that have the cachet of being modern. She even sings and plays the ukulele. When she drives her car, her police dog, Lobo, sits up on the seat beside her to the envy of her wirehaired fox terrier, Buddy. Once she went down in a submarine—the S51, then lying in Providence harbor. She has a brother, younger than she is and much bigger, who also plays golf, but not so well. Nowadays, she lets her father and mother follow her when she is playing, but when she was younger she never permitted it—they had to hide behind trees to watch her. She lives in Greenwich and New York in the summer and fall and in Bellaire in the winter.

In her French clothes, with her quiet manner, her friendly, sun-strained eyes, her short laugh, there is nothing about her that reminds you she is a golf champion except her hands with their short, strong fingers and the little pack of muscle on the outside curve of the palm. She is, as I said, nice-looking. A great deal of tripe has been written in the last few years about the Modern American Girl. I'm not sure what that phrase means, but when I think of Glenna Collett I can't help connecting that phrase with her as another writer connected it a few weeks ago with Helen Wills. It seems to me that if some committee were trying to find a girl who was herself a definition of what it might mean, at its best, they couldn't pick a better definition than Glenna Collett.

# Joyce Dominates the Scene

## Bernard Darwin

"Golf Between Two Wars"                    Chatto & Windus, 1944

What is there new and true to say about Miss Joyce Wethered's methods? I really do not know. I should pitch on the qualities, which are perhaps complementary to one another, crispness of hitting and economy of movement. As for the latter she originally stood so still that her left heel stayed glued to the ground, but later she eased it a little, with gain, I think, both in grace and power. This economy of movement was to some extent delusive. She had in fact plenty of body turn, but it was done so quietly and naturally as not to be very noticeable. As a result, I believe that when she went to stay and play at one place where she had never been seen before, the reverent ladies who watched decided in awe-stricken conclave that "Miss Wethered did not pivot". They remodelled their own swings accordingly, with catastrophic effect. Another quality of Miss Wethered's methods was what, for lack of a better word, I will call its uniformity. There were days, as there must be with anyone, when she seemed to swing a little faster than others, but generally she stuck to a uniform, unhurried and rhythmic pace with a consistency that very few other golfers have equalled. Perhaps this accounted for her accuracy, for she was hideously accurate if one were her opponent, blessedly so if her partner. If ever she did hit a somewhat crooked shot, her ball seemed to have a knack of keeping just out of the bunker. It was part of the fun of watching her at Worplesdon that she was to be seen, through the agency of her male partner, in places where she would never have gone on her own account. It was one of the agitating features of being her partner that one was sure to put her there. If I add that she had an admirable temperament, strung up by the great occasion to exactly the right degree, capable of seeing the humor of the most lamentable situation, and having a power of pegging away and hoping for things to come round, I have done with eulogy and will come back to history.

The Ladies' championship of 1924 at Turnberry, which I had the

*Joyce Wethered at impact.*

pleasure of watching, was a memorable one, with Miss Leitch the out-standing figure. In the very first round she had to meet Miss Alexa Stirling, a beautiful player, then American champion, bred in Atlanta, Georgia, where Bobby Jones comes from, and more or less a contempo-rary of his. It was hard that these two should meet so soon. That was the thought in everybody's mind. The wind roared and swept before it across the links a storm of rain. I cannot remember watching on a more unpleasant day, and when at last at a late hour I had completed my account of the match on sopped pieces of paper, it never reached Lon-don. There was then an impression that American golfers were not at their best in bad weather. This is a complete delusion. Miss Stirling did not blench; she played well, but Miss Leitch was in an irresistible mood. I have a vision of her with her familiar bandeau and some sort of handkerchief knotted round her neck affronting the tempest, revelling in her defiance of it. The wide stance, the little duck of the right knee, the follow-through that sends the club through low as if boring its way through the wind—all the characteristic movements stand out in mem-ory against the grey and lowering background.

*Joyce Wethered congratulates Cecil Leitch on the fifteenth green at Turnberry in the finals of the 1921 British Ladies' championship.*

Meanwhile Miss Wethered was going through in the other half comfortably enough, and the two duly met in the final. Miss Wethered played unworthily in the first round. She had, as I remember it, been a little inclined during the previous day to cut her shots, and this she could not afford to do against Miss Leitch. She was out-hit and generally outplayed, and was seven down at lunch. No second marvel of Sheringham was vouchsafed: she played up well in the afternoon, but her adversary was not letting go and won by 4 and 3, her third successive championship.

I did not see the championship in the following year at Prince's, Sandwich, when the draw was again kind, so that the pair met in the final. Miss Wethered had perceptibly strengthened her game by this time, and, after a hard struggle to begin with, there came a rapid landslide of holes and she won by 9 and 7. Neither was I at Burnham in the following year when the Ladies' championship was held there. The Amateur championship at Deal took place at the same time. Miss Wethered looked like winning again till in the semi-final she was beaten by a beautiful golfer, lacking nothing but a little power, Mrs. Macbeth, who as Miss Muriel Dodd had been the champion in 1913. If Miss Wethered had watched the next day's final, it would have been the only round in any championship during her career that she ever could have watched as a spectator and not a player. As it was, she did not see it, because she travelled through the night to see her brother win at Deal.

In 1924 Miss Wethered won again at Portrush. The next year saw the fourth and last final between the two dominating figures, this time at Troon, and it was the best of all. It ended on the thirty-seventh green, and everyone felt that it was a great pity that the championship could not be halved and the throne shared for the ensuing year. From the start of the championship Miss Wethered was clinging to fours and killing her enemies stone dead. There was one big match on the way to the final against that fine American player, Miss Glenna Collett. Miss Collett held her own for a while, but the fours came too consistently at last. Meanwhile Miss Leitch was fighting her way through to the final. Several people had a chance of beating her and were perhaps too frightened to administer the *coup de grâce*. So Miss Leitch was in the final at last, but this time there was no general expectation that she could stay with her adversary.

The morning saw a complete change in her. The painful ascent to the summit had been laboriously achieved and she emerged on the heights a different golfer. Confidence, dash, rhythm—all had come back, and from the very start she attacked. Miss Wethered was still playing well, not quite so victoriously well as she had been, but even the very best can have their game to some extent dictated to them by their opponents and only play as well as they are allowed. So after ten holes Miss Leitch was quite deservedly, though surprisingly, three up. She continued to play fine golf, but she could not help losing a little ground to her enemy's great counter-attack. Miss Wethered came home in 35, finishing with a long putt, and the match was square.

The more sanguine of Miss Wethered's supporters believed that now she would draw steadily away, but a grim struggle all the way out saw her one up going to the ninth. Here Miss Wethered had a putt to win but was stymied. She decided to put it to the touch and risk two down; she went out for the shot and lofted it into the cup. A risk thus taken and successfully overcome is seldom without its effect, and now Miss Wethered did forge ahead. Going to the long sixteenth hole, she was two up and had hit two good shots, while her adversary was more or less doomed to take six. She had an iron shot, such as she had been playing perfectly, to reach the green and win the match. "She had only to hit a straight iron shot," as some writers are a little too apt to say, forgetting how much easier these things are for the people who don't have to do them. Perhaps Miss Wethered herself became conscious of how apparently little separated her from victory. At any rate, she hooked her ball into some hummocks to the left, and the hole was halved in six. That, too, had its effect. Miss Wethered played two rather weak holes. Miss Leitch took her chance, won them both and halved the match. That, as I said, ought to have been the end. Both players had palpably had all they wanted, but the law is inexorable and out they had to go again with a mighty crowd lining the course all the way to the first hole. Miss Wethered reached the edge of the green with her second and then laid a very long putt stone dead. A very fine putt it was, but there are occasions when the extra holes have a feeling of anticlimax, and this was one of them.

Miss Wethered then retired for a while to private life, but in 1929 she again donned battle armor, unable to resist the lure of playing in that year's Ladies' championship. It was scheduled to be held on the Old Course at St. Andrews.

# The Greatest Women's Match of All Time

## Al Laney

"Following the Leaders"                    The Classics of Golf, 1991

The British Ladies' championship was held at St. Andrews the week after the Open that summer of 1929, and it held special interest for both American and British correspondents. Glenna Collett, who had won three U.S. Women's titles and would win three more, had come over to make another bid for the British. That was reason enough to be on hand, but it was only half of it. Joyce Wethered, called by nearly everyone the greatest female golfer ever, had come out of retirement, the British papers said, "to repel the American invasion". There was a lot of feeling in England about British titles going overseas, but the British Ladies' title had never been won by an American girl, and they wanted to keep it that way.

They had feared for the worst, however, when Miss Wethered had retired. She had beaten Miss Collett at Troon in 1925 in her last tournament, so the popular press made quite a stir over Miss Wethered's "patriotic gesture". She herself said it was just that she had always wanted to win at St. Andrews, and the championship had not been played on the Old Course since she was a child. It made a good story, though, and we all went along with it.

I was reluctant to leave Edinburgh unexplored so soon after Muirfield. Brief glimpses had been fascinating. Edinburgh is one of the most majestic cities in all Europe, still very much the capital of a kingdom that has not existed for two centuries. Here the pulse of an older Scotland seems still to beat. More than two hundred years of a common language, the same currency, and the same history have not made the two people the same. The Scots gave golf to the English but retained their Scottishness.

Walking the Royal Mile from Edinburgh Castle high above the town to Holyrood, it needs little imagination to call up the tragic Mary Stuart, who played golf, and to feel the flow of Scottish history. And besides, those other famous courses along the East Lothian coast demanded attention: Dalmahoy, with its three-storied Georgian club-house, and the Royal Burgess Golfing Society of Edinburgh, founded in 1735. This pleasant duty had to wait, and late on the day after Muir-field, I followed my British colleagues north of the Firth of Forth and on to the marvelous old town of St. Andrews and to what seems to me now one of the pleasantest weeks in a long string of British summers filled with storm and sunshine. This was the first visit on which I had time to loaf, and I wandered about the town in the long Scottish twilight when work was done and in the early mornings before it began, getting ac-quainted with a surprising number of townspeople. I must have fallen under the spell of St. Andrews as so many others have.

The Old Course was full of people when I arrived on the Saturday before the Tuesday when the tournament was to begin. They mingled freely with the entrants in the Ladies' Championship who were taking their final warm-up. I did so, too, and had a long, leisurely Sunday to look over the celebrated course. I had seen it and walked it before, but I could not say I knew it until that tournament. As is well-known to golfers, the Old Course, one of four courses wedged into the thumb of land between St. Andrews Bay and the Eden River, is a public course on which anyone may play for a small fee. Members of the local golf clubs also play it. The principal club is the Royal and Ancient whose club-house stands like a fortress, or a railroad station, behind the first tee.

It was in 1834 that King William IV was prevailed upon to become the patron of the golf club in St. Andrews, the second club to be formed in Scotland and already the respected leader in guiding the growth of the game. William IV agreed to become the club's patron, and it could henceforth call itself The Royal and Ancient Golf Club of St. Andrews. I was not admitted to this royal, sandstone clubhouse on this occasion, since the R. & A. had not yet recognized the right of the press to occupy the clubhouse. I did not pass the threshold for some years, but, in this respect, I was well ahead of every British Open champion except Harold Hilton and Bob Jones. Professionals still were required to remain out-side. When the sanctuary finally had been opened to us, Henry Long-hurst, that delightful and perceptive correspondent of the London *Sunday Times*, declared under oath that the first words he heard after crossing the threshold into the "Big Room" came from an old gentleman seated before the fire, who said, "I must agree, Sir, that a certain lack of discipline is to be observed among the younger generation today."

It also is well-known that many people love the Old Course and some do not, but most of those who do not generally come to do so if they study it and play it long enough. Some excellent golfers have testified to a deep disappointment on their first visit. Others have indulged in ecstacies without knowing the place at all, and some have called it great because they were reluctant to say otherwise. The course is all it is said to be. While it appears to have been laid out casually centuries ago, it still is a fine test today, although players now use a ball that travels a hundred yards farther from every tee. My own first impression of the Old Course was that no architect in his right mind would think of laying it out the same way if he were starting from scratch.

Golf reporters in my early days saw comparatively little play by women. There always seemed to be something else going on that needed to be covered, and the events women played were considered inconsequential from an editor's point of view. There was no women's professional golf at all, and only the local, district and sectional tournaments were regularly reported by the papers. I had never covered a women's national event and had seen few of the best girls in any kind of tournament play. I had observed Miss Wethered on a few non-championship occasions, which had been her only appearances after 1925, and once I saw her in a mixed-foursome competition with her brother Roger as her partner. Like everyone else, I had been impressed with her style, but I did not suppose she would be good enough to beat Glenna again after four years away from tournament golf. This now seems a bit strange since I had not seen Glenna at all, and I knew very well that Bob Jones looked upon Joyce as practically an equal. I accepted Glenna on faith, and I realized that her record was the finest compiled by any lady golfer who had risen to the top in our country. I felt certain that Glenna would win, although she had returned empty-handed from her other journeys to Britain.

The meeting of these two young women was built into a terrific international confrontation comparable to the meeting of Suzanne Lenglen and Helen Wills on the tennis court at Cannes a few years earlier, and the press corps on hand was comparably large. When their names appeared on opposite sides of the championship draw, it was taken for granted that they would meet in the final, a development much less certain in golf than in tennis. Happily it came about, and that Saturday remains the most memorable day of women's golf for me.

I did not see as much of Miss Wethered's play through the early rounds as I should have, because I was trying to see every stroke Glenna played. Besides being rather taken with Glenna, it was she about whom I would write each day, and there was no other way to learn about a match than to follow it, noting the key strokes and the holes won and lost. You had to hustle if you wanted to know these things before writing, and those who write the best golf still hustle.

I saw a good deal of the two girls off the course. In St. Andrews you were bound to see them since everybody went to the same places. Glenna was stopping at the Grand Hotel, where I also had a room, and she and Joyce seemed to be very friendly. They were together a lot, two very attractive young women and the two best golfers of their sex in all the world. Both were perfectly natural, friendly, and charming, but I made no effort to impress myself on either because I believed then that athletes were entitled not to be bothered unduly by morning-paper reporters. There were always plenty of afternoon-paper reporters, tabloid and wire-service men who really needed to speak with them. They did not lack attention, and they both went through it with a good deal of dignity considering that everything was overdone in the Fabulous Twenties.

So, having got the two of them safely through to the final, we all were set for two rounds over the famous course that Saturday in May with high hopes of a good story to write for the Sunday paper. I was confident it would be about an American victory. That was because Glenna's last two victories on Friday over eighteen holes had been most impressive. She had come to the big test with her best game well in hand.

I wonder still if any girl anywhere in the world ever played finer golf than Glenna did at the start of their match. For eleven holes she did not make a single mistake. The hole-by-hole notes I made had that piece of information written opposite the figure 12 on the card. I made this note as they were standing on the 12th tee with the River Eden at their backs. This is where the course, having made the celebrated "loop"— the seventh through the eleventh—turns back, and the golfers now play to the pins on the right-hand side of the double greens as they head back to town. Glenna was three under level 4s and five up. These figures represent terrific golf on such a course, and I was thinking it would not be such an exciting story to write if this kept up. What strange thoughts we entertain during a long match, when there is plenty of time to play with them! The 12th is a short par-4 whose green is shared with the sixth hole. Both girls avoided the trouble on it and were comfortably on the green with their seconds. Glenna, putting first, rolled her ball close to the cup. She had left herself little more than two or three feet for her par.

Miss Wethered said afterward that the 12th was "the crux of the whole game". She thought that if Glenna had not missed that three-foot putt, which would have won the hole and made her six up—Joyce herself had been guilty of "criminally taking three putts"—the results never would have been in doubt. I do not know about that, but I still can feel the shock of Glenna missing her putt for her par. I had noted it as being shorter than three feet, and it certainly wasn't a difficult putt.

Thinking it was a sure thing, I was moving away from the green to be in position to watch the drives from the 13th tee. I saw the miss over my shoulder. I stopped still, and I must have exclaimed, too, as the crowd let out the kind of noise that always accompanies unexpected failure— half gasp, half shout—quickly followed by a wild scramble to get to the next vantage point.

I thought, "Good Heavens! How could Glenna have been so careless!" Then I had a first faint glimmer of foreboding. I had seen Miss Wethered react quickly and punish mistakes, especially in defeating Molly Gourlay, one of the best players in Britain, a couple of rounds earlier. Nothing was lost, though. Glenna had got a half, and that one little mistake in twelve holes indicated how well she was playing. If she could go in to lunch five up, that should insure victory in the afternoon.

As I walked slowly with the uncontrolled crowd swirling past me toward the 13th tee, I realized with something of a shock how badly I wanted Glenna to win. It was all right to hope for an American victory because that would make a better story, but this went beyond that. And for the first time also, as they played the thirteenth, I entertained the thought that Glenna might not win.

It is hardly proper to say that Miss Wethered had been let off the hook by that missed putt, but she must have been encouraged by that error after the way her opponent had been playing. She promptly holed a twelve- or fourteen-footer to win the 13th, and then got back two more holes before they finished the morning round. So the probable six up at the 12th had become only two up when we set out after lunch on the second journey around the course. Word of Joyce's recovery had got about the town, and the crowd now was large—ten thousand, they said, although that seems exaggerated. People were telling one another in jubilant voices loud enough for Glenna to hear, "She's only two doon noo". The match was turning right around as play progressed, and our girl's position was becoming desperate if not hopeless. I fought this thought all the way to the ninth, where Glenna had been five up only a few hours earlier. That seemed another match altogether when we came there again, for now she was four down with only nine to play. Over the fifteen holes from that unhappy morning turning-point, nine had been won by Miss Wethered. And Glenna had not given them away.

There was still to be some excitement. Glenna gave us hope by winning the 10th and 11th in 3s, and magnificent 3s they were. So she came to the fateful 12th only two down and seven holes left in which to get them back. From this point in the morning, Miss Wethered had got back three, so it was entirely possible. Joyce went back to three up by winning the 13th, but she lost the 14th, the Long Hole In, to Glenna's par 5. What encouraged us here was that Glenna could have won the hole with an even bigger score, so poorly did Joyce play it. Then, at the 15th, the match reached its highest point of excitement and its climax.

This hole, a little more than 400 yards, shares an enormous green with the third hole, and its right edge is up against the railroad line. Miss Wethered, still apparently shaken by her experience at the 14th, sliced her drive, a rare thing for her. It ended up close to the rail line, and this prevented her from reaching the green. She played short of it and then left herself a putt of 18 or 20 feet with a half-flubbed run-up. This made four poor shots on the last five holes. For the first time all day, she was not hitting the ball well.

Glenna meanwhile had followed a fine drive with a shot to the green with a wood, and then, with Joyce still so far away in three, she sensibly ran her ball close for her par 4. Only one down with three to play seemed certain now, and, with Miss Wethered playing so nervously, anything might happen. What did happen was that Miss Wethered holed the putt and undoubtedly won the match then and there, four holes from home. The putt was a really hard one, slightly uphill and over uneven ground. I would have given odds it could not be made, and even after she had struck the ball, I was sure it would not drop. She had hit it much too firmly, and it would have gone a long way past, but, of course, that was the only way to hit it. If the ball didn't go into the cup, it mattered not at all how far past it might go, since Glenna already was certain of her 4. It appeared to be another nervous stroke that Miss Wethered had played. The ball bounced a couple of times on its way, and I still do not quite see how it managed to get into the cup. Perhaps it can be explained by the fact that for the great ones or the ones favored by the gods these things seem to happen at critical moments, and you could cite a dozen occasions in a dozen sports to prove it.

If you wanted Glenna to win, though, it was hard to take, because, only a moment before the ball dropped, hope had flared. Miss Wethered may have thought herself lucky that Glenna had missed a three-foot putt at the 12th in the morning, but in the afternoon she created her own luck by running down a putt six times as long as the one Glenna had missed. Anyhow we all knew when it dropped that this was it, and the shout with which it was greeted showed that. Miss Wethered remained two up, and now she needed only a couple of halves for the match. There was a feeling that she was bound to get them, and one came immediately at the 16th, making her dormie two.

The crowd now was having trouble controlling itself. I followed well behind when the ladies had driven on the Road Hole, and, after seeing Glenna make two somewhat less than perfect shots, I worked my way

*The closing act in one of golf's most famous matches. Glenna Collett*
*congratulates Joyce Wethered at the finish of their thrilling 36-hole struggle in*
*the final of the British Ladies' championship at St. Andrews.*

through the throng and onto the road behind the green. It was obvious
that, when the time came, this crowd was going to break and rush
toward Miss Wethered, and I wanted to be well out of the way. I could
not see them play out the hole, but this wasn't necessary. There was no
doubt that this was the actual end, with Miss Wethered winning the
17th, or 35th, hole to close out the match, 3 and 1. I stood far back as the
crowd, with a loud burst of cheering, rushed onto the green, sweeping
players, caddies, and officials into a swirling mass. The two girls disappeared in a sea of people, and years passed before I saw either of them
again.

I waited until I could walk along the road, then went slowly back to

my room at the Grand. I felt depressed and didn't want to write the
story. I don't see how it would have been possible not to want Glenna to
win that match, and it was only prolonged contemplation of Miss Wethered's excellencies that brought the proper perspective. I had been gradually coming to a realization throughout the afternoon that Miss Wethered had won because she was the better player, and now I had to face
that thought before sitting down to write of her victory. I had cared
more than I had realized, but the evidence was in.

I sat for a long time in the late afternoon going over in my mind Joyce
Wethered's wonderful shotmaking and trying to find words for it. I tried
out such phrases as "serene and gracious swing", swiped from somewhere, and her "elegant and faultless style". (I can still picture to myself the perfection of those low-flying mashie shots and the dead certainty of those putts.) At the 17th green, just before the end, a spectator
in front of me had said, "She's wi'oot maircy". Yes, nae maircy when the
battle was joined but otherwise gentle, unpretentious and immensely
popular. Most of these words of praise might also have been said of
Glenna, and it occurs to me that there never have been two more attractive players and personalities to contest a championship.

For me, Miss Wethered remains the finest woman golfer I have seen.
Those who did not see her may dispute this judgment, and I feel sure
they will. Some will have it that Babe Zaharias was the best. Others
will vote for Mickey Wright or some other of the terribly good girls on
the tour. The record books will support them, and if you are going to
argue these things, you have to lean on the record. Women's golf has
changed so much since Miss Wethered's day that comparisons are difficult if not altogether useless. There was no women's professional golf
at all in the playing sense then. The talented women golfers of that
time, and there were a good many of them, played only one or two major
tournaments a year. They played regularly if informally at their clubs,
in their own sectional events and in the national championships. That
was about it. The girls on the Ladies' PGA Tour today actually play
more big tournaments in one season than Joyce and Glenna played in
their entire careers. This, in itself, indicates the tremendous changes
that have come about.

The girls of the 1970s score sensationally, but scores do not tell everything, and I think both Glenna and Joyce would score with the
champions if they were playing now. The golf we saw on the Old Course
confirms this, I think. Glenna and Joyce were amateurs who played
mostly for the pleasure of it, and yet their skills were at the professional
level.

Perhaps not even Glenna and Joyce could play better golf than Babe

Zaharias did in winning her last U.S. Open title at the Salem Country Club, in Peabody, Mass., in 1954 with a 72-hole score of 291, when she already was in the later stages of the cancer from which she died. They would be equally hard put to match Mickey Wright's performance in winning the same title at Baltustrol in 1961 with 293. I suspect that Miss Wright's third and fourth rounds on the final day, 69-72, were, in fact, the most dynamic golf played by a woman in my time in a championship event over such a long and difficult course.

Still, I think it took something comparable to beat Glenna that day at St. Andrews, and from the simple standpoint of striking the ball with various clubs and doing it beautifully, I think I must stick with Miss Wethered. She could drive the somewhat less lively ball with wooden-shafted clubs as far as they drive the ball in recent years, and she could make the ball "do" things that today's women's champions don't seem to know about at all. It should not be forgotten in this era of so-called power golf that Miss Wethered drove level with Bob Jones on many holes when they played together, and that she could get home with her second on holes somewhat longer than 500 yards. She did not have that useful club, the wedge, but she solved that problem by never getting into places where it would be needed.

I realize that I have seen comparatively little women's golf above the district level and that there are many women professionals I have not seen play. But I hold to my perhaps stubborn belief that Miss Wethered was the best, and I am bolstered in it by two pretty good men whose experience of lady golfers was more extensive than my own. Henry Cotton has said of Joyce, "In my time no golfer, male or female, has stood out so far ahead of his or her contemporaries," and Bob Jones, after playing a friendly foursome with Miss Wethered on the Old Course at St. Andrews before the British Amateur of 1930, testified in writing as follows: "She did not miss one shot. She did not even half-miss one shot, and when we had finished, I could not help saying that I never played with anyone, man or woman, amateur or professional, who made me feel so utterly outclassed. I have no hesitancy in saying she is the best golfer I have ever seen."

# Miss Wethered versus Miss Collett

## Enid Wilson

"A History of Golf in Britain"     Cassell and Co., Ltd., 1952

The lure of St. Andrews was too strong for Miss Wethered, who came out of her self-imposed retirement when the British was held there in 1929. It also attracted Miss Glenna Collett and several other prominent Americans. Miss Wethered, with characteristic honesty, denied that her motives in entering were patriotic ones to keep the invaders away. The historic associations of the Old Course were more than she could resist. Only her intimate friends were aware of the quality of her golf, and the rest of the world had to wait patiently until her arrival in Scotland to see if any changes had taken place during the past four years. About Miss Collett there were no uncertainties; we knew she was at her zenith and that she was easily the best and most powerful woman golfer on the other side of the Atlantic. She was fully acquainted with our courses and climate, and we were not a little afraid that she would achieve her ambition and carry off our cup. With Miss Wethered and Miss Collett in opposite halves of the draw, the concern of the entire golfing community was centred on the final to come. Had anyone upset the apple-cart and prevented the drama from taking place, they would never have been forgiven—especially in the light of what followed. The earlier rounds were training canters to build up form for the vital combat. Certainly nothing else was talked of at St. Andrews that week. The opinion prevailed that 'she' would win; and yet, with all the implicit faith we had, there was a little gnawing worm of anxiety. Miss Wethered arrived at St. Andrews with no idea of the impending strain; but as the week wore on, she must have been fully aware of the hopes which she carried, and on the morning of the final the tension of this terrific meeting must have been very real to her.

The weather had wavered during the earlier part of the championship and then relented, so that when the enormous crowd gathered to witness the *pièce de résistance*, the sun was shining from a cloudless sky. This lovely morning must have helped Miss Collett. In the previ-

72

*Tense moments in the great final at St. Andrews: Joyce above, Glenna below.*

ous rounds, the American had not quite produced the golf of which we knew she was capable. Now, with everything at stake, she rose to the occasion, and without a vestige of a mistake she reached the turn in 34. Such golf was almost unbelievable, and Miss Wethered, who had played neither very well nor very ill, was five down. Up to the twelfth, Miss Collett was a woman inspired, beyond mortal reach. And then, with a putt to become six up, certainly no more difficult and not as long as some which she had holed with ease that morning, she missed. The spell was broken, and she became human once more. This was what Miss Wethered must have hoped and waited for, and slowly but surely she took command of the game and won back three of the six holes that remained before lunch.

A thoroughly scared and chastened crowd went to find nourishment and fortification for what the afternoon might have in store. The consensus of opinion was that Miss Wethered had passed the storm and would sail home with moderate comfort. The Elders of St. Andrews must also have been shaken by the best ball of the two distinguished ladies, which was 71. Nothing to equal this had been produced in a women's final before.

After lunch, Miss Collett's lead evaporated. The position at the twenty-seventh was Miss Wethered four up. She had taken 73 strokes for the homeward half of the first round and the outward half of the second one. All seemed secure, and then back came Miss Collett with two birdie threes, to make a fight and show that she still had shots left in her locker. Crisis loomed large on the thirty-third hole for Miss Wethered, who looked likely to lose it and be only one up with three to play; however, a six-yard putt rescued her, and provided the vitally-needed half. The match concluded at the Road Hole. Miss Wethered had achieved her ambition of winning the British at St. Andrews, and the fulfilment of the wish had come to pass with superlative golf. Miss Collett never capitulated, never ceased fighting, every inch of those thirty-five holes. What a glorious game it was!

Every generation swears that its sporting heroes and heroines are better than any before or since, and one spectator at least will always be happy in the belief that nothing could surpass the final of the British in 1929. Superb skill, artistry, sportsmanship and drama for an entire day! These qualities, and the classic setting in which they were framed, make this the finest moment in British women's golf.

# The Origin of the Curtis Cup Matches

## Margaret Curtis

Golf Journal                                    September, 1954

A few years after World War I—in 1924, to be exact—the women's inter-city team match among Boston, New York and Philadelphia was held in Boston. As was customary, a meeting took place in the afternoon to discuss any matters that might have come up in relation to the match or to the Women's Eastern Golf Association championship, which had grown out of the practice rounds preceding the match.

These matches were great fun, and it was considered quite an honor to represent one's home city. We were a very congenial crowd. At this particular meeting someone said, "What fun it would be to play international team matches!"

Several British girls had earlier come over to play in our championship, including Miss Rhona Adair, Miss Dorothy Campbell (later Mrs. Hurd), and the extraordinary Miss Lottie Dod, who had been five times the ladies tennis champion at Wimbledon, retired unbeaten, took up golf, won that championship in 1904, and also won the British figure skating championship.

Mrs. Hurd, who became a resident of this country, was going to England that summer and said she would take it up with the Ladies' Golf Union, in London. The Union reported that, while it liked the idea, its treasury was too depleted as a result of the war to consider it.

But the idea was started.

As a matter of fact, we had long since had a taste of the fun of international golf.

In the spring of 1905, Miss Frances C. Griscom, of Philadelphia, suggested that it would be a very pleasant experience to go over and play in the British championship at Cromer, England. Eight of us went. The championship was held early in the season. Since this was before the days of southern tournaments, most of us had put our clubs in moth balls from November to May and hadn't much practice.

It was customary for the British to play their international matches,

*Two redoubtable sisters, Margaret and Harriot Curtis, did more than anyone else to launch international team competition.*

among England, Scotland, Ireland and Wales, just before their championship. A Britisher suggested that we play their combined strength. We were just eight friends, but in a gay, hopeless mood we took them on.

Miss Georgianna N. Bishop, of Bridgeport, Conn., then our national champion, was the only one of us to win, but we greatly enjoyed the match and the occasion. Of our eight, four had been or were to be United States champions. They were Miss Griscom, Miss Bishop, my sister, Harriot, and I. Miss Molly Adams, of Boston, was a runner-up. The other members of our group were Mrs. Samuel Bettle, of Philadelphia, Miss Griscom's sister, Miss Emily Lockwood, of Boston, and Miss Ethel Burnett, of New York.

Miss Griscom, an ardent follower of our golf, had also arranged a team match with Canada in 1904.

In 1927, Harriot and I attempted to give the idea another push by offering a cup for an international match. Miss Fanny C. Osgood, of Boston, was appointed a committee of one to take up the matter once

*The first American women to participate in an international team match were photographed at Cromer, England, in 1905. The four in the rear are Miss Ethel Burnett, Miss Frances C. Griscom, Miss Harriot Curtis, and Miss Emily N. Lockwood. The three in the middle row are Miss Georgianna N. Bishop, Mrs. Samuel Bettle, and Miss Margaret Curtis. The young lady in front is Miss Molly B. Adams. Miss Bishop was the only one to win her match, but this international competition eventually led to the bienniel matches that bear the Curtis sisters' name.*

more with the LGU. While the British still felt the idea might be premature, a tentative plan was made for a match in 1928. This match never materialized, however, because of financial obstacles.

In 1928, the USGA Women's Committee appointed a sub-committee to consider plans for conducting and financing an international team. Mrs. Charles Fraser, of New York, was chairman, and the other members were Miss Florence McNeely and myself. Although this committee found interest among our golf associations favorable, it, too, was stymied by the financial problem abroad.

Although that committee was dissolved in 1930, the situation thereafter took a turn for the better. The USGA Executive Committee approved the match in principle.

On February 7, 1931, the LGU suddenly accepted an offer we had made to go to England for the first international team match. It also

*The first United States Curtis Cup team: back row, Mrs. L. D. Cheney, Mrs.
D. S. Hill, Mrs. Harley G. Higbie, Miss Virginia Van Wie, Miss Helen Hicks;
front row, Glenna Collett Vare, Miss Marion Hollins (captain), Miss
Maureen Orcutt.*

agreed to continue the matches here in 1934. Shortly thereafter, the
USGA agreed to assume financial responsibility for our side.

The selection of the first team proved unexpectedly simple, probably
simpler than any since. Each member of the USGA Women's Committee was asked to submit the names of fifteen players whom she considered of international-team caliber. Eight, and only eight, names appeared on every list; and since they represented the unanimous opinion
of the committee, they became the team. They were: Mrs. L. D. Cheney,
Miss Helen Hicks, Mrs. O. S. Hill, Mrs. Harley G. Higbie, Miss Marion
Hollins, Miss Maureen Orcutt, Miss Virginia Van Wie and Mrs. Edwin
H. Vare, Jr. Miss Hollins was chosen Captain.

Wentworth, England was the site of the first match, and it was completed in one day—May 21, 1932—with three foursomes in the morning
and six singles in the afternoon. It was a day of real gratification for us.

# A Cartoon from Punch

Punch Magazine                                          1929

PROFESSIONAL (AT INDOOR SCHOOL OF GOLF): *"Are you going to have a lesson, Madam?" MADAM: "No, but my friend is. I learnt last week."*

# The Final Warm-Up before the First Official Curtis Cup Match

## Pamela Emory

Golf Journal                                              May/June, 1992

"By the grace of God, May Day of 1930 in the village of Sunningdale was a beautiful day, a really lovely English spring day." That's how Molly Gourlay, the celebrated British golfer, described the setting to me in a 1985 interview. It was there, some twenty-five miles southwest of London on Sunningdale Golf Club's venerable Old Course, that the American women amateur golfers played a British team in what became known as the 1930 Unofficial Match—five foursome matches in the morning followed by ten singles in the afternoon.

The 1930 Unofficial Match was the last thing Sunningdale really wanted or needed: women golfers tramping over the magnificent layout in a match that created much publicity, excitement, and crowds. On this glorious spring day, over 2,000 spectators showed up, along with countless dogs—some unleashed—and a Movietone camera crew. It was quite a sight. Here was this seemingly brash American group, with their wild-colored clothing, in contrast to the British women in their neckties, attracting this monstrous crowd on the staid playing fields of Sunningdale—but after all, it was for the "good of the game" and all that.

The match was organized by Glenna Collett, the American Women's champion that year (and in 1922, 1925, 1928, 1929, and finally in 1935). Glenna had corresponded with Joyce Wethered, her longtime friendly rival and the British Ladies' champion in 1929 (and in 1922, 1924, and 1925), and asked her to round up a team to play a group of American women who were coming over for the British Ladies'. Molly Gourlay recalled how she became the captain: "For some reason or another, Joyce said she couldn't do it; she was beginning to tire from golf. I was the English champion at the time, and she asked me if I'd do it. So I said I would with pleasure, little realizing what I was taking on. I was a committee of one, the sole selector. I had anonymous letters saying I was only choosing my friends and was most unfair. I had two proposals

*The American team on the R.M.S. Berengaria: from the left, Rosalie Knapp, Maureen Orcutt, Edith Guier, Mrs. Lee Mida, Opal Hill, Mrs. Leo Federman, Helen Hicks, Glenna Collett, Virgina Van Wie, Bernice Wall, Louise Fordyce, Fritzie Stifel, Peggy Wattles, Virginia Holzderber, Mrs. Stewart Hanley (coach), and Mrs. H. A. Martelle.*

of marriage from people I didn't know. I wrote back, 'Thank you very much. I'm sorry I haven't got time.'"

Gourlay's procurement of Sunningdale was no easy task. Although she lived nearby, she was not a member. "Women couldn't be members in those days," she explained. "They were very anti-women *then*. So, I sailed over to see the Secretary. He was very pleasant until I said, 'We'd like to play a match here.' He said, 'Oh, don't you know, we don't have women's matches?' I said, 'Oh, you'll have this one, won't you?' After some argument, he decided he'd ask if we *could* play there. And they agreed we could, thinking we'd putt ourselves potty as hell."

Most of the American team set sail from New York on April 22nd on the R.M.S. *Berengaria* of the Cunard Line. They had a grand time on board: reading, napping, eating, walking, playing shuffleboard, dancing, and even managing to practice by hitting golf balls into the ocean. Rough weather delayed their arrival by a day.

The Americans were housed at the Savoy Hotel in London. Speculation greeted them when they arrived at Sunningdale. Enid Wilson, a member of the British team, wrote, "They interested us immensely by bringing with them huge quantities of clubs and balls—the latter for practice purposes—which were carted about the countryside in the most awe-inspiring voluminous leather caddie bags."

Every move the team members made was a potential subject for the Movietone film crew. Even with black-and-white film, the Americans were popular subjects because of their clothing. One headline proclaimed, "Rainbow Hues of U.S. Girl Golfers." Wilson wrote, "Another novelty was their brightly colored clothing. We were tempted to scoff— and, like so many scoffers, soon followed suit."

One of the biggest issues the Americans faced was which shafts to use, hickory or the newer steel models. Helen Hicks, it was reported, brought with her six steel-shafted drivers, brassies, and spoons which she could choose from, depending on the wind and turf. Captain Collett carted both kinds across, but was using hickory during practice.

Given the Americans' late arrival and the mob scene on the ruggedly glorious Sunningdale heathland, it was no wonder that the result of the team match seemed anticlimactic. The final score was 8½ to 6½ in favor of the British.

One of the greatest individual matches was played by the two captains, Collett and Gourlay. The latter told me recently, "It was the best match I *ever* played, under the circumstances. I'd had all the hassels of arranging the thing, a great responsibility. No ladies' tees but I went round in 75. I was two down near the end and finished rather well. [She won, 1 up.] It was great fun. We halved the foursomes, so everything depended on the singles, and we ultimately won the singles." In Collett's defense, she, too, went round in 75. *The Times* reported in its coverage of the match, "Miss Gourlay . . . had all the worst of it from the second hole to the 13th against Miss Collett, but in the pinch she produced such golf as any 'class' man player would be pleased to show, and turned what seemed inevitable defeat into a great and gallant victory."

When I contacted a number of the 1930 team members back in 1982, their recollections as to who had won the match were interesting. One American commented, "I didn't even know it was a match," while several others thought the United States had won. Since this informal match was the forerunner to the Curtis Cup, there was no cup to present. That would have to wait till 1932.

# An Incident at Turnberry

## Francis Ouimet

"A Game of Golf"                    Houghton Mifflin Co., 1932

On our way to St. Andrews, we stopped off at Turnberry to watch the Ladies' championship. Turnberry is one of those seaside courses, situated near the Irish Sea. Looking out to sea one's eyes take in a huge rock called Ailsa Craig, completely surrounded by water. It made a tremendous impression upon me as it stood like a huge fortress in the emerald-colored water.

In that championship was a girl, Joyce Wethered, who was fast developing into a great golfer. She was having a close match with a player whose name does not come to me at the moment. Miss Wethered's play in the high wind impressed me most favorably, for she seemed to have superb control of her ball at all times. Playing the seventeenth, she led by one hole. That particular hole was really difficult, since it is a three-shotter, and a nasty wind swept across the line of play from right to left. Such a wind is in my opinion the most difficult of all winds to play against, because the common tendency is to play the ball to the right and allow for wind driftage.

Miss Wethered had hit a fine drive and brassie down the fairway and was left with an iron shot of perhaps a hundred and twenty yards to the green. I have seen any number of first-class male golfers under similar conditions play well to the right, allowing the wind to bring the ball back on line. I observed Miss Wethered closely to see just what she would do. Out came a straight-faced iron club from her bag and she took her stance. A short backswing and a smart, decisive stroke through the ball. It traveled low and started to the left, and then began to turn into the wind. The ball was hit hard enough to accentuate the curve as it bored ahead. The wind tried hard to blow that ball off line, but it was too skillfully struck to permit such a thing. When it landed on the green, it took one hop and stopped dead in its tracks three feet from the cup. That was enough for me. Then and there I decided I had seen the finest woman golfer of them all.

# The First Curtis Cup Match

The United States Golf Association                    1932

*Joyce Wethered tees off in the first Curtis Cup match at England's Wentworth Golf Club. Watching are Glenna Collett Vare, Marion Hollins, and Molly Gourlay. Joyce beat Glenna in their singles, but the United States won the match 5½ to 3½.*

# Playing the Old Course with Joyce Wethered

## Robert T. Jones, Jr.

The American Golfer                                        August, 1930

Ordinarily I would never take advantage of a friendly round of golf by making the play of a person, kind enough to go around with me, the subject of an article. I realize that everyone likes to play occasionally a round of golf when reputations can be forgotten, with nothing more at stake than the outcome of the match and a little friendly bantering afterwards.

Just before the British Amateur championship at St. Andrews, Miss Joyce Wethered allowed herself to be led away from her favorite trout stream in order to play eighteen holes of golf over the Old Course in company with her brother, Roger, Dale Bourne, then recently crowned English champion, and myself. At the time, I fully appreciated that Miss Wethered had not had a golf club in her hand for over a fortnight, and I certainly should have made no mention of the game had she not played so superbly.

We started out by arranging a four-ball match—Roger and Dale against Miss Wethered and myself—on a best and worst ball basis. I don't know why we didn't play an ordinary four-ball match, unless we fancied that the lady would be the weakest member of the four and that in a best-ball match her ball would not count for very much. If any of us had any such idea at the start of the match, it is now quite immaterial, for there is not the slightest chance that we should admit it.

We played the Old Course from the very back, or the championship tees, and with a slight breeze blowing off the sea. Miss Wethered holed only one putt of more than five feet, took three putts rather half-heartedly from four yards at the seventeenth after the match was over, and yet she went round St. Andrews in 75. She did not miss one shot; she did not even half-miss one shot; and when we finished, I could not help saying that I had never played golf with anyone, man or woman, amateur or professional, who made me feel so utterly outclassed.

It was not so much the score she made as the way she made it. Diegel,

Hagen, Smith, Von Elm and several other male experts would likely have made a better score, but one would all the while have been expecting them to miss shots. It was impossible to expect that Miss Wethered would never miss a shot—but she never did.

To describe her manner of playing is almost impossible. She stands quite close to the ball, she places the club once behind, takes one look toward the objective, and strikes. Her swing is not long—surprisingly short, indeed, when one considers the power she develops—but it is rhythmic to the last degree. She makes ample use of her wrists, and her left arm within the hitting area is firm and active. This, I think, distinguishes her swing from that of any other woman golfer, and it is the one thing that makes her the player she is.

Men are always interested in the distance which a first-class woman player can attain. Miss Wethered, of course, is not as long with any club as the good male player. Throughout the round, I found that when I hit a good one I was out in front by about twenty yards—by not so much when I failed to connect. It was surprising, though, how often on a fine championship course fine iron play by the lady could make up the difference. I kept no actual count, but I am certain that her ball was the nearest to the hole more often than any of the other three.

I have no hesitancy in saying that, accounting for the unavoidable handicap of a woman's lesser physical strength, she is the finest golfer I have ever seen.

# Visualizing the Shot

## Joyce Wethered

The American Golfer                    September, 1931

There is a great deal of talk about temperament. We understand that it counts for so much in competitive golf, making the difference between the first and second-class player. Temperament is concerned with our thoughts, and the player has two or three hours of thinking before him while he plays a round.

In watching a big match the spectator can probably learn very little from the demeanor or the expression of the players, but at the time it is evident that their minds are exceptionally alert and keyed up. This is a state which can produce inspired moments, and can, at the same time, produce chaos. The part that the mind plays in imagination is extremely varied and differs with each individual. There is the time spent while the player is walking after his ball, or waiting through what may seem interminable ages while his opponent studies his putt and meditates on the green. At these times it may be a matter of great difficulty to keep the mind still and at rest.

To many the mind is a racing, revolving machine that cannot be quieted when once it is roused. A few favored individuals may possibly be ignorant of these difficulties and may experience no trouble in keeping their minds evenly concentrated on the match, undisturbed by what has happened or what is likely to happen presently. But I suspect that they are rare exceptions even amongst those who declare that they have no nerves. Calmness can be cultivated, and without it the technique of hitting the ball can be seriously affected. If consistent accuracy is to be expected, stroke play must be largely mechanical; the mind must be as free as possible from technical worries and able to concentrate upon visualizing what has to be done.

This personal vision of the shot is a thing which everyone experiences, and it would be of the greatest interest to be able to get behind the minds of some of the most distinguished players and see the shot as they see it.

By vision, I include the whole feeling of the shot, as you are going to play it. Personally I find that certain contours—for instance, in the shape of the greens—have an effect on the imagination, suggesting either a sliced or pulled shot. I must definitely allow for it or correct the feeling in the making of the stroke. The most subtle of golf architects are well aware of this force of suggestion and quite rightly make full use of it in order to puzzle the player and get him in two minds.

It is surprising how difficult it is sometimes to hit a straight shot at a hole where perhaps some hill or contour—not affecting in any way the actual flight or landing of the ball—makes one feel that the ball must curve in its flight also. In most cases you must play the shot as you visualize it in order to make it convincing, but there is a danger also that, if you see the shot wrong, you will be led astray.

If we have a tendency to slice the ball, we are apt to see the shot drifting from left to right; we may even see it running away from us across the green. If we take our golf seriously, we shall not feel satisfied if we allow ourselves to yield to the inclination to play the shot in this way. We must resist and counteract the tendency by visualizing the shot as being held up firmly with even a suspicion of draw in order to strengthen our resolution. The club generally follows the inclination of the mind. We must positively see the ball flying as we wish it to, and the time will come when our technical ability will triumph over the weakness which previously would have mastered us.

On the putting green the mind can be a grave source of trouble. Begin to dislike the look of a putt, and the chances of holing it at once become less.

I can recommend only one frame of mind which might help us. We can, if we wish, pretend to enjoy the shots which frighten us. We can positively make ourselves look forward to playing as many of them as possible. Instead of fearing them, we can stimulate an interest in them. A delicate pitch over a bunker can be converted by a little judicious mental effort into a delightful adventure. We can assure ourselves that we enjoy using our putter, even if we feel incapable of holing a putt.

You may say that is only a method of self-deception, but if we can make ourselves believe what we wish to believe, we shall in a very short time have restored our confidence. Our pitches will then be deadly and the two-yarders will drop satisfactorily. There is more in the question of liking and disliking than one thinks. We all enjoy the shots we can hit successfully, and it is only, a step further to approach unpleasantly doubtful shots in the same spirit.

# Grantland Rice Introduces Me to Golf

## Babe Didrikson Zaharias

"This Life I've Led"          A.S. Barnes and Co., Inc., 1955

Shortly after I had moved to Dallas, Colonel McCombs had driven me home one Saturday afternoon, the way he often did. I'd been practicing basketball or track—I forget which. I was still in my sweat suit and tennis shoes. Anyway, Colonel McCombs said, "Babe, do you mind if I stop at a driving range on the way home and hit a few golf balls?"

I told him to go right ahead. I believe I added something about how silly I thought it was for people to hit a little white ball and then chase it. I was talking the way kids will talk when they don't know how to do something and so they pretend they're not interested in it. I don't suppose for a minute that I fooled Colonel McCombs. I imagine his whole idea was to get me thinking about golf, just as he'd taken me out to that track meet when I first moved to Dallas.

We stopped at the driving range, and Colonel McCombs hit a few drives. Finally he invited me to try one. Or maybe I asked him to let me do it. I took my stance in front of a light post. I reared back and swung with all my might. I caught that ball square, but I came around so hard that the club hit the light post on the follow through and broke in two. The little Scotsman who ran the driving range came running up to us. He was shouting. I thought he was mad because I'd broken the club. But instead of that he was yelling, "Wow! Look at that! See where she hit the ball!" They measured it, and it was about 250 yards.

But I don't think you could count either of those times I've mentioned as actually playing golf. So when Grantland Rice, the famous syndicated sports writer, invited me out to the Brentwood course during the Olympics, I'd never played a round of golf in my life.

Granny came around in a car early in the morning and picked me up at the hotel where I was staying, the Chapman Park. He had three other sportswriters with him—Paul Gallico, Westbrook Pegler, and Braven Dyer. Did it make me self-conscious to be with well-known

90

people like that? No, it's never seemed to bother me whether the people I meet are famous or not. All I was worried about was how good they were as golfers. I didn't want to look like a fool on that golf course.

While they were having some coffee before we teed off, I excused myself. I said I wanted to change my shoes and borrow some clubs. That wasn't all I wanted. I ducked out to the pro shop and hunted up Olin Dutra, the Brentwood pro, who won the PGA championship that year.

I said, "Mr. Dutra, I'm going to play golf with Granny Rice and Pegler and the boys. I want you to show me how it's supposed to be done so I won't look too bad out there."

He lent me some clubs, and he showed me as much as he could in a few minutes about the grip and the stance and the swing. He demonstrated how you should pivot when you swing. And he kept telling me, "Look at the ball real hard. That's the most important thing."

Finally we went out to play our round. Granny Rice was taking me as his partner because I was the beginner and he was considered the best player in our group. We played the other three. It was a best-ball match, so he'd have a chance to win for our side even if I didn't do any good.

I said to him, "I don't know how to play this game. So don't bet too much money!" He told me they were just going to play a dollar Nassau.

We flipped a coin, and Granny and I won the toss, so I was the first to drive off. I just put my ball down and was going to hit it right off the ground, but Granny said, "Hey! You have to tee up the ball before you drive." And he teed up my first ball for me, which I've always felt was quite an honor.

I drove, and the ball sailed straight out there about 240 yards. I outdrove all the men on that first hole. They'd thought I was a great natural athlete, and wanted to see how I'd do at a new sport. But after that first drive, they couldn't believe I'd hardly ever swung a club before. They said, "You must have played a lot of golf."

A majority of my drives that day were between 240 and 260 yards. Of course, I had some bad shots in between. I've read since that my score for the round was eighty-six. Actually I think it was around 100.

Granny played some good golf, so he and I were ahead. As I remember it, we were two up coming into the sixteenth, short hole. There was a big dip down from the tee, and then the green was way up on top of a hill.

Paul Gallico hit the best tee shot. It looked like he was a cinch to win the hole. So Granny whispered to me, "Babe, why don't you challenge Paul to race you down and up that hill?" Paul's a real good sport, and he accepted the challenge. Of course I beat him, because I was in peak condition, but he raced me all the way. He was so winded he had to lie down on the grass and catch his breath. When he finally got up, he four-putted the green. Granny and I won the hole and the match.

I'd thought about being a golfer before, but I think that was the day that really determined my future. Grantland Rice told me, and wrote in his column, that he'd never seen a woman hit a golf ball the way I could. He thought that I had the ability to be a great player.

Well, after the Olympics were over, I got back into the old office and basketball routine at Employers Casualty. I was still liking it. But the pressure got pretty heavy during the fall of 1932. People kept telling me how I could get rich if I turned professional. That big-money talk sounds nice when you're just a kid whose family has never had very much.

What I really wanted to do at this point was to become a golfer. I was going to make an appearance at the Dallas ball park, and they were going to present me an expensive watch. I went by the Cullum and Boren sporting-goods store in Dallas one day and saw this beautiful set of golf clubs in the window. It was like a girl seeing a mink coat. I was just dying to have those golf clubs, but I couldn't possibly afford to buy them.

I went in and handled the clubs. I know they'd have been glad to present them to me at the ball-park ceremony instead of the watch, which cost just about as much. However, it might impair my amateur standing in golf if I accepted those clubs. So I took the watch.

Early that December my name and picture turned up in a newspaper ad, with the statement that I liked the new 1933 Dodge automobile. The Southern branch of the Amateur Athletic Union declared me a professional. That would have been fair enough if I'd given permission for my name to be used in that ad, or taken pay for it. But I hadn't. A Dodge man in Dallas had set it up on his own. He didn't realize that it would cause any trouble.

I'd already started another basketball season with the Employers Casualty Golden Cyclones. This made me ineligible for that. And it meant I couldn't compete in the A.A.U. track meets any more. The Dodge man in Dallas wrote the A.A.U. explaining that I wasn't to blame, and so did the advertising agency that handled the ad. And later on that month the A.A.U. annouced that it was reinstating me as an amateur.

By then I'd decided to turn pro anyway. I started out by doing some work for the Chrysler Motor Company, which makes the Dodge car. They were sorry about what had happened, and they wanted to make it up to me. They brought me up to Detroit, with my sister Esther Nancy as chaperone, and got us a suite of rooms in the Book Cadillac Hotel. We

*Young Miss Mildred Didrikson takes up golf after proving unbeatable in the Olympic Games.*

met all the Chrysler people—the president, K. T. Keller, and everybody. And they were real nice. They hired me to appear at the Dodge booth at the Auto Show in Detroit. I signed autographs and talked to people. I even played the harmonica to attract the attention of the crowd and draw people over to the booth.

Chrysler also got George P. Emerson of the Ruthrauff & Ryan advertising agency to act as my agent and arrange some bookings for me. It didn't cost me anything. He got me a contract to start out making stage appearances on the RKO circuit after the Auto Show was over. I opened with a week at the Palace Theatre in Chicago. I had top billing in a stage show with Fifi D'Orsay and Bob Murphy and his Collegians. I was given the star dressing room. Somebody told me that Fifi D'Orsay didn't like that. I went to her and said, "Miss D'Orsay, I'd like for you to have my dressing room."

She said, "How sweet of you! But I wouldn't dream of it." We didn't change dressing rooms, but we became good friends after that.

I'd never done any kind of theatrical performing in my life. I thought I wasn't scared until we drove up to the theatre the first morning and saw a crowd of people lined up down the block. I said, "My Lord, I can't go through with this!"

I had an eighteen-minute act. A performer named George Libbey was working with me. He'd be up there on the stage to get things started. He'd play the piano and do an Eddie Cantor imitation. Then I'd come down the aisle wearing a real cute panama hat and a green swagger coat and high-heeled spectators. The idea was that I was just back from Florida. We'd swap a few lines, and then I'd sing a song. It was a take-off on "I'm Fit As A Fiddle And Ready For Love." It went:

> I'm fit as a fiddle and ready to go.
> I could jump over the moon up above.
> I'm fit as a fiddle and ready to go.
>
> I haven't a worry and haven't a care.
> I feel like a feather just floating on air.
> I'm fit as a fiddle and ready to go.

After I got through singing, I'd sit down and take my high heels off, and put on rubber-soled track shoes. Then I'd remove my coat. I was wearing a red-white-and-blue jacket and shorts of silk satin. I'd demonstrate different kinds of athletics.

One of the things I did was run on a treadmill. They staged it real nice, with a black velvet backdrop and a great big clock to show how fast I was going. They had someone running beside me on another treadmill. At the end they would speed up my treadmill a little bit. I'd break the tape and go on to win.

I was surprised at how good a notice that show got the next day from Clark Rodenbach in the Chicago Tribune. This is what he said about my act:

"Friday afternoon was the 'Babe's' first time behind footlights, and the girl from the Lone Star state took the hurdle as gallantly as she ever did on the track. If her heart was thumping from the dread disease of stagefright, it wasn't apparent from the audience. After a bit of preliminary clowning by her partner, George Libbey, 'Babe' sings a song over the 'mike,' and then goes into her equivalent of a dance.

*Gene Sarazen taught Babe Didrikson the explosion shot.*

" 'Babe' skims a hurdle, jumps a couple of times, drives imitation golf balls, and runs on a treadmill. Mr. Libbey bemoans the fact that the limited scope of the stage forbids her showing more of her extraordinary prowess, such as heaving the discus, flinging the javelin or tossing a basketball. And Mildred ends her turn by playing a harmonica with no mean skill."

On the harmonica, there were just three numbers that I'd practiced to play with the orchestra. I believe that "When Irish Eyes Are Smiling" was one of them, and "Begin the Beguine" was another. I forgot what the third one was. One night the audience wouldn't let me off until I'd given some encores. I didn't know how I could do it, until they whispered to me from the orchestra pit, "Babe, you just go ahead with any numbers you want, and we'll fill in and make you sound good."

I could carry a tune pretty good. In fact, one of the Chicago newspaper critics didn't believe it was really me singing. He wrote that maybe they were piping in somebody else's voice while I stood in front of the microphone and went through the motions.

I got out there at one of the evening shows and said, "I see where some of these critics don't believe I'm doing my own singing. I'm going to sing tonight without a mike." So I did, and the audience gave me a real ovation.

Before the week was out, I was beginning to enjoy myself. I liked the feeling of that crowd out there. I had bookings after Chicago in Brooklyn and Manhattan at something like $2500 a week.

And yet I still wanted to be a champion golfer. I could see I'd never get to do that with these four and five stage shows a day. I was spending all my time either in the theater or in my hotel. And I didn't like having to put that grease paint on for every show.

I talked it over with my sister Esther Nancy—we called her Nancy. She said, "Babe honey, you can make a lot of money on this circuit. It's just a question of whether you want to do it."

I said, "Nancy, I don't want the money if I have to make it this way. I want to live my life outdoors. I want to play golf."

Nancy agreed that it was best for me to pull out if I felt that way. So we canceled the New York and Brooklyn dates.

# The Essence of Scottish Golf

## Joyce Wethered

"Golfing Memories and Methods"
Hutchinson and Co., Ltd., 1933

## East Lothian

Every one, including Doctor Johnson, must have recognized the distinction between the road leading out of Scotland and the one leading into it. No one appreciates the difference in emotion when pursuing these opposing routes more than I do. For the last ten years or so, I have been an inveterate visitor to this neighbouring country; and although I cannot claim a drop of Scotch blood in my veins, I own to a feeling of absolute content whenever I cross the border. I have motored to and fro by as many as three separate ways, and that by Berwick, over the great bridge, is to my mind most like the correct gateway into a holiday land for the majority of English people. From Berwick it is only a short step to East Lothian, and the first stopping place for the golfer is generally North Berwick.

One reason, though not by any means the only reason, why I love Scotland, is perhaps the unworthy one that I feel I play better there than anywhere else. That is an inducement that no true golfer can resist. A course or an atmosphere that encourages one to play well, and flatters one's game, is a place to hurry to at all costs. It is not that Scotch courses are necessarily easier than our own. For one thing, they are usually less closely guarded round the greens, it is true, until perhaps an architect is called upon to alter them. This brings to my mind Muirfield. I played it once in the old days before it was altered and have played on it many times since. Sometimes it is said that penally-bunkered courses are easier for low handicap players than what is termed the "strategic"; but I am not always quite convinced of the argument, though it has been well drummed into my ears at home by an eminent architect of our acquaintance whose chief happiness in life is to puzzle golfers and leave them in doubt as to the right shot to play. A "strategically" constructed course will probably produce these dilemmas for those to whom the experience of a course is still new; but once it is mastered, will it always continue to exert its misleading influence?

Whatever may be the truth of the matter, I have far too great a respect for the dangerous hazards at Muirfield to pretend that their only effect on the good player is to give away the correct length of the holes. On this particular links, when the greens are undulating and exceptionally fast, the slightest inaccuracy will land the ball in trouble only too readily.

Muirfield, North Berwick and Gullane, are the three courses in the corner of East Lothian most familiar to me. In spite of lying so close to one another, each of them retains a certain individuality. Muirfield presents the serious, business-like aspect of the game. The matches played on it are usually four-ball matches amongst the men. As the headquarters of the Honourable Company of Edinburgh Golfers, and a course on which amateur and open championships are played, it stands in a high position in the golfing world and naturally takes its responsibilities seriously.

North Berwick, a few miles down the coast, has a totally different atmosphere. North Berwick, as I see it, possesses a dual character—when it is in the season and when it is out. Sometimes it manages to combine both. Looking out on a bright sunny day over the sea to the islands raised high out of the water, like monstrous jewels in a low setting, and at the harbour, a pile of picturesque, russet-red houses turning grey at the water's edge, is to be carried away by the beauty of the colour, the vividness and the striking reality of it all.

Suddenly out of this dream of beauty one is roused by a name shouted from the Starter's Box. The picture changes at once to a new North Berwick. Now the wild and primitive fishing town is transformed into a meeting place of countless friends and acquaintances—a scene of bright coloured costumes, press photographers, and all the modern paraphernalia of a more sophisticated world.

I am not suggesting for a moment that it is not delightful to step into the midst of this light and spontaneous atmosphere for the space of a week or two. At the same time, there is an inevitable overshadowing of the genuine charm of North Berwick itself and its links; the feeling becomes almost too pronounced that the latest creations of Chenil and Fortnum and Mason are occupying the centre of the stage. Even golf seems for the time being to be relegated to the background; it becomes merely a medium of sociability. The invasion of visitors, however, ceases almost as suddenly as it appears, and North Berwick becomes its old original self once more. I have fortunately been able to visit it also in May, and then one can enjoy to one's heart's content the prospect of this glorious coast line.

Gullane, the last of the three, has not yet lost the quaint and rural character of the first tee. The way of approach is down the village street. One steps straight off it, as it were, on to a village green, to tee up beneath the shade of plane trees, their brown leaves dry and crackling underfoot. Seldom is one allowed to linger. The sound of a buzzing bell and the stentorian voice of the starter summon the player to tee off and leave this pleasant spot. The holes lead one straight up to the top of Gullane Hill to unfold on every side a view famous throughout the land for its wonder and distance. Away up the Firth can be seen Arthur's Seat rising above the smoke-laden haze of Leith; to the southward lie the Lammermoor Hills spread in a protecting belt which encloses a plain of corn and barley fields; to the east and north the sea and the Firth lie glimmering beneath us, dotted with ships and islands; and over and across the water the slopes of Fife fade peacefully into the distance.

# St. Andrews

What a joy it is to jump into the train in the evening at a London terminus, with one's clubs on the rack overhead, and to wake the next morning to the sounds of Edinburgh and then the strange hum of the train rumbling over the Forth Bridge. A few battleships lie quiet and still far beneath, dull shapes in the hazy morning light which is slowly uncovering the stretches of the Firth and the little groups of houses clustered along the shore.

It is a journey as full of charm and interest as the destination we are bound for. The last mile or so runs down the side of the links and the first exciting glimpse of St. Andrews is caught. All too soon the train carries us ahead, wreathing the seventeenth tee in its smoke as it chugs into the gloom of the station.

I cannot imagine a greater contrast to North Berwick than St. Andrews. Its distinction lies in its being not so much a social as a scholastic centre. The University rises, an impressive pile of buildings, in the very heart of the town. Students provide an effective note of color in their bright scarlet gowns, whether in the dark grey streets or mingling in a gallery on the links. Nor are the more juvenile scholars forgotten. They may be seen in scattered groups on Sundays, invading the empty course and the sands on their afternoon walks. On the very big occasions they sometimes join the golfing galleries, peering with apparent zeal through openings provided by their elders. I can remember in the Ladies' championship being kept an embarrassed prisoner in the midst of a swarm of little dark-blue figures flushed with the fever of auto-graph hunting.

The older inhabitants of St. Andrews may be indifferent to auto-graphs, but all of them are golfers bound together in one common en-thusiasm for the game. It is talked of, thought of, practised by all. When I have stayed there, even in the shops I have found the same lively interest. The chemist hopes I am finding the course to my liking; the stationer asks me how I am playing; and the hairdresser, to whom I have paid a hurried visit, is plainly more interested in my golf than in my coiffure.

It is useless to try to pretend that St. Andrews appeals to everyone. To some it may appear cold and unattractive, the links may seem a flat and dreary expanse, with too many blind holes, hidden bunkers and bad lies. An unfortunate collection of faults to begin with, you might say. To others St. Andrews appeals in all the glory of its past history, a course requiring a never-ending stock of intricate and cunning shots to defeat the broken quality of the ground.

The first of my many visits was paid a number of years ago. I re-member arriving in a state of considerable excitement as to what my first impressions would be. I had, of course, gathered certain ideas about the course, as only the year before my brother tied for the Open championship on it. I must admit that my first sight of the Valley of Sin, into which Roger's ball fell in his last round (costing him a five and the championship) caused me a sense of acute disappointment. It was pointed out to me from the window of the hotel—a small, uninspiring hollow. I could not help inwardly hoping that Hell Bunker and the famous eleventh hole would come nearer to my grim expectations.

Driving from the first tee on the following morning, I was not altogether free from terror. My knees were inclined to be un- steady; the tee seemed a vast and empty space; and my ball and myself very small and insignificant in the middle of it. To make things more disturbing still, the large plate glass window in the club overlooking the first tee was filled with faces. My brother more than once that morning had called my attention to the fountain to the right of the fairway, and I knew that the object of his remarks was to inveigle me into hitting it, or at any rate drifting in that direction. However, I saw plenty of room away to the left and managed to pull a low drive into a region of safety. The second shot happened to be a long one that day and I barely carried the Swilcan Burn with a brassie.

By the fourth hole I was completely befogged, lost and bewildered. On the last course I had played, the greens and the bottom of the pin stared comfortably at me. Here I seemed fortunate if I could catch a glimpse of the top of the flag. Certainly so far, except for the first hole, I had not yet seen any of the greens to which I was approaching.

At this point, resigning all claims to independence, I entrusted myself completely to my caddie. For the rest of the round I played obediently over bumps and bunkers, at spires and hotels in the distance, and finally at the seventeenth hole—with no spirit left to differ or to question—over the top of a large shed which clearly belonged to a railway goods yard. At the last hole, to my opponent's evident satisfaction, my ball fell into the Valley of Sin, no doubt a fitting conclusion to a bewildering round.

St. Andrews usually treats a visitor in this fashion. At first sight it is almost impossible to grasp the idea of the course. The good drives end in bunkers; the straight approaches run away from the hole; the putts wander all over the greens. To become a genuine lover of St. Andrews requires time and experience. I stayed a fortnight on my first visit, and the last week passed in a flash—one heavenly day after another. It took the whole of the first week to sort out the holes and begin to understand the links, but ever since the Old Course has stood alone in my estimation, and I love every hummock of it.

The only way to discover what a course is actually like is to play it. When I actually saw the famous holes, I found that they were quite different from what I had expected. I can safely say that the two holes that frightened me more than any others I have ever seen were the eleventh and seventeenth.

If I were asked which holes on the course I like the best, I should find it hard to say. Of the less famous holes, the second, perhaps surprisingly, has always intrigued me. The few bunkers in it are most uncomfortably placed and seem to lie in wait ready to gobble up a good drive or trap a too gentle or over-confident approach.

Another favourite of mine is the thirteenth. A good drive may land one just to the right of the Coffin bunkers, under—but not too near—the steep bank running across the fairway. Then comes a glorious spoon shot to be smacked right up to the large flat green, followed by a rush to the top of the rise to see if the ball is over the jaws of Lion's Mouth and yet has not faded away into the Hole O' Cross Bunker.

That is the great attraction of St. Andrews: nowhere else is there a course so able to thrill, excite, depress or frighten. You can begin confidently enough at the first hole with the best intention in the world of keeping steady and returning a presentable card. By about the fifth and sixth other ideas may be creeping into your thoughts: the greens seem unaccountably large; the twenty and thirty-yard putts give the impression that three putts will be an inevitable certainty. But until the Loop is passed, hope never dies. If only a few threes can be collected, then the score is balanced for the time being.

After all, it is the long and magnificent homecoming that makes St. Andrews the wonderful test of golf that it is and gives the best player a chance of making up ground lost in the first half. The Long Hole In is famous the world over; the fifteenth, once the drive is safely steered from the tee, presents perhaps the easiest iron shot coming in. The sixteenth, distinguished by the Principal's Nose—a nest of three bunkers blocking the centre of the fairway—drives the player, unless he is possessed of inordinate courage, away to the left, from which point the approach to the green requires a very perfect shot of its kind to finish anywhere near the hole.

The seventeenth threatens the successful scorer. The green can be approached gingerly, so that the Road may be safely counted out of the picture. But the bunker lying just to the left of the hole remains a danger up to the very last moment—until the ball has finally been coaxed up the treacherous bank guarding the green. What a heartbreaking turn the ball can take to the left just when the haven of the central plateau is thought to be reached! How many aggravating sixes can be recorded by being over-cautious! As for the last hole, it can scarcely be described as dangerous, although it is certainly not as simple as it looks. The Valley of Sin before the green has not earned its title without good reason. Many times I have watched this hole being played in a championship week when a player, standing dormy and on the point of victory, is seen walking wearily to the nineteenth tee after failing to secure the necessary half.

The greatest triumph I have witnessed on this fateful green was in 1926, when Bobby won the Open by six clear strokes. His long putt for a three just lipped the hole, and the crowd, many thousands strong, could barely control its enthusiasm while he holed the little short one. Then they mobbed him, closing in with a rush and a burst of cheering which was almost frightening in its spontaneity. Looking down on the seething mass I saw Bobby hoisted shoulder high and carried round and round, the center of waving hats and outstretched hands. Such a welcome for the new champion, American by birth and in a land where the success of a Scot is usually the first and only consideration, spoke eloquently for the winner's popularity. Later, in front of the clubhouse, he described in his deep American drawl what to him was the charm and character of St. Andrews' links, for which he holds an affection perhaps as great as that of any living person.

St. Andrews never changes. It is the same every time that one visits it. The holes remain as they were; the same old characters greet one; the same long stream of townsfolk drive off the first tee when the day's work is finished.

# North and West

In the north of Scotland golfing geography seems to repeat itself in rather a curious fashion. Just as Muirfield, Gullane, and North Berwick look across the water in the direction of St. Andrews within a circle of roughly thirty-five miles, so Nairn and Lossiemouth and Dornoch are contained within a similar area, with a belt of water between them, a few hundred miles further up the East Coast. There golf is played in even grander surroundings. The land becomes more primitive and rugged. On the Moray coast, every one would linger if they had the opportunity for a game at Lossiemouth and at Nairn, its less exposed neighbour, which runs along the shore among the stretches of purple heather. I have spent many a happy (and exceedingly cold) day on both.

But Dornoch, to the north of Inverness, is my oldest and greatest friend of all the Scottish courses. In the first early stages, when golf seems perhaps more difficult than pleasurable, Dornoch taught me to grow fond of the game and showed me some of the delights it held in store. It would be difficult to imagine a greater incentive for the beginner than the low blue line of distance reaching beyond Dornoch Firth to Tarbot Ness, on the further side of which lies Cromarty and away inland the higher peaks frowning on the landscape. The first twelve holes of Dornoch are perhaps amongst the best twelve holes to be found anywhere. They follow the line of the coast towards the fishing village of Embo where the land seems equally good for as many links as might be desired.

It was here that I played in my first tournament. In the middle of August every year, the ladies struggle through a medal round and then qualify to meet each other in match play. That is where I won my first gold medal. That knock-out tournament was chiefly memorable for the series of Miss Sutherlands, Mackays, Murrays and Grants who came forward to offer battle. Visitors took part in these competitions, but the local celebrities formed the main bulk of the competitors—and very dour and accomplished opponents they proved to be on their native turf, whins, and sand dunes.

It was at Dornoch, too, that I first experienced the blissful sensation of breaking 70. An ambition to score a full-length course in 69 or under

had been a secret longing for years. I have since done it elsewhere, but
the great day arrived when I played with Mr. Beaumont Pease who
came with a party to lunch with us. I hope Mr. Pease will forgive me for
boasting that I beat him four and three after he had gone round in 74.
As he has had his revenge more than once, I feel sure he will be quite
unmoved by this disclosure. Our best-ball for the first six holes was
even threes.

At any rate, I have for some time loved a medal round. To rival or
equal par never fails in its satisfaction. It means that one has played
well as there is no hope that this inflexible opponent will ever be off his
game. The happiest three days of golf I have ever experienced were
when I played six consecutive rounds—five on the New Course at Turnberry and one on the Old—and stood one over fours at the end.

In the northern parts and nearing the West coast, my golfing visits
are never quite complete without at least a few days of fishing—another of the grand attractions of Scotland. On most of the rivers running behind and above Dornoch I have fished at various times, but the
Langwell and the Berriedale were the first rivers I ever dipped a line
into, after some preliminary but realistic practice on the front lawn
while the rain was coming down in sheets. Then there was the Carron
in Rossshire where I used to fish for two weeks every spring from the
early hours to late at night, never giving a thought or care for anything
else in the world, except, I remember, once for some slight intermission
in trying to improve a nine-hole course in the park. This was the first
time I ever tried my hand at golf architecture, and I cannot say that it
could be counted as altogether a success. The advice I gave about cutting down a clump of silver birches was not too well received; the lady
of the house, now seriously alarmed, declared she did not care a rap
about the golf but she did care very much about the birches.

Mention of the West Coast brings me to Ayrshire, a county famous
throughout the world for its courses. Just to the north of Ayr they run
along the coast in an almost unbroken ribbon, the long and narrow
strips of links even touching their neighbours at some points. Prestwick
and Troon are the two outstanding courses and have been the scenes of
the most crowded and congested championships that have taken place
anywhere. So great is the interest taken in this part of Scotland, lying
only a short distance below Glasgow, that the numbers who swarm to
the great matches have become a serious problem.

Ayrshire is a land of wild landscape, woods and rolling hills. In the
most adorable of houses, set back in a wooded valley from the sea, I
have joined in the happiest of golfing parties. The nearest links is

Turnberry, a glorious, undulating space looking out to sea and to Ailsa Craig and the jagged peaks of Arran.

The new course at Turnberry is our favourite. There could be no better place for the good-humoured matches, and the amiable bickering over endless new styles and methods.

# A Singular Triumph at Worplesdon

## Bernard Darwin

The American Golfer                                    December, 1933

Miss Wethered has just been making her one eagerly anticipated yearly appearance in the Worplesdon Foursomes, and she won them for the seventh time. I shall sing her praises, but I am afraid I shall have to come into the story myself to a small extent, because I had the honor of being her partner.

When I had to make a speech afterwards (she resolutely declined), I alluded to the "annually increasing body of persons whom Miss Wethered drags through by the scruffs of their agitated neck." Well, that was certainly true this time, and, in a lesser degree, it is always true. She has a fresh partner nearly every year, and she nearly always pilots him to victory.

Miss Wethered now works all the week and only plays at weekends. I think that has made her keener and, if possible, better than ever. I am sure I have never seen her play better, and I do not see how anybody could. We played eight rounds, and I could enumerate almost in a sentence the imperfect shots she played: two drives, as far as I can recollect—or was it three?—that just trickled into bunkers; a few short-ish putts that she missed (her partner ought to have put her closer); and a few long ones not laid quite so near the hole as he—poor frightened fellow—would have liked.

As to iron shots, I can't think of a single one to criticize. She nearly finished the final by holing one outright for a two, and the only thing that surprises me, in retrospect, is that some of the others did not go in also. And it was all done with an ease and smoothness that made it seem magical. Her partner had but one duty; namely, to avoid the coarse forms of sin, keep out of heather and woods (there are plenty of both at Worplesdon), and leave the rest to her.

This is not much to ask, but that, in a sense, makes the responsibility a heavy one. As far as I can form an opinion, he performed his duties adequately on three days out of four, but blotted his copy book one day, when defeat came horribly near.

*Joyce Wethered wins the 1933 Worplesdon Mixed Doubles championship*
*partnered with the greatest golf writer of them all.*

Eighty-six couples entered and never, I think, has there been such a field of champions in this tournament. There were Miss Enid Wilson, Miss Cecil Leitch, whom it was a pleasure to see again, Madame Lacoste (who used to be Mlle. Simone de la Chaume and is the best lady player to have come out of France), Miss Pearson, the new English champion, and a variety of other good lady players.

Miss Wethered and her partner marched majestically through the first day—7 and 5 and 5 and 4. Then came the day of that partner's misdeeds and a scrambling win by 2 and 1, followed by a really desperate one in the dusk at the twentieth hole.

The third day was comfortable enough—5 and 4 and 3 and 2—and then in the thirty-six-hole final, where a desperate fight was expected, Mrs. Garon and Andrew McNair kindly had an off-day. We were three up at lunch and won by 8 and 7. The more holes we were up, the more ruthlessly magnificent Miss Wethered became. She holed that iron shot before mentioned to make us eight up. What a partner!

There was a big crowd and, as long as Miss Wethered plays in it, this will be what it has now become: the most popular tournament of the whole year in the south of England. It provides wonderfully interesting watching, and, on the whole, I always think the ladies come out the best. They appear more blameless and less destructive than their partners, and their wooden club play through the green, in which they have more practice, is extraordinarily good.

At the same time, let me say a word for the poor men. I am not thinking of the few lucky ones who are allied with super-ladies, as I was, and so perform the part of second strings. Generally they are first strings, and then they have to try for two things at once. They must get length, or else the holes cannot be reached in two. They must have accuracy, because the heather and the woods are most tenacious, and the ladies may not have the physical strength to recover.

Broadly speaking, *the* thing to do in a mixed foursome is to keep the ball in play. It is always a supreme foursome virtue, and in this game its value is accentuated. Miss Wethered has it to the $n$th degree.

# Virginia Van Wie Holds onto Her Title

## Howard Barry

The Chicago *Tribune*                               September 3, 1933

Virginia Van Wie, a gracious lady in green and white, walked off the fifteenth green of the Exmoor Country Club course yesterday into a horde of admirers who pressed forward eagerly to shake her hand, take her picture, and get her autograph. She had just defeated Helen Hicks, 4 and 3, in the final round of the United States Women's golf championship, thereby winning the title for the second consecutive season.

Whereas boxers and hockey players like to imply that they are perpetually indulging in grudge fights, a different situation prevails between the two leading women golfers. Miss Van Wie and Miss Hicks are good friends who spend a great deal of time visiting at each other's home and playing golf together.

Miss Hicks took the attitude that she was sorry to be defeated but glad that it was Miss Van Wie who beat her. Miss Van Wie was glowing with satisfaction over her triumph and was glad that her friend had been the one to accompany her into the final. So every one had something to be happy about.

In this tournament Miss Van Wie gave a convincing demonstration of her right to occupy the throne left vacant by Mrs. Glenna Collett Vare, who, as Miss Collett, won the championship in 1922, 1925, 1928, 1929, and 1930. In 1931, it was Miss Hicks who beat her for the national championship, and last year it was Miss Van Wie. This season these two youngsters again proved themselves the best women in the game, and it seemed a toss-up as to which would forge ahead.

In yesterday's encounter Miss Van Wie proved that she had the fighting qualities of a true champion by coming back from four down on the 15th to four up on the 33rd. Throughout the match Miss Hicks was smiling and chatting with her caddy, while Miss Van Wie was playing in a more serious fashion, her only expression being one of disappointment when a long putt missed the cup by an inch or two.

Miss Van Wie has been interested in sports ever since she was able to

*Virginia Van Wie*

toddle around. On her tenth Christmas she received a big league base-ball, a bat, a catcher's mask and a football, preferring gifts of this kind to dolls, candy and dresses with pink ribbons. She took up tennis, swimming, and basketball, showing talent for each sport.

She lived on the south side of Chicago and attended Lindbloom High School. Her father Ernest had a liking for golf, and he passed this interest on to his daughter. He retired from active participation in the affairs of the Board of Trade and established a winter home at Deland, Florida, and a summer residence near Big Rapids, Michigan.

When she was twelve years old, Miss Van Wie began playing golf in Florida, taking lessons from two well-known professionals. Her first notable accomplishment occurred when she was sixteen. She won the Western Junior championship and went to the final of the Ormond Beach tournament. The following year, at the age of seventeen, she startled the golfing public by beating Glenna Collett, the national champion, in the final of the Florida East Coast tournament.

From that time, she continued to advance, winning the Chicago District championship in 1926, 1927, and 1928; the Florida state in 1926 and 1928; the Florida East Coast again in 1929 and 1930; the South Atlantic in 1928, 1929 and 1930, and the Mid-South in 1928.

Virginia began playing in our national championship in 1925. She was defeated in the first round that year. The following season, she was again eliminated in the opening round, but in 1927 she reached the semi-finals. In 1928 she went to the final where she was overwhelmed, 13 and 12, by Glenna Collett. In 1929, she got only as far as the second round, but in 1930, she reached the final again, only to lose once more to Miss Collett, 6 and 5. In 1931, Miss Collett defeated her 2 up, this time in the semi-finals. In 1932, her long campaign was crowned with success, for she beat Miss Collett, 10 and 8, in the final.

When Miss Van Wie was beaten recently in the Western tournament at Oak Park, it was thought that she might be slipping and would encounter considerable difficulty in defending her title in the national championship, but she improved throughout the tournament and in the final she played as well as she ever has.

This morning Miss Van Wie will motor to her family's summer home in Big Rapids, Mich., and will remain there for several days.

# A Remarkable Golfing Record

## Joseph C. Dey, Jr.

The American Golfer                    January and February, 1934

## Part I

At the age of fifty, Dorothy Campbell Hurd played eighteen holes of golf over an orthodox course in 69 strokes. It is the best score this golfing grandmother has ever made, although she breaks 80 almost as often as not. It is an apogee at which she has star-gazed all her life.

At the age of fifty-five, the Hon. Michael Scott, a son of the fourth Earl of Eldon, won the British Amateur championship, becoming the oldest champion in the tournament's history. H. Chandler Egan, a graybeard of forty-nine, our Amateur champion in 1904-05, throttled our reigning Open champion, Johnny Goodman, in the first round of our Amateur at Cincinnati in 1933. John D. Rockefeller on his ninety-fourth birthday played his usual nine holes.

Those facts constitute not so much a case against Youth as a commentary on an athletic game in which it is possible to scale the heights despite advanced age. Further, they embody a sketchy introduction to the outstanding character in women's golf—a player who, at the half-century mark, is even more skillful than when she was champion of the world. Presenting—Dorothy Iona Campbell Hurd, a member of the Merion Cricket Club, Haverford, Pennsylvania.

Golf critics have been applying to Mrs. Hurd the label "wonder woman" at intervals spanning more than two decades. They first had occasion to use it twenty-three years ago when Mrs. Hurd completed the unprecedented and still unequaled feat of winning the American, the British, the Scottish, and the Canadian Women's championships. In 1924 they cast conservatism overboard again. After a twelve-year hiatus in which she had been denied a major championship, Mrs. Hurd came back with a reformed, modernized swing, recaptured the United States title, and set an all-time record of winning eleven national championships in four countries. She was then forty-one.

*Dorothy Campbell Hurd*

In 1926 she established a new world record for putting, using nineteen putts in an eighteen-hole round.

Last spring she celebrated her fiftieth birthday by scoring a 70 over the Belmont Manor course in Bermuda; a few weeks later, on the same course, she recorded the best score of her life, a 69. Belmont Manor is 6,172 yards in length and has a men's par of 70. Three months later, Mrs. Hurd qualified for permanent possession of the Griswold Trophy by defeating a field of younger players for her third victory in the Shennecossett Country Club's annual invitation tournament at New London, Connecticut. Then, in September, she won the classic Berthellyn Cup and created an all-time record of four triumphs in the series of invitation events conducted by the Huntingdon Valley Country Club, in Abington, Pennsylvania.

Today, after thirty-four consecutive years as a scratch-handicap player, Mrs. Hurd still is the game's "wonder woman." It is characteristic that she is blissfully unaffected by the pretty things said and written about her. She is an encyclopaedia of golf, unstinting in advice and encouragement to fellow-players, but beyond a certain pardonable pride, she is rather girlish in her naïve outlook on her accomplishments.

On the course, Mrs. Hurd is thoroughly businesslike; off it, quite unassuming. Once she has finished a day's play, she invariably discards her clubs in favor of knitting needles, retires to a quiet corner of the clubhouse veranda, and looks as if she might be a mother, only mildly interested in golf, waiting for her daughter to finish her round.

Mrs. Hurd isn't "just a golfer." She is an omnivorous reader, a clever writer, and a diverting conversationalist. One of her two chief complaints is that she never achieved her ambitions as a singer and a pianist. The other is that her golf swing is not stylish.

After she defeated Florence Hezlet in the final of the 1909 British Ladies' championship at Birkdale, she was about to enter the enclosure where the prize-giving was to take place when her way was barred by a six-foot commissionaire with a row of medals on his chest.

"Are you," he asked with a supercilious stare, "a golfer?"

"I don't think so," was the completely serious reply, "but I believe they will want me inside to receive the championship cup."

Nor is Mrs. Hurd a relentless machine. Defending the Philadelphia women's championship last year, she started by breaking the qualifying-round record with a 79. She won her first match, then in the second round met a young clubmate, Mrs. John J. Mitchell, 3d. Although a tyro at championship play, Mrs. Mitchell began brilliantly and was four up after seven holes. At this point, the match acquired a gallery in the form of a lone reporter. Mrs. Mitchell suddenly became self-conscious. She lost the next two holes and at the turn was only 2 up. She was faltering fast. Thereupon, Mrs. Hurd whisperingly suggested to the one-man gallery that he make himself scarce. "I'm afraid your presence is disturbing Mrs. Mitchell," she explained. "This is her first match of any importance, and she's unaccustomed to playing before anyone. She should be given every fair opportunity to win." The reporter took the hint and departed. Mrs. Mitchell did win, 1 up, in nineteen holes.

It is the opinion of most qualified critics that two players have exerted truly epochal effects on women's golf in the United States. One is Mrs. Hurd; the other, Mrs. Edwin H. Vare, Jr., the former Glenna

Collett. Eleven years ago "Glorious Glenna" won the first of her five American championships. The influence she spread was derived from her demonstration that it is possible for a woman to hit a golf ball as far as the average man and to run off long strings of pars.

Thirteen years before that, a pretty young player came over from Scotland and took the country by storm. Old-timers need little prompting to recall Dorothy Campbell's victory in the United States championship in 1909. She created the first important impress on American women's golf by aiming directly for the hole with her approach shots and not in the general direction of the green. Almost a quarter-century later, she still is able to compete with younger, more vigorous players. How does she do it?

This observer would note that golf is a rarity among athletic games in that it does not tend to "burn out" the player. Mrs. Hurd has kept pace by readjusting her swing from time to time, conforming to effective modern ideas.

She confesses ignorance as to the reasons for her protracted success, "unless it's because my short game is almost second nature to me."

For the benefit of the uninitiate, the "short game" signifies play on and around the greens—chipping, pitching, putting. It is that economical means by which three strokes can be compressed into two, and two strokes into one stroke. Mrs. Hurd's short game is regarded by many experts as outstanding, not excepting that of any man.

A carping critic might quibble with the statement that she has been playing golf all her life, so for the sake of strict truth it must be admitted Dorothy Campbell had attained the ripe old age of one and one-half years before she first swung a club. However, her family's golf background extends well over a half-century. Her paternal grandfather as well as her eight uncles all played the game over the links at North Berwick.

The links at North Berwick, a strip of land between the gardens of houses and the Firth of Forth's high-water mark, was common ground whereon the townspeople permitted their cows to graze. The golf course was quite crude. "In the old days," Mrs. Hurd reminisced, "the pins were simply sticks of wood to which skeins of scarlet worsted were attached. Every Saturday night, my mother told me, the sticks were collected and brought in, so that the townspeople might not see them and thus be distracted from the sanctity of their Sabbath thinking. There were no tees, no markers, no putting greens as we know them today, no tins for holes. Fresh holes had to be cut in the 'greens' every Monday morning. Each golfer as he came along took sand from each hole in order to tee up his ball preparatory to driving down the next fairway. Thus, by Saturday night all the holes were as big as wash-tubs. This was the case long before my day. "I played my first match when I was five years old, and a memorable contest it was," she was remembering recently. Two of my six sisters, Madeline, then eleven, and Muriel, ten, were partnered against me and Arthur Dewar, a young man whose family owned the Scotch whisky interests of the same name. Mr. Dewar, of course, 'carried' me, both colloquially and literally. I was so tired by the fifteenth hole, he picked me up and put me on his shoulder until we arrived at my ball."

Miss Campbell gradually became stronger of limb. It was well for her that she did, for when she formally "grew up" at the age of eighteen, she might not have been able to lug around the heavy tweed skirt she was required to wear. The skirt stopped just one inch short of the ground. In those Victorian days it was considered immodest to appear in briefer attire. In retrospect, Mrs. Hurd cannot comprehend how she and her contemporaries swung clubs in such tent-like habiliment, which not only was cumbersome but became quite heavy in rainy weather.

It may readily be imagined that Mrs. Hurd needed considerable practice with this sort of costume before she was able to win her first national championship, the 1905 Scottish Ladies championship, played at North Berwick. Four thousand persons saw the final. Mrs. Hurd won it after an extra hole of play.


The greatest of Mrs. Dorothy Campbell Hurd's many golfing thrills was her third triumph in the United States Women's championship in 1924 at the Rhode Island Country Club, near Providence. She had not won a national title in any country for a dozen years. She was forty-one years old. The Scribes and the Pharisees were beginning to count her out. Then along came Providence, Rhode Island. It was an eminently gratifying comeback. In winning, Mrs. Hurd defeated a star-studded field which included Mary K. Browne, the ultimate runner-up, who, besides being a good golfer, had been the United States Women's Tennis champion in 1912-13-14.

Paradoxically, the most dramatic event connected with her triumph in 1924 did not occur in the tournament itself but antedated it by nearly a year. A chubby caddie was the unwitting hero.

"It happened in the fall of 1923," Mrs. Hurd recalls, "while I was playing in the Berthellyn Cup invitation tournament of the Hunting-don Valley Country Club, in the Philadelphia suburbs. Until then my swing had been of the old-fashioned, stiff-wristed, sweeping type. I gripped the club in my palms, much as a baseball player grasps a bat and directly contrary to the modern method of holding it in the fingers. My hands were extended fully.

"I simply swung at the ball with the one idea of hitting it. I knew nothing about golf theory, and, mind you, I already had won ten national championships. Why, I was nineteen years old before I first heard the golfing terms 'pull' and 'slice.' The old idea merely was to hit the ball—few attempts were made at theorizing—and I'm not so sure it wasn't a blessed good idea.

"But my swing was definitely outmoded when I started the qualifying round at the 1923 Berthellyn Cup tournament. Moreover, I was laboring with a devastating left-to-right 'fade' which deprived me of possibly twenty yards on each full wood shot.

"In this discouraging manner I went along for a while. Then, after two or three holes, I noticed a look of disgust on the face of my caddie. His expression was so extraordinary I felt sure something was wrong. I asked him what it was. 'The boys,' he replied half-scornfully, gesturing toward the caddie-house, 'all say you could win the national championship if you could hit the ball straight. Your short game's unbeatable, but your woods are bad. You will have to learn to hit farther and straighter with them.'

"The charge struck home. In a sudden flash, I saw my golf game in its true light—saw, for instance, why women equipped with modern swings outdrove me. I was far behind the times with my old-fashioned, stiff-wristed, sweeping method.

"But was I completely through? The thought was depressing. I began to wonder whether I could change my style and acquire an up-to-date swing in which hand action plays an important part, as does the keeping of one's hands close to one's body to obtain accuracy and power. In fine, could I at my age—I was then forty—re-educate muscles long in disuse to execute a new type of swing?

"I asked George Sayers about it. George is the professional at Merion and a son of the late Ben Sayers, the famous club-maker and professional at North Berwick. He was born and brought up in my home town, and I have known him since he was a boy. He told me he *could* help me to change my swing but that it would entail inordinate practice. I was fearful of the consequences if I did not at least try, so, with some misgivings, I decided to have a go at it."

The month of November, 1923, remains as something of a nightmare in Mrs. Hurd's memory. Throughout that month she haunted the practice tee at Merion and underwent a painful golfing metamorphosis. After two days, a joint of her left hand's index finger was reduced to a raw wound by constant friction with fingers of her right hand due to the

Vardon or overlapping grip, which she was using for the first time. She wanted to stop, or at least to return to the old "painless" palm grip. Sayers advised against either form of back-sliding. She stuck it out. Finally, the once-bleeding finger-joint grew hard and calloused, and Mrs. Hurd became more at ease with her completely revised grip and stance and swing.

Did the ordeal pay? "I think it did," said Mrs. Hurd. Less than a year later, she had won the U. S. championship at Providence. And to this day she feels deeply indebted to a chubby caddie who lighted the way to her greatest achievement in golf.

In this connection, she believes it was purely accidental that she happened to secure and to keep the old photograph showing her with the cups emblematic of the three national championships which she held at one time.

"I had a Canadian cousin, William Hendrie, the son of a prominent racehorse owner," she recalls. "He insisted I be photographed with my three cups." "You'll want a picture of it when you're old," he predicted.

"I had no desire to have this sort of a photograph taken, thinking such boldness would be unladylike. But William Hendrie's insistence prevailed. I was so ashamed, however, that just before the photographer squeezed the old-fashioned rubber bulb of his camera, I looked off to one side, so as not to appear as if I had anything to do with so pretentious an array of trophies.

"Regardless of my misgivings and embarrassment then, William Hendrie's prediction came true. I value the photograph rather highly now."


Eight years ago, a woman opposed a man in a friendly yet serious match over the Shennecossett course. Before hostilities began, it mattered not to the man that his adversary was one of the greatest feminine golfers. After all, she was just a woman. He was a man. How could he lose?

The woman scored a 74. She won the match. No sooner had the man departed for his soothing shower than his wife, an interested if silent spectator of the contest, rushed up to the victor and cried out, "Oh, Mrs. Hurd, however can I thank you?"

"*Thank* me? Why, I *defeated* your husband."

"Yes, but . . . but . . ." the wife stuttered in her excited jubilation, "but from now on he's going to be so much easier to live with!"

Should that anecdote stray into a men's locker-room, it will be struck on the head promptly and forcibly with a heavy niblick, and that will be its end. Meantime, it carries a high charge of significance, though of a reverse sort: a strong implication that golf, the great leveler, has helped to foster the emancipation of the female sex.

There is much evidence of a positive nature pointing to the same conclusion. Mrs. Hurd is convinced the game is ideal for women in mental and temperamental as well as physical training, and, most importantly, that it has aided in destroying an unwarranted feminine timidity. She cites this point: "When I first came to the United States in 1909, sand traps were the *bête-noire* of most women golfers. I regarded it as virtually a foregone conclusion that, when any one of my opponents hit her ball into a bunker, the hole was mine. Since I had been playing golf all my life, the necessity of making a trap shot did not create a mental hazard for me. But the great majority of my contemporaries were pitifully timid then. They lacked a certain courage, born only of experience, that is needed to execute a bunker shot properly. Nowadays, the average woman player has no more fear of sand than the average man does."

One of her earliest and most important mentors was a member of the nobility, Lord Denman. "Until I was sixteen," Mrs. Hurd recalled, "my swing was just a half-swing, and my possibilities as a player were relatively restricted. Lord Denman called my attention to this weakness. But he did not stop there. At a time when my ambitions were flagging, he gave me my first encouragement by helping to change my swing to a full one. Fortunately, this happened in June, a month in which it is light almost all evening in that part of Scotland, so I was able to practice many hours under Lord Denman's observation. His assistance was invaluable. Incidentally, Lady Denman, his wife, lately has been president of the British Ladies' Golf Union."

Young Dorothy Campbell early learned to profit from the experiences of others, notably May Hezlet, who served as one of her first inspirations. When Miss Hezlet was seventeen, she won the British and the Irish championships within a fortnight. She was champion of Ireland five times.

"At the age of twenty-one, Miss Hezlet wrote a book," said Mrs. Hurd, "in which she stressed the absolute necessity of concentration, of eliminating all thought of a badly-played hole before beginning the next. Her ideas made a profound impression, because she was one of the finest golfers of all time. Even today her game would have stood up with the best. However, when she was still a young lady she married a bishop and gave up golf."

Mrs. Hurd did not teach herself the full value of concentration until a lapse cost her the chance to hold four national championship cups at the same time. Returning to Britain in 1911 with "hangover" American and Canadian championships gained in 1910, she won her second British title and would have owned four major trophies simultaneously had she captured the Scottish championship.

"But I did not win the Scottish, which was played at St. Andrews," Mrs. Hurd went on. "I was eliminated on the eighteenth green by the ultimate winner, partly because I had not concentrated sufficiently in the week preceding the tournament. Instead of practicing and readying myself mentally, I spent my time in shopping, paying visits to the dentist, seeing my mother's old friends, and in other distractions. The result was fatal to my aspirations, but the lesson was a good one."

Of all those who have aided Mrs. Hurd in her efforts to become a finer golfer, none has lent a more helpful hand than a gentleman named "Thomas." He is her pet club, an odd-looking, goose-necked mashie she has owned for twenty-four years. He has the instincts of a putter, possessing an unusual ability for holing-out. When Mrs. Hurd last won the North and South championship at Pinehurst in 1921, "Thomas" sank two approaches in the final against Mrs. F. C. Letts. In his younger days his average was two holed-out shots in every three rounds, but he's older now.

"Thomas" was the hero of one of Mrs. Hurd's most cherished performances, the creation of a new world record for putting at Augusta, Georgia, in 1926, when golf's "wonder woman" used only nineteen putts in an eighteen-hole round.

"The record until then was twenty-one putts," said Mrs. Hurd. "It was held by the late Walter J. Travis, a great player of Australian birth who thrice won the United States Amateur championship and who was the first American to take the British Amateur trophy from the Isles by winning at Sandwich in 1904.

"I must confess I deliberately set out to break Mr. Travis's record in that round at Augusta. To make a long story short, I teed off at the eighteenth hole needing one putt on the home green to surpass Mr. Travis' mark and two putts to equal it.

"Into the breach stepped 'Thomas', the mashie. I did not putt at all on the eighteenth, for 'Thomas' holed out my approach shot, just as he had done once previously in the round—and there was the record."

# Swinging the Clubhead

## Virginia Van Wie

The American Golfer                                    April, 1934

Golf is so simple it is difficult. That may be a strange statement, but I believe a true one. When Mr. Ernest Jones tied a jack knife to a corner of a large handkerchief and proved to me what swinging actually meant and what a real swing felt like, I proceeded to forget a multitude of so-called fundamentals and worked solely on one thing—learning to swing the clubhead with my hands and letting the rest of my anatomy follow the swing.

From that day on, not only did my golf improve to the extent that I was able to win the national championship, but I learned that the game could be a joy and a pleasure, instead of a mild form of torture.

For years, every time I missed a shot, I would immediately take inventory of my well memorized list of fundamentals: Had my elbows been in the proper position at the top of the swing? Were my wrists cocked at the same point? Had my head remained stationary while the rest of my body turned? Was my weight distributed correctly? Possibly I had just turned my body too fast during the down swing. I would try the next time to remember all of these things, and perhaps, if I didn't die from brain fever, my next shot would be a good one.

You can imagine what a pleasure it was to learn that all of this was as unnecessary as it was impossible. I do not mean to say I immediately knew what swinging meant. Not at all. I had as much difficulty as anyone making that jack knife in the handkerchief travel in an arc instead of figure eights. But once I could swing it, the sensation was such a delightful one I could hardly wait to get my club in my hands to swing it the same way. So much concentration was necessary to feel the clubhead swing, as I had felt the knife swinging, that I had no time to remember any list of fundamentals.

Besides, this was fun. I was getting a sense of controlling that clubhead, which was an entirely new experience. There is no sensation in golf quite so delightful as feeling the clubhead swing. I have had days

121

when I did swing the clubhead without realizing I was doing so, and, as a result, played very well. The next day my shots could fly all over the place, and I didn't know what was going wrong. If a slice had crept up on me, I could stop it by applying a little trick which, in a short while, would start me hooking. Then I was no better off than I was before.

Tricks are very tempting because they are quick cures, and at first they give the impression that you have solved your problem, but I have served my time trying them. There is no trick to swinging the clubhead. It is a most difficult action to master, but anything that can add yardage and accuracy to my golf shots and also give me a sense of control is well worth the time I have spent learning it.

The most amazing as well as amusing thing about it to me is this: since I have made a practice of forgetting fundamentals and tried only to learn to swing, professionals and good golfers have repeatedly told me how apparent these very fundamentals now are in my swing. This, above all else, has proven to me that the fundamentals of a golf swing, which are taught the world over, are undoubtedly correct, providing you forget them, learn to swing, and just allow them to happen.

All of this applies to my every day golf but, more significantly, to my tournament golf. Tournament golf is far more difficult because of the psychological factors involved. One is under a terrific mental strain, and, during the course of a week, this pulls one down physically. When my mind was encumbered with the fundamentals, I found myself under great tension. No brain is capable of concentrating on more than one thing at a time, so when I discovered that swinging the clubhead was the one fundamental to concentrate on in order to possess the others, a large part of the mental disturbance was eliminated.

I won the first tournament I entered after adopting this method. It was the first time in my life I had been able to win a thirty-six-hole final. A weak back has been a handicap to me for years, and when I would tighten my muscles in an effort to keep my head still, my left arm straight, etc., the strain upon my back was too much. I would tire quickly and could not last thirty-six holes. By trying only to swing and allowing my body to follow that motion, as it naturally will if not forced to do otherwise, the strain ceased and I discovered that thirty-six holes were not difficult. I also discovered that I could practise three times as long without tiring.

The mental advantages proved just as great. Anyone who rode to the Wentworth Club with the American team on their way to play the International Team Match against Great Britain would never state that a top-class golfer has no nerves. Nervousness is shown in various ways, depending upon the temperament of the person. I do not know how many of the girls noticed this certainly during that short ride, but it was apparent to me. Some were talking incessantly, others not saying a word. The majority of us were yawning, a true sign of nervousness. I dare say none of us were quite sure what we had eaten for breakfast.

There is no nervous strain in golf equal to playing an International Match. A true champion, regardless of whether her nervousness is apparent or otherwise, plays better golf under a strain. It rather keys one up for the battle. I have never enjoyed a match more than the foursome that morning. Helen Hicks and I were paired against Miss Wilson and Mrs. Watson. Neither of us ever played better. It was a two-ball foursome, and when we finished the match on the seventeenth green we had a four for a 72 and had only won two and one.

In the singles that afternoon I was paired against Miss Wanda Morgan. I found myself three down at the end of nine holes, and two down going to thirteen. Here was a splendid opportunity to see if concentrating only on swinging would prove sufficient. I know that the best way to hit a golf ball is to concentrate on one thing. It worked, and I won two and one.

This last national championship in which I met Miss Hicks in the final was another test. I was four down on the fifteenth green, and I had to sink a ten-foot putt to keep from going five down. That putt dropped fortunately, and I ended the first eighteen holes only two holes behind. I still refused to concentrate on anything but swinging the clubhead, and, with my share of good fortune, managed to win the championship.

When any method proves itself so successful under two such circumstances, I am not inclined to cast it aside lightly. I shall never again try to do anything but swing the clubhead.

# Learning How to Compete

## Virginia Van Wie

The American Golfer                                   October, 1934

During my stay in Florida last winter, I motored over to St. Augustine to watch the final round of the Florida East Coast championship. And who should I meet in the gallery but Harry Evans—formerly managing editor of *Life* and now editor of the *Family Circle Magazine*—who had been my partner in a two-ball foursome over that same course as a preliminary to the same event several years before.

Quite naturally, our conversation turned to the past tournaments— the fading out of the old crowd and the entrance of the present field. Mrs. Hill and Miss Orcutt were the only two players entered in the Florida East Coast tournament who had also played there in the not so distant past. Mr. Evans had been present during the entire week of the 1934 tournament, and he wondered whether it was because he did not know the new players that his interest in the tournament had lessened, or whether it was that the attitude of the players had changed. The golf was as good. The scores proved that in spite of adverse weather conditions. He asked me if I had noticed any difference in competitive golf, and when I admitted I had, he asked me why I had not written an article about it. It is a difficult subject to broach, and it is hard to express oneself clearly on it without some possible misunderstanding. However, for the sake of those starting to play competitive golf, I am going to try to define this difference.

There are many capable young golfers coming into prominence now, all of them grasping for every bit of information that will hasten their rise to the top. I know this because I was once in the same position. Now that I have arrived at my destination, there is only one bit of information which I feel is truly important. Consequently, I am writing this in the hope that it may help some of them.

The girls Mr. Evans knew when he was so interested in that tournament were the girls I met in competition when I started tournament

124

golf. The same group met in practically all of the Southern tournaments and became good friends. We played for several weeks in succession—a different tournament each week—exchanging honors for first place quite often unless Glenna Collett played. She undoubtedly surpassed us in ability, which none of us objected to recognizing. Her sportsmanship was as great as her mastery of golf shots.

My turn to be fodder for Glenna's ability came rather abruptly. It was my first meeting with her, and a great fear arose within me. The same fear haunts any new competitive golfer—that of having to match your shots against someone with better ones. You fear you cannot do your best, unless she is having an off-day. Under a strain of this sort, I went to the course that afternoon and discovered it was possible to play very well with such a turmoil within me. I won that match on the nineteenth hole. Naturally, I shall never forget it, but, what is more important, I shall not forget the consideration shown me by Glenna that day. She knew how nervous I was, but, rather than take advantage of it, she honestly made an effort to get me over it. She is the type of golfer who prefers to match shots with you rather than see you mentally upset to the extent that you are incapable of playing good golf shots.

The majority of our group had the same attitude toward competition. It was your ability against theirs that mattered. The fact that we were all good friends and that many of the titles we were playing for were not too important undoubtedly had a great deal to do with this attitude, but it made competitive golf delightful. I played well that first year and had my share of victories in the more serious tournaments. Then came the inevitable slump which almost every beginner experiences.

During that period, I ran into one defeat after another. This was unpleasant and at times discouraging. However, the art of losing is a fine thing to learn. It is during such a period that well-meaning acquaintances offer so much advice. Due perhaps to my good fortune in winning quite a few matches earlier that year, my ability to execute golf shots was not questioned. It had to be my attitude that was wrong. I had no fight. My opponents felt too comfortable playing against me. I made it too easy for them.

I tried to acquire the "fight attitude." Someone had once told me I would have to decide whether I wanted to be a great golfer or a sweet kid before I could ever win a big title. This seemed an odd decision to be called upon to make. Fortunately, I eventually found it unnecessary. I did want to become a great golfer, but the disposition I had been born with could not be made over. Concentration does not come easy to me, and I was apt to talk to friends in the gallery too much, thus losing a certain amount of concentration in thinking out and playing my next shot. My attitude toward the people around me during a match had to be changed. I now do my conversing after the match is over.

Fight! Fight! Fight! Why is that always preached to a young golfer? After all, if you hold the majority of the good cards, you stand a fine chance of beating Culbertson at bridge. My theory is this: if you perfect your golf shots, your opponent will need more than an unfriendly attitude to defeat you.

One's fighting ability is generally judged by the number of difficult matches one wins. Yet the first time I heard myself being judged a poor fighter came after a week of winning four of the hardest matches I ever played. I lost the fifth by a margin of 13 and 12, and that match apparently erased the merits of the other four. To be a good fighter means but one thing, as I see it: never stop trying to hit your shots perfectly. The good breaks won't always come your way—make the most of them when they do—and when they don't, keep trying to do your best. Should you lose, chalk it up to experience and take your defeat graciously. The good breaks will come your way another day.

It irritates me no end to hear a good golfer who has lost a match called a "poor match player," which is just another form of saying "poor fighter." That player eventually hears the remark and promptly adopts the attitude of "I will show you I can fight" and in the next match starts out with the sole intention of downing his or her opponent any way possible. With this aggressive attitude prevailing, the game turns into a battle of personalities and golf is placed in the background.

It is my belief that this attitude of aggressiveness is far more prevalent in competitive golf today than it used to be. It creates poor sportsmanship and spoils the joy of the game for the players and the pleasure of watching a shot-matching game for the gallery.

This is not true of all matches, but more of them are played in such a manner today than was true a few years ago. The reason for this, I believe, is the constant preaching of Fight, Fight, Fight, and the lack of understanding what the word means when used in connection with a golf match. Since I started tournament golf, no one has won so consistently as Glenna Collett Vare, yet I have never seen Glenna anything but friendly and considerate in a golf match. If you can play better golf shots, the match is yours. If not, it's just too bad for you.

Last year Helen Hicks and I faced each other in the final round of thirty-six holes for the national championship. We had been team mates in the International Matches held in England in 1932. We had been training together for this championship for several weeks. In fact, we were both house guests of the Ralph Bards in Highland Park, Illinois, during the championship.

*Helen Hicks and Virginia Van Wie, friends
and competitors.*

We had breakfast together the morning of the final, drove to the
course in the same car, and, though the match was equally important to
each of us, there was no feeling of enmity. Helen played the better golf
during the morning round, and I was two holes behind when it ended.
The afternoon round started, and I happened to have a streak of the
best golf I have ever played in my life. On the last nine holes we played,
Helen took 36 strokes and I took 32. The match ended in a 4-and-3
victory for me. The entire match had been a battle of golf shots—a
pleasure to play and, unless a great many people were being untruth-
ful, a pleasure to watch.

# Reunion: Wethered and Jones, East Lake, 1935

## O.B. Keeler

The American Golfer                    August, 1935

Miss Joyce Wethered, on her first visit to America, has played in a dozen noteworthy exhibition matches at golf as these lines are written, and before they appear in print she will have played in many more. She may have scored more brilliantly than even her beautiful 74 on the old course at East Lake, Atlanta, where, on the afternoon of June 18, Miss Wethered and Charlie Yates halved the match with Miss Dorothy Kirby and Bobby Jones. But of one thing I am sure—Miss Wethered will not have played, and perhaps will never play, in a match with so pretty a background and affording so vivid an inspiration for the two greatest golfers of their time.

You see, it was Bobby Jones who arranged the Atlanta match, which he requested the Atlanta Women's Golf Association to sponsor for charity. Bobby had been invited to play as Miss Wethered's partner in her first appearance in this country at the Women's National Golf and Tennis Club on Long Island. Shortly before that date Bobby was taken ill with an attack of appendicitis.

It never leaked out that Bobby was quite ill a week before the last championship competition in which he engaged, the national Amateur at Merion, the last trick in his Grand Slam in 1930. It was rumored that he had suffered a slight attack of ptomaine poisoning. Only a few heard of that rumor, though an Atlanta surgeon, Dr. Lon Grove, accompanied Bobby to Philadelphia. At any rate, a week before he was scheduled to appear on Long Island with Miss Wethered on May 30, Bobby was compelled to cancel the engagement.

Bobby recovered sufficiently the next week to make a business trip to Chicopee, Massachusetts, and to attend the Open championship at Oakmont, which he was covering for a newspaper syndicate. He insisted that he was feeling all right, though he had obviously lost much weight. He declined to consider suggestions that he might not be in shape to play the match at East Lake on June 18.

*The two greatest amateur golfers of all time get together for a game at East Lake, in Atlanta, in 1935.*

In New York following the Open, Bobby suffered two more attacks, sufficient to keep him in bed several days at the Vanderbilt Hotel, where his father joined him. The last word I had from Bobby was a telegram with the information that Miss Wethered and her companion, Miss Dorothy Shaw, would arrive by plane after her match at Baltimore on June 16. Presently Bobby turned up, having returned by train. He announced that he was feeling fine and was certain to go through with the match unless he broke a leg. At that time he had already reserved a room in an Atlanta hospital and had got the operation scheduled for the second day after the match.

Bobby and his party met Miss Wethered and Miss Shaw at the airport. At dinner that evening Miss Wethered and Bobby talked golf incessantly, and she told him how Bobby Cruickshank had suggested a change in her putting grip for the American greens—the reverse-overlap. It appeared to me to be almost identical with that suggested to

Bobby so long ago by the late Walter Travis. Tuesday was fair, and a fine gallery turned out to see the match.

I have watched many exhibition matches, but none like this one. Miraculously, Bobby's putting touch, deplorably off-color these later years, had returned. He laid a long one dead over the tricky Bermuda at the first green and holed a thirty-footer for a deuce at the second to put his side 2 up.

Miss Wethered, after hitting her drive two hundred and forty yards into a light headwind, laid her pitch four feet from the flag at the third and holed the putt for a 3. At the 565-yard fifth, with the wind behind her, she was level with Bobby after two great wood shots just short of the green, and she squared the match with another fine pitch and a seven-footer for a birdie 4. Then it was Bobbys turn. He holed a fifteen-footer for a birdie 3 at the seventh and pitched dead for another birdie 3 at the eighth. Then Miss Wethered, just short of the green with two wood shots at the 596-yard ninth, gained back a hole with an exquisite chip that left her no putt at all.

Bobby was out in 34, Miss Wethered in par 36. He was just 1 up on the English girl. Between them they had a best-ball of 31, and while Dorothy Kirby and Charlie Yates were playing admirable golf—the fifteen-year-old Atlanta girl had a 41 from the back tees—the battle between the two greatest golfers of all time was what the gallery had come out to see, though never expecting anything so utterly dazzling as the play on the front nine.

Miss Wethered, driving level with Bobby across the lake and up the long hill of the tenth fairway, squared the match. At this point, she was square also with par from the back tees. Her driving was simply tremendous. The wind was coming up, and when she was facing it, she was hitting low, raking drives with great carry and astonishing run. And at the fourteenth, a hole of four hundred and forty-eight yards, there was for a moment a half-gale from the west straight in her face. And there—well, Bobby and Charlie Yates struck two of their best, and Miss Wethered's ball was well in front.

Against the sweeping wind, Miss Wethered was flag-high with her second shot, the ball curling off to the left into a bunker. Miss Wethered, of course, was unfamiliar with East Lake bunkers in summer. When she tried to blast the ball out with her niblick, the blade ricocheted off the sun-baked surface under the thin layer of sand, clipped the ball fairly in the back and sent it flying fifty yards over the green and the gallery, to the frank amazement of the latter and of Miss Wethered herself. But she trotted down into a little valley, found the ball in a difficult place, pitched back beautifully, and holed a 20-foot putt for a 5, a stroke over par. Bobby won the hole with a 4.

Charlie Yates mopped his brow. "This is the first time," he said with a puzzled expression, "I ever played fourteen holes as a lady's partner before I figured in one!"

The two sides halved the four-hundred-and-thirteen-yard sixteenth with 4s all around. Charlie squared the match at the seventeenth in pursuance of his announced policy when Bobby's long drive was hooked to a ditch by the roadway, and Miss Wethered, for the second time on the strange Bermuda greens, took three putts.

And then came the climax of a great match.

The eighteenth hole of the No. 1 course at East Lake is two hundred yards, across the lake, from a hillside tee to a hilltop green.

"I know a one-shot finishing hole is not usually well regarded," Big Bob Jones, Bobby's father, once said to me. "But when a player stands on that tee at East Lake, with the match square or dormie—that drive calls for all there is in the delicatessen department."

Miss Wethered drove first, a spoon into the wind, and her ball was dead on the line, stopping twenty feet in front of the flag. Yates's shot was the same distance beyond the pin. Dorothy's was short and to the right. Bobby's was shoved a bit, and his wee pitch from the side of the hill caught the slope and trickled down five yards below the hole. Dorothy had to settle for a 4. Miss Wethered putted and just missed a 2. Charlie likewise. And the gallery pressed closer, for it was up to Bobby.

As I stood there watching Bobby line up that putt, I saw him again on the same green, and in the same spot, at the close of a round in a famous Southern Open eight years before—the tournament he won from a great field with eight strokes to spare. I saw him sink that putt, eight years ago, and then—well, the roar of that faraway gallery went out under the roar of the gallery that stood all about me. Bobby had holed this putt, too. The match was square.

Nothing devised in a scenario writer's shop in Hollywood could have improved on that climax. Bobby had a par 71 on his home course. Miss Wethered, a 74. Young Dorothy Kirby was around in 84, and Charlie Yates in 76.

Miss Wethered's play was beyond praise. On Bermuda greens, which she was playing for the first time, she had needed three putts twice. She had been a trifle off-line with two drives. And that was all that stood between Joyce Wethered and a level 70 the first afternoon she had seen the 6600-yard East Lake course. The individual match with Bobby— the gallery, of course, kept that in mind—was won by Bobby, 2 and 1.

Going down the fairway toward the sixteenth green, I was walking with Miss Wethered, and, naturally, I was complimenting her on her brilliant play.

She smiled and then became suddenly grave.

"I had to play well here," she said, simply. "Bobby arranged the match, you know. And he's said and written so many kind things about my game. Then he was ill, and then he insisted on playing. . . . I wish I were sure he *should* be playing, now. . . . It's the most sporting thing I've ever known. I had to play well. I couldn't let Bobby down, you know."

Yes—I knew. And I know, too, that I saw something that afternoon at East Lake that will stand out as the prettiest picture of a lifetime in sport—the two greatest golfers, putting all they knew into every shot, in a generous and gallant complement to one another in the greatest match I have ever witnessed.

# Joyce Wethered's Swing

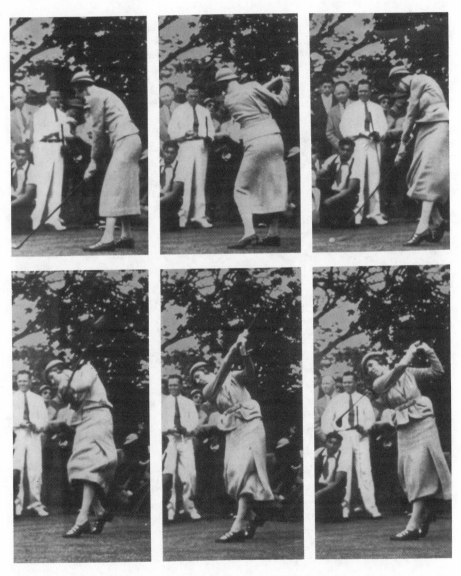

*This sequence from* The American Golfer *was taken during her American tour in 1935.*

# Glenna Collett's Swing

The American Golfer                    1935

*This sequence was taken in 1935. The occasion was our national championship, which Glenna won for a record sixth time.*

# Number Six for Glenna

## Bernard E. Swanson

The American Golfer                                      October, 1935

Mrs. Glenna Collett Vare, of Philadelphia, won the National Women's championship for the sixth time at the Interlachen Country Club, in Minneapolis, during the last week of August, but youth, with all its vigor and impulsiveness, insisted on sharing the spotlight. If ever golf correspondents had something to write about, it was spread before them at Interlachen. Despite stretches of cold and rainy weather, an unprecedented turnout of over fifteen thousand spectators was on hand during the six days of the 1935 championship.

If there is one thing a doting public loves, it is to see a noble figure emerge from the shadows of the past, return to the spotlight, and lead the parade again. Mrs. Vare was not very far back in the shadows. In 1933 she retired from competition to attend to bringing up her young children. Last year, returning to the tournament scene, she went to the semi-finals of the Women's National championship where she lost, 3 and 2, to Virginia Van Wie. Miss Van Wie went on to outplay Dorothy Traung, of California, in the final, 2 and 1, and, accordingly, won the crown for the third straight year. She elected not to defend her title this year, and she has participated in no tournaments. Miss Van Wie has not disclosed her plans for the future.

Mrs. Vare has said that her present game compares favorably with her play in her peak years. She believes that her golf these days is perhaps steadier and more consistent than during the long stretch when she was the unchallenged leader of the American women golfers. She is of the opinion that she is not as long off the tee as she used to be, but her friends disagree. At Interlachen, one of them told her, "I think you're driving the ball farther than you ever did. I've never seen you hit your tee shots as long as you did today in the final against Patty Berg." Mrs. Vare had to be at her best to cope with Miss Berg's sturdy challenge in the final and to close out their match, 3 and 2, with a birdie on the 34th green. In rating the new young players she had watched in the

*Seventeen-year-old Patty Berg put up a stiff fight against Mrs. Vare in the final of the 1935 Women's championship, but Glenna prevailed with a birdie on the 34th.*

championship, Mrs. Vare said, "Patty Berg, I think, is quite a distance ahead of the others. Then would come Elizabeth Abbott, of Los Angeles, and Beatrice Barrett, of Minneapolis."

Patty Berg is seventeen years old and weighs only a hundred and fifteen pounds. She hits a surprisingly long ball. Having played golf only three years, her iron game—particularly on her run-up shots—is not as good as it will become with experience. On the other hand, she is already very sound on the greens. For instance, she won her match with Mrs. Dan Chandler by sinking a 45-footer from the identical spot from which Bobby Jones had made the birdie that clinched his victory in our National Open in 1930. When Patty played Charlotte Glutting in the semi-finals, she squared the match by making a 25-footer on the eighteenth green. These remarkable clutch putts fanned the ardor of Patty's home-town admirers.

Patricia Jane "Patty" Berg was born in Minneapolis in the winter of 1918. She gained her competitive flair from playing in boys' games. When she was fourteen years old, she coached a boy's football team since her parents refused to allow her to play football any longer and she just had to have a hand in it. Three years ago she was introduced to golf by Patricia Stephenson, a former Minnesota State champion. Urged to enter the Minneapolis City tournament, she gathered together a makeshift set of clubs from her father's collection, packed her own lunch, and thumbed a ride to the course. She shot a 122 and decided then and there that she liked the game and wanted to master it. Two years later she won that tournament.

The Misses Berg, Abbott, and Barrett do not stand alone as youth's complete contribution to the 1935 National Women's championship. There were a number of other young women of obvious talent: Marion McDougall, a twenty-one-year-old girl from Portland, Oregon, has won the Women's Western Open and the Pacific Northwest; twenty-one-year-old Marion Miley, who has won the Western and the Trans-Mississippi championships; and seventeen-year-old Betty Jameson who won the Southern Amateur when she was fifteen. There will be many others.

A further word about Mrs. Vare and the National Women's championship, which was first held in 1895 at the Meadow Brook Club in Hempstead, Long Island. In 1919 when she was a nineteen-year-old from Rhode Island, she posted one of the thirty-six lowest scores in the eighteen-hole qualifying round and entered the heart of the championship, the daily rounds at match play. In 1922, she went all the way to the final where she defeated Mrs. William Gavin, of England, 5 and 4, at the Greenbrier Golf Club, in West Virginia. She won her second national title in 1925 at the St. Louis Country Club and her third in 1928 in Hot Springs, Virginia, where she overwhelmed seventeen-year-old Virginia Van Wie 13 and 12 in the final. Glenna had by then firmly established herself as the best woman player in America. In the 1929 championship at Oakland Hills, outside Detroit, she outplayed Mrs. Leona Pressler, from southern California, 4 and 3 in the final. She made it three straight in 1930 at the exceedingly long and exacting Los Angeles Country Club. For the second time the opposing finalist was Virginia Van Wie. In 1931, the year that she married Edwin H. Vare, Jr., the championship was held at the Country Club of Buffalo. In the semi-finals, she defeated Miss Van Wie, who had become her most dangerous rival 2 up in the semi-finals, but in the final she lost a hard-fought match 2 and 1 to Helen Hicks, one of the longest hitters in women's ranks. Mrs. Vare got to the final again in 1932 at the Salem Country Club's spectacularly beautiful course, designed by Donald Ross, north and west of Boston. She and Virginia Van Wie met in the final. On this occasion there was no stopping Virginia. Playing one precisely struck golf shot after another, she simply walked away from Glenna, 10 and 8.

For the first time in fifteen years, Glenna was not on hand in 1933 when the National Women's championship was hosted by the Exmoor Country Club, near Chicago. To no one's surprise, in Glenna's absence Virginia Van Wie—she was then twenty-four—carried off the title for a second time. She outlasted Helen Hicks, the defending champion, 4 and 3 in the final. Over the years Virginia had developed an impressive golf mind and a handsome swing that stood up under heavy pressure. She had studied the golf swing with Ernest Jones, the astute English professional who was best known in this country for the success he enjoyed in making good women golfers better golfers. At Exmoor, Virginia was in good form but not at her best. In the third round she survived her one hard match: Leona Cheney carried her to the eighteenth hole. She had no trouble with Enid Wilson, the British champion, in the semi-finals. She was in charge all the way in the final in which she defeated Helen Hicks, 4 and 3. The following year, 1934, Virginia made it three championships in a row. The field assembled in early October at the Whitemarsh Valley Country Club outside Philadelphia. For decades that area had produced an almost endless stream of young ladies—and older ones, too—who really understood the game and enjoyed competition. Mrs. Vare was on hand again, and a new format was introduced. The low *seventy-two* scorers in the qualifying round, twice as many as in the previous years, played four rounds of eighteen-hole matches to arrive at the two golfers who would meet in the 36-hole final to see who would be champion. In the upper half of the draw, Miss Dorothy Traung of Olympic, Washington, defeated Mrs. Opal Hill, of Blue Hills, Missouri, 3 and 2. Both Miss Van Wie and Mrs. Vare had been placed in the lower half of the draw, and, as it worked out, they met in the semi-finals. Miss Van Wie carried the day, 3 and 2, and went on to edge out Miss Traung 2 and 1 in the final. Shortly after winning her third straight national championship, Virginia retired from competitive golf.

The following year, 1935, as has been described, Glenna Collett Vare won her sixth United States championship at the Interlachen Country Club in Minneapolis, edging out a talented home-town girl, Patty Berg, who was then seventeen. At Interlachen, Mrs. Vare made her eighth and last appearance in the final round of the championship.

# The British Champion, Pam Barton, Adds the U.S. Amateur

## A Report from the New York *Herald Tribune*

Golf Monthly (U.K.)                                          November, 1936

Champion of two nations, Pam Barton won the adulation of the American spectators when in the United States Women's championship final she beat Maureen Orcutt, of Coral Gables, by 4 and 3. Graphic pen pictures of the final scenes were written by New York golf experts, and our bright description is from the New York *Herald Tribune*:

"Clinching victory at the thirty-third hole of play when she made her most sensational putt of the match, a thirty-five-footer that took the undulations like a scared rabbit and went plunging home for a birdie 4, the British champion earned the double crown of the links.

"Before a crowd of several thousand spectators, the English girl added that sensational climax to a grand exhibition of golf on the fifteenth green of the Canoe Brook Country Club's south course. Erasing the memory of many other long ones that she often had failed to lay dead, that brilliant thirty-five-footer started the Cox Trophy, emblematic of the championship, in a direction that it has not taken since 1913. In that year Miss Gladys Ravenscroft, of England, defeated Miss Marion Hollins in the final at Wilmington, Del. Miss Ravenscroft, however, did not hold the British title at that time.

"Miss Barton spanned a period of twenty-seven years to tie the double made by Miss Dorothy Campbell, later Mrs. H. V. Hurd, when that star, holder of the British Women's championship, captured the United States title at the Merion Cricket Club in the suburbs of Philadelphia.

"Pam Barton has nerves of steel—she is passionately devoted to the most hair-raising sport on foot, skiing in Switzerland—not that she went through the final with the easy-going unconcern she showed throughout her preceding matches.

"She was very definitely concerned when Miss Orcutt began cutting down her dormie-margin after the turn. But during the rest of the match, she still presented a remarkable picture for a national finalist,

*Pam Barton*

grinning over her mistakes, like a child taking a lesson, and stepping up to her shots as relaxed as if she were on the practice tee.

"The only sign of below-the-surface tenseness the English girl showed at all consistently was what seemed a degree too much casualness on the earlier greens. She spent so little time sighting the line of her putts and making her strokes that often her misses had to be ascribed to rushing.

"Quite the most extraordinary thing at the championship is the trophy the women play for. In the first place, instead of being the fruit of American enthusiasm, it was donated by a Scot, and in the second, it is an *objet d'art* of unforgettable *mien*.

"Robert Cox, from the heather country, passed a year here forty years ago, and, opining that American women's golf needed a boost here and there, he put up the trophy for the first Women's National championship in 1896.

"The trophy is all it was meant to be. One look at it and it's hard to think of anything one wouldn't do to have it to show admiring friends. In fact, a look at it is worth the price of admission.

"It stood, the proud cynosure of attention, two and a half feet tall on the table at the club-house lawn presentation, venerable and resplendent in a manner all its own. Its lean silver sides are embossed all over with green enamel thistles and medallions of painted porcelain depicting a Scottish castle and meadows with sheep grazing.

"A band at the top is studded with giant topazes and supports a pointed silver cover that bears a porcelain woman golfer, vintage 1896, on its side. Spiring above the whole, on the very top, is a lavender enamel thistle.

"Miss Barton had all she could do to stand up under the trophy's weight when John G. Jackson, president of the United States Golf Association, presented it to her to take back to its native island. She told the massed half-circle of admirers that she was thrilled to have won and was sure she couldn't have done so without the friendly attitude the galleries had shown her. Then she capped this sporting gesture with ten minutes before photographers and newsreel men, sagging under the weight of the trophy, with her Cuban heels sinking into the rainsoaked earth.

"It was an hour after the match was over on the fifteenth hole before the presentation ceremony started, largely because the crowds wouldn't let Miss Barton alone. She was driven to the club-house from the final hole, and the enthusiasm for her final thirty-five-foot putt that staved off loss of the hole and gave her the championship was so great that the gallery broke out with a fresh wave of wild applause as she drove away.

# Two Cartoons from The New Yorker

The New Yorker                                   1940, 1992

*Drawing by P. Steiner; © 1992, The New Yorker Magazine, Inc.*

*"Now you and I are going to share a little secret."*

Drawing by Helen E. Hokinson; © 1940, 1968, The New Yorker Magazine, Inc.

# My Swing

## Patty Berg, with Otis Dypwick

"Golf"                                A.S. Barnes and Co., 1941

Although it is not altogether true, I sometimes feel that if the hands perform correctly, the other components of the golfing mechanism will automatically function properly. The wrists are also important for they are the hinges co-ordinating the arms and hands.

The wrists carry enormous power. Unless they are allowed to play their part, a great loss of distance and crispness will occur. The power in the wrists is applied only when the swing has reached the "hitting area" when the hands are about hip-high in the down-swing. It is then that the power of the wrists, which have been held in a cocked position since reaching the top of the backswing, is unleashed at the ball.

Many players fail to make use of their wrist power, for they neglect to "break" their wrists fully at the top of the backswing. They seem to feel that as a result of cocking their wrists fully, they will mis-hit the ball.

So much has been spoken and written about "cocking the wrists" that I believe some players are confused as to the real meaning of the term. I like to think of this action as a "breaking" or bending of the hands on the backswing to aid one's hitting potential.

I want to caution beginners against misconstruing what is really meant by "cocking the wrists." Some beginners tend to overdo this action. They *lift* the club on the backswing and flip it around loosely in their anxiety to add to their wrist action. The usual result is a rolling-over or "collapsing" of the left wrist and hand at impact. Correct wrist action is *very* important. I like to think of the wrists as a spring that permits the hands to "break" underneath the shaft at the top of the backswing, placing them in position to add their power to the down-swing.

As important as the work of the wrists is, the hands are much more important in the act of hitting the ball. For utmost efficiency, you must have "live", responsive hands. Train them to function properly.

144

This is the address for the drive, front view. Feet, hips, and shoulders are square to line of flight. Stand fairly erect, with a slight stoop of the shoulder and back. This allows arms to hang downward lightly, with a minimum of body interference.

Flex knees slightly for smooth knee action in pivoting and shifting body-weight. I determine the distance from the ball as follows: Stand as outlined above, with your arms hanging down just clear enough of the body to avoid interference. Then "sole" the club-head directly behind the ball. Variations in this procedure must be left to your judgment. They are governed by individual differences in physique.

Try to develop a sense of standardization in your address on every shot.

This is the address for the drive, rear view. Note the squareness of the stance. You will observe the chin is "cocked" behind the ball.

I would like to stress the importance of maintaining the angle or relationship between the lower and upper part of the body throughout the swing. To elaborate—you should retain the same "break" in the knees; the same stoop of the back and shoulders; the same position of the hands and head; and the same position of the feet, except for raising or lowering the heels to facilitate the pivoting of the body.

If the knees dip or "lock" as a result of forcing them too far back, you will likely make ineffective contact with the ball.

I want to stress the importance of the left hand's controlling the downswing through the ball. Don't let the right hand overpower the left. Study the pictures of the swing and you will see the left hand is firmly in control.

*This picture shows the club at a stage of the backswing where the hands start upward and the wrists begin to break, placing the hands in position to hit the ball.*

*Up to this point, the wrists and hands remain about as they were at address, and there should have been* no sensation of lifting *the club.* Feel that you are swinging *it up.*

*As I start the clubhead back and away from the ball, I have the feeling that my left hand and left side are starting the motion. The clubhead is taken back on a straight line from the ball, but because of the pivot away from the ball, the clubhead is actually taken around in an arc inside of the "line of flight," to a point approximately parallel to the right hip. At this height it starts upward.*

*Note in this picture the straight left arm which remains fairly straight throughout the entire swing.*

*Here we see the start of the backswing (front view). It is the same motion illustrated by the previous photo, but from a different angle.*

*The left shoulder is moving underneath and around, while the head is "cocked" behind the ball. The left eye is fixed on the ball throughout the backward and downward motion.*

*This is the initial move in the backswing. I have taken the club back to this point from its address position with my* left *hand in control. Some players say they take it back with both hands. My belief may be due to the fact I am concentrating so intently on* starting back both my left hand and my left side at the same moment. *Both hands take it back.*

*I seem to feel that I start pushing the club back with my left hand* and *left hip; in fact, my whole left side.*

*Here you see the club at the top of the backswing, an important point in the swing. Note that the wrists are now fully "set" and both hands are directly under the shaft.*

*From this position a distinct pull-down of the club with the left hand occurs, the right following until reaching the "hitting area."*

*The wrists should remain "cocked" until the left hand has pulled the club down to a point where it is approximately even with your waist-line. The wrists "un-cock" instinctively from this stage through the impact with the ball. The right hand comes into play simultaneously, adding its power to the stroke and thereby speeding up the club-head for the impact. The left hand* must be in control *so that it can guide the club-head through on a straight line.*

*If you allow your wrists to "un-cock" before reaching the "hitting area" you lose the benefit of your wrist power.*

*This figure portrays the club (a 3-wood) just after the start of the downswing. The hips have already begun their forward movement. From this position the transfer of the weight to the left leg will begin. As the left heel descends to the ground, the left knee will straighten to carry the shifting weight.*

*Now, let's try to visualize what happens in the forward swing. First the hips begin to slide forward. You must have a distinct sensation of* pulling the club down *with your left hand and arm, meanwhile keeping you right elbow close to your side.*

*When your hands reach the "hitting area," wrists should start "un-cocking," with the right hand smashing through the ball. Your left hand should guide the club in an arc from the "inside" and underneath toward the right (or seemingly out across the line of flight).*

*Head should remain stationary and chin back of ball until after impact.*

*This represents a position as the club approaches the "hitting area." The wrists will now begin to "un-cock" to lash through the ball. The weight is flowing from the right to the left leg. The left arm is fairly straight. The left heel has returned to the ground. The head is back of the ball.*

*Note that the right elbow is in close to the right side of the body. This is to help maintain a swing which will carry the club-head from the "inside" toward the "outside" of the line of flight.*

*Note the right leg pushing forward to aid in the power of the swing. It is from this point that the right hand adds its power.*

*Observe how the hips slide forward, then automatically turn, clearing the path for the left arm.*

*At this stage of the swing, be careful to avoid staying back too much on the right leg, or "dipping" the left knee, thus causing wildly-hit shots.*

*Note here that the club-head is travelling upward from a distinctly "underneath" hitting-action. The right shoulder is moving from "underneath" while the left shoulder continues upward.*

*Keep the head fairly steady, for the head is to your arms as a hub is to a wheel. Obviously, if the spokes are to move consistently in the same orbit, the hub must remain fixed. A "bobbing" head spells disaster to any golf shot.*

*Note that the feet and head have maintained their original relative position. This "anchoring" is vitally important in developing a "grooved" (consistent) swing.*

*On the follow-through and completion of the swing, note the hands held high above the head, indicating that there has been* no effort to stop the club until the swing has reached completion. This is important. *It shows that power from the shoulders, back, arms, hands, and legs has flowed without restraint into this stroke.*

*I would like to elaborate at this point on the follow-through, or the action of the clubhead through the ball to the finish of the swing. Many players virtually cease application of power after the clubhead meets the ball.*

*The predominant factor in the follow-through is* uninterrupted speed. *If you impair the speed, you fail to take advantage of your potential hitting power.*

# Ernest Jones: Ladies' Man

## Philip W. Wrenn, Jr.

The New Yorker                                    September 20, 1941

Three guesses as to who had the most to do with winning the 1941 Women's National Amateur championship, held last week at The Country Club in Brookline, Massachusetts. Hal Pierce, president of the United States Golf Association? Nope. Mrs. Elizabeth Hicks Newell, the winner? Again, nope. Miss Helen Sigel, the runner-up? Nope a third time. It was Ernest Jones, formerly the pro at the Women's National Golf and Tennis Club at Glen Head, Long Island, and today the pro at the Cedar Creek Club (same place), which is the result of the merger earlier this year of the W.N.G.T.C. and the Creek Club.

It all goes back to an evening about two weeks ago—four or five days before the start of the championship—when Mrs. Newell, a Californian, was a guest at the Long Island home of Mrs. Helen Hicks Harb, a former champion. Mrs. Newell, Mrs. Harb, and Miss Virginia Van Wie, another former champion, were sitting around the Harb living room after dinner discussing, of all things, golf. Mrs. Newell had gained the floor and was saying, in effect, that her game was shot to hell. She couldn't seem to get the feel of the swing any more, she said, and her best score since mid-July was a ninety-four. Miss Van Wie said that was too bad, but why didn't Mrs. Newell, since she was right there in Rockville Center, drive over to Glen Head and take a lesson from Ernest Jones? Miss Van Wie was so strong in her praise of Jones that Mrs. Newell spent two hours with him the following morning learning how to "swing the club head," as Jones puts it. After that workout, plus a few practice sessions based on the Jones principles, Mrs. Newell headed for Brookline, her ninety-four complex forgotten, and disposed of half a dozen of the country's best golfers, including Miss Clara Callender, Mrs. Estelle Lawson Page, and Miss Sigel.

Jones has dedicated the better part of his teaching career to instructing women golfers. If any proof were needed that he is just about the best women's instructor in the business, this year's championship provides it. Counting his two-hour student, Mrs. Newell, three of the quarter-finalists were Jones products. The other two were Mrs. Reinert M. Torgerson and Mrs. Sylva Annenberg Leichner.

Mrs. Leichner, incidentally, is someone not to get in the way of. A lot of the contestants stayed at Boston's Hotel Somerset during the tournament, and when a copy of the draw for match play was posted on the bulletin board in the lobby Monday evening, one of the many men who gathered around shouldered Mrs. Leichner aside as she was trying to read the name of her next day's opponent. She plucked at his sleeve and asked, "Who do you play?"

# Remembering Pam Barton

Golf Monthly (U.K.)                    December, 1943

*Flight-officer Pamela Barton was killed when an R.A.F. plane in which she was a passenger crashed in taking off at an airfield in Kent on November 13, 1943. She won the British Ladies' championship in 1936 and 1939, the American Women's championship in 1936, and the French Ladies' championship in 1934. She was born on March 4, 1917.*

On the all too few occasions that I met Pam Barton and played with her, I was struck at once not only by her ability as a golfer but by her simplicity and charm. It is because of these qualities that she will be so greatly missed in the golfing world. Her achievements and her character so obviously fitted her to take again a leading part in ladies' golf after the war when, I am sure, fresh triumphs awaited her. She will remain as a fine example to all young golfers, and we shall remember her with real affection.

LADY HEATHCOAT-AMORY (JOYCE WETHERED)

Pam Barton's record as a golfer is one that will never be forgotten. Her record as a sportswoman is equally great. Her method was to walk up to the ball and hit it with the minimum of fuss, and never by gesture or demeanour did she indicate good fortune or adversity. She was always radiating cheerfulness, and men and women, old and young, were captivated by her unfailing courtesy and charm. It is possible that only a few people realize how much Pam Barton did for charity, and many funds are indebted to her for playing in matches all over the country. Her death will be mourned by golfers throughout the world.

ENID WILSON

The tragic death of Pam Barton leaves a great gap in the ranks of the lady golfers and of the many others who knew her. Winning or losing, she was equally charming to play with, for she had a truly wonderful temperament for the game. Her cheerful personality will be sadly missed.

DIANA L. CRITCHLEY

By the death of Pam Barton the golfing world has lost a great personality, with a character that was developed and strengthened by the strain and stress of war, in which she had never shirked a full share of risk and danger.

Pam's great achievements on golf courses in many parts of the world will long be remembered, but I venture to think that when these have been forgotten, a happy memory of her radiant gaiety will remain with us. There were naturally occasions when the tremendous strain involved by endless matches, tours, and championships told on her nervous strength, but it was never long before the combination of a natural courage and a dauntless gaiety re-asserted itself.

What an attractive way Pam had of talking, as if she could hardly restrain the infectious laugh that was such a charming characteristic of hers, and which must have helped and encouraged the airwomen who served under her in the W.A.A.F.

Let us remember her, as I am sure she would wish to be remembered, with laughter and not with tears.

MOLLY GOURLAY

# Impressions of the 1948 Curtis Cup Trip

### Glenna Collett Vare
### Captain, 1948 U.S. Curtis Cup Team

Golf Journal                                        August, 1948

The good send-off luncheon given by the USGA. . . . Frannie Stebbins's wonderful job as Chairman, and Willie Turnesa's speech telling us of his British golfing experiences. . . . The four-leaf-clover charms which Frannie Stebbins gave us, worn with our USGA Curtis Cup pins.

Crowds on the *Mauretania* to see us off. . . . The three rough days that put some below decks. . . . Cobh Harbor looking mighty green in the early morning, and the fog shielding Cherbourg and Southampton.

Tea on the train to London and our first glimpse of the countryside, full of pheasants. The chimney pots and Big Ben. . . . Welcomed at Waterloo by Doris Chambers, Enid Wilson and Mrs. Wallace-Williamson. . . . Our first attack of baggage. . . .

Pleasant quarters at the Lady Golfers Club, flowers, messages and dinner. . . . Two rushed but exciting days seeing London, meeting people, ridding ourselves of sea legs, and getting acquainted. . . . A good day arranged by Doris Chambers at Roehampton, and more pleasant games at Berkshire with the Critchleys. . . .

Mad dashes to make the theatres' seven o'clock curtain. . . . Supper afterwards with Dorothy Pearson at Crockfords. . . . Dinner with Roger Wethered, Joyce and her husband. . . . Jean Hopkins and Peggy Kirk trying to decide about going to Paris. . . .

Arrival at our real destination, Southport and Royal Birkdale, with the Union Jack flying in front of the Prince of Wales hotel and at the club. . . . The golf course looking strange to us with its huge sand dunes, continuously undulating fairways, and no trees.

Estelle Page spending every spare moment writing letters. . . . Grace Lenczyk singing. . . . Enid Wilson and Dot Kirby snap-happy, taking pictures by the score.

The Big Day, with everyone keyed to a terrific pitch. . . . Luncheon away from the crowd with our table decorated with balloons and Amer-

154

ican flags. . . . Our two victories in the foursomes to put us in a comfortable position. . . .

Singles day, with a complete reversal of weather, high winds and unbelievably cold. . . . Fine finishes by all and especially Louise Suggs's last two holes. . . .

Elaborate and formal luncheon by the L.G.U. afterward, and Southport's Lord Mayor and major-domo bedecked with medals. . . . Speeches and toasts. . . . Doris Chambers' fine sportsmanship. . . . Dinner at the hotel, our cup filled with the bubbly by an English friend, and more toasts by the assembled multitude. . . . The friendliness and marvelous hospitality of everyone at Birkdale. . . .

A brief trip to Scotland. Snow-capped peaks surrounding Gleneagles, and a game at St. Andrews with a privileged visit inside the Royal and Ancient Club.

Return through the beautiful English lake country to Lytham St. Anne's to prepare for the championship. . . . Two matches a day for four days, and Louise Suggs's splendid win over Jean Donald of Scotland on the 36th hole in the final. . . .

Statue of Liberty lighted to greet us. . . . Home!

# Are Our Courses Right for Women?

## Margaret Curtis

Golf Journal                                            Winter, 1949

We women play our golf on courses laid out for men. In everyday life and in other sports, it is taken for granted that men are stronger than women. We ask our menfolk to unscrew the recalcitrant jar cap because their fingers are stronger than ours. We never did expect Helen Wills to beat Bill Tilden, nor Alice Marble to beat Don Budge. Of course not.

But, *relatively*, don't our Good Girls play as fine golf as the Good Men? When you watch Louise Suggs, Glenna Vare, Estelle Page, Dot Kirby, or Grace Lenczyk, to mention a few, it is hard to think otherwise. And this leaves out Babe Zaharias, who is unique.

If talented women golfers play as well as talented men, why are their scores so far apart? Let's start with scores in the 60s. Estelle Page has played in the 60s four times in competition. Louise Suggs three times. Glenna once, and that included a hole in one! The Babe many times. But never has any woman broken 70 in the USGA championship. The lowest score ever made in the qualifying round was 74.

Turning to the men. Last year in sectional qualifying for the Amateur championship there were at least twenty-five rounds in the 60s.

What's the explanation? Mightn't it be that the courses as set up for women are a good deal harder than the architect intended and relatively much more demanding than for men?

Both national amateur championships have been played recently at Pebble Beach in California, the men's in 1947, the women's in 1948. A beautiful but stiff course. The official scorecard shows that on six of the first nine holes the women played from the men's tees with identical yardage. The three women's tees shortened the other holes a total of 85 yards. On the second nine, the women played all but one hole from the men's tees: the 17th was shortened from 218 to 190 yards.

In fairness, it should be noted that women's par was 76 as compared with 72 for men. But the course was only 113 yards shorter for women. Could this be a rather cruel compliment?

The crux of this problem isn't the drive but the *shot to the green* and

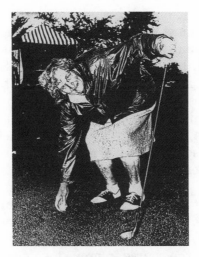

*Margaret Curtis*

the trajectory (isn't it a grand word?) of the ball—what club *should* be used and what club *is* used by the low-handicap women for that shot?

If we are agreed that women are mostly playing golf courses that are out of tune, mightn't we start a modest campaign?

Several groups are concerned: (1) the Ladies in Authority, both the USGA Women's Committee and the state and district committees which run championships; (2) the men on the thousands of club committees; (3) finally, and in some ways the most important, the big bunch of us rank-and-file players.

It isn't reasonable to expect much support from the championship players. They are in their prime and rejoice in their strength. They are young, and only the thoughtful ones will be interested or see any need for change.

Let's begin our studies on our home course's one-shot holes. It seems to be accepted that courses should have two one-shot holes in each nine. They usually call for shots of precision, although not necessarily iron shots. They are trapped accordingly. They range from the closely guarded "dropped-egg" hole to one that might call for a 4-wood by men.

It should be remembered that, let's say, a 7-iron for a man is quite a different shot from a 7-iron for a woman, in both length and trajectory.

Let's watch our low-handicap men play these holes. Let's inquire what clubs they use, and ask the pro, too. If you have girls in the championship class, find out what clubs they use for each short hole.

After that, let's consider the longest holes on the course. How do the hazards and lengths suit the women golfers?

There is one hole at our club that's over 500 yards long. A brook crosses the fairway at just the questionable distance for two good woods. In medal play and usually in match play, a sensible woman elects to lay up short of the hazard using a 5-iron to be safe. She must then play a 2-wood to reach the green. There is no women's tee.

What are the steps that can be taken? First, a careful study of the course. Then, a definite program. Nowadays most courses have several women's tees—some beautifully placed, others still not setting up a proper shot to the green. The cost of moving an existing tee or installing a new one in a proper place must be considered.

In the main, men's golf committees have been very sympathetic to women's needs. The fault has been that the women usually haven't asked what would be good tees for them. If the men are interested but don't see where the money is coming from, see if there aren't enough women keen to have the course improved who would chip in or have a special "day" and use the entry fees to start the improvements.

I believe a surprise is in store for the women on any reasonable request that is put before the men. Chivalry isn't entirely dead yet, and there is a willingness to give the gals a break.

With these considerations in mind, thought can be given to placing tees for championships. At a state championship not long ago, the markers on a fascinating but tricky water hole were moved back to the men's tee for the final. One player attempted the difficult carry and went splash with a 4-iron. The pro was asked what the low-handicap men used for this shot. "A number 9," was the answer. In this instance, it wouldn't have been difficult to advance the women's tee so that they also could play a number 9 or something like it.

Will the ladies on the USGA Committee give the rest of us their thoughts on this matter? Will they have the tees placed for our championship where it is possible for the girls to have the thrill of scoring, like the men, in the 60s? It will take courage. Of course, we don't want our courses made too easy. Stiff courses develop good players. But why not the same par for men and women on each course?

# "You're Always Learning New Ideas, New Methods. It Keeps You Young."

## Patty Berg

"Gettin' to the Dance Floor", by Al Barkow     Atheneum, 1986

When I was a little child living in Minneapolis, about seven doors down from me lived a fellow by the name of Charles "Bud" Wilkinson. He was a guard on the University of Minnesota football team, and in his last year was the quarterback. So anything he did, I had to do. We had a football team called the 50th Street Tigers. Bud was the guard, coach, and captain, and I was the quarterback because I was the only one who could remember the signals. We had one, 22, and when I yelled it out, everyone ran whichever way they wanted. Well, Bud finally told me I had to quit because I was too slow and short and there wasn't any future in it for me.

So I went into speed skating and did a lot of that. I skated in the national junior championships, intermediate division, and in the state championships; won some medals, too. Then there was a time when we were skating in some little town in Minnesota and, oh, it was cold! I remember coming to the finish line going so fast I ended up in one of the drifts. My dad came over and said, "Your mother and I are going to Florida tomorrow," and I told them to wait for me.

I was about twelve years old when I started swinging a club. I would swing away in the backyard, and my father was always wondering who was taking the divots—see, my sisters also played a little golf. Well, Dad caught me out there one day knocking up the grass and said, "How would you like to get that clubhead in back of a golf ball?" I said I'd like that, and that's when it really began. We were members at the Interlachen Country Club, which was where Bobby Jones won one of his Grand Slam championships in 1930—the U.S. Open. I wasn't there for that. I was in 6B at John Brown's Elementary School at the time, running in a track meet—won the thirty-yard dash.

Anyway, I took my first lessons at Interlachen from Willie Kidd, the head professional, and Jim Pringle, his assistant. Then for about forty years I took lessons from Lester Bolstead, who was the golf professional at the University of Minnesota. He coached the men's golf team. His team won the Big Ten championship one year, which was quite something to do in Minnesota. He was a real taskmaster with me. He would stand there and say, "Now, Patricia Jane,"—he never called me Patty—"you've got to strive for perfection, you must conquer your flaws, you must use your legs." And every time he said my name he would clap his hands: "Patricia Jane," clap, "Patricia Jane," clap. But he is a great golf professional and a very knowledgeable man. He knows a lot about anatomy and uses that in his teaching.

I won the 1934 Minneapolis City Ladies championship, which was the most memorable event in my golf career because I probably wouldn't have had a golf career if not for what happened. I played in my first City Ladies championship the year before, when I was fifteen, and shot 122. That qualified me for the last flight, and in my first match some lady beat me on just about every hole. After that defeat I walked back to the clubhouse and said to myself, "I'm going to spend the next 365 days trying to improve." The next year all I did was eat, sleep, and play golf. I thought if I could move up a flight or shoot better than 122, that would be an improvement. Well, 365 days later I was medalist and won the Minneapolis City Ladies' championship.

It's very possible that if I didn't improve on my 122, or didn't move up a flight or so, I might not be in golf today. But I didn't think I'd win that tournament. When I did, I started to dream. I thought, maybe I'll be able to play the Minnesota State Women's championship; maybe I'll be able to play in some of the tournaments in Florida, maybe even play in the Trans-Mississippi and the Women's Western Amateur and the United States Women's Amateur. I really started to dream that golf was my future, and that's exactly how it turned out.

That's a long time to spend on one endeavor, isn't it—365 days? But I'll tell you, it was worth every freckle on my face. What did I learn during that time? To hit the ball straighter by improving my tempo, timing, and rhythm. I got to know more about the swing, so I could correct myself during a round—you're the quarterback out there. And I spent a lot of time chipping and putting, because I knew I wasn't going to hit all the greens—no one does—especially when you were as small as I was.

We had a short golf season up in Minnesota. If we were lucky, we would start playing in the first part of May. A lot of times we'd play through October and November. If I made any swing changes at all, it was in October and November, because, by the time we could play in the spring, there wasn't time for that—the tournaments started coming up. I'd hit balls into a canvas, indoors. In 1935 my family starting going to Florida for a good bit in the winter. I spent a month in Florida the winter of '35, and that helped a lot in my winning the Minnesota State Women's championship and getting to the final of the USGA Women's Amateur championship. I would make up the schooling I missed, and when I was selected for the U.S. Curtis Cup team in my last year of high school, I was gone so much that my dad got a tutor for me.

My father had a grain company, the H. L. Berg Company. He was a member of the Chicago Board of Trade, the Minneapolis Board of Trade, and the Winnipeg Board of Trade. He was a businessman-golfer and had a ten handicap. My brother was a fine player. He played in the city league and the state championships. But he had come down with scarlet fever when he was a boy and that left him with a bad heart. He died at forty-three.

I went for two years to the University of Minnesota but didn't play golf for the school. There was just a men's golf team. But after I won that city championship, my father sent me to tournaments. I played in the Minnesota State, of course, then the Trans-Miss, which was my first major event. I qualified for the championship flight and got beat by Opal Hill in the second round. I did win the driving contest though. My prize was a beautiful mirror. Then, in 1935 I was runner-up to Glenna Vare in the Women's National Amateur. In 1937 I was runner-up in just about everything, and somebody wrote an article calling me the uncrowned champion. In 1938 I turned it all around and won ten out of thirteen tournaments.

I played amateur golf for part of 1939. Then, while I was on my way to defend one of my championships and having a wonderful year, I had an emergency appendectomy and was in the hospital for almost a month with a private nurse. I was finished for the season. In September I went on some trips for the University of Minnesota to raise funds. What I did was play in exhibitions that we wouldn't charge anything for, but at night we'd have dinners and collect contributions for the Student Union building. We went out into the Dakotas, and Montana, and California, about eight or nine states, contacting alumni. That's when I played Pebble Beach for the first time and met Bing Crosby and Richard Arlen. And Helen Lengfeld, who has done so much for women's golf. She put on a lot of golf tournaments, including one for the LPGA, and does to this day at the age of eighty-five. A lot of the girls on the tour today played in Helen Lengfeld's junior tournaments in California.

After I got back from that trip, I went to college for another year. Then in 1940 I turned pro. I went with the Wilson Sporting Goods Company. They offered me a job, and it was a very good arrangement. My father went to Chicago and discussed it with Mr. L.B. Icely, the president of Wilson. You know, at that time you didn't have any managers, so your father was your manager, or at least helped you. My dad was the greatest.

I wasn't the first woman pro, though. There were several before me, including Helen Hicks, and Bessie Finn. Bessie became the pro at The Breakers in Palm Beach, where she succeeded her dad. She taught but I think she mostly did administrative work. Then there was Helen Dettweiler, Opal Hill, and Hope Seignious. When I turned pro, I think there were something like three tournaments—the Western Open, the Titleholders, and maybe the Asheville Invitational. Sometimes some other tournament would come along. The total prize money was about $500, and we had a field sometimes of only five players, plus outstanding women amateurs.

We gave a lot of clinics for Wilson. I was used to doing clinics. I learned how to do them during the eight years I played amateur golf. My father had me play around the state of Minnesota giving clinics and exhibitions on weekends for different charities. A pro would give the instruction, while I hit the balls. I listened to how the pro made his presentation and picked up the technique that way.

What tour there was we did by train or bus or car. In 1941 I had a terrible accident going from Corsicana, Texas, to Memphis. This was to play an exhibition for British War Relief. I was on the passenger side of the car, Helen Dettweiler was driving. Somebody hit us and I went into the dashboard and broke my left knee in three places. And, of course, my face hit the windshield—no seat belts in those days. I was laid up for eighteen months. When they took the cast off, I couldn't get the leg bent because of the adhesions. The knee started to turn blue, so they gave me gas and ether and hit it, or manipulated it. They did that twice, and I fell once, so I ended up with about seventy-five percent use of the leg in terms of bending it.

When I got out of the hospital, I went down to Mobile, Alabama, and took a training program with a prize fighter named Tommy Littleton, who had a gym down there. I rode a bicycle and did two hours of gym work each day with Tommy. I got so I could hit golf balls, then so I could pick them up, and, finally, so I could play. The first thing I did after that was play an exhibition at George S. May's Tam O'Shanter Country Club in Chicago. He had a nice luncheon for me, and I shot 78 from the men's tees. The course played long because it had rained a lot, so I thought I was back.

The doctors now think that my hip may have been displaced a little from that accident and I didn't know it. I walked for thirty-nine years with it that way. The doctors now ask me if I ever felt the displacement, or the pain. I didn't, but I guess that after a while you don't feel pain. In 1980 I had a total hip operation, and now I have an artificial left hip. In 1971 I had a battle with cancer. I had a massive tumor close to the kidney. But I'm fine now.

I joined the Marine Corps during World War II, and was an officer. I went to Camp LeJeune for officer's training, then to Philadelphia where I worked in public relations and recruiting. I entered the service in 1943 and came out in 1945.

In 1946 we had an organization called the Women's Professional Golf Association. Later, Babe Zaharias and her husband, George, Fred Corcoran, and myself reorganized it into the Ladies Professional Golf Association, which is the LPGA today. In January, 1948, we met at the Venetian Hotel in Miami. We wanted to line up more tournaments to play, and that was Fred Corcoran's job. He had been the PGA Tour manager and knew everybody in the game. The first thing we did was change the name from Women's to Ladies Professional Golf Association. Fred thought it would be better to be Ladies than Women.

Wilson Sporting Goods gave us money for six years, not for prize money but for administrative costs and to pay Fred and his expenses. He was paid well for that time, but he did a very good job. Then other manufacturers put in some money, and, well, the LPGA just grew and grew. It was hard to envision then that women would soon be playing for $9 million in purses.

Babe Zaharias was a tremendous asset in the early days of the ladies tour. People wanted to come out and see her play golf. She was a household name. She gave them a show, too—a great competitor, a great player, and fun. I remember the time we played a team made up of the top British men amateurs at a famous course outside London, the so-called Burma Road course at Wentworth. In the morning Babe and I lost our match to John Beck and some other fellow. Betsy Rawls and Betty Bush lost, too. But Peggy Kirk and Betty Jameson tied their match, so we're behind two and a half points to a half-point. At lunch we're sitting around the table with all the little American flags on it, and I said, "All of those who expect to win their singles, follow me." Babe said, "Come on, follow Napoleon." Anyway, we went out and all of us won our singles match and beat the men, six to two. Babe played Leonard Crawley, the golf writer. Leonard had this big red mustache, and before they teed off Babe said to him, "If I beat you, do I get to cut your mustache off?" Leonard said, "You sure do." So after Babe beat him that afternoon, she was running around the parking lot with a scissors trying to find Crawley. She never did.

People have said that the Babe was a little crude once in a while, but

I didn't see that in her. No, I saw a wonderful athlete and someone with a lot of class. I remember when she was suffering from cancer so badly, she'd tell everybody it wasn't so bad, we're all going to get better. She knew she didn't have a chance, but she went around to hospitals telling patients they were going to get better, and so was she. You think that's a lady with class? Yes, sir. She gave everybody hope.

I guess a woman athlete in my younger days had to deal with the tomboy image a little more than nowadays, but I never got ragged for being an athlete. I had a tremendous amount of support from everybody. And the men pros always welcomed us with open arms when we played a tournament or gave a clinic at their clubs. In fact, I would get a lot of good instruction from some of the men. Johnny Revolta had a magnificent short game, and I took a lot of lessons from him whenever I was around Chicago during the summer or out in California. Sam Snead helped me a lot. I think he's a marvelous teacher. He has a keen eye, and I always liked the way he rolled in with his left foot; that movement he did with his feet and ankles was terrific. But I'm not tall—only five feet two—so I had to swing like Gene Sarazen, who was a terrific competitor and player. I watched him a lot.

If there is one thing I would tell all golfers about technique, it would be that the grip has a tendency to change even during the course of a round. You have to keep checking this day in and day out. The grip is the foundation of the swing. There's another thing. You must work constantly on timing and tempo. You know, some days you just cannot do anything with your tempo—it gets too fast. I tend to do everything quickly because that's my nature. So if I get too fast and don't complete my backswing, I'd just swing the club with my left-handed practice swing. Then, without stopping, I'd put my right hand on the club. That's how I'd get my tempo back. You see players on the tour doing this all the time, trying to get their tempo back. It's the best way I know.

# It All Depends on the Backswing

## Louise Suggs

"Par Golf for Women"  Prentice-Hall, Inc., 1953

*Illustration 1*

In Illustration 1 I am addressing the ball for a tee shot. The ball is played slightly forward of center of my stance. I generally use a square to slightly closed stance. Note the straight line formed between my left shoulder and the ball by my left arm and the club. My weight is equally distributed between my right and left feet, and between the toes and heels of both feet. My knees are slightly flexed for comfort and freedom of movement.

*Illustration 2*

I have a mannerism with my hands and wrists just before the start of the backswing that is designed to break the tension and pave the way for a smooth-flowing, rhythmic backswing. What I do is carry my hands forward in unison just an inch or two while the clubhead remains stationary. My right knee flexes slightly at the same time. The return of my hands and knees to their original position at the address of the ball develops in a continuous motion into the backswing. This "forward press", as it is known, is essential to avoid the jerking motion that is apt to result from a cold, rigid start on the backswing.

You will note in Illustration 2 how I have started my backswing. The clubface is still square to the ball and is being pushed back in a low trajectory. My weight is just beginning to go over from my left to my right foot. You can see that the clubhead has not been "picked up" by my right hand, for my left arm and the shaft still form a straight line. My hands are working together, but I have the feeling that my left hand is *pushing* the club back away from the ball. My right hand is just "riding" at this point.

*Illustration 3*

Every part of my body is working as a unit. Observe that the left knee is beginning to flex to accommodate the turn of the hips and the shoulders which starts at this point. My right leg is bracing (not becoming rigid) so that it can bear the weight of my body as the transfer to the right side takes place. This transfer continues during the backswing.

Illustration 3. At this point in the backswing the wrists are just beginning to "cock." This is not a conscious effort. It is caused by the upward pull resulting from the momentum of the clubhead. At this point, as well as all others in the backswing, the motion is a rhythmic, graceful one. During the course of the backswing there should be no thought of how you are going to "murder" the ball when you finally get back to it. The best insurance for a well-hit shot is a backswing that puts you in position to have full control of the downswing and thus insure maximum hitting efficiency.

The turn of my hips and shoulders continues, as does the transfer of weight from my left to right side. While my head is turning with the shoulders, as it must to avoid rigidity and tenseness, it remains in its

*Illustration 4*

original position, and my eyes are fixed on the spot on the ball I expect to hit.

My left arm remains straight and firm, but not tense. My right arm is breaking at the elbow but remaining comparatively close to my body.

As shown in Illustration 4, my weight is now pronouncedly over on my right side and the inside of my left foot is now carrying what weight remains on my left side. My left knee continues to give with the turn of my hips and shoulders. My head is still turning, but remains in its original position, and my eyes are fixed on the ball.

Note particularly that my left arm is still straight. The momentum of the clubhead continues to carry the clubhead back into more of a cocked position.

In Illustration 5 I have arrived at the top of my backswing. In so doing I have set the pattern for my downswing into the ball. It is the opinion of every golf authority that if the backswing is properly executed, it is virtually impossible to hit the ball poorly.

*Remember this:* the errors that throw a golf swing out of kilter de-

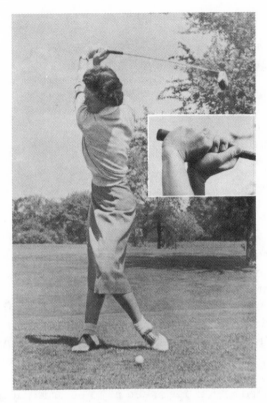

*Illustration 5*

velop in the course of the backswing. It is virtually impossible to cure them by remedies in the downswing. If the backswing is faulty, it is impossible to hit the ball consistently straight and far.

My back is now turned toward my objective. The turn of my shoulders has pulled my head seemingly out of position. Such is not the case. It has had to turn on its own axis with the turning of my shoulders, but out of the corner of my left eye, I can still see the point on the ball at which I am aiming.

Many golfers have entirely the wrong notion of what the head is supposed to do. They have been warned: "Keep your head down." "Keep your eye on the ball." "Don't move your head." This leads them to stay in a fixed position which is completely unnatural. It is humanly impossible to turn your shoulders into the desired position and still keep your face pointed straight down at the ground. In doing this, you would disastrously restrict the backswing. However, your eyes should still be on the ball.

# The Babe Comes Back

## Al Laney

New York *Herald Tribune*                                    July 4, 1954

Mildred Zaharias, who is known to all as The Babe, won the second Women's United States Open golf championship at the Salem Country Club today by the overwhelming margin of twelve strokes and with the very fine seventy-two-hole score of 291.

Mrs. Zaharias, leading by seven strokes as the final day began, played two closing rounds in 73 and 75, and the mere figures of her four rounds—72—71—73—75—speak eloquently of her quality as golfer, athlete, and competitor. The total is three strokes above a really difficult course par, and all three were dropped on the final few holes when she was very tired and so far ahead as to be practically out of sight.

The positions of those who were behind her in a field, which included all of the best professionals and many of the fine amateurs in the country, does not really matter, but here is the order in which they finished: Betty Hicks, a former U.S. Amateur champion, was second with a total of 303, and Louise Suggs was third at 307. Tied at 308 with Mickey Wright, the low amateur, was Betsy Rawls, the defending champion, and then came Jacqueline Pung, who lost a play-off to Miss Rawls last year. The remainder of the forty who qualified for the last two rounds were strung out, some with well-known names but very high scores.

It is impossible to praise too highly the play of the new champion, for what we saw here probably was the finest consecutive four rounds of golf on a championship course under the most demanding conditions ever played by a woman. Mrs. Zaharias was the only one of the ladies who understood how the difficult Salem course should be played and had the shots to do it. She alone negotiated the strenuous three-day journey without once faltering until near the end when she was very tired and had many strokes in hand. She played the same fine brand of golf in every round, never once yielding to the pressure and tension that an Open championship, under the banner of the U.S.G.A., must always

170

*The Babe*

bring. She was tied with Claire Doran, the Cleveland amateur, at the end of the first round, and she moved to a 7-stroke lead at the halfway mark. This enabled her to coast home today. By noon her lead had increased to 10 strokes.

The Babe's name will be engraved on the new U.S.G.A. Women's Open trophy just below that of Miss Rawls, who won the first Open at Rochester last year with a total of 302. The Babe did not play in that one. Everyone will remember that she was then just recovering from a cancer operation, and the fact that she has come back in so short a time to play such wonderful golf makes her victory the more remarkable.

There is no doubt that The Babe's excellence took something from the tournament in the way of tension and excitement, but it stands alone as a performance to be admired by all. After she had fired her 71 on

Friday, the tournament was over so far as the winner was concerned, leaving only the battle for second money by way of a contest.

But the struggle for second place in a big golf tournament is not really very interesting, and nobody bothered much about what the other girls were doing on the last day. They were, in fact, having a nice quiet little scramble for position which, if The Babe's score had been removed from the top, could have developed into an exciting event.

The champion's play, however, was most interesting from several points of view. With so big a lead to start the third round this morning, she was in a position to play safely and conservatively for a moderately good score. Even a 75 or a 76 would have made her position practically impregnable at lunch time.

She did play it this way for the most part, but with the caution dictated by circumstances she mingled great boldness at times. First she made sure that on no hole would her score get out of control, but she was forever seeking opportunities to save a stroke. Many times she went straight for the pin when everyone expected her to play safely to the middle of the green for par. Sometimes this cost her strokes but at other points she got them back by the same methods. Going out this morning she was over par twice and under once; coming home she was over once and under once. She was in the happy position of being able to lose a stroke without the slightest worry, knowing she could probably get it back somewhere along the line and not caring much if she did or didn't.

This made every hole a little adventure for her and the crowd. The Babe thoroughly enjoyed the day and so did all of us who went with her. We all knew that we were seeing the best there is, a real champion giving an outstanding performance. She acted the part of a champion to perfection, and her progress twice around the course was a queenly procession with her nearest pursuers, already dimly seen in the far distance at the start, fading more and more out of the picture as the day wore on.

At the very end the champion's quality stood out strongly. Over the last four or five holes, The Babe had begun to fly the first faint distress signals. Her tee shots, which had been wonderfully accurate for three days, began to both fade and hook, a sure sign of fatigue.

At the final hole, with all the people lining the course and waiting to escort her home, she sliced her drive into a wicked place among the trees. She could have used as many strokes as she pleased, and the sensible thing to do was to sacrifice a stroke and play back to the fairway. But The Babe took the position that this was no way to finish. She found a tiny opening and she took a long iron and went through it

**The scores**

| | |
|---|---|
| Mrs. M. Zaharias, Niles, Ill. | 72-71-73-76—291 |
| Betty Hicks, Durham, N.C. | 76-76-75-77—303 |
| Louise Suggs, Atlanta | 76-77-78-76—307 |
| *Mary K. Wright, La Jolla, Calif. | 74-79-79-76—308 |
| B. Rawls, Spartanburg, S.C. | 77-73-78-80—308 |
| Mrs. Jacqueline Pung, Glasgow, Ky. | 81-77-78-73—309 |
| *P. Ann Lesser, Seattle | 79-73-78-80—310 |
| Beverly Hanson, Fargo, N.D. | 77-80-78-75—310 |
| Fay Crocker, Montevideo, Uruguay | 77-82-79-73—311 |
| *Claire Doran, Cleveland | 72-79-80-80—311 |
| *Mrs. Mae Murray Jones, Rutland, Vt. | 79-81-74-78—312 |
| Patty Berg, St. Andrews, Ill. | 78-76-78-81—313 |
| Betty Dodd, Louisville | 77-77-78-82—314 |
| B. Jameson, San Antonio, Tex. | 78-78-80-80—316 |
| Bonnie Randolph, Linworth, Ohio | 82-81-74-79—316 |
| Mrs. Betty Bush, Hammond, Ind. | 79-79-83-75—316 |
| *Mary Lena Faulk, Thomasville, Ga. | 77-76-84-79—316 |
| P. O'Sullivan, Orange, Conn. | 76-79-81-82—318 |
| *J. Ziske, Waterford, Wis. | 78-82-78-80—318 |
| Marilyn Smith, Wichita | 83-75-79-82—319 |
| Betty MacKinnon, Savannah | 78-80-82-80—320 |
| *Mrs. Helen Sigel Wilson, Bala, Pa. | 80-82-84-76—322 |
| *Jean Hopkins, Cleveland | 78-79-83-86—326 |
| *Mrs. Edward J. McAuliffe, Newton, Mass. | 82-83-81-84—330 |

*Amateur.

toward the distant green. A champion's shot, and a great roar greeted it. It gave her a chance for a par-4. She missed it by an inch, but she had finished in a champion's way.

The Babe has now completely outclassed all her challengers. She has set the pattern by which a champion should act on the course and off it, and in the future all women golfers must be judged by how well they measure up to that standard.

# Berg, Jameson, and Suggs in Havana

Sports Illustrated                                    February 27, 1956

These winter months, while the men's professional golf tour is transcribing its customary dusty arc across the southern states east to Florida, the Ladies PGA as usual is plying its own cold-weather circuit. Life on the LPGA tour requires a few less suitcases, Val-A-Paks, and clothes hangers than the men's tour does, for the girls pursue a fairly compact itinerary: Sea Island, Tampa, Havana, Miami Beach, St. Pete, Sarasota, Jacksonville, and finally their equivalent of the Masters, the Titleholders at the Augusta Country Club in early March. These tournaments, for the most part, are orthodox strokes-play events but occasionally the format undergoes mild variations. For example, at the Havana Biltmore Yacht and Country Club, where the sorority was encamped early in February, on the last two rounds each of the girls went out in a foursome that was made up of three club members partnered with her in a best-ball event, the members using their respective handicaps and the lady pros playing at scratch.

A playing arrangement like the one that obtained at Havana puts more of a burden on the key player, the pro, than may appear at first glance. Patty Berg, for example, drew as her partners: 1) a dashing young air force major who serves as President Batista's personal pilot; 2) a delicate middle-aged señora who wore a colossal vizor that shielded her entire face from the sun—a bronzed complexion is less highly prized in Cuban society than in ours; and 3) a peppy, sociable little fellow who was in the throes of that international virus, the slice.

This season some twenty-five players are making the women's winter tour, ranging from Patty Berg, the ranking veteran, to Diane Garrett, a slip of a girl from Houston who is quite an accomplished player. The women professionals devote the same long, wearying hours to their business that men do. The Havana Biltmore, for example, offered them every opportunity for escaping from work—it is a really wonderful *country* club which provides its 1,800 members with ocean swimming, a sandy beach, a yacht basin, a swimming pool, a riding stable, tennis courts, a softball field, a baseball field, a basketball court, and bowling alleys aside from a golf course with a stimulating clubhouse. Yet, with very few exceptions, the girls were out on the practice fairway before and after each day's round, stoically accepting the inescapable fact of golf life that you're only as good as your practice sessions.

There is an interesting difference in the ways the men pros and the women pros practice. The women spend less time working on their full shots with the irons and woods, about the same amount of time as the men do on their putting, and a lot more time on their chip shots. They have absolutely astounding short games, and they must in order to score, for women's circuit golf is essentially a different proposition from the men's. On most of the circuit layouts that the men visit, just about the only times a player needs a fairway wood is on the par 5s. On the high percentage of the par 4s, a seven-iron or even an eight is all he requires to get home after a good drive. At Havana, where the course played longer than most of those the girls visit, a strong hitter like Louise Suggs can play a five-iron or less for her second shot on only two of the ten par 4s. A long iron or a spoon or a brassie was necessary on the rest of the 4s, and sometimes when the wind was blowing against her, two good woods still left Louise yards short of the green. To pull out your par under such conditions, you have to be able to get your chip within reasonable holing distance, and the girls do it time after time. That is one of the great treats of watching them. Another is the beautiful slow rhythm which sets up their clubhead power. A few of them—Fay Crocker, Mickey Wright, Betsy Rawls and Beverly Hanson come first to mind—have strong wrists and hands and can power the ball almost the way a man does, but sheer "hands golf" is beyond the capacity of even the most sturdy females. They must swing the club head, extract the full power from a correct body turn, and integrate the action of their body and hands with precise timing. Patty Berg, Betty Jameson, and Louise Suggs, the best of the lady pros, possess strong, repeating swings, and to follow them for a stretch of holes as they produce one beautifully struck shot after another is to get very close to the heart of the game.

For the past decade or so, Patty, Betty and Louise along with Babe Didrikson have made up what was known as the Big Four of women's professional golf. The Babe, to be sure, was the tour's primary attraction, what with her flair for showmanship and her zest for competition gilding her big and frequently brilliant game. The tour is certainly not the same without the Babe, but Berg, Jameson and Suggs have taken up the slack and are carrying it very well. Their styles are quite dissimilar. Louise, the youngest of the three—she won her U.S. Women's Amateur title in '47, Patty hers in '38, and Betsy her two in '39 and '40—has an exceedingly modern technique. A trim, athletic girl, she takes a generous cut at the ball on her full shots and develops her club-head speed in much the same area as the men pros do. The shot that Louise plays best—she not only plays it better than the other girls but better than most of the men—is the short approach with the six-, seven-, and eight-irons. Not too long ago, she and Toney Penna, teamed up in a selected-drive Scotch foursome, went around a medium-length course in 64. They took Toney's tee shot on just about every hole, and then, with that nice, crisp, uncomplicated style of hers, Louise would smack the approach five feet or so from the pin. That simplifies life. She is a very good player to watch if you happen to be in a slump yourself, for she has the knack of reducing the hitting of firm golf shots to their basic essentials. All you have to do is cock your chin as you figure out your line, then get the feel of your clubhead in your hands while you size up the distance, place the head of the club soberly in front of the ball for a second or two as you square up to the shot, and move into your swing in one piece. *Whack*! It's an easy game.

Betty Jameson is far and away the sorority's most knowledgeable technician, an honest-to-goodness scholar who can weave her way through theory with the likes of Tommy Armour. Not unlike Tommy, who is one of her best friends in golf, she has the uncommon gift of not letting her erudition throw her and of being able to determine what slight departures from orthodoxy work best for her. Betty has groomed her swing sedulously for years, and it shows. She is extremely deliberate about finding a solid stance, which amounts to an eccentricity for her since the rest of her style is so polished: a truly impressive grip, a backswing a little on the upright side where all you are conscious of is how perfectly the left hand does what the left hand is supposed to do, and, as she moves into the ball, an acceleration which keeps building so smoothly that it is hardly perceptible. With the one possible exception of Hogan's golf at the Masters in 1953, I cannot remember watching as straight a player as Betty Jameson. On her opening round at Havana— she missed a three-footer on the home green which would have given her 18 straight pars—I followed her for about eight holes and at no time was she more than ten yards from the center of the fairway.

It hardly seems possible but two decades have whistled by since the third member of the triumvirate, Patty Berg, first came to prominence by reaching the final of the Women's Amateur. Patty has proved to be nothing less than one of the great golfers of all time, men included. It isn't just her durability or her overall record or her figures on any one

*Before she turned professional, Betty Jameson in
1940 won the U.S. Women's Amateur, the Women's
Western Amateur, and the Women's
Trans-National Amateur.*

round. It is how she plays, and you must watch her make her way
around a course for at least nine holes before you can begin to appreciate her wonderful gift for hitting golf shots. She can handle a club in
her fingers like no one since Hagen. Her mannerisms at address and as
she rocks into delivering the shot are highly reminiscent of Sarazen.
Like these champions of an earlier era, as distinct from the leaders
today who are first and foremost masters of precision, she is the intu-
itive shot-maker who plays each shot to fit its particular require-
ments—buzzing a low approach into the wind when it is blowing
against her, floating a short approach into a banking wind, girding
herself on another hole for an extra-long drive when it will take her two
big clouts to get home, and getting an added ten yards by punching a
long iron to roll onto the green when a wood would not have held the
green.

# Make Way for the Girls

Sports Illustrated                                    October 15, 1956

Events this past season have made it unmistakably clear that women's golf in America is on the threshold of a genuinely golden age. It has been a long time since there was anything like the present proliferation of excellent and engaging players—in fact, one has to go back to the 1920s, when the sports public was forced to take notice of the skill and flair attained by Glenna Collett and her contemporaries.

Today, however, there are signal differences. The number of talented players is considerably larger than in the '20s. Their technique, much closer to the men's, is advancing all the time. And, largely due to the USGA's institution of the Girls' Junior championship some seven years ago, the stars are now blooming at astonishingly young ages. Wiffi Smith, the reigning French and British champion, is nineteen. Anne Quast, the victor in the 1956 Western Amateur, is also nineteen. The national Women's Open was won by Kathy Cornelius, twenty-three, after a playoff with Barbara McIntire, twenty-one. The top money-winner on the pro circuit, Marlene Bauer Hagge, is all of twenty-two.

In the last major event of the 1956 season, the United States Women's Amateur, the rush of youth reached its peak. In the final, opposing the eventual winner, Maureen Stewart, the twenty-two-year-old Canadian champion, was JoAnne Gunderson, an extremely impressive seventeen-year old. Today, in truth, a veteran is anyone over twenty.

*Amazingly relaxed throughout the morning round of the 36-hole final, JoAnne repaired to the clubhouse (where flowers awaited her from her home town, Kirkland, Wash.) holding a 1-up lead. On the 24th she went 4 up when she holed a 30-yard chip. Her inexperience then began to tell, and Marlene, rallying stout-heartedly down the stretch, won on the 35th, 2 and 1.*

*New Amateur Champion, Marlene Stewart, is a petite (5 feet 1 inch) Ontarian who also took the 1953 British title at 19.*

*Youngest player in modern history to reach Amateur final, JoAnne Gunderson is rangy (5 feet 8½ inch) Girls' Junior champ.*

*The finalists presented contrasting personalities and techniques, and this added a decided punch to a championship that has become a flavorful affair. Marlene, christened "Little Miss Hogan" by the Canadian press because of her coolness under fire, makes up for her lack of power through the accuracy of her wooden-club play and a very precise short game. Her head always remains "down" well after she has stroked a putt or a chip. JoAnne, a sprawlingly natural girl (especially when she is earnestly lining up a putt), is a very strong player who averages 230 yards on her drives.*

# 1956—Marlene Hagge's Year

Golf Digest                                December, 1956

Not since Babe Zaharias has anyone dominated women's golf as did Marlene Bauer Hagge during the 1956 season. Entering all twenty-four LPGA events, Marlene was easily the cash leader. Never finishing worse than twelfth and over sixth only six times, Mrs. Hagge won eight of the events. Victories in the Sea Island, Babe Zaharias, Pittsburgh, World, Denver and Whittier (Calif.) Opens, plus the LPGA championship, gave the pert blonde her remarkable record.

These eight championships tied her with a pair of great golfers in the number of individual titles won in a single year. The late Babe Zaharias, in 1951, and Louise Suggs, in 1953, also won eight. Marlene also set a new 72-hole scoring record for LPGA members in the Mile High Open at Denver. At the Lakewood Country Club, Mrs. Hagge brought in rounds of 75-69-71-69 for a total of 284. That sensational burst broke the record owned by the 1956 U.S. Women's Open champion, Kathy Cornelius, who had fired a 287 at St. Petersburg earlier in the year.

In 1955 Marlene did not win a single tournament, although her performance was steady enough to net her $7,051 in prize money, good for ninth place. Her Performance Average was .775, placing her fourth. This year she has won $20,162 to be the leading money-winner, and she ranks second in Performance Average with .860.

A professional since 1950, the 22-year-old native of Eureka, S.D., had won only two LPGA events before 1956—the 1952 Sarasota Open and the 1954 New Orleans Open. Previous to that, she had won two events in 1949, the Western and the USGA Junior championships.

Oddly, Marlene's status as a professional golfer was in some doubt only last year. She left the tour in July to accept a position with an eastern grocery chain. However, after she was married to Bob Hagge in December, Marlene made up her mind to go after the golfing dollar. She hooked up with the Ben Hogan Co. as a playing representative, signed contracts with several clothing manufacturers, and took off like a scalded cat. Her very first start produced a victory at Sea Island, Ga.

*"It is hard to imagine what women's golf was like when my sister Alice and I first begin to play the game. Our father, David Bauer, was a Russian immigrant who became tremendously interested in golf and built a nine-hole course—with sand tees and sand greens—in our hometown of Eureka, South Dakota, in the 1930s. He was wild about golf. He read everything he could find on the game, especially on instruction. He pored over books and magazines that wrote about the great men players of his day, but I believe he also was influenced tremendously by reading about the great women players—Glenna Collett Vare, Joyce Wethered and Babe Didrikson Zaharias. Soon he envisioned the day when Alice and I might learn to play well enough to make a living touring around the country giving exhibition matches. I started to play golf when I was three. Alice was nine. Six years later, Dad loaded the family belongings into a Model-A Ford pick-up and moved all of us west to California, where the plan was for Alice and me to play year-round on real grass courses. We lived in a tiny house they'd bought in Lakewood City so Alice and I could play golf at a Long Beach public course—I believe there was $8 left in the family bank account when we finally got settled."*

*Marlene Bauer Hagge*

Over the next few months her play was good but not the thing of beauty it was to be later.

It wasn't until April that she won her next event, the Babe Zaharias Open at Beaumont, Texas. Including the Zaharias event, she won seven of the sixteen events she entered through Kansas City.

Mrs. Hagge admits that she has more zest for golf these days. "Now I really want to play golf," she says. "I used to avoid it whenever I could—especially practice golf."

Under the tutelage of her father, Dave Bauer, Marlene has been playing tournaments since she was seven. Mr. Bauer advocates a tremendously long backswing for Marlene and Alice, her older sister, and both have always been noted for their extremely free swings. Dave believes the long backswing and full pivot gives women golfers much more distance.

# Bobby Jones and Joyce Wethered
# Play the Old Course

## S. L. McKinlay

The Glasgow *Herald*                    December 18, 1957

When the legendary cricket player, Sir John Hobbs, was describing
the great innings of his career on television the other night, he gave as
his personal choice not one of the many centuries he scored in memorable Test matches but a score in the 80s he had put together against
the full might of Australia in a match that was not commonly classed
as a major fixture.

Lady Heathcoat-Amory might do likewise if she could be persuaded
to come before the cameras now that she has retired from the presidency of the English Ladies' Golf Association and thus broken her last
official link with the game which, as Miss Joyce Wethered, she adorned
for so long.

All the world of golf knows of her two tremendous matches in the
final of the British Ladies' championship—one against Miss Cecil
Leitch at Troon in 1925, the other against Miss Glenna Collett at St.
Andrews four years later. Both of these matches she won, but only just,
for she had to lay a very long putt dead at the thirty-seventh to beat
Miss Leitch, and against Miss Collett she was five down after nine holes
and still two down at lunch.

This was against nature, and no wonder a stranger to St. Andrews,
who was walking the streets of the city in search of the cathedral and
the university, "was surprised to find himself addressed by a postman
in a depressed tone of voice as he passed gloomily on his rounds, 'She's
five doon.' "

I would like to think that Lady Heathcoat-Amory's own personal
choice of her greatest round would be of another game at St. Andrews.
In 1930 the American Walker Cup team came to St. Andrews for the
Amateur championship after the match at Sandwich, and the two captains, Jones and R.H. Wethered, set out one day for a practice round
that has carved a niche in golfing history.

It happened that I was on the first tee of the Old Course talking to

Wethered and his sister when Jones and the late Dale Bourn arrived. Miss Wethered said something to Jones that I shall long remember because it was an indication of the character and modesty of this remarkable woman. "It is very kind of you to play with me," she said, and Jones's reply was equally characteristic: "On the contrary, it's kind of you to play with me."

So they set out, Jones and Miss Wethered playing together against Wethered and Bourn, and what a game it was. Miss Wethered holed the Old Course in 75, Jones was 72. The others did not matter, for clearly it was a contest, if not a match, between the two greatest players of their age, some would say of any age.

Miss Wethered played beautifully. She was easily the straightest of the four, her iron shots were crisp and wonderfully controlled, and if she had holed only a few putts she would have equalled Jones's score. No wonder that later he described with something like awe the great impression she and her golf had made upon him—and that, we must remember, was Jones's *annus mirabilis*, the year when he won all four major championships.

A year later I had an excellent opportunity of assessing the essential quality of Miss Wethered's play. During practice for the Amateur championship at Westward Ho! I played round that formidable course in a stiff breeze, and immediately behind our foursome came another four— Miss Wethered, J. S. F. Morrison, "Monty" Pease, and a fourth whom I cannot recall.

Every time we moved off after playing our seconds, there would be a thump and a ball would land in mid-fairway. Whenever we holed out on a green and moved away, another thump and a ball would land a few yards from the flag. Looking back we could easily see that this was Miss Wethered rifling shot after shot dead on the target. Morrison told me afterwards that she had holed the course in 72 without being lucky, and we, who had holed some good putts in scrambling round in the middle and high seventies, were thankful she was not competing in the championship.

Just how would she have fared in the championship if she had played? Clearly she would have frightened the life out of most of the competitors and she might very well have won several matches. But I am not persuaded that she would have reached even the closing stages. She was long among women golfers but not among men, and length is very important indeed on courses stretched to the limit for a championship. She was a wonderful striker of every shot, and her medium ironplay was first-class. Above all, she had a superb match-play temperament.

She looked to be ice-cool but she was really all fire and anxiety inside. "I know the feeling," she has written, "of standing on a tee with real fear in my heart, the match slipping away and the club feeling strange and useless in my hand, and yet I have fortunately been able to laugh at myself for the absurdity of such intense feelings and the perversity of one's own thoughts."

Joyce Wethered had known many crises in a career which included four victories in the British Ladies' championship, five in the English Women's championship, and no fewer than eight victories in the Worplesdon mixed foursomes with seven different partners. Inevitably the legends about her grew up, and none is more pleasing—though ill-authenticated—than the story of her holing a putt on the twelfth green at Troon against Miss Leitch just as a passing train blasted on its whistle. "Didn't the train upset you?" she was asked, and the reply, so the story goes, was "What train?"

# Your Head Must Move

## Helen Dettweiler

Golf Digest                                    May, 1958

There is not much difference between the terms "steady head position" and "still head position," but it is a difference of great consequence to the golfer. You should make a distinction between "steady" and "still."

The bugaboo of "sway" frightens many players into an unyielding head position with so much rigid cooperation from the body that the natural windup of the hips and shoulders is blocked.

Your head must be permitted to move in the swing.

It should not bob up and down, of course. But there should be a certain freedom granted to the head in the interest of good body action.

Your head may move slightly to the right on the backswing and to the left on the downswing. It may also be permitted to turn on the backswing.

Louise Suggs is the finest example of freedom of head motion that I have seen among professional players. She lets her head rotate as her body rotates on the backswing, and the result is the beautifully unhampered swing for which Louise is so famous.

Sequence photographs of Miss Suggs show graphically how she does move and turn her head. The pictures may be profitably studied by anyone wishing to improve his game.

To swing correctly, you must allow some lateral movement of the body—a shifting to the right on the backswing. This is accompanied by body turn. It should be as natural a movement as possible. You should allow it to happen, neither restricting nor forcing it.

To feel this correct action, forget your golf swing for a moment. Stand erect. Gently move a good portion of your weight to your right foot and then to your left.

As you do this, you will note that your shoulders and head move with your body because, as the song explains so well, the neck bone connecka to the head bone. The human spine extends from the base of the skull

to a point below the hips, and trying to hold any part of it still while you torture the remainder of it is both futile and dangerous. As you shift your weight, your shoulders and head move with your body; they cannot remain still while the weight shifts.

Now, address a golf ball and feel the same type of shifting movement. Of course, when you swing at a ball, the proper arc of the club inside the line will also cause the body to turn quite naturally, if you will just permit it to do so.

Movement of the head is blamed for many poor golf shots. But I believe that many poor shots are caused by trying to keep the head still.

# The Tragic Fourth

Sports Illustrated                                                July 8, 1957

You will probably never see an unhappier group of people at a golf championship than was gathered at the Winged Foot Golf Club in Mamaroneck, N.Y., last Saturday evening at the close of the United States Women's Open. This gloom came hard on the heels of a very deeply felt elation. Mrs. Jackie Pung, the 235-pound Hawaiian lady, who is quite a golfer and quite a person, came ripping down the final 18 (after a par 75 in the morning) to catch the leader, Betsy Rawls, and edge her out by a stroke, 298 to 299. The gallery's great delight in Mrs. Pung's triumph was occasioned partially by the magnificent 72 she had played when nothing short of the most brilliant golf could have won for her. And it was occasioned partially by the knowledge, common to just about everyone present, that the rotund Hawaiian, a self-taught golfer whose talent for the game is as instinctive as the young Sarazen's, really needed the money which victory would bring.

After Mrs. Pung, then a complete unknown, won the U.S. Women's Amateur in 1952, she turned professional as the logical means of getting the where-withal to pay for the education of her two daughters. In 1953 she lost the playoff for the Women's Open to Betsy Rawls. Some two years ago, physically and emotionally far from well, she went back to Hawaii to try to reorganize her life. She returned to the States and to the pro circuit only two months ago. This is just brushing the surface of Jackie Pung's story. There have been many hard knocks in it, but she has managed to survive them all quite valiantly. In this day and age of public-relations personalities, her manner, always natural and altogether honest, is extremely refreshing.

About 40 minutes after Mrs. Pung had walked off the 18th green, the apparent winner, the United States Golf Association announced—with the most genuine unhappiness—that she had been disqualified for reporting an incorrect score on one hole (the fourth) on her final round. It is hard to describe the feeling this created at Winged Foot. First, it

189

*Winner, daughter—before the blow.*

seemed incredible, like a bad dream. Second, it seemed grossly unjust, however defensible legally. Mrs. Pung had handed in the correct total for her final round—72. Her card showed a 5 and not the 6 she had taken on the fourth, but her addition took into account that it had been a 6—her total was correct. The shocking news of Mrs. Pung's disqualification filled everyone with a personal sense of impotent anger and with compassion for the victim of so important a ruling based on so insignificant a technicality. The members of Winged Foot spontaneously undertook a collection for Jackie, and within a very short time over $2,000 had been contributed. Some of the most generous contributions came from the USGA officials, who, in pursuit of their duty as they saw it, felt compelled to uphold the rules, whatever their personal feelings. It had all the elements of classical theatrical tragedy. Mrs. Pung spoke at the conclusion of the ceremonies at which the cup was presented to the official winner, Betsy Rawls. Earlier, on hearing the bad news, she had broken down and left the club with her 15-year-old daughter, then she had calmed herself down and returned, honestly stoical about the whole hard experience. "Winning the Open is the greatest thing in golf," she began her remarks at the presentation ceremonies. "I have come close before. This time I thought I'd won. But I didn't. Golf is played by rules, and I broke a rule. I've learned a lesson. And I have two broad shoulders. . . ."

Let us now get the facts relating to the infraction clear. On the final day of the Women's Open, the contenders go out in twosomes (Jackie Pung was paired with Betty Jameson). Each player has a scorecard on which she keeps the other's score (Jackie kept Betty's; Betty kept Jackie's). Each twosome is accompanied by a woman scorer, but she has no official function. The scorecard she keeps is for the convenience of the press. At the conclusion of a round, each player is handed her scorecard by her playing partner. It is each player's job to check and see that her score for each hole has been correctly recorded before signing it. (A player is responsible for reporting her score for each hole—not for the total). According to USGA regulations, once a card is signed and handed in, it is an official return. If it is later discovered that a person has reported a wrong score for a hole, the penalty is disqualification. As it happens, this matter was given especial attention only this past winter by the Executive Committee of the USGA. In the 1956 Men's Open Jack Burke and Gil Cavanaugh both handed in incorrect cards and were penalized two strokes by the USGA. Same thing with Betsy Rawls in last year's Women's Open. Many old golf hands felt this lenient penalty to be an evidence of laxness on the part of the USGA, certainly the most conscientious and standards-guarding of all governing bodies in sport. The majority of the members of the USGA Executive Committee also felt this way. The present disqualification rule was passed.

Returning to the fourth hole of the final round—the fourth is a par 5—both Pung and Jameson took 6s. Each, preoccupied under the pressure of the Open with her own game, mistakenly credited the other with a 5. Each knew that she herself had played a 6. Jackie knew she had a 6, the gallery knew she had a 6, and the keeper of the blackboard scoreboard following the match knew it and changed Jackie's standing with par for the round from 2 under par (she had birdied the second and third) to 1 under par. During the next three hours, everyone on the course knew correctly how she stood in relation to Betsy Rawls, who had started the final round with a three-stroke lead and was playing some two holes ahead of Pung. Everyone knew correctly that ultimately, when Jackie came to the 18th, she needed the 4 she got to win by one stroke. (As she was playing the 18th, an executive of the USGA announced to the gallery packed around the green that she had to get a 4 to win.) The round over, Betty Jameson gave Jackie her card, and Jackie gave Betty hers. Though neither caught the mistake on the fourth, both totals were correct—both knowing well how they stood with par. Each signed her card.

In disqualifying Mrs. Pung (and Miss Jameson), the USGA was legally correct. Each player had broken a rule. It is very questionable, though, if in serving the letter of the law the USGA served justice. There were some exceptional circumstances which the USGA could well have taken into account. Mrs. Pung's failure to spot her incorrect score for one hole—which, it should be repeated, had no bearing at all on her correct total score—came not at the end of a routine early round of a tournament. The moment she holed the winning 4 ½-footer, happy pandemonium broke out, made all the more joyous by the sight of Jackie's young daughter running out to greet her. It was a very exciting moment, and no doubt the press and radio men were wrong in rushing Jackie away as soon as they could to the press tent for the usual interview with the champion. In such a hurly-burly of happiness, it is small wonder that Mrs. Pung, glancing through the figures on her card which Miss Jameson handed her, could only note that the totals were indeed correct, sign her name, and turn her thoughts to the full significance of her winning the Open.

Just about all of us at Winged Foot felt that the unusualness of the circumstances and the irrelevance of the technicality to Mrs. Pung's known performance were sufficient grounds for the USGA to break its own rules and to justify this on the grounds that the error in bookkeeping had truly affected the winning and losing of the tournament by not so much as a gnat's eyelash. Sufficient grounds, also, to be indeed thankful that there were these good reasons for disregarding the technicality and officially accepting as the winner the golfer who has completed the 72 holes in one shot less than her closest rival. Had the technicality of disqualification been waived, the rules of golf would not have been weakened, and, I really believe, the spirit of golf more honestly served.

# Les Girls: Life Under Pressure

Sports Illustrated                                    September 8, 1958

At 8:30 on the morning of the second and final day of the recent Curtis Cup match at the Brae Burn Country Club, west of Boston—as you may remember, the team of women amateurs from the British Isles retained possession of the cup by splitting the nine points (3 foursomes, 6 singles) with our American team—the two players in the first of the six 36-hole singles matches drove off. Since a 36-hole match can take innumerable twists and turns, the group of us who walked down the fairway with this first twosome were counseling one another not to bear down too closely during the morning rounds—one should always keep as much energy in reserve as possible for the afternoon, when the really meaningful moments arrive, and especially since this Curtis Cup (with the British Isles leading 2-1 after the foursomes) had all the earmarks of developing into another of those cliff-hanging affairs in which the ultimate result is suspended in the balance until late in the afternoon. "As a matter of fact," Frank Pennink of the London *Daily Mail* observed at 8:35 a.m., thinking of the many holes and crucial moments ahead, "I suppose it will all hinge again on the match between Polly Riley and Frances Smith." Mr. Pennink was referring to the last time the two teams met, at Prince's in Sandwich in 1956 when, with all the other matches concluded, the losing and winning of the cup depended on the dramatic duel between these two veteran internationalists. They had gone to the 36th tee all square, and Mrs. Smith had won it there by hitting a great iron to that difficult home green. Now at Brae Burn in the 1958 meeting, they had been drawn together again, each having been placed by her captain in the final singles spot.

At 5:20 p.m., roughly some nine hours after the long day's play had begun, Miss Riley and Mrs. Smith came trudging up the hill to the 16th, or 34th, fairway—and once again the outcome of another international competition rested on them. This is an almost insupportable

193

amount of pressure and responsibility to have weighing on a player's shoulders. Each stroke is critical, and there are moments when even the most seasoned and positive-minded competitor, thrust into such a spot, can think only of the heavy consequences of playing a bad stroke. As they walked up the 34th, Mrs. Smith was holding a 1-up lead over Miss Riley. I think we all know Polly well by now—she has been the outstanding match player among our women amateurs for quite some time—but a word at this juncture about Frances Smith might not be amiss since she is hardly known in this country.

Frances Smith—she was Bunty Stephens when she first came to prominence in English golf about a decade ago—is now in her early middle 30s. She has a most unimpressive swing. It includes what surely must be the longest pause at the top of the backswing in all of golf. After that, she whips the club through to the finish in good style, but, taken all together, her swing, neither rhythmic nor powerful, is the type one would usually associate with a mid-90s shooter. Mrs. Smith, moreover, is a fraily built person. When you watch her play a grueling 36-hole match, your sympathies go out to her: she looks like she will be lucky to finish, let alone produce anything resembling her best golf. Somehow she does, just about always. As a matter of fact, this slight, quiet, entirely undramatic person has come through with more first-rate shots in the clutch than any other golfer, man or woman, over the last ten years.

On the 34th, a rugged par 4 for the ladies, Frances held her 1-hole margin when both she and Polly took fives. In truth, she was lucky to get this half, for Polly just missed dropping a 20-footer for her four, and Frances, after too bold an approach putt, had to hole a hard-to-read five-footer coming back for her five. The 17th (or 35th) at Brae Burn is a difficult par 3, 212 yards long, that drops downhill all the way from a high perched tee to a green protected by trapping along both the left and right sides and by the contours of the fairway which break toward the traps. Up first, Polly, using a three-wood, played a very fine shot. Hit low, it bounded onto the green, but it was a shade too strong and just did trickle over the back apron into the rough behind. This was a bad break for Polly, but she is a redoubtable chipper and would no doubt manage her three. With this stern probability confronting her, Mrs. Smith hit an even better shot, a high four-wood that was right on the flag every yard of its flight. It floated down onto the front apron and finished about twenty feet short of the flag. Both made good bids for their birdie and halved the hole with threes. On to the 36th, 360 yards long, most of them uphill. Mrs. Smith still 1 up. Here, as composed as if she were merely out for an evening walk, Frances won the hole and the match, and insured the 4½-4½ tie in the team match by hitting a straight drive down the right side of the fairway and following it with a beautifully hit 3-iron that almost struck the base of the flagstick.

Frances Stephens Smith is the daughter of a Lancashire professional, Fred Stephens of the Bootle Golf Club, outside Liverpool. As one of her countrymen put it during the week, "Frances is very plain of face and figure. In a gathering she is retiring to the point of invisibility. You hear talk of negative charm, and maybe this is what she has, but I think it is more than that. She has such a lovely manner about her that you like her immensely, and there is such fortitude in this girl that you admire her immensely." Frances has won the British Ladies' championship twice and the English Ladies' championship three times. Some three years ago, she married Roy Smith, a test pilot for Scottish Airways. It was an extremely happy marriage. Last summer he was killed in a plane crash, a few months after the birth of their daughter. Frances started to play golf again this spring. In her first tournament, the Lancashire County championship, she was eliminated in the first round. She looked better in the inter-county matches, and, when her play in the British Ladies' championship convinced the selectors she was very much her old self, she was named to the Curtis Cup team for the fifth time.

To come through in the clutch just once, as Frances did at Brae Burn, is no small accomplishment. To come through as regularly as she has— well, I don't really know what one can say. In any event, here, for your astonishment, is her record in Curtis Cup competition:

1950. At the Country Club of Buffalo, she won her foursome (with Elizabeth Price) 1 up. In the singles she faced Mrs. Mark Porter. Three down with three to play, she won the 34th, 35th, and 36th to halve the match. On the crucial 36th (390 yards) she put her approach six feet from the hole.

1952. The match was held at Muirfield. Partnered with Jessie Valentine, Frances was beaten in the foursomes. In the singles, something went wrong, and she didn't go to the 36th green, only to the 35th, in defeating Marjorie Lindsay.

1954. At Merion, Frances again lost her foursome but, playing in the No. 1 slot in the singles, outlasted Mary Lena Faulk, 1 up. Frances won the 36th with a birdie 4. After pulling her second into the rough, from an awkward sidehill stance, she contrived to manufacture a shot that got the ball onto the green, five feet from the cup.

1956. In this match, played at Prince's in Kent, Frances won her foursome (with Elizabeth Price) and became the direct agent of the

British Isles' 5-4 victory when she won the decisive singles match from Polly Riley on the 36th.

1958. Brae Burn. A victory in the foursomes with Janette Robertson and, as we have described, once again all the way to the 36th in the deciding singles.

How does Frances Smith do it? What does she have that enables her to work such wonders? Her friends explain it something like this. She holds onto her timing in the most nerve-wracking situations because she has superb concentration. She holds onto her concentration because she has a purposefulness that never wavers and a wondrous heart. I suppose that this is all there is to it except for a fine talent for golf.

Frances Smith had to fly back to England the day after the 1958 Curtis Cup match was over and did not play in the Women's Amateur championship which started a week later at the Wee Burn Country Club in Darien, Conn., in the heartland of what sociologists call the Gracious Living Belt. There a Martini is usually referred to, in an intimate tone, as a Martin or even a Mart, and a few old-timers are still persevering with automobiles operated by an automatic gear shift. Had Mrs. Smith been able to appear at the championship, I am sure she would have been struck by the size of the field (a record 189 entrants owning handicaps of 6 or less) and by the thought-provoking youthfulness of the large majority of the entrants. Two of the best golfers at Wee Burn were Judy Eller, the 17-year-old National Junior champion, and Sherry Wheeler, the 17-year-old runner-up in that event.

Anne Quast, the 21-year-old charmer from the state of Washington who won the championship at Wee Burn, is a perfect illustration of what this tournament has been coming to. She was all of 14 when she made her first appearance in it at Portland in 1952 (and, incidentally, won her first-round match). Between then and her notable victory at Wee Burn, she has twice been a quarter-finalist and once a semifinalist. En route to becoming a champion she has had to work hard, not so much on her game as on her competitive temperament. High-keyed by nature—she is an unusually aware and responsive girl—she has had to learn how to muffle her intensity and allow herself enough breathing space to enable her obvious aptitude for playing golf shots to come through. Over the years Anne's swing has remained pretty much the same. It is a good sound swing, but by the best standards not a really pretty one. There is a sense of lift in the way she takes the club back and a fairly pronounced dip in the downswing as the shoulders turn the arms into the ball. I mention these aspects of Anne's swing because they are usually part and parcel of the technique of a scatter-hitter and she is exactly the reverse—as straight as a string. On her afternoon

*Quast and Gunderson eat and telephone after their semi-final match.*

round in the final against Barbara Romack, the 1954 champion, Anne
hit every fairway when she was playing a wood off the tee.

Anne is nearly always this straight, and my guess is that her enviable accuracy comes from the superb "square" position on the club her
left hand commands from the beginning of the address and from her
cultivated instinct for driving her hands and the clubhead square
through the ball. She also has the gift, which is not common among
women players, of judging distance very well on her iron shots, and this
as much as any one factor set up her 1-up victory over JoAnne Gunderson, the defending champion, in their semifinal match, in which
Anne was outdriven by twenty-five yards on the average and on one
hole, where she did not miss her tee shot, by sixty-five yards. JoAnne
does that to everyone. Her wonderful hip drive puts her hands in the
strongest position possible, as it does for the best male players, and she
can powder that ball 265 yards on occasion, swinging within herself.
She probably averages about 240 yards off the tee.

JoAnne—to digress for a moment—is the most colorful personality
women's golf has produced in quite some time. On the course, in addition to playing such full-blooded shots, she goes at the game as if it were

a game, approaching the whole complicated business with a genuine friendliness of spirit that makes the speeches on sportsmanship by self-appointed character-builders seem positively Victorian. On the 14th hole in her semi-final with Anne Quast, Anne outdrove her for just about the only time during the match. JoAnne had just lost three holes in a row, and you could certainly have excused her if she had been all grimness at the moment, but, as she walked past Anne on her way to the ball, she said with a private wink, "Hello, slugger." She has apparently limitless energy. In the Curtis Cup, she was carried to the 36th green by Jessie Valentine in an exhausting match. The next minute she was running full tilt onto the course and up the steep wall of the hill on the 17th to root home her teammates who were still deeply embroiled in their matches. At Wee Burn in her semi-final, when her drive on the crucial 16th ended in an unplayable lie in the rough, she loped all the way back to the tee, laced out a magnificent drive, and came loping all the way down the fairway again. She is something, this girl!

Anne Quast was 4 under par for the sixteen holes of the afternoon round—and four under for the beautifully played final seven holes in which she went 443 443 3 against a par of 544 543 4. It is not easy to remember a finish in the final of an important match-play championship to compare with this.

# On the Road with the Pros

## Barbara Heilman

Sports Illustrated                                    June 19, 1961

I arrived in Dallas, and the next day an interview with golfer Gloria Armstrong was published in the *Dallas Times Herald*. Gloria said the girls played poker and gambled with club members, and she described a birthday party in which she, her friends, and her grandmother were all down on their knees shooting craps. Some of the girls on the tour, who are earnestly concerned that the world realize women professionals are really delicate blossoms, are in shock. Gloria's close friends are shaking their heads. Gloria just keeps saying helplessly, "The things that are there I said, but I didn't say them that way." The upshot is the girls are writer-shy. When they see me, they stop talking about whatever they have been talking about, and tell me some more about what a grand group of girls it is and how they love each other like sisters.

As a matter of fact, they do get along very well, as much as anything else because of the way they keep apart. The existing cliques don't accept anyone easily. It is not like an office, where it is no worse than tiresome to have someone intrude at lunch. On tour an intruder would be with you all the time—breakfast, lunch, dinner, golf course and motel room. It illuminates a remark by Betsy Rawls, "We get along real well. Some of the girls I won't have dinner with for a whole year," which at the time sounded like a *non sequitur*. The units into which the touring pros break down seem to be the bridge players, the poker players, the new girls, the loners, and Patty Berg.

The few further generalizations that seem to be defensible are: 1) Most of the girls were good athletes as children (it's degrading, I think, to call them "tomboys"—they were valid athletes, as much as Joe DiMaggio and Kyle Rote were) who took up golf when their parents wrested away their footballs and baseball bats as being unbecoming to young ladies. 2) Whether they care for touring or not, they now get restless after several weeks in one place. 3) Allowing for no exceptions, they love the game of golf profoundly, more than anything else. And 4)

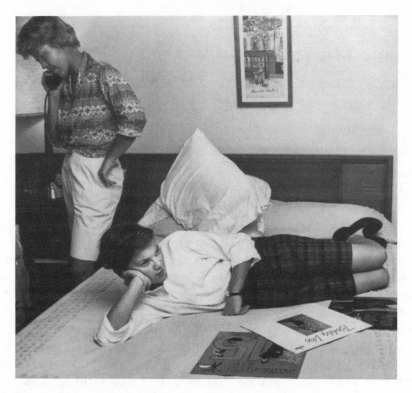

*Their home is the motel of the week. Barbara Romack telephones.*
*Sandra Haynie listens to records.*

their enthusiasm for a life on tour varies according to their ages. Seventeen-year-old Sandra Haynie, twenty-year-old Carol Mann love it. "You get to see so many places! And to meet so many people!" But 28-year-old Jo Ann Prentice says, "When I started out it was fun. Now it's work." And 41-year-old Betty Jameson, "If I had it to do over again, I think I would marry and have a family."

Perhaps it doesn't mean much. Ask 17-year-olds and 40-year-olds how they like life in the ribbon factory and I suppose you'll get the same kind of answers.

April 16. The Dallas Civitan tournament is over. Suggs won it (for the third consecutive year), and Sandra Haynie came in third. Sandra is so small (105 pounds) it seems unlikely that she could have the strength to be properly in competition with the Rawlses and the Wrights, but she is strong and in time may be one of the really good golfers.

The weather was windy and cold, and the Glen Lakes course apparently lies on real hardpan; hitting down into it brought out a grand crop of old injuries. Sore hands, wrenched backs, bad knees all reappeared as if by magic. Tremendous gallery, though, so the girls were pleased. I followed Betsy Rawls, Betty Jameson and Barbara Romack on the final round. Romack was finishing out the tournament despite the news that her father had died on the previous day. Pity she was paired with Betty Jameson, who is a perfectionist—high-strung and apt to be nervy and imperious on the course. Betsy was beginning to sharpen up after an indifferent start when, on the 10th hole, a fine drive bounced off someone inexplicably running across the fairway. Judy Kimball appeared from nowhere to say fiercely, "That just cost her the tournament," and disappeared again. Very hard on 22-year-old Judy, who worships Betsy and suffers and dies over every stroke of her game. They even look alike.

Betsy's 32, a Phi Beta Kappa from the University of Texas (major, physics), and she and Mickey Wright head up the bridge players. At the moment, Betsy is president of the Ladies Professional Golf Association, an honor which is acknowledged to cost the holder money. The time it takes, the responsibilities on the golfer's mind seem to add an almost calculable number of strokes to the president's game. Betsy's is erratic in the first place—she will be on, and then way off. It seems likely to me that the presidency may be responsible for some of her disappointing tournaments this year.

April 17. Drove halfway to Beaumont with Shirley Englehorn, counting tractors. Her father is a John Deere distributor in Caldwell, Idaho, so the fact that we saw more Ford tractors than John Deere tractors was a matter of concern. They're tearing up the highway out of Dallas, and we had to pick our way through some messy construction. There are bluebonnets and Indian paintbrush all along the road, though, and the country turns green and wooded toward Beaumont.

Shirley's 21, has played golf since she was 6 and has always known she wanted to be a pro. She's sponsored by the Athletic Roundtable of Spokane, and she was signed by Golfcraft, Inc. in 1959. That, of course, is the sort of arrangement which is the financial backbone of the pro system—the salary from the sponsor and the deal with a company, which varies according to the company and the stature of the pro. (Berg and Suggs have salaries, expense accounts, income from autographed clubs, clothing bearing their names, etc.) The pro gives clinics in her company's name, attends luncheons and generally is supposed to play brilliant golf to the greater glory of the Spalding Dot, or whatever.

The girls who don't show promise enough to arouse the interest of a company probably are going to finish consistently out of the money. Living on the tour isn't cheap. Marilynn Smith, a former LPGA president, estimates that a girl shouldn't take to the road for a season without $5,000 and her own car. If she finishes regularly in the money she can manage comfortably. Last year first-place Louise Suggs made $16,892; Marlene Hagge, 10th place, $7,212; and Kathy Whitworth, down in 17th place, $4,901. Few of the girls travel together any more. They used to, but though they may share motel rooms to cut down expenses, most find it easier on the nerves to come and go as they like. Also, four seasons' worth of clothes and all your golf equipment take up a good deal of room.

Halfway to Beaumont we overtook a car, which Shirley finally recognized as Murle MacKenzie's, keeping a none too straight course down the highway. Murle was sleepy, so I was given to her to keep her awake. A small-boned blonde, Murle is fastidious in that enviable way that makes neatness not something one achieves but is. She's 22 and going to be married in the fall. She said of the older golfers, "I wonder what they think about homes and children. They seem so lonely. Nothing to look forward to, to come home to." Precisely what one does wonder and can't ask.

We stopped for ice cream, at a place where no one had heard of any such flavor as coffee, and arrived at the motel about 5.

Beaumont, April 18. Went to a Rotary luncheon. The Rotarians are sponsoring the tournament here in Beaumont, and it's customary for the girls to go to luncheons and speak briefly. Mickey Wright and Betsy Rawls aren't going to get to Beaumont in time for their appearances, which is unfortunate. It means a great deal to the sponsors to have the bigger names among the girls. But Patty Berg was here for this one, with Murle, Carol Mann and Judy Kimball. Very nice to see the girls in dresses, with their feet showing white where their golf shoes stopped and their pumps didn't begin. The young ones were stouthearted, if bashful, about their speeches—giggled a little, were fervent about the extraordinary pleasure of finding themselves in Beaumont. Patty spoke at greater length, and obviously out of a great many years of experience. She told golf jokes, and delivered them beautifully, spoke soberly of the Babe (Babe Zaharias was born and is buried in Beaumont—the tournament is the Babe Zaharias Open), was funny about her age and the girls' ages and Carol Mann's height. Carol Mann happens to be 6 feet 2. "Carol Mann still holds a record—she was the *longest baby born in Buffalo, New York!*" Patty trumpets, and everyone roars with laughter. Not just because it's funny, but because of Carol, who out of some well of essential good nature, makes it fine for people to laugh. At clinics, at luncheons, at dinners, Carol stands there ducking her shock head and twisting her hands, knowing it's coming and turning red and

*Jo Ann Prentice, crouched in the trunk of her automobile, stuffs her shoes away in her only permanent closet on the tour.*

shrieking. "Oh, Patty!" just before Patty gets to it: "Carol Mann still holds a record. . . ." Patty also upon these occasions reminds us that it isn't if you won or lost but how you played the game.

On the course Patty is Winston Churchill; shaped like him, doughty, peering out from under a visored cap set at Sir Winston's angle, requiring his exact lift of the chin to see out from under it at all. Her game is steady and solid. Amidst the chirping and excitement about what Wright may be doing and what Suggs probably is doing, Patty will always be found to have surfaced stolidly into the money. It is said that she relies heavily on her caddies—that her eyes aren't too strong any more, and she won't wear glasses.

Off the course she is an eternity of blue suits. Carol says Patty can't buy a blue suit in the city of Chicago, there not being one she doesn't own. The skirts of all of them come to a chaste four inches or so above the anklebone, and the material has been tested for irresponsible behavior in a wind. "What do you want any more of that stuff for?" her father is supposed to inquire in gloomy mystification when bills arrive for dresses or underwear. "You can't need any more of those things."

"My dad's a terrific reader," Patty says of him. "He's president of a grain company, retired. He's the busiest retired man I know. Daddy raises roses, in Fort Myers, Florida. Mother raises orchids." "Mother" is Patty Berg's step-mother. "My own mother dropped dead on Christmas Day," she says, with a certain clarity. It was a heart attack. But then, "One day I was out playing golf [Patty says goff] and I introduced Dad to this lady, and they've been married 19 years. She has red hair and freckles, and looks just like all of us." Of tour life Patty says, with earnestness and love, "The girls are wonderful—they're very, very high class. The worst thing, of course, is that you're not with your family as much. I don't get to be with my father and mother and sisters, and my little nieces and nephews. But I have their pictures and everything, and they write on my birthday. My nephew wanted to go in the Air Force, so I got some books about it. . . ." Patty herself was in the service, during the war—the Marines, from 1943 to '45. Now in her 43rd year, and her 20th year of professional play, Patty handles things carefully, conserves her strength. She gets to bed by 10 o'clock and travels now by air. "At my age I can't very well get into an automobile and drive 900 miles to Augusta. I try to stay as relaxed as I can and not to worry. This is the life I chose. I have to think it's wonderful."

April 20. Talked with the wicked, wicked Gloria Armstrong—31, blue-eyed, mild and amiable. She said of her customary amusements, "I read a lot, and watch television, and knit. It's only changing towns that keeps it from being dull. When I'm home doing the same thing it gets boring. On tour the things we do that are most fun are unplanned. We had a lot of fun in Gatlinburg, Tennessee. We had a picnic and went up into the mountains, and two bears came and stole the bread right from the table. We were all together, having a picnic. The most fun is always just getting together and having a party we've made up ourselves."

Of the difference between her contingent (poker-playing) and the others, Gloria says, "The big difference is that we aren't in training. I love golf, but I'm not going to sacrifice everything for the game. If some people want to, I think that's wonderful. But if I want to date, to stay out till 3 in the morning, I'm going to, and if I want to have a drink, I'm going to. I'm not going to stop talking to people because of golf. Some people get themselves into a trance on the course, but I may be thinking about my wash. The first couple of years I thought this was a good life—you got a chance to travel across the country. Of course, you wouldn't *do* it if you didn't like it, but it's a lot harder than some people think, waking up in the morning and you can't remember what town you're in.

"A lot depends on how you're playing. If your game goes sour on you, it's miserable, and all you want to do is go home. When I was playing

*Bob Hagge dines amidst the girls: (from left to right) Ruth Jessen, Jo Ann Prentice, wife Marlene and Gloria Armstrong.*

badly it got to my nerves—I was grouchy. I went home and said, 'I'm getting out of golf.' But what can I do? I had a year and a half of college, and you can't do anything with that. Sometimes a job you might like comes up when you're traveling, but you look hard at what it involves, and the first thing you know you're back on the tour. About 80% of the girls want to get married and have a family, but we aren't in a position to do anything about it, and here we are."

It's hard to determine why the chance to see the country pleased Gloria so. She says, "I'm not a sightseer. I can't think of anything I hate to do worse. I did look at the place where Custer had his last stand, because it was where you could kind of see it as you go by. And you can look at Mt. Rushmore, and I did stop at Old Faithful. We were very lucky—we got there about two minutes before it let loose. Otherwise I wouldn't have waited around."

Carol Mann, the night she arrived in Beaumont, got back into her car and drove till she found the oil refineries, because she had heard that oil refineries were what there was to see in Beaumont. Then she drove 40 miles to look at the Gulf of Mexico, and drove up and down the beach. "I found two *sharks*. They were washed up on the beach, and I tried to cut them open with my pocket-knife, but they were too tough, so I took the car and ran over them, but that didn't work either. I mean, I never *saw* the inside of a shark."

April 21. Beaumont is a beautiful course—narrow, defined by its trees—and the weather is good. I followed Ruth Jessen, Louise Suggs and Sandra McClinton. Sandra is new to the tour, was obviously rattled and hit some painful shots that had to be hacked out. Suggs and Jessen both moved in and surrounded her, making comforting, reassuring noises. With few exceptions, the girls play together without strain or any grimly specific competitiveness toward their partners. Golf, of course, has a curiously private element, the sense of competition between oneself and prevailing conditions in addition to the competition between oneself and anyone else. Even so, the accord in which the girls play and their genuine interest in each other's game are remarkable. Marlene Bauer's husband, Bob Hagge, apt to be the only man in this sea of professional lady golfers, says, "I've seen it happen that one girl will help another who's having trouble with her swing, knowing that next week she may go out and beat her because of it. They'll come in after a round of a tournament and go back out to watch somebody else play. They play against each other, and they're playing to eat, and they come in and are good friends. I defy the men to do it, at least without a couple of shots of whisky." (Bob isn't the only one who finds the women steadier than the men. Fred Corcoran, who founded the Ladies PGA, left the men's PGA because they were too temperamental.)

Hagge, 6 feet 5, with almost translucently blond hair, intends to be a golf-course architect but now shepherds Marlene through the tour. Before she tees off, he leaves. "Where are you going, Bob?" "I got to warm up," he says, a touch wryly. "Unwrap the balls, give the caddie hell, test the wind. . . ." And when Marlene comes in, grim and self-castigating, calculating in dollars and cents what the last hole cost her, Bob reminds her of the good shots she played. No light breaks through. He points out that tomorrow is another day. Nothing. He sighs, says with the greatest gentleness, "Grem, keep playing it, if it makes you feel better. Go ahead and twist the knife." And Gremlin Bauer Hagge subsides, not happy but as comforted as anything but time is going to make her. Marlene is small and careful and pretty. She diets, takes vitamins, gets enough sleep and dresses with a flair short girls are rarely capable of. She is a sort of den mother to some of the girls, so there in the Hagges' room they are, hair in curlers, in front of the TV set, playing cards.

Augusta, April 25. Carol Mann and I left for the Titleholders on Sunday, before the Beaumont tournament was over, Carol having finished out of the money and Augusta being 900 miles away. Murle MacKenzie and Kathy Whitworth left with us, and we picked up some others when we got to Baton Rouge on Sunday night. They called back to congratulate Mary Lena Faulk when they heard she'd won in Beaumont. We left early for Augusta. It was hot. Louisiana looked like Texas, Mississippi looked like Louisiana, Alabama looked like Mississippi and, I suppose, Georgia looked like Alabama, but it was too dark

*Alone in a motel lobby, "loner" Louise Suggs reads a local daily newspaper.*

to see. We dragged in exhausted, but at any rate early, so the girls who had never seen it could get used to the Augusta Country Club course. And then for the next few days it rained.

When it rains you polish your shoes and play cards and look at television.

April 26. Talked to Louise Suggs, the definitive loner. Louise Suggs is a *grown-up*. I was suddenly conscious when I met her that life in this sororal society (the evenings of bridge in one another's rooms, bull sessions, and dining together) has the air of college or summer camp. Louise is a woman of 37 ("I can't lie about my age, because I was born the night the ball park burned down") who is not about to live as though she were still in school. She finds out where the younger element is staying and goes somewhere else. She drinks Martinis before dinner and does not see in it a topic for group thinking. She does not talk about golf. She is not interested in the tempests in the tour's teapot, or in going to Fun Night, or in promoting some image of the professional woman golfer in the mind of the public, or in having 5% taken off the top of the purse to divide among the girls who finish out of the money. ("I worked for my money, why shouldn't they? Why should I support them now—if I get sick, are they going to feel an obligation to support me?") Louise is entirely forthright and alienates people on occasion. "I guess I'm terrible," she says wistfully, "an awful bear." (A bear of whom Ruth Jessen says, "Louise is always doing things for you, and never lets you know she did.")

Fond of her or not, everyone respects her absolutely—personally and as a golfer. Louise was last year's leading money winner, is in the Ladies' Golf Hall of Fame, has been the National Amateur champion, the National Open champion, the British Amateur champion, and the Ladies Professional Golf Association champion. She's won the North and South championship, the Southern, the Western Amateur and Open championships. This year she has won five of the 10 tournaments she has played in and finished second or third in most of the ones she didn't win. In February, in Palm Beach, on a par-3 course, she turned in a total of 156 for 54 holes, beating Sam Snead's 158 and Dow Finsterwald's 165. It's a feat about which she feels particularly gleeful.

Louise has put in her time as president of the LPGA and assuming association responsibilities. She is at present their member-at-large but says, "I've served my apprenticeship. Now is the time for me to be able to slack off." She finds it hard being obliged to relate to people, whether she is feeling like it or not, because tournaments, clinics and business luncheons demand it. "Does it affect your own friendships?" I asked her. And Louise said, "I have no friends." She made nothing of it. The friends she did have when she was a girl have married, and she sees them only once a year. There happens not to be on the tour anyone her age she feels close to. There is a friend, Jean Hopkins, who joins her briefly when possible, but, with this exception, Louise means it: she doesn't have any friends. "It's not too bad, once you've made up your mind that it's necessary," she says of the life. "But basically it's no way for a woman to live. Don't get me wrong, I wouldn't trade it." So there she is, with her Cadillac and her traveling clothesline, her collapsible cooler, her clothes that don't need ironing, and no friends, in a motel room. A motel room at the top though, and if she has no friends she has a troop of admirers, in the front row of whom is me.

April 27. It was still raining this morning. They moved the starting time back, and there were rumors that they would cancel the round and play 36 holes on Saturday, or even cancel for good, but finally it was decided to begin in the rain. The girls teed off and moved out in mournful pairs. There was no gallery but the officials, in identical raincoats and pith helmets, and the press. I followed Sandra Haynie, who played badly. It turned out that she had caught the flu, so she got to spend a couple of days in bed in a motel room—in a motel where room service refused to involve itself in anything more elaborate than sandwiches. (Carol Mann did get a dish of ice cream, but they didn't extend themselves so far as to provide a spoon.)

April 30. The 72-hole Titleholders is one of the important women's tournaments, and there was relief when on the second day the weather cleared. On the last day it was perfect. The course was dry enough, and it was a marvelous final round. For a while, just before the turn, there was a four-way tie—Berg, Suggs, Mickey Wright and Kathy Cornelius. The gallery milled around the posted scores, unable to decide to follow any one of them and miss what the others were doing. In the end, Mickey Wright took it from Louise by one stroke and won her first Titleholders. For years people have expected her to subdue this long course to which her long (longest in women's golf, in fact) drives seemed particularly suited. Very big day for Mickey, who received her green Titleholders' blazer, the Vare Trophy, the LPGA Babe Zaharias Trophy—about everything in sight. There were speeches and awards, and a good deal of ceremony, but Murle MacKenzie wanted to duck out as early as she could, and she took me back to the motel. She was exhausted, and dissatisfied with her game; she wanted her supper, and to get to bed. She had to leave for Spartanburg in the morning to get her washing and ironing done there before practice. After Spartanburg come Columbus, Nashville, New Rochelle, New York, Dillsburg, Pennsylvania, and Baltusrol, New Jersey, Leesburg, Indiana, Rockton, Illinois, Minneapolis, Minnesota, and Waterloo, Iowa. Etc. I am going *home*.

New York, May 1. What do I think? Well, I see empty dinner trays in motel corridors. I can hear Del Shannon singing "Runaway" from Texas across Louisiana and Mississippi and Alabama, down 900 miles of highway into Augusta; I see tall Carol Mann working a gas pump herself, in the middle of the night, 200 miles out of Augusta, and in a fit of laughter letting it run over; I see self-exacting Betty Jameson sitting up in bed, hugging her knees and grieving over a bad shot, and Bob Hagge leaning on this side of a door marked Men Only. And golf courses, stretching away, sunny and green, in that astonishing silence that can attend 30 people engaged in their life work and 5,000 others excited enough to come and watch. I don't know what I think. It's a life you can make anything you want to of, if it doesn't make anything it wants to of you first.

# Anyone Can Hit a Long Ball

Mickey Wright with Gwilym S. Brown

Drawings by Frank Mullins

Sports Illustrated                                      February, 1962

For the weekend golfer a good driving round will be a good scoring round, since a long, straight tee shot usually will bring the green within reach and create a good chance for a par or even a birdie. Most golfers, however, have never really tried to learn how to hit for distance. Women in particular think that they do not have the necessary size or strength. Not true, says U.S. Open champion Mickey Wright, who has become the longest hitter in the history of women's golf by incorporating into her swing seven distance-building elements. She guarantees that anyone of normal size and coordination, whether man or woman, can learn to drive a golf ball consistently 200 yards or more. On the following pages Miss Wright teaches the seven vital elements in seven simple steps. Once studied and mastered, they will make it easy for anyone to achieve the distance off the tee that is so essential for winning golf today.

## Step 1: The grip

There are two important points to keep in mind about the grip. First, it should be natural. By this I mean the position of your left hand on the club should be more or less the same as its position when your left arm is hanging loosely at your side. This is absolutely the strongest position it can be in, but I learned this the hard way. In 1960, in order to develop a soft, controlled fade, I weakened my left-hand grip by moving my thumb over onto the top of the shaft. After a few months I began to feel a strong and persistent pain in my shoulder which vanished only after Earl Stewart, the Dallas pro, persuaded me to return to my natural grip. "You are probably forcing too hard to get the club face back on line," he pointed out.

*When her left hand hangs limp at her side before gripping the club (left), Mickey Wright's thumb is turned slightly to her right. This is its strongest position, and it remains there when she grips the club, thus contributing to distance and accuracy.*

Just as important as the position of the left hand is the placement of the right index finger. This finger should be around the shaft slightly apart from the middle finger, just as it would be if you were set to squeeze the trigger of a rifle. This position is especially important for women. It helps tremendously in keeping the club face square at the start of the backswing, and it supplies a much stronger hold on the club at the top of the backswing than a grip that doesn't emphasize this trigger-finger action of the right index finger.

**Suggested practice routine:**

Practice for a minute or so daily just putting your hands on the club in the correct manner. Check the trigger finger closely. Then keep re-checking it against the drawings until the grip becomes automatic. Re-check frequently.

# Step 2: The stance

*Ball* (arrow) *placed under the shoe just inside the outer row of spikes will force weight to fall correctly on right instep.*

*At address* (right), *Miss Wright's arms are held firm but not rigid, with most of her weight carried on rear portion of the feet.*

*The right knee is braced toward left so that muscular tension* (shaded area) *is felt on instep of right foot and inside both legs.*

The right foot is the key to a strong stance. It is both a buttress around which you will build a great deal of your swing and a starting block from which you can accelerate into the shot quickly and smoothly. The rest of the stance is pretty routine, but I'll go over it briefly. Play the ball opposite the instep of your left foot with your weight distributed over the rear portion of both feet, from the balls of the feet back through the heels. No weight should be on the toes. At address your arms should be firm but not rigid, neither pressed in against the body nor reaching out for the ball. You will lose a great deal of distance if you have to reach. The sole of your driver should be flat on the ground. When it is, you know you are handling the club the way it was designed to be used.

To produce extra distance you must learn to use the right foot efficiently. The weight planted on the right foot should be carried entirely along the instep. The right knee should be braced inward so that you can feel tension all up and down the inside of the calf and thigh, as if you were holding a volleyball against your left leg with the right knee. Bracing your right foot and leg in this manner will keep the leg from buckling during the backswing and thus prevent a left-to-right sway. It will also furnish a powerful jumping-off place from which to start the downswing. To reproduce exactly what I want in this respect, I often hit practice shots with a golf ball tucked under the outside spikes of my right shoe. The immediate increase in distance using this gimmick is astonishing.

**Suggested practice routine:**
Spend at least 15 minutes each week hitting shots with a golf ball placed under the outer edge of your right shoe. This will also help improve footwork.

## Step 3: The wide-arc swing

A swing with a wide arc will give you more opportunity to build up clubhead speed without hurrying the swing. To achieve this wide arc it is vital to start the backswing correctly. I start mine by taking the clubhead straight back from the ball and low along the ground for a distance of about a foot, at which time the turn of the body will naturally bring the club to the inside of the line. This low, straight takeaway sets the mood for the entire swing. To get this takeaway firmly implanted in your mind during practice, place a tee in the ground 12 inches behind the ball. A correct backswing will knock down the tee.

The rest of the wide-arc swing should follow almost as a matter of course. You should not consciously cock your wrists at any time. In fact, you should not be thinking about your hands or arms during the entire backswing. I keep the inside of my left elbow facing straight up as the club starts back. This helps to keep the club face on line as long as possible and it helps keep the right elbow in front of the right hip. Once the right elbow starts getting outside or behind the right hip it means that you are swinging the club back with your arms alone—and too fast—rather than allowing the weight to shift and the hips, shoulders and arms to turn in unison. At the top of the swing, you should have rotated your hips about 45° from their position at address, your shoulders about 90°. The turning of the hips and the shoulders, combined with the clubhead's own momentum, automatically send the clubhead to the top of the swing. This natural, one-piece motion will guarantee a wide-arc swing and will promote a smooth, gradually accelerating backswing and downswing, an essential item when you want distance.

**Suggested practice routine:**

Twice a week take 10 swings with a tee placed in the ground. Then hit at least 10 drives while thinking of nothing but the low, straight takeaway.

## Step 4: The right elbow at the top

Bringing your right elbow into the correct position at the peak of the backswing may be the most valuable step to master. When you learn it, you will be taking a giant step toward being able to swing the club as hard as possible without destroying the groove or the rhythm of your swing. At the top of the swing the right elbow should point directly toward the ground and the right hand should be directly under the shaft of the club, its edge pointing up. One way to help remember this position is to swing the club to the top and then, making sure your left arm is straight, attempt to press your two forearms together. The right elbow position is crucial for two reasons: 1) anticipating getting the right elbow into this posture will make it much easier to produce a one-piece backswing; 2) on the downswing you will find it easier to bring your right elbow down in front of your right hip, a point I'll discuss in Step 5.

Getting your right elbow into the correct position at the top should be an easy enough move to visualize, but it may prove quite difficult to perfect. It is hard to resist letting the elbow fly out. But with practice this step should start to become natural within a few weeks.

*At top of backswing Miss Wright's right elbow resists impulse to fly out* (dotted line)*, points straight toward ground, fleshy edge of the right hand points up.*

**Suggested practice routine:**

Take six swings in front of a mirror three times a day, getting your right elbow into the correct position and keeping your left-hand grip firm. This will also strengthen the key muscles.

## Step 5: The right elbow on the downswing

If your right elbow is in the correct position at the top of the swing, the proper downswing will follow automatically as soon as you shift your weight off the right foot and onto the left. Most women uncock the hands too soon because they are not strong enough to delay this. But with the right elbow pointing straight down it is almost impossible to make this error. When you have started your downswing correctly, the right elbow should work down in front of the right hip. This is crucial. The move will properly delay the uncocking of the hands and bring the club down on the desirable inside arc and the clubhead into the ball from straight behind. You will be able to swing hard without a resulting loss of club control. Once the elbow gets behind the hip on the

*Miss Wright's elbow* (circle)
*comes down in front of the*
*hip, correctly delays*
*uncocking of hands, keeps*
*club on inside arc.*

downswing, the result is often a slice and a disheartening loss of distance.

**Suggested practice routine:**

For a minute or so each day, starting from the correct position at top of the swing, stand in front of a mirror and practice 1) bringing the right elbow down in front of the hip properly and 2) keeping the hands fully cocked as long as possible.

## Step 6: Footwork

Where distance is concerned, the force exerted by the right foot is critical. The weight planted on the right foot should be carried along the instep (1). As you sweep the club back you should gradually and consciously push your weight off the left foot and onto the instep of the right (2). The right foot and leg, in fact, should act like a buttress, resisting the pressure of the backswing, and the right leg should maintain pretty much the same position that it held at address. Also keep this in mind about the left foot: as the weight is transferred to the right foot, the left should roll over sideways, onto the instep. If the left heel is lifted too high, or even if it remains planted on the ground, too much weight will tend to remain on the left foot. At the top of the backswing

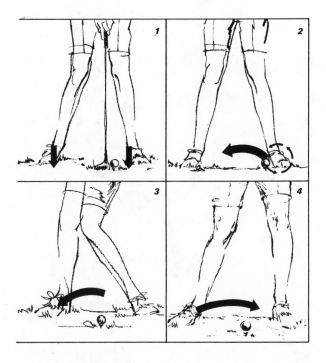

(3), most of your weight should be felt along the right instep and along the inside of the right calf and thigh.

You start the downswing by pushing your weight off the right foot and onto the left (4). The hips will turn almost simultaneously, but there should be no violent pivoting action. Initiating the downswing by turning the hips—the popular method—too often leaves the right elbow behind the hip. This throws the clubhead into an outside-in arc and is likely to produce a slice.

**Suggested practice routine:**
Spend five minutes a day swinging your driver back and forth, concentrating on footwork. Hit at least 15 shots with your driver each time you practice, concentrating entirely on this weight shift.

## Step 7: The head behind the ball at impact

It is not exactly revolutionary to state that you should keep your head behind the ball throughout the swing and at impact. But it is still an important point to stress, because failure to do so will drain off all the power, rhythm and momentum built up by the first six steps. You must

*Miss Wright's follow-through indicates how force (arrows) is applied. Hips, legs shift to left; head, shoulders stay behind ball (cross). Hitting power goes through and toward target.*

feel from the very start of the downswing that your head is remaining behind the ball, that you are looking at the back of the ball when it is hit. Thus, though your weight will be moving over to the left side, your right shoulder will be under your left shoulder and in perfect position to keep the explosive hitting force you have produced behind the ball where it belongs. If your head has slid to the left of the ball before or at impact, this means that your shoulders have also moved to the left. The movement can produce only two results, both bad. First of all, your hands also will have moved ahead of the ball. The clubhead, accordingly, will not have reached its maximum speed at impact. What little power remains will be applied downward instead of through and toward the target. Second, hitting at the ball from in front of it, instead of from behind it, will open the face of the club at impact, with the obvious result that the shot will be pushed to the right or, worse, will result in a slice.

**Suggested practice routine:**
Spend 10 minutes of every practice session drilling on keeping your head steady. Ask an observer to tell you each time whether you have succeeded.

# SUMMARY

In explaining how it is possible to increase dramatically the distance of your drives, I have made no attempt to describe all the basic fundamentals of the golf swing. I have sought only to isolate and clarify the areas in the swing from which distance hitting springs. There are other factors that will help, too. Ball games—tennis, paddle tennis, ping-pong, etc.—are good for your timing, because they accustom you to the act of striking a ball. Pitching or chipping a golf ball around the backyard also helps in this respect. So will exercises with hand grippers and dumbbells. With them you can increase your hand and arm strength. A woman, fortunately, can do a good many strength exercises before they begin to have any effect on the shape of her arm muscles. If you are a weekend golfer, by merely handling, swinging and feeling the weight of a club every day, you will help your game. If you should go further and master even two or three of the seven steps I have described on the preceding pages, you are bound to improve. When you have incorporated all seven into your swing, the result in longer drives and lower scores is likely to be astonishing.

# Anne Quast Welts and the Hogan Touch

## Frank Hannigan

Golf Journal                                    September, 1963

There are more good women golfers today than ever before. This is as obvious as the latest statistics on the current golf boom which show record number of rounds played by women every year. An increasing number of competitions affords the better players more opportunities to sharpen their skills; the modern female style of play reflects the aggressive go-for-the-flagstick methods of the famous males who perform on television; and the scores in women's events go down and down.

In the midst of this Golden Age of feminine golf talent, it is all the more remarkable that Mrs. David A. (Anne Quast) Welts, of Mount Vernon, Washington, continues eminent in our Women's Amateur championship, for the title is certainly harder to win today than at any time since the championship was first played in 1895. Mrs. Welts became champion last month at the lovely Taconic Golf Club of Williams College in Williamstown, Massachusetts, just as she did in 1958 and 1961. When Mrs. Welts does not win, she comes awfully close to winning. She has been a quarter-finalist in the Women's Amateur in all of the last nine years, starting in 1955 when she was seventeen.

The loser in the 36-hole final at Taconic, 2 and 1, was Miss Peggy Shane Conley, of Spokane, Washington, the youngest player ever to reach the final round. Sixteen years old last June and playing in the championship for the first time, Peggy is a prototype of the bubble-gum set who make it so difficult now for the ancients in their mid-twenties to maintain their reputations.

Mrs. Welts's splendid record is not the result of continuing trial by fire. Quite to the contrary, she has played in only eight competitions the past three years. It is not straining a comparison to think of Mrs. Welts as the Ben Hogan of women's golf. Hogan, it will be recalled, played in precious few tournaments during his greatest years but prepared himself exquisitely for those he did enter.

Mrs. Welts arrived at Taconic a full week ahead of time. Her analysis

*Anne Quast Welts*

of the course led to the conclusion that it would be wise to approach some of Taconic's greens with a left-to-right fade on her iron shots, since those greens slope in the opposite direction. She worked diligently on the fade shot daily and on many others for long periods of time; then she practiced putting; then she practiced putting a little longer; and then, for good measure, she hit a few more putts. The fruit of this preparation was 123 holes played in only ten over par on a course where she was seldom able to reach any but the par-5 greens with less than a 5 iron. The course played at 6,195 yards to a par of 72.

On the few occasions when Mrs. Welts's drives and irons faltered, she was able to call for help from a remarkable short game, somewhat like a baseball manager beckoning his ace relief pitcher in the late innings.

During her thrilling semi-final match against Miss JoAnne Gunderson, the defending champion, Mrs. Welts was, for Mrs. Welts, very wild over the first seven holes. She strayed from the fairways seven times yet walked off the seventh green one under par and 1 up. Then she resumed bisecting the fairways and greens, and won 3 and 2.

The jovial rivalry between Mrs. Welts and Miss Gunderson—also a native of Washington—has become a modern classic. Each won the championship three times in the last seven years. Miss Gunderson, who also plays in few tournaments nowadays, was appealing as always with her relaxed course manner and her booming drives. Taconic members of both sexes will long speak in awed terms about her performance in the fifth round against Mrs. Charles (Helen Sigel) Wilson, of Philadelphia. Mrs. Wilson, the runner-up in 1941 and 1948, was once again at the peak of her game and often outdrove the powerful Miss Gunderson. But Miss Gunderson birdied four of the first eight holes, went out in 33, and won 5 and 4.

The other semi-finalist was 20-year-old Carol Sorenson, of Janesville, Wisconsin, who eventually lost to Miss Conley, 1 down, in an exciting contest that concluded with the last five holes halved in par. Miss Sorenson, the 1960 United States Girls' Junior champion, won both the Western Amateur and the National Collegiate titles in 1962.

Mrs. Welts's route to the final round was blocked not only by Miss Gunderson but by Mrs. Scott Probasco, Jr., of Chattanooga, a semi-finalist in the past; by Miss Janis Ferraris, the 16-year-old whiz from San Francisco, whose string of fourteen consecutive match-play victories included winning the United States Girls' Junior championship in August; and by Miss Nancy Roth, of Elkhart, Indiana, the scourge of the Florida tournaments last winter. Mrs. Probasco lost 6 and 5; Miss Ferraris, 4 and 3; and Miss Roth, 2 and 1.

The type of golf now being played in this event was exemplified by the match between Mrs. Welts and Miss Roth. The first six holes were halved, five in par. Mrs. Welts chipped in on the seventh to go 1 up. After the eighth was halved in par, Mrs. Welts hit a long iron to the par-3 9th within 10 feet of the hole. Miss Roth put her ball even closer to the cup. Mrs. Welts missed and Miss Roth holed to square the match. Holes 10, 11 and 12 were halved—all with pars. Miss Roth birdied 13 to go 1 up; Mrs. Welts came right back with a birdie on 14. Mrs. Welts then added three more pars, two of which Miss Roth could not duplicate, and the match ended on the seventeenth.

The quality of play in the final was equally good. Mrs. Welts hit 24 of 35 greens in regulation figures, and Miss Conley hit 20 on a day when a brisk wind was always a factor. Miss Conley's victims included Miss

Phyllis Preuss, of Pompano Beach, Florida, and Miss Judy Bell, of Colorado Springs, Colorado, both members of the 1962 Curtis Cup team.

Miss Conley began the final day in uncertain fashion, losing the first hole when she three-putted from eight feet. On the second green she was faced with a seven-foot putt for a half, one that few will make with the memory of failure so recent. Miss Conley banged it into the cup. She went ahead on the seventh hole.

Mrs. Welts did not regain the lead until the 27th hole. Eventually, the consistency of her game was decisive. Miss Conley, who had been driving wonderfully, suddenly started to miss the fairways and fell three holes behind. Mrs. Welts, by the way, missed the fairway off the tee only three times in 35 holes.

Just when a complete collapse by the teen-ager seemed likely, Miss Conley rallied for one final burst of superb golf. She ripped a full wood shot four feet from the hole on the 31st but got only a half when her putt didn't drop; she birdied the 32nd by hitting a medium iron dead to the flag and holing a four-footer; she halved the 33rd and 34th, the latter with a do-or-die 10-foot putt; and she seemed on the verge of winning the par-3 35th when her tee shot reached the green and Mrs. Welts was bunkered. Miss Conley putted three feet short. Mrs. Welts blasted out about seventeen feet from the pin. She holed her putt, and there is no greater tribute to her skills than to say that no one seemed very surprised that she did.

The champion will now concentrate on teaching such things as the date of the Norman Conquest to her senior high school history class. She will be fortunate to come upon a roomful of students on the same level as Miss Conley, a B-plus scholar whose personality is a rare mixture of true poise and teen-age humor.

Miss Conley came across wonderfully in her daily interviews with the Boston press, which must have set some sort of record for rapport since the questions were tossed at a lass named Conley by reporters named Looney, Fitzgerald, Monahan and Barry. The questions and answers went something like this:

Q. And what does your father do, Peggy?

A. He's a dentist who plays pretty good golf.

Q. Have you talked to your parents this week?

A. I called home last night.

Q. What did they say?

A. My mother said I should change my putting grip.

Q. How long have you been playing golf?

A. Five years, except that I gave it up last year for awhile.

Q. Why?

A. I was playing rotten, so I decided to see how the other half lives.

Q. And what does the other half do?

A. Oh, they ride horses, swim in the lake, go to barbecues. You know, stuff like that.

All this occurred in an idyllic setting. The Taconic course, with the Berkshires as a backdrop, was wonderfully groomed under the supervision of Dick Baxter, who is about to retire after forty years as golf professional and course superintendent to Taconic.

All in all, the 1963 Women's Amateur championship was both a successful and charming event. There must be nothing in sport quite like a golf match involving girls. Take the fourth-round contest between Miss Conley and Miss Sue Lance, another sixteen-year-old, from Woodland, Calif. When they reached the eighth green, Miss Lance lagged her approach putt to within two feet of the hole. She looked at her opponent, who was standing motionless at the side of the green. "Aren't you going to give me that putt?" Miss Lance asked. Miss Conley turned on her very best map-of-Erin smile, shook her head, and replied, "I know how you putt, Susan." Thereupon Miss Lance, with a great show of disdain, walked up to her ball and rapped it in backhand. The opponents walked together to the next tee giggling.

# Barbara McIntire: At Her Best at Prairie Dunes

## Frank Hannigan

Golf Journal                                September, 1964

There is a time to take risks in golf and there is a time to be conservative. The tactics are really quite easy to learn, but the self-discipline needed to apply them properly is another matter.

Miss Barbara McIntire, of Colorado Springs, Colorado, has both the ability to think clearly and to control her swing under stress, and thus she was able to win the United States Women's Amateur championship last month at the Prairie Dunes Country Club in Hutchinson, Kansas. She defeated the redoubtable Miss JoAnne Gunderson, of Kirkland, Washington, 3 and 2 in the 36-hole final.

When Miss McIntire addressed her ball on the tee of the 22nd hole, she was 3 down to Miss Gunderson. The fourth hole at Prairie Dunes is an uphill par-3 of 165 yards. Trouble of the direst sort awaits the player who misses the green to the right. The hole was cut fairly close to the right side that day.

Miss McIntire, who normally is a great fan of discretion, hit a full-blooded wood shot right at the flagstick against the wind. Her ball came to rest 10 feet from the cup, and she proceeded to win the hole.

Six holes later, Miss McIntire, playing bold strokes, had come from behind to lead by two holes with only eight to play. It was clearly time for a change in tactics.

Aiming away from the trouble areas, Miss McIntire repeatedly drove down the fairways. She then carefully selected targets on the greens which would leave her in a position to get down in two for her pars. It was as though a public announcement had been made to Miss Gunderson that a couple of birdies on the final nine might bring her back to even but that nothing less would do the job. Miss McIntire parred her way in, and the match ended on the 34th green when Miss Gunderson failed to hole a putt of seven feet.

The morning round of the final was notable for Miss Gunderson's work around and on the greens. Even though she was somewhat erratic

*Barbara McIntire*

with her driver—and, as a result, hit only ten greens in regulation figures—Miss Gunderson was able to come up with two birdies and fifteen pars. She went to lunch 3 up.

In the afternoon Miss Gunderson's errant drives cost her dearly. She was in the fairway only six times off the tee and hit only five greens in regulation figures. Miss McIntire, on the other hand, was accurate all day. She never holed a putt in the final longer than six feet, but she still was able to play thirty-four holes only three strokes over par.

This was Miss McIntire's second victory in the Women's Amateur. She won in 1959 at the Congressional Country Club in Washington, D.C., and went on to win the British Ladies' championship the following year. She has come closer to winning our Women's Open championship than any amateur. In 1956, she lost in a play-off to Mrs. Kathy Cornelius at the Northland Country Club in Duluth, Minnesota.

Miss McIntire, Miss Gunderson, and Mrs. David (Anne Quast) Welts, of Mount Vernon, Wash., comprise the Great Triumvirate of contemporary women's amateur golf. Not one USGA Women's Amateur championship in the past eight years has escaped them. Miss Gunderson and Mrs. Welts have won the title three times.

That three young ladies have been able to dominate the championship during an era in which there surely must be more first-rate players than at any previous time is quite remarkable. As an illustration, consider the highest qualifying score of 160 at Prairie Dunes. When the USGA last employed a similar format in 1946—thirty-six holes of stroke-play qualifying for thirty-two spots in match play—the highest qualifying score was 177, seventeen strokes higher than this year. The drop to 160 occurred, mind you, on a course that Jack Nicklaus has played nine times both as an amateur and a professional and has yet to match par although its length from the back tees is only 6,522 yards. For the Women's Amateur championship the yardage was 6,001.

Anyone who thinks he has seen all the distinctive American courses is mistaken if he has not yet visited Prairie Dunes. It is a little bit of Scotland on the Kansas Prairie. All the characteristics of a Scottish seaside course are there—except the sea. There are rolling sand hills, fierce-looking native grasses allowed to grow waist high, frightening rough created by prickly yucca plants and wild plum thickets, and winds that sweep across the prairie almost incessantly. If the course were situated near a large urban center, it would surely be one of the most celebrated in the country.

# The Drama of St. Germain

## Tom Scott

Golf Monthly (U.K.)                                    November, 1964

In a four-day tournament (October 1-4, 1964) with 25 teams and 75 players, or thereabouts, it is impossible to go back and review every great round or even a fraction of the brilliant shots. I will content myself, therefore, by recounting some of the dramatic moments as the first competition for the World's Women's Amateur Team championship at St. Germain, near Paris, reached and passed its climax.

With so many players and so many strokes involved, it was amazing that the event should end with a one-stroke victory. After all the work of organization by the incomparable Vicomtesse de Saint Sauveur and the French officials, what could be better than a victory for the home team! The figures were: France, 588 points; United States, 589 points; England, 597 points.

Before play on the fourth round began on a sunny and warm Sunday morning, the United States was leading with a 54-hole total of 440 strokes with France on 441 and England on 446. Much attention was given to Brigitte Varangot and the American Barbara Fay White who were in the same threesome. It was pretty clear very early on that neither of their scores were going to count—the best two of the three scores did—but both were obviously feeling the strain and trying just that little bit too hard, which makes all the difference between a good score and a moderate one.

Much then depended on the two other members of each team, Misses Cros and Lacoste for France and Misses Sorenson and McIntire for the United States. Miss Cros finished with a 74, an eminently satisfactory performance marked by a fine burst of two successive birdies in the middle of the round. Miss Sorenson, who has played so well in Europe, never put a foot wrong. I saw little of it, but I am assured it was a perfect round of golf. It was certainly near perfect, being one over par. She had no adventures and played every shot as it should be played. The United States led France by three strokes with one match remaining. And here was where the element of big drama crept in. On one hand we had the not very experienced Catherine Lacoste, the daughter of two great sports champions, and on the other the calm, ice cool United States champion, Miss McIntire.

Miss Lacoste, the strong little French girl who hits the ball a mile, was playing just in front of her rival, and at the fifteenth hole she was one under par. There she had to wait on the trio in front, and the "Oohs" and the "Ohs", the gasps and the sighs as she missed the green at the short sixteenth were heard all over the course and perhaps beyond. The atmosphere was heavy. But then came two holes Miss Lacoste won't forget in a hurry, the seventeenth and the eighteenth, two strong par 4s. She played both in fours to receive a reception that was almost hysterical in its enthusiasm. She deserved it for the way she had fought back after her disaster.

After the joy of Catherine Lacoste's finish came the tension of waiting for Barbara McIntire, the last American player. She had dropped a stroke at the fifteenth but got her three at the sixteenth, and that meant she had to play the last two holes in nine strokes to give her side the lead. The glum faces of the French followers clearly showed they felt such a feat was certainly within Miss McIntire's ability.

So on to the American's finish. Miss McIntire pulled her second into sand at the seventeenth and took a five. Now she had to get her four at the last hole, a good two-shotter with the bunkers placed at strategic spots. She pulled her second into one of them and slashed it into another bunker. Now the French onlookers could hardly bear to look at her next shot.

Miss McIntire got her ball out of the bunker and was left with a putt of about eight yards to tie. She made a great effort but the ball stayed out of the hole. There was a gasp, a moment of silence, and then many joyous scenes among the winners and their supporters, while the Americans went over to console the completely dispirited Miss McIntire.

It was France's greatest golf hour. Miss Lacoste, who tied with Miss Sorenson for the individual title, was the centre of the scene at the finish, but one must not forget that she was only one of a team. Claudine Cros and Brigitte Varangot both played magnificently.

*The French team won the first World's Women's Amateur Team championship. From left to right: Brigitte Varangot, Claudine Cros, Catherine Lacoste.*

*The American team finished one stroke behind the French. From left to right: Carol Sorenson, Barbara McIntire, Jeannequin de Mallarimé (hostess), Barbara Fay White.*

# A Report on the First Women's World Amateur Team Championship

## Vicomtesse de Saint-Sauveur, President Women's Committee, French Golf Federation

Golf Journal                                                    November, 1964

The reasons for worry during the months preceding the first Women's World Amateur Team championship last month turned out to be the reasons for success in the end.

Where an entry of fifteen to seventeen teams had been our first estimation, twenty-seven countries entered. Twenty-five teams were present, with Venezuela and Czechoslovakia unable to attend. Luck served us: the weather was perfect and the crowds were the largest I have seen in France, last year's Canada Cup excepted. On the whole, scoring was good—women's golf has greatly progressed in recent years the world over. And the finish of the competition, while not surprising, was extremely close.

We had regarded England, France and the United States as favorites with Australia and Canada as possible threats, and these five teams took the first five places with totals ranging from 588 to 613. Each of the twenty-five teams had three players, and the two best scores daily over the four days represented the team total.

After the first round, France was leading by one stroke, and at the halfway mark by two, in front of the United States 295, England 297, Canada 305 and Sweden 309. After three rounds, the situation had changed: USA was leading with 440 with France one stroke behind, England 446, Canada 460, Sweden 462, Australia 463, and Germany 465.

The finish on the fourth day was close with considerable tension and pressure as the final round developed. For France, Mlles. Brigitte Varangot had 77 and Claudine Cros 74, while for the United States Miss Barbara Fay White had 76 and Miss Carol Sorenson, the steadiest of the Americans throughout, had 73. With the United States champion, Miss Barbara McIntire, and the young French star, Catherine Lacoste, still on the course, the United States led by two strokes. After

*A zealous organizer, Vicomtesse de Saint-Sauveur checks preparations
for the first Women's World Amateur Team championship.*

fourteen holes, Miss McIntire was even with par. Until the par-3 16th,
Mlle. Lacoste was one below par.

Mlle. Lacoste had 5 at the 16th. She played on in a haze of anger and
depression, quite sure she had ruined all chances of her team winning.
This young girl of nineteen played superbly all week, but she did nothing better than the two perfect par 4s on 17 and 18 that enabled her to
finish with 73.

It was a sad ending for the USA players. Miss McIntire was bunkered
on each of the last two holes, and finished 5-6. The United States lost by
one stroke with a total of 589 to France's 588. The French and American players have become close friends and, in spite of the joy of winning, Claudine, Brigitte, and Catherine felt strongly for Barbara. At
the prize-giving, one could sense a deep sympathy and understanding
between all of the players present.

The low individual scorers for the seventy-two holes were Miss Sorenson of the USA, who shortly before had won the British Ladies'
Amateur championship at Prince's, Sandwich, and Mlle. Lacoste. Both
had 294—six strokes above par for the St. Germain Golf Club.

The first Espirito Santo Trophy was run on a small budget. We managed to get much for nothing, especially from non-golfers to whom the
words "World Championship" had a special meaning. I firmly believe

*The Vicomtesse de Saint-Sauveur, formerly Lally Vagliano, was an outstanding golfer. She represented France in international competition from 1937 to 1965 without a break. She won the British Ladies' championship in 1950 and the French Ladies' championship in 1948, 1950, 1951, and 1954.*

that the success of an amateur championship does not reside in vast expenses. A good basic organization is essential as is a feeling of friendship and sympathy between the host country and the visiting teams. Both of these are in danger when too much importance is given instead to ceremony and when receptions try to be too impressive. There is a French saying: "Le mieux est l'ennemi du bien." In English: "Overdoing is worse than just doing."

**Order of finish in first Women's World Amateur Team championship**

| | | | | | |
|---|---|---|---|---|---|
| 1. | France | 588 | 15. | Italy | 641 |
| 2. | United States of America | 589 | | Philippines | 641 |
| 3. | England | 597 | | Holland | 641 |
| 4. | Canada | 606 | 18. | Chile | 645 |
| 5. | Australia | 613 | 19. | Japan | 649 |
| 6. | New Zealand | 616 | 20. | Argentina | 658 |
| | Sweden | 616 | 21. | Spain | 663 |
| 8. | Germany | 621 | 22. | Portugal | 668 |
| 9. | Mexico | 624 | 23. | Denmark | 682 |
| | Scotland | 624 | 24. | Bermuda | 689 |
| 11. | Belgium | 626 | 25. | Austria | 713 |
| 12. | South Africa | 627 | | | |
| 13. | Wales | 634 | | | |
| | Ireland | 637 | | | |

# Lacoste: Old Name, New Glory

## Anonymous

Golf Journal                                    February, 1965

A little more than eleven years ago, a young French girl began to be initiated into the joys of golf—and its tribulations. From her mother, she received three "words" of advice—be physically fit; start with a correct grip; and hit the ball hard, as the Americans do. From her father, three more words: observe, note, and work.

Now, at age 19, Mlle. Catherine Lacoste is lifting to the heights again one of the most famous names in French sports history. In the past year, Mlle. Lacoste won the French Girls' championship, led her country to victory in the first Women's World Amateur Team championship, and challenged mightily for the British Women's Amateur title, including a decisive triumph in the second round over the United States champion, Miss Barbara McIntire. All who have seen her in competition are predicting a day not too far off when she may stand as tall as the two other Lacostes in French sports.

Her father, René Lacoste, was one of the world's leading tennis champions in the 1920s: twice winner at Wimbledon, twice United States champion, an outstanding Davis Cup player, and three times champion of France. Her mother, the former Mlle. Simone Thion de la Chaume, was nine times French Ladies' golf champion, winner of the British Girls' title at age 15, and in 1927 the first foreign winner of the British Women's Amateur championship.

To Catherine they deeded not only the tradition of winning but the oft-overlooked importance of preparation. When René Lacoste was a youngster new to tennis, he suffered a particularly humiliating defeat in the first round of a local tournament. His immediate impulse was to abandon the game. But after a week he retrieved his racquet from the corner of the room into which it had been flung, and he announced to his father that he was determined to try again. After each defeat, he made careful note of why he was beaten. He filled page after page in small notebooks. Through sheer will, he made himself a champion and was ranked No. 1 in the world from 1926 through 1928.

In his book "Tennis," Lacoste wrote: "Will power in tennis is, as in everything, the best and least expensive insurance against failure. To play tennis you should have certain natural qualities. To become a great champion, it is necessary to have the will to use them. Tilden won because he knew how to use his height, his flexibility and his intelligence; Borotra because he was extremely fast; Cochet because of wonderful reflexes. I don't have the genius of Tilden, or the physical qualities of Borotra and Cochet, and if sometimes I succeeded in beating them, it was because I wanted to win with all my might, using the means available to me." Of his daughter's success at golf, Lacoste noted with considerable satisfaction that she followed his advice and worked long and hard on her technique before entering competition. He says: "Catherine would not have been able to achieve her victories if she had not spent hours and hours of work on her swing."

Mme. Lacoste brought to golf perhaps superior natural talent than her husband took to tennis, but very early she displayed an attitude of the kind found most often in champions. When she was 14, the London *Daily Mail* correspondent wrote of her performance in an international match between Britain and France: "Against Mrs. Hartill, champion of the Midlands and one of the more lengthy English players, she played a splendid game, accepting a defeat due mainly to lack of luck with the perfect calmness which characterizes a champion."

In 1927, when she won the British Ladies' championship by defeating Miss Dorothy Pearson (her same opponent in the British Girls' final three years before), the correspondent for the London *Times* wrote of Mlle. de la Chaume: "Miss Pearson in the final started a beautiful comeback, but to this magnificient effort Mlle. de la Chaume responded with equal strength and proved in the critical moment to be the absolute mistress of herself, which is characteristic of great champions."

That daughter Catherine possesses similar qualities was demonstrated during the final holes of the first Women's World Amateur Team championship, played at the St. Germain Golf Club, near Paris, in the autumn of 1964. The competition had resolved into a struggle between Mlle. Lacoste and Miss McIntire. They were playing two holes apart. Until the par-3 16th hole., Mlle. Lacoste was one below par and was leading the French girls, as she had all week. Then at the 16th, she took a 5—two over par. She approached the last two holes in a haze of anger and depression, certain she had ruined all chances of her team's winning. Despite this, she took control of her emotions and played the

*Rene Lacoste, former world tennis champion, and Mme. Lacoste, who as Simone*
*Thion de la Chaume won the French and British Ladies' golf championships,*
*congratulate daughter Catherine after she led France to victory in the first Women's*
*World Amateur Team championship.*

17th and the 18th in par 4s. Her 73 brought France the Women's World
Amateur Team championship by one stroke.

In the jubilation that followed, it was left to René Lacoste to signal
the emergence of another bright star in the family. "Nowadays," he
said, "when people talk about me, they do not speak of me as a tennis
champion but as the father of a golf champion."

# When Mickey Wright Did Nothing Wrong

## Gwilym S. Brown

Sports Illustrated                                    November 23, 1964

Mickey Wright, the best woman golfer of all time, is an Alexander the Great in Bermuda shorts. She is only 29, but for her there are very few records left to break, frontiers to push back or worlds to conquer. It wearies her, it depresses her. A couple of weeks ago she confided to the director of the Ladies PGA tour, Lennie Wirtz, that she was in a mood to retire.

"You can't," Wirtz protested, dismayed at the mere thought of the tour's biggest gate attraction vanishing from the scene. "There's a lot you haven't done yet. You don't even hold the record for the lowest 18-hole score."

So the other day it happened that Mickey Wright walked off the 18th green of the Hogan Park Golf Course in Midland, Texas, in a daze, but not in too much of a daze to go to a pay phone and call Lennie Wirtz. "You know that scoring record?" she said. "Mr. Wirtz, I've got it now."

What she had done was shoot a nine-under-par 62 that broke the old LPGA record of 64 held by Patty Berg and Ruth Jessen. She set the mark on a testing 6,286-yard course where the men's record is 66. Some of the best male amateurs in Texas had played from the same tees in a tournament three days before, and the lowest scores were three 69s. Mickey herself had done no better than a 73 and a 72 on the first two days of what was officially called the Tall City Open. Thus her 62 stands, without ifs, ands, or buts, as the lowest round of golf ever played by a woman.

Nor did her day end there. Her 62 only enabled her to tie Sherry Wheeler for first place in the tournament. Mickey went back out and birdied two straight holes to win a sudden-death playoff.

Mickey Wright is tall and blonde and she wears crisp, neat blouses, crisp, neat shorts, and crisp, neat eyeglasses. On a golf course she appears to be all business, like an upper-echelon executive's thoroughly efficient secretary. But in reality she is leaping from emotional cloud to

237

*The final putt goes in on the 18th green, giving Mickey
Wright her record round. Good for a par, it also enabled
her to tie for the lead in the tournament. She went on to
win the playoff.*

emotional cloud. She is such a long hitter, so accurate and so dedicated
to the game, that many observers are surprised she doesn't win every
tournament she enters. For Mickey Wright, however, the toughest person to beat has always been Mickey Wright.

"Sometimes I lose control of my emotions so completely," she has
said, "that I don't even know where I am or that it's me hitting the
ball."

The other week at Midland the emotional barometer had swung to
another extreme. An inner voice was not only telling her where she was
but that she could break the scoring record.

"It sounds cuckoo," she said later, "but I remember it clearly. I'd say
to myself: 'O.K., don't let it slip away a shot at a time. You have an
opportunity to shoot a really great round. Work hard. Bear down. Keep
going.' "

Ordinarily Mickey keeps her emotions to herself, but on this Sunday
she was feeling so high that she had to share the exhilaration with the
crowd that followed her. "I don't usually emote much in public," she
said, "but for some reason, after the first few holes, I'd grin and laugh
each time I tapped a putt in. And the crowd really seemed to be with
me. I've never felt so much electricity. Between shots the gallery was so
quiet I could hear myself breathe."

On the first tee on Sunday morning she had stood eleventh in the
tournament, ten shots behind the leader, Kathy Whitworth. She had
only the barest hope of materially improving her position. Practically
every hole on the Hogan Park course is a dogleg. The rough is sage,

mesquite and sand, the greens large and fast. Mickey had gambled recklessly on her two previous rounds trying to cut the corners of the doglegs but ending up in the sage-strewn rough instead. Now she resolved to play safe and keep the ball in the fairway.

On the first hole, a 457-yard par-5, she reached the green with a second shot that stopped only 18 inches from the pin for an easy eagle 3. She birdied the second hole with a tight wedge shot and the third with a 15-foot putt. This was a very fast start, but clubhouse grillrooms echo with stories about golfers who have started fast on the first three holes and fizzled on the next fifteen. Mickey Wright's round went into the golfing equivalent of overdrive on the 4th hole. To make another birdie, she had to roll her 25-foot putt into a cup that was on the side of a mound. "Son of a gun, it went right in," she said later. "Now I started getting scared. I knew I was onto something."

She certainly was. She had played many rounds like this before, when every drive was prodigiously long, when every iron shot bore directly toward the flagstick. But this day, for a change, her putting matched the rest of her game. After four pars, she rolled in a birdie putt of 12 feet on the 9th green. Her outgoing 30 tied the LPGA record. On the 10th she hit a courageous sand wedge off bare dirt to set up another birdie, and her momentum carried her smoothly past the only bogey of the day, on 11, where she missed the green with a five-iron and chipped weakly. She birdied the par-4, 407-yard 14th with a 15-foot putt, and another putt of 15 feet gave her a birdie on the 15th. Her last birdie came at the 17th, where she tapped in a curling eight-foot downhiller.

"Not until I stood on the 18th green," she said, "did it enter my mind that I could win." The record had been in her mind all along—which shows what interests Mickey Wright these days. She two-putted for a par on the 18th and then brought herself down to 11 under par for the day with the birdies on the two extra holes.

Mickey has only the barest recollection of accepting the winner's check of $1,350. She was in a warm fog, and the mist did not clear until the next day as she cruised along the highway toward Dallas in her new sedan. She put on the brakes, swung the car onto the gravel parking lot of a roadside cafe and fished in her purse for a piece of scratch paper. Most touring golf professionals can recall for years even the very routine rounds, club by club and putt by putt, but Mickey was not about to trust her precious 62 to anything so capricious as memory. She found a letter and on the back of it jotted down the number of every club she had used on her glorious round. Now the challenge falls to LPGA Director Wirtz. When Mickey feels in a mood to retire again, what can he tell her?

# A New Leading Lady

## Don Weiss

Golf Journal                                               August, 1965

A remarkable aspect of a women's golf championship is that it can be on the one hand a showcase of exceptional golfing skill and on the other an event of considerable informality. It can be, at the same time, both businesslike and casual.

It is thus more than fitting that the 1965 United States Women's Open champion should be a young lady such as Miss Carol Ann Mann of Towson, Maryland.

Here is a girl who, moments after holing out at the home green at the Atlantic City Country Club, would burst into a genuine torrent of tears; then moments later, in reference to her height of 6 feet 3 inches, ask with an impish twinkle in her eye: "Am I the longest shot who ever won the Open?"

Here is a girl who, in recounting a wedge chip she holed during the very crucial third round, would say: "I absolutely got goose bumps!", and in discussing a poor approach a few holes earlier: "I told my caddie both of us ought to apologize to the gallery."

But here also is a girl who can be precisely what she has chosen to be, a professional golfer. Two days before the start of the championship she was ill with a severe chest cold. Later, she felt so weakened she feared she might not make it through the first round. After 10 holes of that round, she was five strokes over par and struggling to keep her composure.

A lesser person might have given way to discouragement. That Miss Mann did not is evidenced by the fact that from the 11th hole until the end of the championship three days later, she played 62 holes in three under par on a fair but eminently testing golf course. Nothing less would have won for her, since the outcome was in doubt until the last hole when a well-played birdie 4 gave her a two-stroke margin over Mrs. Kathy Cornelius, the 1956 Champion, who had a final 69 for 292.

"Certainly I was disappointed in the way I started," Carol said later.

"I had been playing very well when I won the week before (the Lady Carling Open at Baltimore) and we all try so hard to be ready for the Open. Last year I was forced to miss it because I had back trouble and had to go into traction. This year I thought, 'Oh, no, not again.' I decided to keep my nose to the grindstone and see what happened."

What happened was that Miss Mann fought through to a 78 after her poor start, moved high into contention with a course record 70 the second day, opened a four-shot lead over the field with another 70 Saturday, and withstood Mrs. Cornelius' spirited challenge Sunday.

There were perhaps three "key" points in Miss Mann's victory—her third professional triumph since she left the amateur ranks in the fall of 1960. The first came during the third round when, paired with Mrs. Cornelius, she made consecutive birdies on the 13th, 14th and 15th holes. On the 13th, a 133-yard par 3, she hit an 8-iron to within four feet of the hole. On the long 14th she reached a greenside bunker in two, exploded to within two feet and holed for a 4. On the 15th she gambled with an approach shot out of a bad lie in the rough, carried the shot boldly over a large pond to heavy grass behind the green, then holed a 25-foot wedge chip coming back.

That shot not only gave her "goose bumps" but considerable momentum that carried her safely through two crises on Sunday's final round. Her cold and cough more troublesome than before, Carol spent a mostly sleepless Saturday night and began quite erratically Sunday. On the first four holes, she was in the rough six times and scrambling for every par. On the fifth tee, she pulled her drive into sandy rough on the left. Here she passed her second "key" point—lofting a 6-iron to the back of the putting surface and then holing a downhill, curling 18-footer for a birdie 3.

Immediately, the crispness of the previous two days returned to her game and kept her moving smoothly until the 70th hole. Here she drove badly to the right (as she had dreamed she would the night before). She barely cleared a ditch on her second, and was 12 feet below the hole with her third. At this point, Mrs. Cornelius was playing the last hole en route to her 3-under-par 69 for 292. A five would have dropped Miss Mann level with Mrs. Cornelius, but she resolutely holed the 12-footer she had for her par and maintained her one-stroke margin. A chip to two feet saved par on the 71st after she again missed the green. And two well-placed, long wood shots made her birdie 4 on the last hole look easy.

Mrs. Cornelius' challenge was highlighted by her remarkable play on the short holes: she was 6 under par for the twenty par-3 holes played, and had an incredible run of four straight 2s at the 163-yard eighth.

The new champion is 24, a left-hander in all but golf, and not at all reluctant to talk about her height—which makes her by far the tallest of the lady professionals ("I really like the attention. I guess I'm sort of a ham"). She was introduced to golf at age 11 by her father, Louis (Rip) Mann, who is 6-2. She has four brothers—Steve, 23, who is 6-2½; twins Gary (6-4) and Gale (6-6), 18 and heading for college; and Bunky, 14, who is over 5-7 and on the way up. Her mother, Ann, no longer plays golf although she is the only one of the family who has made a hole-in-one.

Although she is 6-3, Miss Mann keeps the ball relatively low, and this helped her cope with the wind that is such an important factor at Atlantic City. The wind can—and did—blow from six different directions, changing the way each hole played from day to day. Competitors were unanimous in hailing the course with its contrasting links and inland characteristics as one especially well suited for a championship such as the Women's Open. Much of the credit for the tournament's success should go to Leo Fraser, the president of the Atlantic City Country Club and Treasurer of the Professional Golfers' Association of America.

The best score in the championship was a 67 on the final round by Miss Margie Masters, the Australian professional. It matched the all-time single round record for the Women's Open set by Miss Judy Bell, an amateur, last year at San Diego. Miss Marilynn Smith, who has competed in all thirteen USGA Women's Opens, was third at 294, and Miss Mary Mills, the 1963 champion, was fourth at 295. Miss Susie Maxwell shared fifth place at 296 with the low amateur, Mrs. Helen Sigel Wilson, of Gladwyne, Pa., ten times Philadelphia champion and runner-up in the Women's Amateur championship in 1941 and 1948. Mrs. Wilson's four-round total was a record for an amateur in the Open.

# The Queen Steps Down

The New Yorker                                    August 8, 1965

This past July, Mary Kathryn (Mickey) Wright, the tall, blond, and handsome Californian who has been by far the most outstanding woman golfer of our day, returned to college after an absence of eleven years. To spell out this unusual sequence in a bit more detail, Miss Wright left Stanford in 1954, at the close of her freshman year, in order to pursue a career in professional golf, and now, having won all the honors there are to be won, she has, at the antediluvian age of thirty, entered the sophomore class of Southern Methodist University, in Dallas, her adopted home town, where for the past several seasons she has been affiliated with the Oak Cliff Country Club. (She has chosen to major in psychology—a decision that is not at all surprising when one stops to reflect on it, for the women's professional golf tour provides some of the country's top preparatory schooling for that field of study.) Miss Wright hopes that she will be able to play a number of tournaments during her summer vacations, but even so her retirement will be all but complete, and it brings to an end an era that began in 1958, when she established herself as something extraordinary by winning both the United States Women's Open and the Ladies' Professional Golf Association championship—the equivalent of the men's P.G.A. championship. From that year on, she dominated women's golf absolutely, just as Bobby Jones dominated men's amateur golf in the nineteen-twenties. For four straight seasons (1961 through 1964), she won the most tournaments, collected the most prize money, and produced the lowest scoring average on the women's circuit. She set new L.P.G.A. records in just about all categories: the most tournament victories in one season (thirteen, in 1963), the most prize money won in one season ($31,269.50, in 1963), the lowest score for a four-round tournament (275, with rounds of 68-68-70-69, in the Spokane Open in 1962), the lowest eighteen-hole score (62, with nines of 30 and 32, in the Tall City Open, in Midland, Texas, in 1964), and the lowest average score per round for one season (72.81, in 1963). During her professional career,

243

*The queen*

she won a total of sixty-five tournaments (including two this year, when an injured wrist severely hampered her play) and close to $200,000 in prize money. Both of these achievements are also records. In brief, just as it was Jones against the field, so it has been Wright against the field, and I suppose the only question that remains to be answered is whether she deserves to be ranked as the greatest woman golfer of all time. A good many sound golf observers think so. For my part, I would like to have a little more time to think it over, but I do know this much: there has never been a better woman golfer.

The probably obvious reason I am hedging on this matter is that prior to Miss Wright's arrival on the scene it was standard practice to regard Joyce Wethered, the English star of the nineteen-twenties, and the late Babe Didrikson Zaharias as being in a class by themselves among women golfers. Since each was phenomenal in her own way and incomparable in her own time, it seems to me that perhaps it is more judicious to rank Miss Wright alongside them, and not above them, in much the same manner that it has become customary to acknowledge Ben Hogan as the peer but not the superior of the two super-champions of earlier periods, Bobby Jones and Harry Vardon. Indeed, it occurs to me that before returning to Miss Wright we might do well to spend a moment or two talking about Miss Wethered and Mrs. Zaharias, for the passage of time has already rendered them into shadowy figures—Miss Wethered in particular. A slim girl just under six feet tall who learned the game on the links of Dornoch, she came into prominence at the age of eighteen, in 1920, when British golf was starting up again in earnest after the First World War. That year, her brother Roger, who was later to win the British Amateur championship, was the captain of the Oxford golf team, and it was the unreserved enthusiasm of Roger and his teammates for her golf that led her that summer to enter her first tournament of any importance, the English Ladies' championship. (Female golfers are always "ladies" in Britain; over here they're sometimes "ladies" and sometimes "women.") Hoping only to perform creditably, she was staggered when she won the tournament by defeating Cecil Leitch, the leading woman golfer of the day. (Miss Wethered subsequently played in four other English Ladies' championships and swept the lot.) In 1921, emboldened by this success, she entered the British Ladies' championship and made her way as far as the final, where she lost to Miss Leitch. Over the next four years, she won the British Ladies' three times, and then she decided that she had had her fill of tournament golf. In 1929, however, when an unusually large contingent of foreign stars, headed by Glenna Collett, three times the American champion, invaded Britain, Miss Wethered came out of retirement and scored a fourth victory in the British Ladies' by defeating Miss Collett, 3 and 1, in the thirty-six-hole final at St. Andrews in what could well be the finest match in the history of women's golf. Then she went into retirement again, emerging only to play in the annual autumn mixed-foursome tournament at Worplesdon, which is essentially a convocation of old golfing friends, and to make a brief exhibition tour of America as a professional in 1935, two years before she became Lady Heathcoat-Amory.

Miss Wethered's reputation rests not only on her record of winning nine of the twelve championships she played in during her abbreviated career—in 1921 she was beaten in the French Ladies', her only appearance in a foreign championship—but also on her abilities as a scorer and as a technician. At a time when the top women golfers were only just beginning to break 80 in competition over difficult courses, she usually went around comfortably in 73 or 75. For example, when she and Miss Collett first came up against each other, in the third round of the 1925 British Ladies', at Troon, the American girl rose to the occasion with the best golf of her life and was only one over par after fifteen holes, but by then the match was finished, 4 and 3, Miss Wethered having played the last ten holes in six under par. In their return match in the famous final at St. Andrews four years later, Miss Collett, again in marvellous form, went to the turn in the morning in 34 and stood 5 up. Thereupon Miss Wethered buckled down hard to her task and played the next eighteen holes—the last nine of the morning round and the first nine of the afternoon round—in 73, to take command of the match. The essence of her style, like Jones's, was fluidity and rhythm. There is no such thing, of course, as a natural golf swing—the movements must be mastered by practice—but Joyce Wethered made golf seem as natural and effortless as walking. Her thoughts on what made for a good golf swing were uncomplicated and well ahead of her time. She believed that the club should be taken back a shade inside the line of flight, that the first yard of the backswing set the tempo for the entire swing, that the hip pivot should be more restricted than the shoulder pivot, and that the downswing should be inaugurated by a movement of the hips to the left—all of which, as we now realize much more clearly than we did forty years ago, are fundamental to the correct swing. Most of the time, she played her wood shots with a relatively full swing, and, being a tall girl with a big arc, she hit the ball a long way, averaging about two hundred and twenty-five yards off the tee. On her iron shots, which flew in a low, drilling trajectory, like Gene Sarazen's, she took her hands back only shoulder-high and finished her swing with her hands again no higher than her shoulders; in fact, this is the picture that remains fixed in everyone's mind as most characteristic of her style. During her matches, she talked very little to her opponent and gave the impression of cool detachment, yet actually she was anything but relaxed, and the wear and tear on her nerves forced her to rest for two weeks after each tournament and leave the game strictly alone. This strain was, of course, what underlay her decision to quit competitive golf so early. "A less active role has always suited me perfectly well and made possible the idea of retirement. I can [now] enter into the emotions of the game and enjoy them just as I like without having to preserve a state of elaborate calmness as a player over incidents which are in reality causing me acute excitement and probably no little apprehension and alarm."

As is probably apparent, Miss Wethered was shy and extremely modest. Not long ago, on rereading her book "Golfing Memories and Methods," I was especially struck by the elaborate circumlocution she devised to conceal the fact that in the final of the 1924 British Ladies' she had routed Mrs. Frank Cautley, 7 and 6. "I came in to lunch three up, and the day ended in a terrible deluge of rain," she wrote. "Neither of us, probably, was very sorry when the game finished on the twelfth green." I mention this aspect of Miss Wethered's nature because it presents such a pronounced contrast to the temperament and demeanor of Babe Didrikson Zaharias. Having grown up in public, as it were, after attracting universal attention as the nineteen-year-old track-and-field sensation of the 1932 Olympic Games, Mrs. Zaharias was a happy extrovert who loved the spotlight. At the end of a round of golf, she would linger at the clubhouse chatting with one and all, and if she felt that things were too sombre, she would grab her harmonica and launch into an impromptu concert. She was, to be sure, a beautifully coördinated athlete, but the attribute that made her so formidable a competitor was her fantastic confidence. Her golfing friend Peggy Kirk Bell once told me a story that nicely illustrates this. Shortly after Mrs. Bell had turned professional, she was invited by Mrs. Zaharias to be her partner in a rather important four-ball event. On the morning of their first match, Mrs. Bell had a bad attack of jitters; all she could think about was that she might play very poorly and drag her illustrious partner down to defeat with her. "Forget it," Mrs. Zaharias told her. "I can beat any two players in this tournament by myself. If I need any help, I'll let you know."

Mrs. Zaharias had what amounted to two separate careers in golf. The first began in 1936, when she barnstormed around the country with Sarazen and other well-established men professionals, playing one-day stands in which she demonstrated that she could regularly drive the ball two hundred and fifty yards and could occasionally hit it where she was aiming. After a while, she got down to the tedious business of really learning how to play golf—a game in which natural athletes have an advantage but only after they have toiled enough to master a technique that is quite different from anything required in other games. In 1944, she applied for and received reinstatement as an amateur, and her second career began at the close of the Second World War. She won our Women's Amateur championship in 1946, and the following spring, at Gullane, in Scotland, became the first American ever to win the British Ladies' championship. Then she turned professional again. Between 1948 and 1955, her last year as a player—she died in 1956—Mrs. Zaharias won thirty-one professional tournaments, including three U.S. Women's Opens, the last one in 1954. That Open may have constituted this amazing and gallant woman's greatest performance in golf. A year earlier, she had undergone an operation for cancer, but she nevertheless came through with four altogether superb rounds (72-71-73-75) to finish twelve strokes ahead of her nearest competitor. Throughout her career, one of her most valuable assets, naturally, was the distance she could clout the ball. To cite just one example, on the fifteenth hole at Gullane, which is five hundred and forty yards long, she reached the green one afternoon, assisted by a slight following breeze, with a drive and a 4-iron. She was only a moderately large woman—five feet seven, a hundred and forty pounds—but she had exceptional strength and timing. While her swing was not an aesthetic treat, like Miss Wethered's, it was grooved and efficient. The best thing about it was that however hard she hit the ball, she could not hook it—just about the most desirable failing a golfer could have. (The explanation was that she took the club back on the outside as she rocked into her swing and then brought it directly up; as her hands moved down and through the ball, she never allowed her right hand to cross over her left.) There was a good deal more to her golf than mere power, though. What she strove for on all her shots was feel and control, and, as a result, her short game—particularly her wedge play and her chipping—was definitely superior to that of her competition. "Not many people noticed it, but off the golf course Babe was extremely dainty with her hands," Mrs. Bell, who was very close to her over the years, remarked not long ago. "She would pick up a cigarette as if she were playing jackstraws. When she lifted a fork or a knife or any other small object, she would move it around delicately and feel its weight and balance. I asked her about this once, and she told me, 'It helps my golf.' "

By a happy coincidence, in the 1954 U.S. Women's Open, which was Mrs. Zaharias's last championship, she was paired in the double round on the last day with Mickey Wright, a tall (five-foot-nine), slender, exceedingly nice-looking nineteen-year-old amateur who had won the Girls' Junior championship two years before and was making her début in the Open. Miss Wright was very impressive that day. She kept up with her partner off the tee, broke 80 on both rounds, tied for fourth place, and beat all the other amateurs. This was heady stuff for a young girl, and it had a considerable influence on her decision to leave college and turn professional. At that time, Miss Wright had been playing golf for seven years. The daughter of a well-to-do San Diego lawyer, she had taken her first lessons, at twelve, from John Bellante, the pro at the La Jolla Country Club, who also taught Gene Littler the ABCs of golf. However, the instructor who really developed her swing was Harry Pressler, the pro at the San Gabriel Country Club, outside Los Angeles. Every Saturday for two years—the years she was fourteen and fifteen—Miss Wright drove a hundred and twenty-five miles up to San Gabriel with her mother and took an hour's lesson with Pressler. Basically, he set out to teach her how to hit the ball with the same kind of vigorous hand action that the best men players use; most women tend to sweep the ball away with a swing that is nearly all arms, and are therefore rather short hitters. To this end, he emphasized three points for his young pupil to work on: at the beginning of the downswing her weight should start moving across her right foot to her left foot; on the downswing, also, her right elbow should be tucked in close in front of the right hip; and, third, as her hands moved toward the ball, her wrists should remain cocked as long as possible. Miss Wright adhered faithfully to these three fundamentals throughout her career. At certain periods when her swing went sour, she sought out various professionals whom she respected—chiefly Harvey Penick, Les Bolstad, Stan Kertes, Paul Runyan, and Earl Stewart, Jr.—and asked them to check on how well she was executing the moves she wanted to maintain as the core of her swing. She was never seriously tempted to alter the guiding mechanics of the swing she grew up with.

When Miss Wright joined the women's professional tour in 1955, the goal she set for herself, like any red-blooded American girl, was to become the best woman golfer who ever lived. During her first seasons on the tour, she was grim and fretful, beneath an innate politeness, because she was not at all sure she could come anywhere close to her ambition. For one thing, she was reminded daily of how far the veterans of the tour surpassed her in skill. The Babe was gone by then, but the other members of what had come to be known as the Big Four—Patty Berg, Louise Suggs, and Betty Jameson—were still very much in evidence. (By the way, I would without any hesitation name Miss Berg as the most accomplished woman shotmaker—and, for that matter, one of the very best shotmakers, male or female—that I have ever had the pleasure of watching.) For another thing, Miss Wright was having her troubles with her own game. While she hit her full shots farther than any other player on the tour, she was generally erratic. In trying to achieve the maximum delay in uncocking her wrists, she developed a habit of dropping her hands too sharply at the start of the downswing and hitting the ball with a flailing action. On top of this, her short game was very weak. "Mickey had no touch at all on her chip shots, and she was absolutely the worst putter I have ever seen in professional golf," Betsy Rawls, her closest friend on the tour, recalled this summer. "Her mental attitude was all wrong. She was preoccupied with playing flawlessly from tee to green. If she didn't hit fifteen of the eighteen greens in the regulation stroke, she was disgusted. She had complete contempt for scrambling. It took her at least two years to learn to respect the short game and realize that even the top players have to be able to get down in two from off the green. Then her chipping and putting started to improve, and, of course, her scoring did."

In 1956, her second year on the tour, Miss Wright won her first professional tournament—the Jacksonville Open. She won three tournaments in 1957, five in 1958 (including the U.S. Women's Open), four in 1959 (including the U.S. Women's Open), and six in 1960. In 1961, she really arrived. She won ten tournaments that season, but it was the quality of her play—especially in the Women's Open, which she won for the third time—that revealed her as a golfer eminently worthy of comparison with Joyce Wethered and Babe Zaharias. That year's Open was held on the Lower Course of the Baltusrol Golf Club, in Springfield, New Jersey—a difficult, heavily bunkered layout over arduous terrain that measured 6,372 yards for the championship and played a good deal longer. Miss Wright began with a 72, even par, but an 80 on her second round, mainly because of poor putting, left her four strokes behind the leaders at the halfway mark. On the third day, when the last thirty-six holes were played, she moved out in front of the field with a spectacular 69 in the morning and then added a very solid 72 to finish six strokes ahead of the runner-up, Miss Rawls. En route to her 69, she had no fewer than six birdies, but, in a way, her closing 72 was every bit as brilliant, for she was on every green except two in the regulation stroke; the difference was that she needed only twenty-eight putts in the morning and took two putts on every green in the afternoon. These figures, eloquent as they are, do not begin to suggest the near perfection of Miss Wright's play on the double round. Throughout a long day of pressure, swinging as fluently as if she were on a practice tee, she boomed one long drive after another down the middle of the narrow fairways. For all her length, she had to use a lot of club to get home on her approaches—3-irons, 4-irons, 5-irons, and 6-irons, for the most part—but on hole after hole, hitting very pure shots, she put the ball within twenty feet of the pin. Had she been holing putts in the afternoon, she could have been around in 66, easily. It can be stated categorically, I believe, that no other woman has ever played a long, exacting course quite as magnificently as Miss Wright did that last day at Baltusrol. In fact, I can think of only one comparable exhibition of beautifully sustained golf over thirty-six holes in a national championship—Ben Hogan's last two rounds at Oakland Hills in the 1951 Open.

After her remarkable performance at Baltusrol, Miss Wright went on to become an even more proficient golfer. The next three years, she led the L.P.G.A. tour in every department; indeed, her domination was so complete that a tournament became news only when she lost it. Everything considered, her competitive ardor held up well. Whenever she was in contention in a tournament, she was able to summon the shots she needed to carry the day. In the 1964 Women's Open, she had to par the last hole, a tough 395-yard par 4, to gain a tie with Ruth Jessen, and she did it, after pushing her 2-iron approach into a greenside bunker, by exploding six feet from the pin and then rapping the putt into the center of the cup; she won the playoff with a 70, an almost errorless round. During those years, Miss Wright could have made a small fortune if she had wanted to, because golf clubs around the country were clamoring for Mickey Wright personal appearances and would gladly have paid her upward of five hundred dollars for an afternoon's work, but she turned down nearly all these offers. In temperament and general sensibility, she is very much closer to Joyce Wethered than to Babe Zaharias, and the thought of complicating an already punishing schedule just to make money appalled her. A highly self-critical and emotional girl, she masked her feelings so well on the golf course that she presented a picture of unruffled calm, but playing the role of the queen had no attraction for her, and off the course she went her way quietly, as she always had. Her idea of a gala evening was to have dinner with a few friends, preferably of an intellectual bent, who were entertaining talkers. Between rounds and tournaments, she spent a good deal of her spare time listening to music—she always carried a portable recordplayer on the tour—and, in addition, she read exhaustively, studied French and the guitar, and occasionally went fishing. As far as her golf went, she was not a particularly avid practicer, but, like many of the women professionals, she was fascinated by the theory of the swing, and she loved to articulate her thoughts on it in long, rounded sentences.

Then, during the 1964 season, professional golf quite suddenly began to lose its appeal for Miss Wright. Though she continued to maintain her high standard of play, the constant pressure of knowing that she was expected to win every tournament she entered finally wore her down so badly that she developed ulcers. By 1964, moreover, she had been leading the nomadic life for ten full years, and she found that she was enjoying the off-season months in Dallas, where she shares an apartment with two girls who are social workers, more than the long, arid stretches on the tournament circuit. There was one other reason for her change of attitude—a most important one. She had done everything she had set out to do in golf, and her enthusiasm was waning. (One day last autumn, she mentioned this to Leonard Wirtz, the tournament director of the L.P.G.A., and he astutely called her attention to the fact that there was one record she didn't hold—the lowest score for eighteen holes. In her very next tournament, she shot that incredible 62.) For all these reasons, she had her mind pretty well made up a year ago that she would carry on for one more season and then retire. She would naturally have liked to go out in a blaze of glory, but last winter she was unlucky enough to suffer an injury to her left wrist, which she had sprained the previous autumn, and she had to favor it conspicuously even in the two tournaments she managed to win. In June, a fortnight before the Women's Open, which was the tournament she had been waiting for all year, the injury—a form of tendonitis—became so painful that she couldn't hit a ball without wincing. She rested her wrist until it was time to go to the Atlantic City Country Club, where the Open was being held, but after her first practice round her hand was in such bad shape that she had no alternative but to withdraw from the championship. It was a very hard way to step down.

After Bobby Jones retired, at twenty-eight, in 1930, following his Grand Slam, he played no tournament golf until he appeared in the first Masters championship in 1934. Everyone was wondering, of course, whether he would then be able to take up where he had left off and lead the field, but the best he could do was tie for thirteenth. In his subsequent appearances in the Masters he was never a threat. He had been out of the crucible of competition too long, and, as he readily acknowledged, had lost the knack of concentrating on his shots under the strain of tournament conditions. In Mickey Wright's case, it is difficult to predict what effect her present plan to play serious golf only during her summer vacations will have on her game. One might logically suppose that she would have some trouble regaining her old concentration, but ten months away from the lists is not three years, and I don't think that either her rivals or her devoted following would be exactly bowled over if she won a couple of tournaments next summer.

# The Babe in Retrospect

## Enid Wilson

"The Golfer's Bedside Book"          B.T. Batsford, Ltd., 1965


Mildred Ella Didrikson, subsequently Mrs. George Zaharias (pronounced Zar-harris) and "The Babe", was a legendary figure in track and field and in other sports before she occupied a similar position in the world of golf. A great athlete and a fine woman, she died of cancer at the age of forty-two. Since then there has been some controversy as to her status in the hierarchy of the great women golfers, but none can dispute that, when she passed away in the autumn of 1956 after a prolonged and valiant battle with the dread disease, she had established herself as the outstanding competitor of her time.

The dynamic personality of The Babe was largely responsible for the success and development of the Ladies' Professional Golf Association in America. Her phenomenal power proved a great draw for spectators, and one of her delights was to wisecrack with the galleries. She attracted the limelight and adored it, and an example of her outlook may be gathered from her remark one morning to the starter on the East Course at Wentworth just as she was about to drive off in a tournament. Babe spotted his gesture of admonition towards an over-zealous photographer who wished to get an action shot. "I would have worried if he didn't want my photograph", she remarked, and the picture was duly taken.

With the passing years there has grown up a generation who never saw The Babe, and to them she is a mythical figure, the first American to win the British Ladies' championship. Of her early days and background they are completely ignorant, apart from knowing that before she turned her attention to golf, Mildred Didrikson broke world records and made history in the Olympic Games at Los Angeles in 1932. There she won gold medals in the javelin and hurdles; she also broke the record for the high jump by several inches, but the judges would not allow this to stand because she used the then controversial style known as the Western roll.

*Possibly the greatest female athlete of all time, Babe Didrikson is shown here on July 31, 1932, just prior to setting a world record in the javelin toss of 143 feet and 4 inches. She was eighteen years old. She also set a world record in the 80-meter hurdles.*

As her maiden name of Didrikson would indicate, she came of Scandinavian stock. Her parents were Norwegians who began their married life in Oslo. Ole Didrikson was for a time a seafaring man, and during one of his voyages he was attracted by Port Arthur in Texas on the Gulf of Mexico. His wife, Hannah Marie, approved of the idea of emigrating, and their family had grown to three by the time they had saved enough money to go to America.

When the Didriksons made their home in Port Arthur, Ole went to work in a furniture factory. The family increased, there were twins; then in June, 1914, Babe was born, and she was followed by another child, so there were seven young Didriksons, five girls and two boys. Before Babe's fourth birthday, they had moved to Beaumont, and it was there ten years later that she began to make a name for herself as a star on the Beaumont High School basketball team. Her one big stroke of luck was being born in a land where there were plenty of opportunities for those with outstanding athletic abilities, and although her early days were fraught with poverty, she came of a happy family. On leaving school she went to work for an insurance company in Dallas, where she paid five dollars a month for a room and sent more than half her salary home.

The story goes that it was on a driving range in Dallas that she made her debut as a golfer, and in keeping with the many legends of her fabulous athletic prowess, she is reputed to have swatted the ball 250 yards on her first attempt. During the 1932 Olympics at Los Angeles, Babe was the darling of the sportswriters, and it was they who took her out on a golf course, where she proceeded to astonish them by her powerful drives.

After the Olympics The Babe had several tempting offers from firms interested in publicity promotions. Acceptance meant the loss of her amateur status as an athlete, but the bait proved too tempting. Among other things, she did a variety turn on the stage in Chicago, and was lined up for a tour of the big cities. Although her act went down well, she began to pine for fresh air and an out-of-doors occupation, so she quit the theatre and returned to basketball. By then she had made up her mind to learn to play and to win the United States Women's Amateur championship within three years. When she made this decision, she thought she had enough cash put by, but it soon dwindled and she returned to her old job with the insurance company in Dallas. To augment her income she tried her hand at baseball and tennis. Then, after watching Bobby Jones in an exhibition match, her desire to excel at golf was rekindled. Her firm co-operated handsomely by arranging for her to become a member of the Dallas Country Club and to take lessons from the club professional, George Aulbach.

In the autumn of 1934, The Babe entered her first tournament, the Fort Worth Invitational, and made headlines by winning the medal with a score of 77. However, she was eliminated in an early round of the match play. She then set siege on the Texas State title the following spring, and during the week-ends practised up to sixteen hours a day. The venue of the tournament was the River Oaks Country Club, in Houston, and Babe achieved her ambition by defeating Mrs. Dan Chandler two up in the final over thirty-six holes. Her feat received country-wide publicity, which was unfortunate because three weeks later the United States Golf Association ruled that she was a professional, and declared her ineligible to participate in amateur events.

So, in the spring of 1935, Babe signed up with a sporting goods company and was booked to go on a tour of exhibition matches with Gene Sarazen. She could not have had a more understanding partner, and Gene spent a great deal of time helping her to improve her game.

During that tour, Babe twice played in matches against Miss Joyce Wethered. At Oak Park, Chicago, Britain's greatest woman golfer was paired with Horton Smith, and the scores of the quartette were Sarazen and Horton Smith both 71, Miss Wethered 78, and Babe 88. Meadowbrook was the course of their other encounter, and on that occasion Miss Wethered was paired with George Nagell. The scores were Sarazen 72, Nagell 73, Miss Wethered 77, and Babe 81.

Two more contrasting characters than Joyce Wethered and The Babe could not be imagined, and their methods were also totally dissimilar. The perfection of Miss Wethered's timing and her effortless swing, control, and artistry were lost on The Babe, who was then more concerned with getting distance than anything else. Miss Wethered's impression of the young American was that she had not had sufficient time in which to polish her short game. The Babe was then too inexperienced to appreciate the English woman's skill, and her recollection of those exhibition matches was that she could hit as far with a two-iron as Miss Wethered did with a driver.

There was nothing in the rules to prevent a woman from entering the Los Angeles Open, a 72-hole medal event for which there was no qualifying test. In January, 1938 the idea of playing in it appealed to The Babe, and the officials arranged for her to play with the Reverend C. P. Erdman, a Presbyterian minister, and George Zaharias, a professional wrestler. It was the beginning of the romance between Mildred Didrickson and George Zaharias. They announced their engagement in the summer and were married the following December.

*The climax of a memorable week that endeared Babe Zaharias to the British people. She was the first American to win the British Ladies' championship.*

Because of her renown as an athlete and the many different sports in which she had competed against men, the majority of people were apt to gain a wrong impression of Mildred Zaharias. Most tended to imagine her as a big-boned, overly muscular, strident-voiced Amazon, whereas, in fact, anyone meeting her for the first time would have had no idea that she was endowed with an abnormal physique. Above average height, slender and straight-backed, The Babe moved gracefully. Although she was generally photographed in sports clothes, which were not always becoming, she took a great interest in how she dressed. She had done so from childhood when she often made her own clothes.

In the autumn of 1939, The Babe was anxious to improve her golf with further competition, but only two tournaments were open to her, the Western and the Texas Opens. With George earning enough to give her all the golf she wanted, they came to the decision that the best thing she could do would be to send in an application to the United States Golf Association requesting reinstatement as an amateur. This course remained open to her as she had not been a professional for five years, but time was running out and her application had to go forward before May, 1940. The Babe had to wait three years before she became eligible to compete in amateur events. Before this probationary time expired, the war had put an end to the traditional national championships.

It was not until 1946 that The Babe played in her first U.S. Women's Amateur championship, which was held at the Southern Hills Country Club in Tulsa, Oklahoma. The match-play stages followed a 36-holes qualifying test which reduced the field to thirty-two. Dorothy Kirby headed the qualifiers with 152, Louise Suggs was second with 154, and Babe's score of 156 put her in third position. A series of easy victories brought her to the final, and there she annihilated Mrs. Clara Sherman, 11 and 9. Before winning the national title, The Babe had captured the Trans-Mississippi, Broadmoor Invitational, and the All-American tournaments, and she concluded the season by winning the Texas Open to put together a run of five prestige events.

In the spring of 1947, she mopped up the Florida tournaments as well as the Titleholders and the North and South. When she had notched ten more victories to make it fifteen in succession, she looked abroad for further worlds to conquer. The obvious plum was the British Ladies' championship which had never been won by an American.

When The Babe arrived at Gullane on the east coast of Scotland in early June, there were still evidences of the exceptionally severe winter. The frost had not worked out of the ground, so the top surface was unusually soft and heavy. These conditions suited her admirably, and the tremendous carry of her drives were utterly disconcerting to her opponents. She often out-drove them by 100 yards. An instance of her power came in her match with Miss Frances Stephens. On the 540-yard fifteenth hole, Babe's second shot with a 4-iron pitched over the back of the green. Another instance of her tremendous power was her method of dealing with the fifth at Gullane, some 460 yards uphill. She carried the corner of the dogleg with her drive and flipped her approach with a wedge onto the green.

On the tee, Babe stood straight up and, from a square stance, delivered all the power she could muster. Her only mannerism was the curious one of licking the thumb of the glove on her left hand, which she then wiped on the slate-blue corduroy slacks she wore throughout the championship. Her swing was too forceful to be pretty, and many of her strokes finished way off line. When they did, it didn't matter, for she had the strength to get home with her seconds from almost any position. After the instruction she had received in her early days from Sarazen, bunkers held no terrors for her.

The main road from Edinburgh to North Berwick runs through Gullane, and the first tee of Gullane's Number One Course is close to where the road bends at the beginning of the main street of the village. The tee is surrounded by a fence of white posts with a top rail on which the natives like to lean and watch the players drive off. Babe's custom was to walk down to the course from her hotel at the far end of the village and to vault lightly over the top rail onto the teeing ground. She did this without any perceptible effort to the considerable amazement of town folks.

Having spent so much of her life travelling, Babe was in no way disconcerted by having to play on a type of course that she hadn't seen before. She was supremely confident of winning, buoyed by her unbroken run of successes over the past year. She came to Britain at a time when the post-war austerities were still prevailing. The older players were past their peak, and the up-and-coming players were seeking to find their feet. Miss Helen Nimmo, a member of Gullane, was her opponent in the first round, and Babe beat her 6 and 5. She then met Mrs. Sheppard, a sturdy English Midlander with a good record in match play, but Mrs. Sheppard's courage and fine short game were of no avail against Babe who beat her 4 and 2 . In the third round, an ex-Irish champion, Mrs. Val Reddan, who had represented Britain in the Curtis Cup match at the Essex County Club in Massachusetts in 1938, was hammered by the American, 6 and 4. Another Scot, Mrs. Cosmo Falconer, who had represented her country (and Britain also) against France, fared slightly worse, losing 7 and 5. Thus The Babe had accounted for four highly experienced golfers in the early stages of the championship. Fortune then decreed that her remaining opponents should be young ones.

In the fifth round Babe had her hardest match and that was with Miss Frances Stephens, whose seeming frailty made people wonder if she would have the stamina to stay in championship golf. The slender Lancashire girl stuck doggedly with Babe for twelve holes, but in the end she went down, 3 and 2.

Babe was through to the semi-finals, and confronted the Scottish champion, Miss Jean Donald, daughter of a local doctor. All Edinburgh and the East of Scotland had been waiting for this meeting of champions, but, although Babe revelled in the size of the crowd and was inspired by it, the effect on Miss Donald was quite different. She began by taking three putts. The American then had birdies on the second, third and fourth, and romped away to win 7 and 5. Her score that afternoon was five under even 4s.

Meanwhile, a strong, determined player from Middlesex, Miss Jacqueline Gordon, had been making her way through the other half of the draw, thereby vindicating her selection in the English team the previous week. On the morning of the final, Babe set off on her accustomed walk down the village street to the first tee, wearing a pair of pink and white check Bermuda shorts. Before she got to the course she was intercepted by the Captain of the Ladies' Section of the Gullane Club, and persuaded to return to her hotel and change into the blue corduroys which she had worn previously all that week.

Miss Gordon was not in the least intimidated by her foe that day and played the first nine in 36, one under par. A birdie on the eleventh enabled her to lead The Babe by two holes, but by the end of the morning round they were all square, both players having gone round in 75. When they resumed, Miss Gordon faltered on the first hole. Babe grasped the initiative and delivered a mortal thrust with an eagle 3 on the second, and when the English girl slipped again on the third, it was apparent that the championship was going to America. Miss Gordon did her best, but the situation was hopeless, and Babe ultimately triumphed, 5 up and 4 to play.

On her return to the United States, The Babe received such tempting offers she was prevailed upon to turn professional again. The greatest of her victories was the U.S. Women's Open championship at the Salem Country Club, in Peabody, Massachusetts, in 1954 when she won that event for the third time. The previous summer she had endured a colostomy. Two years later The Babe was gone.

# Catherine Lacoste: An Amateur Wins the U.S. Women's Open

## Frank Hannigan

Golf Journal                                                    August, 1967

Any amateur who dares to dream of winning an Open competition confronts two obstacles, one mechanical, the other mental.

The first, although formidable, can be cleared by the most talented amateurs, for, despite all the gibberish in golf's literature on the subject of mechanics, there is no unfathomable mystery about striking the ball. The very gifted young amateurs—Bob Jones, Jack Nicklaus, JoAnne Gunderson—were *mechanically* capable of winning an Open while still in their teens.

Where the best amateurs tend to run aground in an Open is on the dark and mysterious psychological side of the game. Rare indeed is the amateur who can truly convince himself that victory against the professionals is a distinct possibility.

The very word "professional" takes on a mystique that conspires against amateurs. The expression "old pro" was coined not to define antiquity but efficiency. When someone consoles you by saying you missed a putt "on the pro side", you are meant to believe that you at least gave it a chance.

The ability of Miss Catherine Lacoste, of Paris, France, to crack the mental barrier as an amateur is what made her victory in the 1967 United States Women's Open championship at Hot Springs, Virginia, so memorable and so stunning.

Indeed, after two rounds, when she led by five strokes, Miss Lacoste somehow had managed to reverse completely the now time-honored relationship of amateur vs. professional. Up ahead of her on the course were the tournament-hardened professionals—cautious, uncertain, not playing up to their potential. Looking back, they caught glimpses of Miss Lacoste bouncing along, poised, alert and, above all, very aggressive.

The grandeur of what she was doing finally affected even Miss Lacoste's blithe spirit. Midway through the final round she began to play a series of sorry shots. Her lead dwindled from seven strokes to one. Then, on the 71st hole, she tapped some hidden resource and came up

*The youngest player, the first foreigner,
and the first amateur to win the U.S.
Women's Open.*

with a birdie, followed it with a par on the final hole, and finished with
a total of 294—two strokes ahead of the runners-up, Miss Beth Stone
and Miss Susie Maxwell.

Just like that, Miss Lacoste, only 22, became the youngest player, the
first foreigner, and the first amateur to win the United States Women's
Open.

Amateurs have defeated the lady professionals before, of course. In
1946 Miss Louise Suggs won both the Women's Western Open and the
Augusta Titleholders championship as an amateur. Peggy Kirk Bell
also won the Titleholders as an amateur, but it's a rare thing.

The 1967 U.S. Women's Open was played on the lovely Cascades
Course of the Virginia Hot Springs Golf and Tennis Club, where the
Curtis Cup Match was held a year ago. This really splendid course calls
for accuracy off the tee because trees and water hazards lurk in the
drive zones; it calls for even more accuracy on the approach shots because many of the greens are flanked by severe slopes. The greens were
firm and fast, as prescribed by the USGA.

On the eve of the championship the experts thought the Cascades
Course would be ideal for the skilled women players because it stressed
control, their strong suit. What happened was that the venerable Cas-

course beat everyone except Miss Lacoste. Many players exercised an unwonted degree of caution. Those fine, firm greens seemed to inhibit most of the field.

On the other hand, there was Miss Lacoste up on her toes, going all out on every drive and then flying her approach shots right at the flag without regard to hole locations. She hit her iron shots in an extraordinarily high trajectory, à la Nicklaus. On the greens she was boldness personified. The putt for the crucial birdie, a 10-footer on the 71st hole, was typical in that it was struck so hard that it jumped after hitting the back of the cup. Her élan inevitably led to a number of three-to-five-foot putts coming back. Nothing to those for Miss Lacoste! She just rapped them hard and at the back of the hole.

How this youngster was able to harness what must have been swirling emotions and make them work for her and against the seasoned field is a question that only Miss Lacoste, and perhaps not even she, can answer.

We can conjecture, however, about two factors that might have been helpful. The first has to do with her heritage. She is the daughter of champions, so winning at games must have seemed natural to her, even as a child. Her father is René Lacoste, the French tennis genius, who won at both Wimbledon and Forest Hills in the 1920s. Her mother is the former Simone Thion de la Chaume, who won the French Women's golf title six times and the British Women's championship in 1927.

The second factor had to do with the way she managed her affairs during the championship when it wouldn't have been surprising to find a youngster, thousands of miles from home, brooding endlessly about her chances. What she actually did was to play with children almost constantly when she wasn't on the Cascades Course, the children being those of Mr. and Mrs. William Preston, of Charlottesville, Virginia, whom she met at the Cascades Inn in Hot Springs. She went swimming, rode horseback, played a bit of tennis, bowled, and danced. As she said later, she never spent a minute in her room except when she was good and tired and ready to go to sleep.

Miss Lacoste's triumph, epic though it was, was not a complete surprise to those familiar with her career. She had led the French team to victory over the United States in the 1964 Women's World Amateur Team championship in France, when she tied for low individual score; in 1965, during a brief visit to the United States, she finished 14th in the Women's Open and placed fifth in a Ladies' PGA tournament; earlier this summer she won the French championship for the first time.

At Hot Springs, where she arrived to practice nine days in advance, Miss Lacoste opened with a par round of 71 to tie for second place, one stroke behind the leader, Miss Sandra Haynie. She followed with a superb round of 70 on the second day. She hit the first fourteen greens in regulation figures. Her lead at the end of the round, which was five strokes, would have been greater had she not found the water on the par-5 16th, where she made a 7. Susie Maxwell and Margie Masters were tied for second at 146.

Miss Lacoste faltered on the first nine of the third round, going four over par, but her pursuers were not able to take full advantage of this. So, when Miss Lacoste rallied with a 34 coming in for 74, her total of 215 was good enough to maintain a five-stroke lead over Miss Masters. Miss Maxwell, Beth Stone, and Murle Lindstrom trailed by seven strokes.

In the final round, Miss Stone and Miss Suggs mounted the most serious threats to the leader. Miss Lacoste finished with a 79. Miss Stone, only one stroke behind with three holes to play, parred in. Miss Suggs, who had begun the round nine strokes behind, was even par for the day through fifteen holes and had made up eight of those shots when her third on the sixteenth imbedded itself in the embankment of a water hazard. Had the ball carried just a foot more, Miss Suggs would have been close to the hole.

It will be interesting to see whether Catherine Lacoste's success will carry over to other skilled amateurs in the Women's Opens that lie ahead. On one hand is the realization that only six amateurs survived the 36-hole cut, fewer than in any previous Women's Open. On the other hand is the feeling that among the ranks of the women amateurs there are many gifted players. Only two members of the last five Curtis Cup Teams are no longer amateurs; over the same period, eight members of the men's Walker Cup teams have left the amateur ranks.

**Leaders in the 1967 Women's Open**

| | | |
|---|---|---|
| Catherine Lacoste* | 71-70-74-79—294 | Pin |
| Susie Maxwell | 71-75-76-74—296 | $3,600.00 |
| Beth Stone | 75-76-71-74—296 | 3,600.00 |
| Sandra Haynie | 70-79-77-71—297 | 1,033.33 |
| Murle Lindstrom | 75-74-73-75—297 | 1,033.33 |
| Louise Suggs | 76-74-74-73—297 | 1,033.33 |
| Margie Masters | 73-73-74-80—300 | 750.00 |
| Sharon K. Miller | 76-80-74-71—301 | 630.00 |
| Clifford Ann Creed | 75-75-76-75—301 | 630.00 |
| Marilynn Smith | 75-77-72-77—301 | 630.00 |
| Judy Torluemke | 78-81-70-73—302 | 550.00 |
| Shirley Englehorn | 73-74-76-79—302 | 550.00 |
| Dorothy Germain* | 75-78-79-70—302 | Pin |
| Sybil Griffin | 71-79-75-78—303 | 520.00 |

*Amateur

# Catching Up with Virginia Van Wie (I)

## John Husar

The Chicago *Tribune*                    February 16, 1968

The lady was rubbing the dust from an old hickory-shafted golf club while on a nearby wall hung pictures of a willowy, pretty girl holding a huge trophy thirty-four years ago. "Here," she said, "try this. See how light it feels." Not only was it light but solid, perhaps still solid enough to help someone else win a national title.

The lady, looking not much different from the girl in those pictures, took another club, gripped it gently, drew back and swung. From the hum, one could have sworn there was a bee on the mat. It seemed a perfect swing, but Virginia Van Wie wasn't satisfied. "Time marches on," she grinned, replacing the club and resuming an interview-turned-golf-lesson in her studio at 2653 E. 75th St. in Chicago.

Miss Van Wie, once acclaimed as the world's greatest female golfer, dropped out of sight in 1934 after winning her third United States title in a row, only to turn up twenty-one years later as a teaching pro in Chicago. In between came the ownership of an ice cream parlor in Florida and, later, a job as market researcher for a Chicago foods company. "I had a chance to turn pro when I was twenty-four," she said, "but I didn't want that life. After ten years in golf I'd had it. When I won the championship that third time, I really proved to myself that I had earned it, that it wasn't a lucky break. After that, what was left?"

Apparently very little to a woman whose first love, admittedly, is golf. Her years away from the sport produced mainly a gnawing desire to spread the gospel of the late Ernest Jones, one of the game's great teachers and the man whose lessons fashioned her championship game.

"He taught me the joy of the game," she said. "He preached that 'Golf is meant to be a pleasurable pastime and not a mental tragedy.'"

She teaches students to swing naturally and not worry about keeping the left arm straight or the head still. "You might say I'm a devoted Ernest Jones disciple. All I want is to pass on what to me is the greatest method of hitting the ball correctly."

# A Women's Open That Was Won—Not Lost

## Frank Hannigan

Golf Journal                                        August, 1968

The chronicles of golf are filled with sad tales of the leaders in championships, heavily laden with the burden of trying to hold the lead in the final round, who have staggered and fallen. Those who have read the history of the United States Open championships for both men and women are especially familiar with these morose accounts. Indeed, it is often said that most of our Opens haven't been won—someone just happened to lose them.

Bob Dylan, the bard of our long-haired younger generation, has written, "The times, they are a changin'." Perhaps he's right. It begins to appear that the latest generation in golf, accustomed to playing week in and week out for large sums of money, is more immune to the pressures of great occasions than were their predecessors.

First we saw Lee Trevino, looking right down the barrel of a thunderous 67 by Jack Nicklaus in the last round of the men's 1968 Open, go blithely about the business of shooting a 69 to win going away by four strokes.

Then, in the first week of July, along came Mrs. Susie Maxwell Berning to play the fourth round of the 1968 Women's Open in 71, level par, to capture the championship with 289 at the Moselem Springs Golf Club, near Reading, Pennsylvania.

The Nicklaus role in the Women's Open was played by the redoubtable Miss Mickey Wright, four times the Women's Open champion, whose final round was a brilliant 68 but who never came close to taking the lead. Miss Wright was the runner-up with 292.

Mrs. Berning led right from the start. Playing near the end of the field on the first day, she came in with a 69 to go one shot ahead of Miss Wright. A solid 73 in the second round increased her lead to four strokes, with Mrs. Murle Lindstrom now second. When Mrs. Berning faltered to a 76 on the third day, her advantage was cut to two strokes. Miss Carol Mann was second, four others were within four strokes of

*Susie Maxwell Berning, here with daughter Robin, won three
U.S. Women's Open championships: the first at Moselem
Springs, Pennsylvania, in 1968; the second at Winged Foot
Golf Club in Mamaroneck, N.Y. in 1972; and the third in 1973
at the Country Club of Rochester in Rochester, N.Y.*

the lead, and there was much speculation that Mrs. Berning was beginning to feel the strain. Her reaction was to go out on the third and
final day and play the first nine holes in 35, one under par. By then, no
one was closer to her than four shots, but Miss Wright up ahead was
working on one of her great rounds. Mrs. Berning then proceeded to
play holes ten through fifteen in two under par to effectively destroy all
opposition. She faltered only on the final three holes, all par 4s, by
making three 5s, but, by the time she reached the 16th tee, the only
issue was the margin of her victory. In a word, Mrs. Berning *won* the
Women's Open.

Those final three holes dogged the champion throughout the week. She played them in a cumulative total of 9 over par while playing the other fifteen holes 4 under par. Had she been able to par the last three on the final day, her 72-hole score would have been 286, one lower than the Miss Wright's Women's Open record 287.

Mrs. Berning, a 27-year-old graduate of Oklahoma City University, is an intense competitor. She generates a surprising amount of power for a young lady with a slight frame. She turned professional in 1964 after compiling a good amateur record in Oklahoma, and was chosen the Ladies PGA "rookie of the year". Her progress since then has been steady. Last year, when she tied for second in the Women's Open, she was the LPGA's fifth leading money-winner.

The former Susie Maxwell, Mrs. Berning was a bride of seven weeks on the eve of the 1968 Women's Open and had played in only three tournaments previously. Her husband Dale, who presented her with a 1912 Maxwell automobile as a wedding gift, followed her play throughout the championship and held up very well.

There was an extraordinary amount of public interest in this year's Women's Open because the defending champion was a foreigner and an amateur—Catherine Lacoste, of Paris, who astounded the world of golf by winning the title last year at Hot Springs, Virginia. Miss Lacoste began her defense with a 74, but her second round of 78 put her ten strokes back and out of contention. Her primary failing was her putting. Miss Lacoste finished with rounds of 77 and 73 for a 72-hole total of 302 and a tie for 13th place. It is hoped that she will come back time and again.

# The 1968 U.S. Women's Amateur: JoAnne Gunderson Carner versus Anne Quast Welts

## Frank Hannigan

Golf Journal                                      September, 1968

Every time I see JoAnne Gunderson Carner play golf—which is once a year—the dormant publicist within me wants to cry out, "Hey, wake up, all you golf fans. A genius is among us and not enough people are watching. Get away from your TV sets and come out to watch the incomparable 'Gundy' strike a ball as it's meant to be struck. Watch her rifle two wood shots into the wind and onto the green of a 428-yard hole. See her blast out of wet sand to within three feet of the hole. Observe as she closes the face of a 5-iron and punches the ball under a tree limb to the heart of a green one hundred and fifty yards away. Notice how she fades the ball over the trees at the turn of a dog-leg hole."

All these and many other wonders Mrs. Carner worked last month during her majestic fifth victory in the United States Women's Amateur championship at the Birmingham Country Club, Birmingham, Michigan. Only the great Mrs. Edwin H. (Glenna Collett) Vare, Jr., who won the title six times between 1922 and 1935, surpasses this record.

The committees of the Birmingham Country Club did an exemplary job promoting the event, with the result that the number of spectators was unusually large for a Women's Amateur. There may have been 2,500 at the final, but considering the extraordinary records and the skills of the players, it seems a shame that more public attention isn't focused on the event. Mrs. Carner won her fifth title by defeating Mrs. David Welts, of Mt. Vernon, Wash., 5 and 4. Mrs. Welts, the former Anne Quast, has won the championship three times.

Mass interest in women's amateur golf is probably one of the casualties of this era of commercial interest in the game. The public doesn't know what it's missing. Mrs. Carner is not only a great player but she is a great personality as well, and she plays with a zest and natural flair that captivates everyone who watches her in much the same way that Arnold Palmer attracts his huge army of admirers.

Mrs. Carner probably couldn't care less whether anyone is paying

*The incomparable 'Gundy'*

attention. She is quite obviously playing the game for fun, and this is no small part of her appeal. The same applies to Mrs. Welts.

Mrs. Carner now lives in Seekonk, Massachusetts, but she grew up in the state of Washington not more than 50 miles from Mrs. Welts. During eleven of the last thirteen years, one or the other has reached the final. In addition to her three victories, Mrs. Welts has been runner-up twice and has reached the quarter-final round in twelve of the last fourteen Women's Amateur championships. Mrs. Carner has not only won five times but has been runner-up twice.

One of the more fascinating aspects of their continued success is that both defy the tenet that a player must compete often on the highest level in order to be sharp. Mrs. Welts has played in three tournaments

*In 1952, at fourteen, Anne Quast became the youngest
qualifier in the history of the U.S. Women's Amateur.*

this year—the British Amateur, the U.S. Women's Open and the Women's Amateur, along with the Curtis Cup match and a team contest with the continent of Europe. Mrs. Carner has been unusually active—for her. During a Florida vacation last winter, she entered and won two tournaments, and months later she won the Rhode Island and the Eastern championships. Five for five!

Despite their long association and their strings of victories, these two ladies had never before been opponents in the final of the Women's

Amateur. They had twice met in 18-hole semi-final matches, and Mrs. Welts won both times.

The course played very long for the Saturday final after a storm dumped about two inches of water Friday night. Mrs. Carner's ability to carry the ball unusually long distances was a particular advantage under such conditions. On one par-5 hole, after both players had hit two good wood shots, she was ninety yards ahead of her opponent.

Following the morning round, Mrs. Carner was only 1 up. Mrs. Welts, thanks to some fine putting, was 2 down and very much in it after eleven holes in the afternoon. Then Mrs. Carner produced consecutive birdies on long holes and ended the match by pitching to within 18 inches of the pin for a par and a win on the 32nd hole.

The excitement surrounding the final was fully matched by that of the semi-final round. Mrs. Carner was pitted against none other than Miss Catherine Lacoste, of Paris, who won our Women's Open in 1967, the Women's Western Amateur earlier this summer, and had earned the qualifying medal at Birmingham with a brilliant 36-hole total of 143, four strokes ahead of the field. It tied the tournament record.

Mrs. Carner produced an awesome finish to her match with Miss Lacoste. They were even after eleven holes—then it happened: Mrs. Carner won the 12th with a particularly bold iron over a bunker to set up a winning par; she got down in two from a bunker for a birdie on the par-5 13th; she flew an iron six feet from the cup for another birdie on the par-4 14th; and she holed a 27-foot putt for a birdie on the par-3 15th. Birdie, birdie, birdie—end of match.

Meanwhile, Anne Quast Welts was working her way into the final by beating Miss Joyce Kazmierski, 2 and 1 in the other semi-final. Mrs. Welts concluded the match with a birdie that vividly contrasted her style with Mrs. Carner's. She deliberately played short of the green on the par-4 17th with her second and watched as the ball rolled to within four feet of the hole. Mrs. Carner, faced with the same shot, will fly the ball right at the flag. Both methods seem to work.

The Birmingham Country Club is a creation of the late Donald Ross, the Scottish architect who evidently built nothing but wonderful courses during the early decades of this century. It is very attractive, relatively tight in the drive zones without too much emphasis on sand, and not overly long—even from the back tees. It easily passes the test of a good course, the test which provides that a player should be able to recall all the holes after playing it only once.

# Donna Caponi: Symbol of a Happy State of Affairs

## Frank Hannigan

Golf Journal                                    August, 1969

*The old order changeth, yielding place to new.*
The Passing of Arthur, by Alfred Lord Tennyson

That's the way it is in golf these days, too. Orville Moody wins his first tournament since joining the pro tour, and it's the United States Open; Donna Caponi wins her first title as a professional, and it's the United States Women's Open.

Miss Caponi hasn't been around long enough to appreciate the tenet that United States Open championships are not supposed to be won— someone is supposed to lose them. Well, Miss Caponi *won* her title with an attacking four-under-par final round of 69 for a total of 294 on the very demanding Scenic Hills Country Club course in Pensacola, Florida, last month.

The last few holes were memorable both for the golf and the weather. Six players were jammed within two strokes of the lead when Miss Caponi broke away from the pack with a glorious eagle 3 on the 15th hole. A light rain was falling and a first-class electrical storm was brewing not far off.

The rain intensified as Miss Caponi parred the 16th, but when she lost a stroke to par on the par-3 17th, her lead was down to a single stroke. Just after she drove on the par-5 18th, the storm hit Scenic Hills with a fury that was frightening. Play was suspended. Miss Caponi had to walk in and ponder her fate for an unsettling fifteen minutes or so until it was decided that play could be resumed.

She returned to her ball, which was lying in the fairway, and played a wood shot from a tight lie about twenty yards short of the home green. She pitched deftly above the cup, and holed a tricky downhill four-footer for a birdie. The putt was critical because Peggy Wilson, playing in the final group, also birdied the 18th to become the runner-up, one stroke off the pace.

273

*Donna Caponi is often overlooked, but she won two consecutive U.S. Women's Opens and all four major championships.*

Miss Caponi's first three scores were 74, 76, and 75—nothing very brilliant but nothing very sour either—just good enough to remain in contention without calling much attention to herself. After she won, she confided that she began the final round with the conviction that the course owed her one very low score.

A different player led after each round, so that the focus of the championship was never on one or two players. The cast of characters, in addition to the eventual winner, went as follows:

Peggy Wilson: Led after the first round with a two-under-par 71 and was always a factor thereafter. A second-round 76 put her three strokes behind, and she moved to within two strokes of the lead with a 75 on the third day. She played the last seven holes of the fourth round in two under par for a concluding 73 and a total of 295. That sort of performance is good enough to win most Women's Opens. Miss Wilson is a late bloomer. She's 34 now and just starting to play consistently well, having won her first LPGA tournament last year. She never touched a club until she was 22.

Kathy Whitworth: The heiress apparent to Mickey Wright as the preeminent figure on the LPGA tour, Miss Whitworth's career has been marred by a singularly unsuccessful record in the Women's Open. Prior to this year, she had never mounted any sort of challenge, and at Scenic Hills her frustration continued in the opening round when she scored 76. A 78 on the second day seemed to finish her, but then Miss Whitworth marshaled her power and skills to fashion a 69 in the third round to get back into contention. Like Peggy Wilson, she was at her best when it counted most—on the last nine of the final round she had three birdies and six pars—but she had too much to make up and finished at 296, two strokes behind.

Ruth Jessen: A heroic lady who is again playing well after undergoing surgery for cancer in 1968. She led after 54 holes with a total of 220, but wilted in the extreme heat and humidity of the last round to finish at 298.

Sybil Griffin: Totally inconspicuous for three days but within striking distance of the lead, Miss Griffin—who has never won an LPGA event—almost stole the title with a concluding 72 for a total of 298. She finished relatively early, and there was a good chance that those behind her might falter. Instead, they made birdies.

JoAnn Prentice: Another veteran, and one who has often been a challenger in the Women's Open. She led after 36 holes with 144 and, at 223, was three strokes back beginning the final round. Paired with Miss Caponi, she played a creditable 75 to tie for fourth at 298.

Mickey Wright: Eleven strokes behind beginning the final round and obviously uncomfortable in the heat, this great player, four-times the Women's Open champion, managed to play herself back into a challenging position. After eleven holes she was five under par on Sunday and within three strokes of the lead: she had made up eight strokes. With two relatively short par-5 holes among the last seven to be played, there was reason to believe she might accomplish the most unlikely reversal of form in the history of USGA championships. But no; a bogey on the 12th and a two-over-par 6 on the 14th ended her chances. She finished with a 71 for 302.

The amateurs, who are sometimes a serious competitive factor in the Women's Open, never had a representative close to the lead, but seven survived the 36-hole cut. The low amateur for the second straight year, and for the third time in her career, was Miss Phyllis Preuss, of Pompano Beach, Fla., who fashioned a marvelous last-round 69 for a total of 304 and tied for 16th place. Miss Preuss, like Deane Beman in men's golf, is a wizard with fairway woods.

The second-low amateur was the gifted Miss Shelley Hamlin, of Fresno, Calif., with 306. At 20 she is already a veteran of three international matches. Miss Hamlin, incidentally, had a rather puzzling first-round score of 38-48—86. Thus, she played the last 54 holes in one over par—better than anyone else in the field. Mrs. Scott L. Probasco, Jr., and Miss Connie Day, both of Chattanooga, Tenn., shared the honors for third-low amateur at 312.

As for the leading lady, Miss Caponi is a blithe spirit of twenty-four years who bubbles with enthusiasm and good cheer. Television viewers of the fourth round may have noticed a bandage supporting her right ankle, a result of a sprain she suffered while contorting herself after hours during one of the violent forms of social dance that have supplanted the good old fox trot.

She was born in Michigan, moved to California when she was four. Her father Harry is a professional at a public course in what his daughter refers to as "beautiful downtown Burbank." Miss Caponi joined the ranks of the LPGA in 1965 at nineteen with a thorough background in the fundamentals of the game but not much of a record in California's intense circle of junior competitions to support her aspirations. Nevertheless, she was able, almost from the start, to make a go of it on the tour. She won $6,500 during her first season, and it has always seemed just a matter of time until she learned how to win.

She is a very long and true driver, which she calls the strength of her game. Prior to the Women's Open she had been troubled by a tendency to become skittish under pressure, particularly on the last round, and to make what she calls "silly mental mistakes." Recently, she has been joined on the ladies' tour by her younger sister Janet, 22, who also is a player of promise.

The emergence of players like the Caponi sisters is symptomatic of the current happy state of affairs on the LPGA Tour. The ladies are enjoying a mini-boom in prize money which, while dwarfed by the vast sums played for by the male professionals, is startling in its recent percentage of increase. This year the prize money on the LPGA tour will exceed $600,000; last year it was $485,000. The ladies have limited themselves to thirty events beginning in March and concluding around Thanksgiving. All the tournaments are 54 holes with the exception of the Women's Open and the LPGA championship, and all except the Women's Open are preceded by pro-amateur competitions, which often are vital to the financial health of the sponsors. There is a high percentage of repeat sponsors, and the lady pros are delighted to report that at one or two events this year the gallery actually got out of control. As a result, the number of LPGA players has increased markedly to a point where, at the Women's Open, seventy lady professionals began play—a record.

### Leaders in the 1969 Women's Open

| | | |
|---|---|---|
| Miss Donna Caponi | 74 76 75 69 294 | $5,000.00 |
| Miss Peggy Wilson | 71 76 75 73 295 | 2,500.00 |
| Miss Kathy Whitworth | 76 78 69 73 296 | 1,500.00 |
| Miss JoAnn Prentice | 73 71 79 75 298 | 1,033.34 |
| Miss Sybil Griffin | 73 76 77 72 298 | 1,033.33 |
| Miss Ruth Jessen | 73 72 75 78 298 | 1,033.33 |
| Miss Shirley Englehorn | 72 76 77 76 301 | 850.00 |
| Miss Mary Mills | 75 80 71 76 302 | 718.00 |
| Mrs. Murle Lindstrom | 74 79 74 75 302 | 718.00 |
| Miss Mickey Wright | 76 79 76 71 302 | 718.00 |
| Mrs. Clifford Ann Creed Gordon | 76 76 75 75 302 | 718.00 |
| Miss Louise Suggs | 76 78 75 73 302 | 718.00 |

# Catherine Was Great

## Frank Hannigan

Golf Journal                                                    October, 1969

The chronicles of match-play championships are laden with sad tales of illustrious players who have been ousted in early rounds by opponents of lesser repute. Advocates of match play contend the factor of daily person-to-person competition is one of the virtues of the match-play game; detractors have always argued that the elimination of a great player early in a championship is farcical.

The best players, though, have always seemed to win both at stroke and match play. In fact, one of the most valid tests of greatness may well come in an 18-hole match when the favored player is in danger of losing to an opponent who obviously has thrown caution to the winds while caught up in the excitement of staging an upset.

Catherine Lacoste, of France, who surely must be regarded now as one of the great women players in the history of the game, had to face two such tests this August during the 1969 Women's Amateur championship which was held at the Las Colinas Country Club in Irving, Texas. During the second round she watched Miss Constance Hirschman, of York, Pennsylvania, hole an enormous putt on the 17th green to make their match even. Miss Lacoste proceeded to play three perfect strokes on the par-5 18th to set up a birdie and a 1-up victory.

The next day Miss Lacoste was confronted by the talented Mary Jane Fassinger, a 17-year-old from New Castle, Pennsylvania, who was runner-up in the Girls' Junior championship one week earlier. Miss Fassinger began the match with two birdies and five pars. Catherine hadn't made a mistake and was 2 down. At that point you could almost hear Miss Lacoste telling herself that if pars weren't good enough, she'd have to make birdies. And so she did. Three birdies combined with six pars gave her a 4-and-2 victory. Incidentally, Miss Lacoste hit sixteen consecutive greens in regulation and putted for birdies from 20 feet or less on every green from the 9th through the 16th. This, mind you, on a course that many considered a shade on the severe side for a women's competition.

Standing between Miss Lacoste and the final match was a player whose credentials *are* complete: Mrs. David Welts, the former Anne Quast, a three-time Women's Amateur champion who over the years has won more matches than any other player in the history of the championship. Mrs. Welts, conceding great hunks of yardage off the tee but accurate as can be and brilliant on the greens, built a lead of three holes after the tenth. Then she started to pull her long shots to the left. Miss Lacoste, as is her fashion, grew stronger as the match progressed, and, with a great rush of birdies, came from behind to win 2 and 1.

In the 36-hole final Catherine came up against 20-year-old Shelley Hamlin, of Fresno, California, who had already played on three USGA international teams. Miss Hamlin was unsteady at the start and fell three holes behind on the first nine. Then she began to play exquisitely. In fact, she played the next twenty-five holes in even par. In women's golf, and on a tough golf course to boot, that should do something. It did exactly nothing, because Miss Lacoste was unrelenting and won 3 and 2. With this victory Miss Lacoste concluded a marvelous season which saw her win the championships of France, Spain, Great Britain, and the United States.

Catherine Lacoste became famous in this country when she came over in 1967 and won our Women's Open as an amateur, a foreigner, and a youngster of twenty-two at the Cascade course in Hot Springs, Virginia. Those who saw her play at the Cascades course as well as at Las Colinas are certain that Catherine is now a much better player than she was two years ago. She has always been a long hitter and a putter who holes more than her share of birdies, but she now has added to her repertoire a considerable finesse particularly with her medium and short irons which she plays with a minimum of exertion and maximum of control.

When Miss Lacoste, who was not expected to come to the United States this year, submitted her entry after winning the British Ladies' championship, there were visions of a renewal of her rivalry with Mrs. Donald (JoAnne Gunderson) Carner, who was in quest of her sixth U.S. Women's Amateur title. Mrs. Carner had beaten Miss Lacoste in the semi-final round of the 1968 championship and had added to her reputation by beating the professionals in an LPGA tournament during the winter. Mrs. Carner qualified handily with a total of 150 ("Not bad for practice rounds," she said) and then seemed on her way to a first-round victory over Mrs. Sam (Ann Baker) Furrow, of Concord, Tenn., who was runner-up to Mrs. Carner in 1962. Mrs. Carner was 3 up after ten holes but she then made seven consecutive bogeys and lost, 2 and 1. It was like going to Philharmonic Hall and hearing Vladimir Horowitz hit the wrong keys for a solid hour. Such is the nature of the game.

That championship concluded with an announcement by Miss Lacoste to the effect that she might very well not choose to defend her title and that she might, in fact, forego serious competition in the future. She indicated that she has had enough of the travel, pressure, and attention that goes with the game on the highest level of competition. She also reminded us that her father (one of the greatest tennis players) and her mother (a winner of both the British Ladies' golf championship as well as the French) had both retired when they were in their prime.

We can only hope that Miss Lacoste—like another great French lady, Miss Sarah Bernhardt—will reserve the right to change her mind and will come back to the United States time and time again.

# Catherine Lacoste: Championne du Monde

## Peter Ryde

"The Golfer's Bedside Book"          B.T. Batsford Ltd., 1971

In the autumn of 1969, Catherine Lacoste let it be known that she was retiring from international competition. It was not to be a clean break. She was to marry a Spaniard, but since she would be living in that country she could hardly turn her back on the Women's World Amateur Team championship which was to be held there the following autumn. It looked then, as though she might be the one champion whom the game would allow to remain unhumbled. Her successes had been so numerous during her five-year career that she had hardly had time to play undistinguished golf in a tournament. Her whole story was one of dazzling success, proudly borne.

She had, of course, known defeat, as any great golfer must. Quickly as she rose to supremacy, she had first to establish herself against three of the finest golfers in Europe at that time. The Vicomtesse de Saint-Sauveur was coming to the end of a long and distinguished career; Brigitte Varangot and Claudine Cros were approaching the summit of theirs. All of them were French, and, taking the long view, her rivalry with them was the making of her as a champion. Without such a tough initiation into the competitive world, she might never have prevailed in the United States.

Although she had at the age of nineteen contributed most to the victory of France in the first Ladies' World Team championship, she needed time to prove her superiority. It was not until two years later, in 1966, that she won the championship of France for the first time, overcoming an inhibition about beating Brigitte Varangot that was threatening to turn into a mental block. The following year she suffered what I have always supposed to be her most vexing defeat. At Harlech she led the qualifiers for the second year running in the British Ladies' championship, only to be beaten in the first round by Martine Cochet, a compatriot who had scraped into the championship sixteen strokes behind Catherine over the two qualifying rounds.

Vexing, yes, but that defeat hardly entered into the realm of grand drama. In the ultimate test of strokeplay, Miss Lacoste had already made her mark; the hazards of matchplay were another matter and had always frustrated the best. Bobby Jones, we hasten to point out, had won two British and three United States Opens before he succeeded in winning the British Amateur.

From her childhood she had been cast in a heroic role, having champion's blood in her veins from both sides of the family. The ability to win does not, of course, depend necessarily on inherited talent in that particular field. Sheer adversity may force the genius out of a performer, and sometimes the parents of a champion may excel in another field. But with a father who had been singles champion at Wimbledon, Roland Garros, and Forest Hills, and with a mother who, as Mademoiselle Thion de la Chaume, won a British championship in Catherine's favourite sport, golf, it was not long before Catherine felt at home in the competitive atmosphere. Her father, René Lacoste, confined himself to shrewd observations about her technique. A great theorist of this and other games, he perhaps had the good sense to realize that his daughter did not need instruction—she was too good a natural ball player for that—but an outside eye that could supply what most players need, a gift for diagnosis when things go wrong. Many a good golfer, who can detect faults in others and correct them, can remain curiously blind to the faults that have crept into his own game.

Catherine's string of successes has its roots in the children's tournaments her mother used to organize during the summer holidays at their home course of Chantaco, down the road from St. Jean de Luz in the Basque region of France. Madame Lacoste did her best to see to it that her daughter did not collar the first prize all the time, but it was hard work. They had given birth to a winner. She was young, she was powerful, she was scornful of opposition to the point of giving offence. Add to this some blunt remarks, remarkable more for their honesty than for their tact, and it is hardly surprising that, over and above her maddening habit of winning, she roused occasional animosity. She once admitted to being perhaps 'un peu cabochard'. We must make what we can of that, but 'caboche' is a hob-nail, and riding-roughshod over people's feelings might not be wide of the mark.

But how exciting a trait that was when translated into action on the course! She came to the first Women's World Team championship at the age of nineteen, junior champion of France, and that was about all. The team event, the only one of its kind in which a player represents his country in strokeplay, is the most exacting of all. Yet Catherine played the last decisive round as though it were the height of enjoyment to her.

We said that it was the innocence of youth, but even in full maturity she never lost that quality. Patty Berg was quick to observe it. She wrote: "She enjoys playing golf, and anyone can see that sport is far from being the most important thing in her life." This completely amateur approach helps to explain her victory later in the U.S. Women's Open where so much was at stake, and it also helps to explain her ability to play her best when it mattered most. "I need a high stake to bring out the best scores in me", she once said. Such a remark may sound like tempting providence, but almost until the end of her career she made it look as though it were the right way to treat providence, and as though an assurance so complete had enabled her to earn exemption from the golden rule of humiliation.

In 1967 came the first thunderbolt, completely unexpected and almost unwitnessed by the game's leaders from this side of the Atlantic. I was in Portugal watching the European Women's Team championship in which Catherine, to the irritation of her colleagues, declined to take part. They were standing in a huddle in the hotel lobby, and when I said in reply to their question that I had not heard the news, they told me that I must first be seated or the shock would be too great. Catherine had won the United States Women's Open championship. The surprise has worn off for all of us by now because we are familiar with the brilliance of her game. We accept that she can hit the ball harder and straighter than any other living woman, that she has more confidence in playing the one-iron than do most men. We know, or thought we knew until that last act in Madrid, that she would always knock in the putts that matter.

What lingers in my mind about that victory is the courage she showed in going over to the United States and maintaining her game to the end. I sometimes pass the time thinking of the great occasions I have missed and would like again to have the chance of seeing. Catherine's triumph at the Cascades club in Virginia is high on the list. She herself is not easily drawn to the subject but a French journalist, Renaud de Laborderie, in *Les Reines du Sport*, has reconstructed the ordeal with sensitivity. For days at the motel and at the course, Catherine was completely alone. The press and the players ignored her existence. The only exception were two young girls seated at the next table to her. They got talking as Catherine sat munching her corn flakes, and they persuaded their parents to stay on until their new friend had won. Her 70 on the second round hoisted her five strokes clear of the field and established her on the road to victory. It was one of the great rounds of her life, comparable to the fabulous 66 she scored at Prince's the year before in winning the Astor Trophy. Before the final round on a day of clouds and humidity, she went to mass, praying no more fervently than usual, for golf is not essential to life. It was this air of detachment that carried her through the final round, that enabled her to keep hold of a slipping lead, to drive across the trees at the seventeenth and to hole a three-yard putt that insured her victory.

Her triumph was as complete as that of the next foreigner to win an American championship, Tony Jacklin. She was the first foreigner to win the United States Women's championship, the first amateur to do so, and the youngest player. It was the championship she most wanted to win, *ça va de soi*. But it was not the one she found hardest to win; that was the United States Amateur. It wasn't the one that gave her the greatest pleasure in winning; that was the British Amateur. She had to wait three more years to carry off those two, and one depended on the other. The British had been the stumbling block in her career, for here her predominance in strokeplay could not assert itself. But in 1970 she went early to the green shores of Northern Ireland to prepare for the championship that had eluded her. Already that year she had won the French championship and also, for what it was worth, the Spanish. She allowed her mother to accompany her. In America she had wanted to make her own way to fame, apart from her parents. Now she wanted her mother with her, because it was down the coast from Royal Portrush at Royal County Down that she had won the same championship forty-two years before. Only Ann Irvin looked capable of stopping Catherine that week at Royal Portrush, a giant course worthy of a true champion. Ann was three up on her after seven holes, and luck went against her when Catherine's approach to the ninth was deflected by a spectator's handbag from the rough to the edge of the green. But luck comes to all, and it is the ability to take advantage of it that marks the champion. Catherine holed that putt and banged her tee shot to the next hole ten feet from the pin.

Coming back to London in the plane afterwards she was uncertain what to do next. She was contemplating marriage, but reluctance to return to America, where, to put it mildly, her triumph had been received with mixed feelings by players and press, was losing ground to the vision of completing the Grand Slam by winning the United States Amateur. This time she would land in that country not an unknown at the start of a great adventure but as someone who was expected to win and whom every American would take delight in beating. "When you are a champion, if you win *c'est normal*; once you lose, everybody says you are over the hill." Moreover, the championship was being held in Texas at the hottest time of year. From the relaxed country-house atmosphere of the Côte Basque she would have to go forth into the furnace, summoning up for a final effort her great competitive spirit. In a temperature of more than one hundred degrees in which the iron clubs became too hot to handle, she clung like a leach to par. As had happened in the British, she found herself three down in the final; again she extricated herself, this time against Anne Quast Welts, a golfer in the highest class, but one she had beaten when our Curtis Cup team had visited Paris.

The grand slam was complete. That year she had won the French, British, and American championships in succession. She was now ready to withdraw from top competition, with the finest record of all time and also the proudest. But by one of those quirks of fate, the Women's World Amateur Team championship was to be held the following year in Madrid, the city where she was going to live and on the course of which she had recently become a member. Complete as her achievement was, this was one last international championship on which she could not turn her back. In the six years of its history, her individual record of tied first, third, and first was second to none; and of all the leading countries, France alone had kept her team intact from the start.

Since the Women's World Amateur Team championship would take place a few weeks after her marriage, she would not be in full competitive trim. Still, half a Lacoste was better than no champion. Slowly and inexorably the situation built up. In that type of championship, where the best two rounds out of three count over a three-day period, the climax sometimes passes unseen out on the course, and the result becomes a matter of statistics. In this case there was never any doubt where the climax lay, and the crowd that found its way out from Madrid, reinforced by members of other teams who had finished, watched the long drawn-out agony of those last nine holes. Catherine Lacoste blew up. She would not, I feel sure, with her own tremendously high standards, want to hide behind words. There were all kinds of extenuating circumstances and she finished with a plucky par at the seventy-second hole which even in ordinary circumstances is not an easy four, but she blew it. I am concerned only to make the point that at the eleventh hour the champion who looked to have got away without being humbled by the game she loved, was made to pay the tribute demanded of all other great players.

We can gloss over the details. The three-strokes lead Catherine held with nine to play vanished, and the United States retained possession of the cup by one stroke. By ordinary standards the French girl did not collapse, but she would not forgive herself the shortness of the putt she missed on the eleventh green or for having been short with her pitches at two relatively easy holes. Her opponent, Martha Wilkinson, was a lovely swinger of the club. She did not have, as did her opponent, packing cases full of unopened wedding presents in a still unfurnished home. Sometimes as a spectator it is possible almost to hate the game you love when you see the full burden of a team event proving too heavy for one person. There had been an example of that the day when Catherine first burst upon the world in 1964 and won the First World Women's Amateur Team championship for France. Then, Barbara McIntyre's failure to retain America's lead sent a chill through the hearts of the spectators. In Madrid the boot was on the other foot as Catherine, waiting for Martha to take two putts and get her four, sat on the bank at the back of the green, her head in her arms.

Catherine, whatever that day may have cost her feelings, is not diminished by it as a golfer. She remains the greatest woman champion of our times, and it would not be surprising if the experience has left her a more complete person.

# The Girls' Junior Championship
# Grows Up

## Harold Peterson

Sports Illustrated                                    August, 1971

Girls' golf, observed a USGA man down in Augusta last week, is a very formful game. Despite the adolescent figures strolling the fairways at the U.S. Girls' Junior championships in those trim, no-nonsense outfits, he did not mean it as a play on words. One of the more durable pieces of male wisdom holds that women don't like surprises, and it seemed to go double for the teen-age girl golfers at the Augusta Country Club.

All of them—the Debbys, Lindas, Cindys, and Candys, the Aprils, LuAnns, Kimberlys, and Mary Beths—came to the Augusta Country Club, next door to the Augusta National where the Masters is played, well supplied with hopes and hair ribbons. One hundred and one came, and after the qualifying rounds most of them went right back home again. The 32 left to fight it out in three days of match play were the 32 everyone expected to be there, including the one—Hollis Stacy—the rest wished had stayed away.

Form was followed with eerie precision down to the very last day. In this quiet, unturbulent pool of feminine order, a cool, braided, California blonde named Laura Baugh made quite a splash. She was an innocent troublemaker, but a troublemaker nevertheless. First, in a field of 13-to-17-year-olds made up of children moving into adolescence and adolescents changing into women, she wasn't emerging at all. Miss Baugh had already emerged. She had one of the most confident walks ever seen, her perfectly tanned, well-formed legs swinging jauntily. The hair on her tapered arms was bleached absolutely white against a milk-chocolate tan. Her platinum hair was pulled smartly back into a Viking-maiden braid. Her tunic-skirted golf outfit contrasted with the essentially neutral uniform often adopted as protective coloration by girl golfers of that age. When Laura stooped down to line up a putt, she

287

did it gracefully, as she seemed to do everything else. Never a moment of uncertainty, nor an awkward gesture. It was quite unfair.

The other girls never actually *admitted* they disliked Laura—whatever antipathy there was seemed to stem from the fact that she seldom conceded a putt, no matter how short. But that was merely part of her conservative game, which was manifested in other ways. She consistently chipped on the safe side of the ideal placement and consistently drove shorter than she was able. Actually, Laura Baugh is quite likable. Her father, Hale Baugh, came up from Florida to be with her in Augusta (Laura's parents are divorced), and his pride was evident. "Her mother has done a wonderful job with her," he said. He recalled how Laura at age four would tag along when her brothers played golf, hitting an occasional ball of her own. "We'd clap for her, then she'd play a hole or two. I made her a little club out of a wood block."

During the tournament she dallied with the idea of breaking out of her conservative mold at least once. "I wanted to wear tennis panties with my dress today," she said one morning. "I was just afraid the USGA wouldn't let me." And then, of course, she almost made golfing mischief. She nearly beat unbeatable Hollis Stacy.

Native to Georgia and a great local favorite, Hollis had won the last two junior championships, only the second player in twenty-five years to do so, and had done it walking away. Up to Thursday's match she had lost exactly two holes in two rounds. She had won her first-round match in eleven holes, and the talk among the caddies was that she could have won in ten, the minimum number, but that would have been rubbing it in.

In her quarterfinal match with Laura Baugh there was no question of rubbing it in. Laura, who started off shakily with a bogey on the first, watched impassively as Hollis seemed to be up to her usual tricks. On the par-3 4th, Hollis hit her tee shot to within a foot of the cup. She went one up. Normalcy. But somehow, Laura wouldn't follow the script. Over the next fourteen holes, she went two under par and did not have a bogey. On every drive she was twenty yards shorter than Hollis, but her short game more than made up for it. On the 8th hole, a short par 5, she drew even. And on the ninth, she holed her pitch shot and went 1 up.

Now the imperturbable Hollis began to trudge. She swung around in frustration after missing a putt on the 14th and almost fell three behind on the 15th before getting down in two from a trap. Hollis also put her second shot on the 16th into a trap, next to a high green looking out over the national forest where all Augusta gathered in 1864 to watch Sherman's March.

*In 1971, Hollis Stacy beat Amy Alcott on the 19th hole to win her third straight U.S. Girls' Junior championship.*

Once again the Yankees didn't make it. Hollis blasted out beautifully, Laura missed a long putt, then another, and Hollis was only one down. When Hollis won the 18th, it was even. Coolly, Hollis hit her best drive of the day on the 19th: Laura pulled hers into a sand trap, and Hollis had won.

Laura congratulated her opponent graciously and walked off the green under perfect control. But when her father told her what a good game she had played, she said fiercely, "I'm terrible! No one could be two up on the 16th and lose." There might have been a catch in her voice as she said it, but nobody could say for sure with Laura. So much for the unforeseen.

In the final Amy Alcott could scarcely be rated an underdog, even to Hollis Stacy. She had played golf since she was old enough to swing a stick, learning the game by chipping from sprinkler head to sprinkler head on the Alcotts' Los Angeles front lawn. Only fifteen, she drives the ball 240 to 250 yards, farther than most women pros. She says she gets her strength from jogging, but one might also add that much of it comes from long years of participation in all kinds of sports.

"I used to think I was a boy," says Amy. "My knees and hands were always skinned. I would play football and baseball with the boys and beat them. They didn't like that. The girls hated me, too, because they had a crush on the sixth-grade teacher, and he liked me best because I liked baseball."

Against Hollis, Amy played one of the most remarkable rounds of golf ever seen in the junior championship. In the course of firing a three-under-par 70 over the 6,052-yard course, she birdied five holes and bogeyed only one. There was just one trouble. While all this was going on, Hollis Stacy was doing the same thing. As a result, Amy trailed most of the way, after going 1 down to Hollis on the first hole. The margin held through the first seventeen holes, and nothing that happened to Amy on the eighteenth seemed to augur an improvement. Her tee shot caught a fairway trap, and her second fell into a bunker near the green. Then she blasted out three feet from the cup and sank her putt. Her birdie put her even with Hollis and into a sudden-death play-off.

Hollis made quick work of it, sinking a fifteen-foot putt on the 19th hole and winning an unprecedented third-straight U.S. Girls Junior championship. Her parents came up to her afterward—her father almost sheepishly because it had been the first time he had come out to watch his daughter in competition, and he perhaps feared he had jinxed her. Her mother came out from behind a bush where she had hidden on both of Hollis' sudden-death holes, afraid to watch. Tillie Stacy gave her daughter an enormous hug.

# Nancy Lopez Lines Up a Big Future

## Sarah Ballard

Sports Illustrated                                    August 13, 1973

Since the oil companies began to move away and the government shut down Walker Air Force Base a few years ago, there has been relatively little to get excited about in Roswell, New Mexico. The town sits in the high dry plains, a pleasant place that because of its climate is now beginning to attract retired people from other parts of the country. Anglo-Americans and Mexican-Americans form the basic population, their lives intertwined, as they have been ever since the Anglos moved into the Southwest. Sixteen-year-old Nancy Lopez of East First Street is Mexican-American, and although she may be the best young girl golfer in the country, in Roswell East First Street is a long way in spirit from the country club.

By sheer force of her achievements Nancy has become an institution in Roswell, a kind of junior natural wonder. She won the New Mexico Women's Amateur Golf championship three straight years, starting when she was twelve, and a lot of other things besides. Last August she went to Jefferson City, Missouri, to try for the big time, the United States Girls' Junior championship. Nancy came away with her first national title and a ranking as the No. 1 girl golfer in the country. She did it the hard way. One hole down at match play with two holes to go, she sank a 25-foot putt on the 17th to draw even and a six-foot down-hiller on the 18th to win and become the youngest champion since Hollis Stacy in 1969. This week in Bernardsville, New Jersey, she is trying for a second junior title, and after that she will go after a bigger prize, the Women's Amateur in Montclair, New Jersey.

She got ready for both those events back in Roswell, basking in a warm celebrity glow. As she tees up on the first hole of the long flat course at New Mexico Military Institute, people honk cheerily at her from passing cars. Senior citizens cross fairways to shake her hands and ask how folks treated her when she was playing in Wisconsin or Illinois or Missouri, or wherever it was they used to live. High school kids wave

*Nancy Lopez lines up a big future.*

to her and she honks back as she "drags Main" in her bright yellow
Ford, a gift from her father.

Domingo Lopez has learned a lot of tricks for keeping a young girl's
interest and competitive drive alive in the eight years since Nancy
began trailing him around Roswell's nine-hole municipal course. The
idea of rewards is one of them. "First I gave her one dollar for As at
school. Then I gave her one dollar for birdies," he says. Now, many

birdies and quite a few As later, the ante has been raised to things like a family trip to Los Angeles for the LA Open last January or mag rims for the wheels of her car. Lopez is a small, wiry, sunbaked man of 50, known widely as "Sunday," an Anglo nickname he picked up playing city league baseball in his youth. He has worked hard all his life, first tenant-farming cotton just outside town and, since World War II, as a body and fender man. On his own he built the East Second Body Shop, at first large enough for only two cars but grown now to take ten or twelve. Working from six a.m. to five p.m. each day, he makes a comfortable living, owns a two-bedroom house a block from his shop, drives an 18-year-old pickup and an 11-year-old Cadillac, and, through very careful planning and severe self-denial, has just enough left over to finance his daughter in the amateur style to which the USGA is accustomed. Nancy's car, he hastens to explain, was partly a reward for good grades, hard work and competitive success. But it was also a great boon to his wife Marina, who for years had spent her days shuttling Nancy back and forth to golf courses.

USGA rules allow junior players to accept financial help toward transportation, housing and caddie fees for junior tournaments from sources outside their immediate families. But until early this summer nobody in Roswell had ever thought to offer Nancy any aid. (The Roswell Country Club to this day has not made her a member, although it has declared that her family can join—for a fee that is obviously well beyond Domingo Lopez' means.) An organization called the Roswell Seniors and Retirees, which includes many newcomers with quite a few golfers among them, finally broke the ice. When Nancy returned from Jefferson City with the junior title, it gave a banquet for her and invited everybody who was anybody in Roswell's business community. The Seniors and Retirees used the occasion to let it be known that it was high time Roswell demonstrated a little gratitude. The Chamber of Commerce responded with $500 toward her expenses at the Women's Western Golf Association junior championships in Wisconsin this summer. Nancy won that event and reached the semifinals of the Western Women's Amateur as well. She was able to return $100 because an interested family named Lindell from Winfield, Iowa, not only housed her between the tournaments but drove her all the way home to New Mexico.

"I'd like to work, to have my own money," says Nancy, who understands about money pressures. "Sometimes I feel guilty. I think I could get a pretty good job. I can type 65 words a minute and I could learn bookkeeping from my mother. She does it for my dad. But my dad doesn't want me to work. He thinks it would tire me and take too much time away from my golf." There are other things Nancy would like to do, too, that are proscribed, such as swimming—"It uses the wrong muscles and softens my calluses"—and tennis—"I played it some, but once I sprained my ankle, and it scared me. My dad said then I should stick to golf." But there are compensations, too.

"My husband tells me, 'Don't let her do the dishes. It will hurt her hands,'" says Marina Lopez, chuckling. "She gets away with a lot."

Last January, as a sophomore, Nancy was allowed to join the Goddard High School boys' varsity golf team. Each Friday through the winter, in every kind of weather, the team traveled by car to such places as Clovis and Hobbs and Andrews and finally to the state championships in Las Cruces. The Goddard Rockets beat Albuquerque High by four shots for the team title, and Nancy placed fifth in individual scoring with 77-82-159. The winner shot 150.

"When we were playing in March in Clovis," said Nancy, shivering in July heat at the memory, "our hands were freezing before we even teed off, and by the ninth hole it had started to rain and we wanted to quit. By the 14th it had begun to hail and we went in, but the pro told us to go on back out. I told myself, 'I have to be a boy now. If I quit, the coach might not let me back on the team.' So I finished with a 41 on the back and then went inside, washed my pants to get the mud off—they were soaked anyway—and just put them back on ready to go home. Then they told us we had to go back out for a playoff. We won on the first hole, thank goodness."

Out of a deep-seated mistrust of motels, Marina Lopez—a short, plump realist who carries an umbrella as a sunshade on the golf course—chaperones her daughter to tournaments where there is no private housing. Domingo stays home in Roswell, hammering out dented fenders and thinking about Nancy's future.

"I want her to be happy if she wins and happy if she loses. I want her to be able to do whatever she decides to do. Maybe she will go to college if she can get a scholarship. But I am saving money now so if she goes on tour she can have three years to win. Some of them, you know, take a long time to get started. Right now I have maybe enough for the first year. I used to be a baseball player, a pitcher, and I believe I was good enough to get to the major leagues. But I never had a chance. That is why I want to give Nancy a chance."

Although he had only three years of school, Domingo Lopez is an instinctive teacher and the only golf instructor Nancy has ever had. "He knows my game better than anybody," says Nancy. "He can tell me what to do even though he can't do it himself." But more and more Nancy now makes her own adjustments. Just this summer she has worked a loop out of her swing, slowed her backswing, and she has shortened her putting stroke. When a friend sent her a snapshot he had taken at a tournament, she was surprised to see that she was up on her right toe at the top of her backswing. Now her heel is firmly planted. And, most important, she has slightly altered the unorthodox grip that was causing her to slice and costing her distance off the tee. Frank Hannigan of the USGA, who watched her play for the first time last summer in the Juniors, said, "Purists would say she needs a radical change, and it's not too late for that. But I think possibly her strength allows her to overpower her bad grip. It will be interesting to see how she develops. She has a superb touch on and around the greens and, wow, what a great instinct to win! She made *all* the important putts in match play."

When she was ten and had just competed in her first Roswell Ladies' golf tournament, Nancy told her father she wanted to be as good a golfer as Mrs. Jo Boswell, who was Roswell's leading female player at that time and had won the tournament. Her father told her, "Yes, you be as good as Mrs. Boswell—and maybe a little bit better." The next year, at eleven, Nancy was runner-up to Jo Boswell by three strokes, and at twelve she won. That was also the summer she won her first state women's championship. In those days her fingernails were chewed down to the quick and she threw up so often before her matches that she made it a habit to get dressed in a bathroom. Experience and accumulated success have given her poise and a pleasantly confident manner that is betrayed only in the nervous jiggling of her legs. The idea that she might have limits hasn't occurred to her.

"Development is unpredictable in junior girls," says Hannigan, who has seen a lot of them come and go. "They mature quicker than boys. I think a lot of girls at fifteen are playing the best golf they'll ever play. They find out, thank God, that there are other things in life beside golf."

For a Mexican-American girl in southern New Mexico, even one who can sink putts under pressure, the alternatives—the "other things in life"—are limited, and the chances are that before long Nancy Lopez will be taking her best shot and trying to make her living on the LPGA tour. And Domingo Lopez back home in Roswell will be hammering and hoping.

# How Nice it Is to Win

## Sarah Ballard

Sports Illustrated                                        August 27, 1973

The first two acts of the Women's Amateur championship last week were drawing-room comedy, the last was drama, but the resolution was plain soap opera. In the end the deserving ingenue won the silver loving cup and dedicated it to her mother, while the Other Woman went home to tend her garden and family.

In its early rounds a USGA tournament for women amateurs resembles a summertime house party. Most of the players have met and played each other before, some of them every year for decades. At midday in the dining room and at sunset on the terraces, they mingle with club members and relatives, and if they have been around a while and know the right people, they spend their nights as guests in the nearby homes of hospitable members. At least that is the way it is when the tournament is played at a venue like the Montclair Golf Club in New Jersey, which is old (1893), affluent and determinedly genteel.

While more than half the field of 149 was shooting 82s or worse and failing to qualify on the first day, or eliminating each other at match play over the next three, the club members continued to play the eighteen holes not being used for the championship, and the tennis players plonked from morning till night, and the children in the pool near the first tee did their best to swallow their squeals. Such galleries as there were made more noise slapping mosquitoes than applauding golf shots.

By Friday and the semifinals, the cast of characters was down to four—the clubwoman, the patrician, the coed and the working girl. Donna Horton, a sophomore at the University of North Carolina at Greensboro, who is small, blonde, unknown and says "yes, ma'am" a lot, was the surprise of the early rounds, mainly because she knocked off Jane Bastanchury Booth, one of the favorites and a veteran of two Curtis Cup teams, 2 and 1. Donna had the misfortune to run into Anne Quast Sander in the semis and lost 5 and 3, but said it didn't matter because "I'm just so happy to be here."

Anne Sander is a new name for a familiar face in golf. In 1958, when she was Ann Quast, a Stanford junior from Marysville, Washington, she won her first United States Amateur championship; she followed that in 1961 with another as Anne Decker, and another in 1963 as Anne Welts. This summer, after a three-year layoff devoted to marrying Stephen Sander, a stockbroker, having a second child, and tending her garden alongside the sixth fairway at Seattle's Broadmoor Golf Club, she was back at 35, determined to put Sander into the record books and playing some of the best golf of her life.

Her comeback began at the British Women's Amateur, where she was medalist by *seven* strokes. A few weeks later at the United States Women's Open in Rochester, N.Y., she finished fourth, her best placing ever against the pros. And she had been mopping up on the hilly 6,032-yard Montclair course, too, closing out each of her matches with at least three holes to go.

The other semifinal was match play at its best. Both players were virtually unknown outside regional events, and each had improved her game impressively over the last year. Bonnie Lauer graduated in physical education from Michigan State in June, having won both the Intercollegiate and Mid-Western Collegiate for 1973 and having been the first woman athlete ever named MSU's Spartan of the Year. The Amateur was her last tournament on the summer circuit before taking a job in California to see what it is like to play the year round.

Carol Semple, her opponent, had reached the semis by beating, among others, Mary Budke, the defending champion. Carol, a tall, loose-jointed 24-year-old blonde with a big rhythmic swing, was born to amateur golf and the life that nurtures it. She was raised on the fairways of Pittsburgh's venerable Allegheny Country Club, and by a father who is a two-handicapper and vice-president of the USGA, and by a mother who has played in some twenty Women's Amateurs, despite never having gotten further than the quarterfinals. Her teacher from the time she took up the game at 12 until she was 20 was none other than Bobby Cruickshank, the little Scottish pro who tied Bobby Jones in the 1923 United States Open and lost in the playoff.

Carol fidgeted her way nervously through the front nine of the semis against Lauer, but even so was one up at the turn. Then Bonnie, who throughout the tournament looked as though she were actually enjoying the game, won three of the next four holes. After they had halved 14 and 15, Semple was two down with three to play. But at the 147-yard, par-3 16th she laced an iron that landed nine feet from the pin and holed a birdie putt that whacked the back of the cup. "That sparked me a little," she said. One down and two to go. When Bonnie left a chip short at 17, Carol won the hole with a par, closing her eyes tight while waiting for her turn to hit. "I try to picture each shot before I hit it, and that's the only way I can concentrate." A well envisioned 60-foot chip that almost went in on the 18th gave her a final birdie, her third straight hole, and the match.

The 36-hole final on Saturday was a genuine blow struck for old-fashioned excellence-for-its-own-sake amateurism, though you would not have known it by listening to the good-sized gallery. The clans had gathered. Semple's consisted of her father, flown in from a USGA function in Canada, her little sister Cherry, Bobby Cruickshank, aunts and uncles, most of the club people, and, of course, the underdog rooters. Sander's was made up of her husband and a few fans with historical perspective.

After the morning round, Sander was one up but unsettled going to lunch, since she had lost the 18th with two shots into the rough and three putts. By the 6th hole in the afternoon, though, all that was forgotten. She had stretched her lead to three holes, and her smooth, economical and effortless-looking swing was working as it had throughout the tournament and the years. But at the par-3 7th, Semple narrowly missed a hole in one, and the whole day began to turn around. Of the next seven holes, Sander was able to take only one. When at the 15th she gambled on a 5-wood out of a fairway bunker and lost, the match was even. At the 17th she was bunkered again to go one down, Carol parring the hole, and when she missed a 35-foot birdie putt on the final hole, the Amateur title belonged to Carol Semple. Anne Sander gave her a hug. She remembered how nice it is to win.

# Gundy

## Sarah Ballard

Sports Illustrated                                        October 21, 1974

Parked under a dry, bony oak at a campground in northern California's mother lode country a few weeks ago was a 31-foot-long Airstream trailer. In the early morning light the silver capsule gleamed ominously against the background of the black-green oak, looking more like an interplanetary visitation than the mobile home of a latter-day gold miner, which it was.

Inside the trailer, her home for the past five years, JoAnne Gunderson Carner was drinking coffee and waking up for the first round of the Sacramento Union Ladies Classic, her 26th tournament of the season and one of the last steps toward the goal she set for herself in midsummer—to earn $100,000 in one year. Carner was in the process of accomplishing on the LPGA tour what Johnny Miller has done this year on the men's, toppling giants. With her sixth win a week earlier in Portland, she had raised her 1974 winnings to $84,019, thereby surpassing Kathy Whitworth's record for a single season. Whitworth has dominated the women's money earnings in recent years much the way Jack Nicklaus has the men's, leading the list eight of the last nine seasons to Nicklaus's six out of ten, but this year she is some $35,000 behind Carner.

The wonder is that JoAnne Carner did not challenge Whitworth sooner. Carner is now thirty-five and she came to the tour in 1969 as the Great Gundy, a big, easygoing woman whose amateur record included six national championships—five women's and one junior—and who for several years rankled the pros by maintaining, aloud, that the tour was not for her because 1) it wasn't fun, and 2) the pros were not all they were cracked up to be, and 3) she and nine other amateurs could beat any 10 pros any old day, etcetera. And just to emphasize her point, she and her husband Don would drive their trailer to Florida from their home in Massachusetts each winter, stop just long enough for her to play and finish well up in a pro tournament or two (once, in

299

*JoAnne as a professional.*

1969, she even won one) and then, leaving the prize money behind for the pros to divide among themselves, they would go fishing.

So, when the Great Gundy did turn pro late in 1969, it was a matter of putting up fast or shutting up for good. She won one tournament in 1970 and was named Rookie of the Year, but her winnings, $15,000 or so, did not approach her expenses. The next year she won two tournaments, one of them the United States Women's Open, but she still earned barely enough to keep the trailer in shag rugs. Then followed two miserable, winless seasons during which her powerful, natural swing went to pieces and with it her confidence. A year ago, she finished out of the money in eight straight tournaments.

"As an amateur I could hit the ball, but I didn't really know how," she says. "In twenty years of golf I'd had never had a slump, so I didn't know what to do when it came. I didn't know how to break down my swing and find out how to hit every shot. And at the same time, I was thinking too much. I couldn't stop analyzing while I was playing. You try so hard and you put so much pressure on yourself."

Something kept her going, maybe pride, or what she calls "my pig-headed Norwegianness." A major factor was Don Carner who, besides being coach, confidant, business manager, and constant companion, is also booster, publicist, fishing partner, and, sometimes, cook. He is an intense, wiry man with thinning blond hair combed over a brown scalp, and he claims he makes the best chicken and dumplings anyone ever ate. One of the other important things he does is make sure there are still some good times to balance JoAnne's hours on the practice tee—like a fishing trip, such as the one he was planning for this week's break between Sacramento and San Diego.

"JoAnne has a swing like Babe did," says Marilynn Smith. In 1949, along with Babe Zaharias, Marilynn Smith was a founding member of the LPGA, and at forty-five she still plays the tour with considerable success. "JoAnne has the power that Babe had and the same sort of three-quarter swing. She also has Babe's communication with her galleries." When they are straight, and sometimes even when they are not, Carner's drives travel 250 yards, which is nearly thirty yards ahead of her playing partners.

JoAnne, for all her power, was going nowhere last winter until she went to Gardner Dickinson in Lost Tree Village, Florida, for help. In two sessions—three hours one day, one hour another—Dickinson laid out his theories for the Carners. He could mimic JoAnne's swing and so was able both to explain and demonstrate what was wrong. "Then he showed me what he wanted me to do," says JoAnne. I guess I'd always been a bad pupil. I think I hadn't ever really listened till I began listening to Gardner."

Dickinson was the beginning. Next came Texas Rangers' Manager Billy Martin, of all people. Through mutual friends, Martin and Carner wound up at the same dinner table one night toward the end of spring training. Conversation worked itself around to golf, and Martin, who knows a lot about getting the most out of the athletic psyche, went to work on JoAnne.

"He asked me if I was scared," says JoAnne. "I said that although I hated the word, I would admit that I didn't trust my swing and I guessed that was a form of being scared."

They talked until 2 a.m. about aggressive thinking and enjoying the game and how to practice. Martin pointed out that because she was practicing in the mornings before her rounds, JoAnne was bringing her analyzing frame of mind onto the course with her.

"He told me that you just can't shut it off as soon as you begin to play," she recalls. "He said I should just warm up, hit 15 or 20 balls to loosen my muscles before I play, and do my analyzing afterward. He

said that then I should go to work with specifics in mind, like bad
fairway woods or poor eight-irons. Now Don and I talk over the round
and decide what I should work on. Then I might hit as few as two
buckets or as many as nine.

In the meantime, JoAnne put herself on a diet. She is five feet seven
and looks taller. She has always had a big frame, but over the last few
years she had put on so much weight that her girlish appearance had
turned almost matronly. By eliminating breakfast and lunch and
Cokes on the course for more than seven months, she has taken off
thirty-five pounds. Her big, direct blue eyes have emerged as the face
around them has receded. She still will not say what she weighs, but
she will say that it is less than Don weighs for a change.

Carner's winning streak began in May with the Bluegrass Invitational in Louisville and continued through two of the next three tournaments—the Hoosier Classic, in Indiana, and the Desert Inn Classic.
In July she went back to Gardner Dickinson for one more day-long
lesson and won again in mid-August in St. Paul. Then came Dallas and
Portland, both in September.

At Sacramento she finished tied for fourth, picking up only $1,700,
and her dream of becoming golf's first $100,000 woman just about van-
ished. If she failed to make it, it is more a reflection on LPGA purses
than her year-long performance. Her six wins, transposed to the men's
tour, would surely have brought her more than $200,000.

Now JoAnne is back on the practice tee and Don is watching her. Her
drives have been veering right all day. He spots the fault in her position
at address.

"You keep that right side down," he says. "When you get that right
hip down, you look so damn good."

Soon the shots she has been pulling start to straighten out and she is
obviously beginning to enjoy herself. She moves quickly through all her
clubs. Everything is working right.

"O.K., JoAnne, let's go home," says Don, seeing she is beginning to
tire.

"Naw," says JoAnne, continuing to swing, hitting one red-ringed
range ball after another. "It feels good."

# Make Way for Mr. David Foster

## Sarah Ballard

Sports Illustrated                                    April 28, 1975

When Sandra Palmer made a commercial for a Colgate-Palmolive detergent, she recited the dialogue in her gentle Texas twang.

"Dumb shot! Lipstick on mah nahlon shirt . . . Hahm I gonna get that out?"

Now Palmer can throw away that nahlon shirt and buy a hundred more, because by the time the Colgate-Dinah Shore Winners Circle LPGA Championship was over, she had made only one dumb shot in four rounds and it was on the 72nd hole when it no longer mattered. She blew a 1½-foot putt in front of a gallery of thousands at Palm Springs and several million more TV watchers, but all it meant was she had won $32,000 by one shot instead of two.

Kathy McMullen came closest to catching Palmer, who led all the way. McMullen is a tall, strong, 25-year-old from Florida who hunts bear in the Everglades and shoots pool to relax. She took advantage of a windless Saturday to fire a competitive course-record 66—as did Sue Roberts the same day—that placed her three shots behind Palmer at the start of the last round. She narrowed the gap to two midway through the back nine on Sunday, but a double bogey on the 14th hole ruined her chances.

Palmer's rounds, 70-70-70-73—283, five-under-par, were a marvel of consistency that reflected two weeks of diligent practice. She arrived in Palm Springs on March 30, and, while living in the townhouse she owns at a nearby development called del Safari, she played the 6,347-yard Mission Hills Golf and Country Club course every day until the tournament began, accustoming herself to the eccentricities of its nerve-grinding greens and the winds that blow down from Banning Pass and roar across the valley floor nearly every afternoon. "I don't have a secret," Palmer said, after accepting the biggest prize in women's golf. "I just work hard."

303

Palmer is only 5′1½″, but she has powerful calves and thighs. Her drives average 220 yards, with an occasional 240, and her hard work has earned her thirteen tour victories and more than a quarter of a million dollars since she turned pro in 1964.

To understand the importance of the Colgate-Dinah Shore to Sandra Palmer, you have to take into account the fact that the total prize money in the average LPGA tournament is $40,000, with $5,700 for first place, so that winning the Shore is worth approximately 5½ average tournaments. Even fifth place is worth more than first in most events. There are few players who would not rather win the Dinah Shore than the U.S. Open, and the devil take tradition.

"Once you turn pro, it's the money you make that you're judged by," says JoAnne Carner, who won the 1971 Open. "I'd like to see the Open be the most prestigious someday, but it isn't now."

Gratitude plays a large part in the golfers' loyalty to the four-year-old tournament. "They've done so much for us," says Sandra Post, the blonde, 26-year-old Canadian who last December won one of Colgate's three new tournaments, the $72,000 Far East Ladies' Open in Melbourne.

"They" is really David R. Foster, the 54-year-old president of the $2.5 billion Colgate-Palmolive Company, the man who gave the world Irish Spring. Foster is a Cambridge-educated Anglo-American who once played to a two handicap and who looks like a balding, slightly stuffy British elf. He is a member of the Royal and Ancient and several other golf clubs here and in Great Britain, and he is an all-round sports buff who, according to an assistant, can name the winner of the shotput at the Melbourne Olympics as easily as he can come up with the sales potential of a new liquid detergent.

Foster got into women's sports in 1972 with the first Dinah Shore event. Colgate put up a $110,000 purse, the first six-figure prize money in an LPGA tournament, and Jane Blalock won $20,000. "We felt a larger purse would serve to upgrade women's golf, bring more young players into it and stimulate higher purses all down the line," says Foster. He did not add, but might have, that women's sports were a bargain then and still are.

"Until we got into golf," says Tina Santi, Foster's director of corporate communication, "nobody would touch women's sports with a 10-foot pole. Late last year we bought the women's free-style ski tour for $90,000 in prize money. Nobody else wanted to sponsor it. We bought half an hour on ABC on Easter Sunday, and the show drew an eight rating, which was 50% better than we or ABC had forecast and which equaled the rating of an NBA game on at the same time." The Dinah

Shore ranked sixth last year out of 31 televised golf events, ahead of both the Masters and the men's U.S. Open.

Though Colgate expanded into women's tennis, skiing and track last year and is looking into other sports, it still indulges the LPGA like a favored first child and probably will continue to do so, at least as long as David Foster is in charge. The purse for the Dinah Shore has doubled since 1972; Colgate has purchased the Mission Hills Golf and Country Club, where the tournament is played, to guarantee the conditioning of the course and to ensure its continued availability; and thirty-six pros, not just Laura Baugh, have been paid to do TV commercials for Colgate products and promotion for the tournament. Kathy Whitworth, who for eight years was the most successful female golfer in the world, is only lately learning what it is like to be recognized. She is shyly pleased when people recall only that she is "the Ajax lady."

There is concern, however, that the preeminence of Colgate is scaring other sponsors away. "Procter & Gamble, for instance, is a company that has a lot of money to spend on advertising," Palmer said after Saturday's round. "Now maybe they want to get into women's sports but are scared of golf. Other companies think they're going to have to take a backseat to Colgate."

"We have to learn how a corporate executive thinks about things," says Carol Mann, the LPGA's unpaid president for the last two years. "We can't just go in and throw a player guide on an executive's desk. We have to get sophisticated." As part of her unending search for additional revenue, Mann is talking to TV people, licensing agents, book publishers, and film makers. "We're a $2 million business, and I want to see us do our business in a more businesslike way. We have 120 players depending on us to make their livings." If some of her business ventures produce, particularly TV, Carol Mann may be able to quit selling golf and concentrate on playing it again.

For the week of the Dinah Shore, though, the pros are invited to forget their problems and let themselves be pampered like movie stars. Colgate puts them up, if they wish, in a slick Palm Springs hotel called The Spa, pays all their expenses, and plans a lavish week of entertainment around them. There are parties every night until the tournament begins, but the style of each is informal and they end early. The pro-am, in which the women are paired with Colgate's other guests—mainly business people important in the Colgate scheme of things—lasts two days, but the prize money is substantial. And best of all, the requisite list of celebrities, without which a respectable pro-am cannot survive these days, excludes comedians. That was David Foster's idea. May he be rewarded in heaven.

# Sandra Palmer Can Handle the Pressure

## Sarah Ballard

Sports Illustrated                                    November 24, 1975

Success has snuck up on Sandra Palmer. It has arrived so unobtrusively that even now when someone asks her, "What next?" she will say, "I want to be No. 1," overlooking the fact that finally she *is* No. 1. With a single tournament to go on the LPGA tour, Sandra has $75,885 in official earnings, and her place at the top of the 1975 money list is secure. JoAnne Carner, last year's leader, is in second place with $64,353 and could not overtake her even if she were to win the Bill Branch Classic this week.

In her twelfth year of professional golf, Palmer not only collected the richest purse on the tour, $32,000, at the Colgate-Dinah Shore event in Palm Springs in April, but she also finished in the top ten eighteen times, or in 70% of the tournaments she entered. In September, Seagram's gave her a check for $10,000 and "a beyootiful trophy this high" for being the best female professional in golf. She sat on a dais at the Waldorf-Astoria among her peers—Joe Morgan, Chris Evert, Mean Joe Greene and others—and chattered over the tournedos with Bernie Parent. "He spoke French and I spoke Texan," she says. "You can imagine what we did to those people."

Most significant of all, in July 34-year-old Sandra Palmer won the U.S. Women's Open and thereby entered golf history alongside Babe Zaharias, Betsy Rawls, Mickey Wright, and the rest. When the Open was finally hers and she came off the long, wind-whipped Atlantic City Country Club course, the winner by four strokes over Carner, Sandra Post, and amateur Nancy Lopez, one of the very first things she said was, "Now that I've won the Open, I want to do it again, just to prove to myself it was no fluke."

Palmer has spent a good part of her life proving, first to herself and then to the rest of the world, that she is no fluke. She discovered golf through a school-bus window when she was 13, and she was determined to play it. But first she had to overcome a few obstacles. One of them

*Sandra Palmer*

was her height—a 5'1½" golfer has problems. It means that just about everybody else is going to be longer off the tee. It also means that hitting a fairway wood, for instance, is going to be a riskier proposition than it is for a taller player.

"The longer a club is, the harder it is to get back to the ball after you've taken the clubhead away," she says. "And the more upright you are, the less chance there is of error. Carol Mann, JoAnne Carner, and Kathy Whitworth should beat me every time. They should be able to repeat the swing more consistently than I do, but because I work harder, I'm more consistent. There are people better coordinated than I am and with more ability, but if I had to choose, I'd take somebody with confidence over somebody with natural talent."

Palmer has always had determination enough for ten golfers, but her confidence was many years in catching up. "I can't tell you why I wanted to play pro golf," she says. "I wasn't any good. But it was a challenge. It's so much harder to hit a golf ball than a tennis ball. It is an art and you can never perfect it." Although she had won the West Texas Amateur five times and the Texas Amateur once, it was seven

years before Sandra won her first professional tournament, an unofficial event in Japan toward the end of 1970. It was the next spring before
she won a tour tournament, the Sealy Classic in Las Vegas.

All those years she had been working on her game without letup.
Even while she was still teaching high school in Arlington, Texas, near
her Fort Worth home, and saving money for her assault on the tour, she
was driving 200 miles each weekend to Austin for lessons with teaching
pro Harvey Penick. Every Friday evening for a year she spent the night
with friends or with Penick's family. She would practice all day Saturday and Sunday and then head back to Fort Worth in time for school
Monday morning. "Harvey taught me the uses of practice and concentration," she says. Nobody on the tour has learned those lessons better.
For a month before this year's Open, she practiced hitting wedge shots
out of high grass in preparation for the USGA rough. And she played at
least 18 holes every day for two weeks at the site of the Dinah Shore,
studying the tricky ways of Mission Hill's tortuous greens.

Out on the tour in 1964, she came under the wing of Mickey Wright,
who sent her to Harry Pressler, another teaching pro, at a driving
range in Palm Springs. Each winter for three years, when the tour
wound down in late November or so, Sandra would drive from Fort
Worth to the Southern California desert. There she would take an
apartment for two months and play every day. Pressler concentrated on
fundamentals. He broke her swing down and then relied on Sandra's
endless repetition to bring it back together again, improved.

"It was a very lonely life," says Palmer. "But making a change in a
golf swing takes a long time, and winter is the time for making
changes. You do it over and over again, and it is so long before you can
see the change that you sometimes wonder why you are doing it at all."

Since then she has worked with Johnny Revolta in Palm Springs and
with Ernie Vossler in Florida. "You need different people at different
stages of your development," she says. "I began with Revolta because I
had had too much separation under Pressler. It was necessary in order
to break down bad habits, but I was ready for something else."

Vossler is a technician, which suits her now. In addition, she is comfortable with him and his golf-knowledgeable family in Palm Springs
as she has been with few people in her far from average life. She seems
easygoing and gregarious at first, but her banter and her girlish Texas
voice effectively cover an extremely retiring nature, the quality that
probably led her to her lonely occupation in the first place. "I was from
a kind of poor family," she says. "My mother has been married a number of times. I didn't know my father until I was six when my mother

remarried him. When I was in college I couldn't tell people about my childhood. I was embarrassed by it. Even my family didn't know how sensitive I was about it."

Her father was a salesman who traveled all year long. After the remarriage her mother joined him, and Sandra was left in Fort Worth in the care of her grandmother. She spent the summers with her peripatetic parents until school opened again in the fall.

She found golf and her salvation when for two years she and her parents settled down on Lake Lucerne outside Bangor, Maine. "I went to a country school with three grades in one room," she says. "The school bus used to pass a golf course, and one day I got them to let me off there. I found out I could make money by caddying on weekends, so I did. I carried two bags and eventually I was making more money than my mother, who was working in a department store."

When she was thirteen, Sandra walked in the front door of her parents' house one day carrying a bag of Jackie Burke, Jr., golf clubs and crying. "I was crying because I was sure they were going to tell me it was a waste of money," she says. That year she played in her first tournament. She cannot remember today where or what it was, but she recalls shooting 98, which her grandmother, back in Fort Worth, thought was wonderful because it was the highest score in the field.

Before she turned fourteen, her parents had separated again and she was back with her grandmother. She was a star on Castleberry High School's basketball team, but the rest of the year she devoted to golf, practicing at Rockwood, a municipal course near her home, and playing whenever she could at the Glen Garden Country Club, the course on which Ben Hogan and Byron Nelson had begun their careers as caddies.

The club gave her a membership when she was in high school, but by then she was living with an aunt and uncle across town and had no way to get back and forth. While she was playing in a West Texas State tournament in 1957, she was befriended by a middle-aged couple named Warren. Ed Warren was then assistant postmaster for Fort Worth and president of Glen Garden. He and his wife Vida lived across the street from Glen Garden's third hole. When the Warrens learned of the chaos that passed for Sandra's upbringing, they offered her a home and their care, and during her junior year she moved in with them. "It was a difficult decision to make," Sandra says now, "but I was fed up with my home life and all the arguments. The Warrens never said an unkind word to each other."

The Warrens saw to it that she went to college and that she stayed there when she wanted to quit college to play golf. "I have a knack of surrounding myself with people who believe in me and give me confidence," she says. "Good things have happened to me, and I don't know why."

At North Texas State she majored in phys ed, joined a sorority, was elected homecoming queen in her junior year, and had a boyfriend who eventually said, "It's either golf or me," or words to that effect. "I've always wondered, what if we'd gotten married?" she says. "Would I be a principal's wife? I can't picture myself wearing white gloves and going to teas." For a year after graduation Palmer taught gym and biology classes at Sam Houston High School in Arlington and was miserable. "The only way they knew me from them," she says of her pupils that year, "was by the whistle around my neck." But she bided her time, saved her money, and drove to Austin for lessons.

At the beginning of 1964 she played her first round of professional golf in Dallas and shot a 78. Ruth Jessen, the veteran star who was playing with her that day, shot a 64. "In college I was happy-go-lucky," says Palmer. "But once I was out on the tour I felt inferior and inadequate. I stayed to myself, wouldn't let people get close to me. I was kind of mean. In fact, I was a bitch. I was such a perfectionist that I got irritated with myself and I took it out on other people. Recently I started putting the blame where it belongs."

She is coming to terms with herself in other ways, too. "I used to be alone a lot but I didn't want to be," she says. "Now I'm doing more things, and I don't mind being alone."

Late this season she played several practice rounds with Kathy Whitworth, who was the LPGA's leading money-winner for eight years. Ordinarily Palmer practices by herself because few other players concentrate as hard as she does. But she sought out Whitworth because she wanted advice. "I needed to express my feelings. I was becoming too aware of my competition. I was checking the scoreboard for Carol and JoAnne. I asked Kathy how to think, and she told me not to worry about them because they might not be the right ones to worry about anyway. You have to keep your mind on your own self."

Sandra sees the last five years, the years since she began winning, as the "great part" of her life. "I key myself to when I'm in contention coming down those last few holes," she says. "It is a miserable, sick, lonely feeling. You're so scared, sometimes you can't see. But when I can pull off a shot on those holes, that's what I look forward to. And I figure I haven't won *nearly* enough."

# "Tillie, I Won the Whole Thing!"

## Frank Hannigan

Golf Journal                                    August, 1976

The first time I ever saw Hollis Stacy she was standing in a puddle of golf balls in the 14th fairway of the Flint Golf Club, Flint, Michigan. It was during the first of two rounds of qualifying for the 1968 Girls' Junior championship. She was fourteen. Her mouth was wide open but nothing came out. It was raining.

As the USGA staff representative at the event, I had been called to issue a ruling. Hollis, acute enough to notice it was pouring, had decided it was time to put on protective clothing. She and her caddie, about the same age and also mute, had managed to dump golf balls, along with the clothing, all over the fourteenth fairway. One of the dumped balls had moved a ball in play.

A member of the USGA Girls' Junior Committee, who had not actually seen the incident, called for my alleged expertise, via walkie-talkie. As this lady understood the situation, Hollis, or her caddie, had caused Hollis' ball to move.

Grumpily, I advised everyone that Hollis had violated Rule 27, that the penalty was one stroke. I suggested that she and the caddie start picking up the irrelevant golf balls, and then remounted my trusty cart and sped off into the gloom.

My thoughts while riding away remain vivid: I had just penalized a fourteen-year-old with eyes like a wounded fawn; having, as usual, left my own raingear in the motel, I was wet, cold, and subject to disease; and why hadn't I listened to my mother and gone to law school?

That evening and early the next morning, rumors began to spread about the penalty. (There are more rumors at golf tournaments than there are at the end of an Army basic training cycle.) According to a reliable source, they are based on erroneous information. It was suggested that the engorgement of golf balls from Hollis' bag had resulted in the movement *not* of Hollis' ball, but of that of a fellow competitor.

311

We found Hollis on the practice tee. Apparently still not able or willing to make sounds, Hollis managed to confirm by a series of head movements that the now-famous moved ball was not hers. She did so to both my satisfaction and that of Margaret Lovell, then Chairman of the Rules Committee.

Now, this makes all the difference in the world under Rule 27 on stroke-play. The Rules of Golf taketh and they sometimes giveth. Since we were still involved in a stroke-play event, the committee was allowed to negate the penalty (see, for example, 62-21 in your friendly tome, *Decisions On The Rules of Golf*, providing you can lift it). We told Hollis she would begin the second round with one stroke less than was posted on her scorecard the first day. She only nodded and opened those eyes wider. At the end of the second round, she lost a playoff for the 32nd and final qualifying place.

The next year, 1969, marked the start of the great Hollis Stacy Triple Slam: she won the Girls' Junior championship three years running. Since this is August, the month of the two USGA Junior championships, and since we may wait forever for someone to duplicate her feat, it seems appropriate to remember Hollis, the teen-age champion.

Her reign began at the Brookhaven Country Club, in Dallas, where she exhibited extraordinary poise under pressure. It was, in retrospect, the quality one associates most with her success and which may have distinguished her then from a very talented group of peers, including Nancy Hager, Laura Baugh, Amy Alcott, Mary Budke, and Barbara Barrow—all of whom have since either won national titles or played on USGA international teams.

Her opponent in the final at Brookhaven was Mary Jane Fassinger, who, as a student of the late Deacon Palmer, Arnold's father, hit every drive as if it was her last and, consequently, carried the ball great distances. Hollis was 3-up through the eighth only to suffer the unnerving experience of watching her opponent birdie four of the next five holes to get even. Hollis, unfazed, just cruised along, parred everything in, and won 1 up.

Since she was the youngest champion in USGA history and was likely to be around for a long time, it seemed worthwhile to find out something about her. First of all, she was one of ten children born to Jack and Tillie Stacy of Savannah, Georgia. She never drove the ball out of play, seemed quite serious about the prospect of holing every putt, and had learned to speak—at least to golf mandarins. In fact, she began to exhibit an impish humor. You couldn't help notice that she seemed to enjoy herself quietly but continuously and that the other kids

*Hollis Stacy*

liked her. The last factor is not to be understated. It is not easy to be a teen-age winner and retain a sense of balance.

The next spring she became a mini-celebrity by winning the historic Women's North & South tournament at Pinehurst against a field of talented adults. *Golf World* waxed rhapsodic. Charles Price of *Golf* was enthralled. The new *wunderkind* of American golf was proclaimed Glenna Collett Vare and Joyce Wethered rolled into one.

Gee, we thought at Golf House, it's just old Hollis.

Her second Girls' Junior victory in 1971 was fascinating. Hollis was hurting—tendonitis in the right wrist. She winced every time she didn't catch the ball just right. Tillie Stacy had by then been put on the Girls' Junior Committee by Margaret Lovell and favored us at meetings with homilies on motherhood and young golfers, such as "If she's dumb enough to play, I'm dumb enough to let her."

Hollis took advantage of the conditions of the course, venerable old Apawamis outside New York City. Gary Caruthers, a very skillful superintendent, had contrived to give the girls a set of greens that would have warmed the icy heart of whatever USGA ogre was in charge of a

U.S. Open championship. These greens were as fast and firm as the law allows. It was an interesting educational experience. What one learned was that teen-age girls, even the best, can't handle greens like those—the medalist, Louise Bruce, shot 163—but that a golfer with a genius for competing at match play can transform strange conditions into an asset. Hollis simply remained cool, minimized her mistakes, and winced her way to the final where she nipped Janet Aulisi, 1 up, just as she had won by the same margin a year earlier.

Hollis would, during those years, show up at Augusta in April at the Masters tournament. It was her duty as a Georgia golfer. She would have in tow some dazzling little sister, we would review the state of her world, and introduce her to the game's princes and acolytes behind the putting green under the great, old trees. One winter she even ventured north to New York City to be honored at the annual awards dinner of the golf writers of the Metropolitan Golf Association. I remember Dave Stockton, then PGA Champion, recognizing her at the pre-banquet reception and making much of her in a tone of genuine admiration. Hollis and I both marked Dave Stockton down as someone special.

When the summer of 1971 came, Hollis was in great form as she prepared to consummate her unprecedented Triple. The site was the Augusta Country Club, adjacent to the Augusta National Golf Club. Most of her family had come over from Savannah.

The Hollis Stacy sense of humor had blossomed. She took to needling USGA officials just for the fun of it. She stopped play in one round to ask, in a tone of fake indignation, if she had to putt over a miniscule bare spot. Having been forced to inspect this fleck of soil and seriously pronounce it to be other than damage caused by the impact of a ball, I suggested that she stop kidding around and putt. "Boy," she said, just loud enough so that her fervent gallery of Georgians could hear, "you'd make a person putt through the Grand Canyon, wouldn't you?"

The final at Augusta was sublime—the best match I've seen in sixteen years of USGA match-watching. Her opponent was the California phenom, Amy Alcott, just fifteen, who decided that week that she was going to be an important golfer.

The quality of the play was breathtaking. After exchanging wins with pars on the first two holes—Amy was so nervous on the first green she picked up her ball when she still had a makeable putt for a half—they went on to play holes three through seventeen without either player making a bogey, and there was never a concession of anything longer than two feet. During that stretch they made nine birdies.

One down playing the eighteenth, Amy got even by almost holing a bunker shot from an awful lie when it looked as if she might barely get the ball on the green. On the extra hole, a par-four, Amy literally drove 250 yards—about forty yards ahead of her opponent. Hollis then ripped a four-iron shot to within fifteen feet of the hole and made the putt for a birdie. Imagine. She holed a fifteen-footer on an extra-hole to win her third straight national title. The results of her three Girls' Junior championship final matches were 1 up, 1 up, and 19 holes.

After the prize-giving at Augusta, an elderly member in a rocking chair engaged Mrs. Stacy in conversation. The old member asked Tillie her husband's line of work. Mrs. Stacy said Jack was an architect. Asked how business was, Tillie said Jack seemed to be doing OK. "That's good," the old member said, "because that child's gonna cost you a ton of money playin' golf."

A year later Hollis matriculated at Rollins. We kept in touch. Once she came to our house for breakfast. My kids, then about six and four, thought it would be terrific to adopt Hollis as an older sister, although I pointed out that she would eat us into penury.

One winter I got a postcard from Hollis, from Moscow, where she had ventured on a class trip. Lenin's Tomb was on the face of the card, naturally. Hollis Stacy in Moscow! What would Trotsky, Bukharin, and Zinoviev have made of Hollis Stacy?

Rollins and Hollis were not mutually compatible. I sometimes think she would have been happier at Antioch or Swarthmore where they would have been more interested in a live Georgian. One spring she showed up, under the big trees at Augusta National, and said, with just a trace of trepidation, "I'm going to turn pro."

"Swell," I said. "You'll probably starve because golf doesn't mean all that much to you, and the maturity edge you had as a junior isn't going to cut it on the tour, but good luck anyway."

Last year Hollis won about $30,000 in her first full year as a pro.

# Mickey Wright: Questions and Answers

## Kathy Jonah

Golf Digest                                    September, 1976

Mary Kathryn Wright holds more records than any other female professional golfer. She's the only player to win the United States Women's Open and the LPGA championship the same year, and she did it twice, in 1958 and 1961. She set and later matched the LPGA 18-hole record of 62. She amassed the most career victories (82). She has the most wins in one year (thirteen in 1963) and she shares the records for the most consecutive wins in one year (four in 1962 and 1963) and the most birdies in one round (nine). She won five straight Vare Trophies for low scoring average in 1960–1964, and was the leading money-winner from 1961 through 1964.

On September 8, Mickey Wright, 41, becomes the fifth woman to be enshrined in the World Golf Hall of Fame at Pinehurst, North Carolina. The other female inductees are Glenna Collett Vare, Joyce Wethered, Babe Zaharias, and Patty Berg.

A wrist injury and a painful nerve disorder in her left foot forced Wright into semi-retirement from tournament golf in 1970. At home in Port St. Lucie, Florida, her new interest is investment analysis. She studies the stock market avidly "to protect what little money I have." A fiery, emotional player in the 1960s, she remains candidly outspoken about golf and what it takes to be a champion. Here Mickey comments insightfully on the pro tours, the current status of the women's game, and her place in golf history.

Your friend Betty Hicks says it tears you apart not to be playing regular tournament golf.

WRIGHT: My frustration centers on not being able to play as well as I once did. I still could play regularly, but I don't want to. I was out here from 1955 through 1969. That's fifteen years of motels and competitive pressure. Now I play only a handful of events. I've played six tournaments this year. Last year I played only two.

How are you hitting it today?

WRIGHT: As well as I ever did. But there is a difference between playing well and hitting the ball well. Hitting the ball well is about thirty percent of it. The rest is being comfortable with the different situations on the course. What used to be automatic—a little shot over a trap, say—isn't automatic anymore. Now I stand there and grind it, whereas before I would step up, grab the right club, and hit it up there.

How has the calibre of play on the women's tour changed in the last decade?

WRIGHT: There are more good players. There are more girls with better scoring averages. But there aren't any more *great* players than there were. Maybe there are not as many great players now. The leading scoring average during the last few years has not been that much better than fifteen years ago. Bigger purses could be one reason scoring hasn't improved dramatically. You can finish third or fifth or ninth regularly in tournaments and make a comfortable living. I've heard players speak proudly of fifth-place finishes. If you can be happy with fifth, it could be you don't have what it takes to win.

In what ways do today's players excel?

WRIGHT: I feel today's players are much better putters and chippers and wedge players compared to a decade ago. Of course, you have to credit the shorter courses they play. They get to hit more wedges; they play more chips.

Why do many observers feel the women pros still are not as good as the men pros from 100 yards in?

WRIGHT: I've always felt that strength plays a part in the game from the driver down to the putter. It's easier for a strong person to control a heavy wedge even if you are hitting it only fifty feet. Second, the men have a more fiercely competitive tour than the women do. And it's a feeling I have that the men seem better able to control their emotions under pressure.

You were challenged to compete in a men's tournament. Why didn't you accept?

WRIGHT: I had no interest in it. I think I'm realistic. Men have always been stronger players and they always will be stronger players. It would profit no one for a woman to take on a man from the same tees.

You're 5'-9" and bigger than some of the men pros.

WRIGHT: Size per se has nothing to do with it. Listen, I could carry—just carry, now—a driver 230 to 235 yards. I played an exhibition in 1956 with George Bayer, who at the time was the big hitter on the men's tour. But I wasn't impressed with what I'd read. Sure, he was big and strong and hit it long, but you wait and see. We played Griffith Park in Los Angeles. There is a dogleg par-5 hole there about 540 yards long. I hit a driver, a 3-wood, and a wedge. He hit a driver over the trees and had a 9-iron second shot. I needed no more convincing.

Some newspaper accounts say Babe Didrikson out-drove you. Others say you were longer off the tee. Would you set us straight?
WRIGHT: I didn't drive it farther than Babe. I carried it farther. She hit a low, running ball, and I hit it high. I hit it longer on lush courses. She hit it farther in Texas and in Florida where the ball rolls.

Do you have any swings you've particularly admired over the years?
WRIGHT: Jay Hebert comes to mind. His swing was similar to Hogan's—short, compact, controlled. He hit the ball so straight. And Gene Littler for his tempo. I feel Patty Berg has the finest golf swing I've ever seen, male or female. She's been playing for forty years and hits it just as straight and solid as ever. That's a pretty good test of a golf swing.

Do you find that any aspect of the swing is especially difficult for the average woman to master?
WRIGHT: The main problem is women often can't move the clubhead fast enough because they're not strong enough. Otherwise I don't feel women swing any differently than men. A good golf swing is a good golf swing whether it belongs to a 10-year-old boy or a 50-year-old woman.

We all hear comments that women professional golfers are more feminine today than back in the 1950s. Would you react to that statement?
WRIGHT: I resent it every time I see it written that the women pros fifteen to twenty years ago were dowdy, poorly dressed, masculine, and cruddy. We had many fine dressers, considering what the manufacturers were making for us at the time. Remember, slacks and shorts were not allowed on most of the good golf courses.
There was never a girl on tour at that time who wasn't a lady. We used to have rules and fines for bad language, for throwing clubs, for rude behavior to sponsors and the public. They didn't cramp anyone's style, and I think some of the rules would not be bad to have around today.

What do you think of the "new" LPGA—the bigger money and the commercial aspects?

WRIGHT: I think it's the only way to go. But it has changed the character of the tour somewhat. There seems to be more interest in making money, commercializing one's name, rather than just playing golf for its own sake. It's very hard for me not to be an arch-conservative. I could say I'd like to see great, long courses and a smaller, more friendly tour. But this would not help the goal of the majority on tour, which is to grow and grow fast. That personally rubs me the wrong way, but it's what's good for the majority on tour that counts.

Do you think someone will dominate the tour again, the way you did in the early 1960s?

WRIGHT: Some say that because of the fine caliber of play today, there never again will be a person who will dominate the tour. Is that implying that the caliber of play in the past was poor and one good player—like me—was able to dominate? I don't think so. I think that anyone who comes along and wants it as much as I did, or Kathy Whitworth did, or Patty Berg did, if that person has the combination it takes to be a winner, then it will happen again. All my records will be broken.

Do you see anyone out here now who is showing signs of becoming such a player?

WRIGHT: That's hard for me to say because I'm not out here enough. But Amy Alcott, from the first time I played with her in Birmingham, impressed me with having some of those qualities—the want-to, the dedication, the desire, the willingness to sacrifice without it feeling like sacrifice. I don't know enough about her golf game. I was impressed with it the day I played with her. Mary Bea Porter certainly has the physical qualities. Beautiful golf swing, big, strong girl. But I don't know her personality well enough to know if she has the other things it takes. Sylvia Bertolaccini from Argentina is a very impressive player. Good swing, high composure.

You were hot-tempered and critical in your early years, weren't you?

WRIGHT: I was a hothead, but I got it taken out of me real fast. I was the first one ever to get a fine on tour. I paid $150 for smarting off to a sponsor. I was young and righteous. But you cannot become a champion without developing the ability to cope with your emotions. That is the most important factor in becoming a winner. This is what it's all about—being able to control every emotion: elation, dejection, fear, greed, the whole lot. I see girls who can overcome anger. They learn not to get mad when they hit a poor shot. But they still go bananas with joy when they make a good putt. You have to control the whole thing. It takes a tremendous amount of energy, because it's not natural.

You've said in the past that you have trouble coping with the lime-light, that you felt that you had to put on a game face in public. Now that you're leading a more private life, are you able to be more yourself?

WRIGHT: Any time I get back out there in front of people, I am on stage. It's just the nature of the beast. And every time I become conscious of that, I'm not going to be myself.

Mickey, what would you do if your game took a downhill turn, as Arnold Palmer's has. Would you continue playing professional golf if you were shooting regularly in the 80s.

WRIGHT: No, I wouldn't. That hurts me too badly. If I can't play good golf, there's nothing else out here for me. For Arnold, I think there's a lot more to tournament golf than just the golf. The people, his relationship with the public—these things are important to him. They are not so important to me that I'd continue if I were playing badly.

What are your future plans?

WRIGHT: For many years I felt I couldn't teach golf. I was too impatient. But I'm beginning to think I can make a contribution through teaching the game. I'm simply thinking about it at this point. I would want the right kind of environment. I'm not sure yet what that is, but I probably will investigate possibilities in the near future.

# High Tee

## Richard F. Miller

Town & Country                                                    July, 1977

The day is overcast. I stand on the same tee, the par-3 13th hole on the Old Course at Sunningdale, where Bobby Jones committed his only mistake—"a flaw like an emerald" wrote the British golf writer Bernard Darwin—in an otherwise errorless round qualifying for the 1927 British Open. If Jones's iron off the tee landed in a greenside bunker here, what will I do? Tense, palms sweating, I begin to strangle the all-weather grip of my 5-iron. Then I remember, "Now hold the club as gently as if you were shaking hands with a lady." And I keep remembering this as I angrily dig the ball out of wry heather at Sunningdale.

I was in an attacking frame of mind before I played Sunningdale, Walton Heath, Royal St. George's, and a half-dozen other English courses late last summer. Fortunately, my mood was eased to a more civilized one—golf is not a game for the angry—because, before I set out to battle the sway in my swing, the wind, and the weather, I had a memorable visit with a lady's lady, a golfer's golfer: Lady Heathcoat-Amory, better known as Joyce Wethered, the greatest by far of Britain's female golfers. Even now with the welcome rise of women's golf—decades after Joyce Wethered first made her mark—she is considered the equal of Babe Didrikson Zaharias and Mickey Wright.

In only seven years of major competition in the 1920s, Joyce won the English Ladies' championship five straight times and the British Women's championship, the premier event of that day, four times. However, her reputation rests on her scoring. At a time when women were just breaking 80, she was consistently scoring close to par. In the Worplesdon Mixed Foursomes, which pairs Britain's top male and female amateur golfers in an alternate-shot, match-play competition, Joyce Wethered was a member of the winning pair an unprecedented eight times during a fifteen-year stretch. She won on one occasion with her brother Roger, an outstanding player in his own right, and in 1933 she scored her last victory partnered by Britain's finest golf writer, Bernard Darwin.

In 1935, after Miss Wethered had played a golfing exhibition with Bobby Jones, he stated, "Joyce Wethered never even mis-hit a shot. Man or woman, she is the finest swinger of a golf club I've seen." Such praise from the man who carried off the Grand Slam of the four major championships in 1930 is not be taken lightly. As for her feelings about women and golf, she once wrote: "I am not talking about ladies' golf because, strictly speaking, there is no such thing as ladies' golf—only good golf or bad golf played by the member of either sex."

This statement spurred a question in my mind about golf between men and women or, more specifically, about men golfers and Joyce Wethered. However, Lady Heathcoat-Amory, as I should call her, doesn't like to talk at any length about herself. She is incredibly modest. In the living room of her small cottage just off the mansion of her estate in Tiverton, Devonshire—it includes a beautiful 25-acre garden and is now owned by the National Trust—there is not one trophy, photo, or book that would indicate that Great Britain's finest female golfer resides there.

She is dressed in navy trousers, a pale pink and white gingham blouse, and an orange wool cardigan. She is wearing a strand of pearls. Her eyes are a soft hazel; her white hair is short and brushed back. Her handsome good looks belie her age. For at 77 she is extraordinarily attractive. Close to six feet tall, her posture is wonderfully erect, her walk brisk. But her most engaging feature is her smile. When she smiles, which is often, she radiates warmth, a feeling of complete self-fulfillment, and a spirit absent of guile. But her bearing remains aristocratic.

I recognize that it is untimely to ask my questions about golf between the sexes, so I ask her how she learned the game.

"Oh," she says smiling. "I learned by copying. My father used to take Roger and me to watch golf when we were youngsters, and I tried to copy the good players' rhythm. Then, when I began playing fairly well, I played a lot with Roger and his friends from Oxford." (Roger Wethered and his Oxford friends didn't exactly play off a 15 handicap. His friends were Cyril Tolley and Ernest Holderness. The three of them won the British Amateur five times and collectively made twelve appearances on Walker Cup teams.)

Though I now feel I can ask the question I've patiently waited to ask, I'm vulnerable to women with warm smiles; I hesitate and ask Lady Heathcoat-Amory if she still plays golf. She answers that she hasn't played in ten years and has forgotten where her clubs are, but she does admit she watches all the golf she can on television. I asked if she had watched the Colgate European Open for Women at Sunningdale. She says she did. I then ask her what she thought of last year's winner, Chako Higachi, who has a finely tuned sway in her swing. "I would like to see her play in the wind," she says sententiously.

"How does one avoid swaying?" I ask.

"Your only hope," Lady Heathcoat-Amory says smiling, "is to keep your head absolutely still."

I'm troubled. It isn't because I have a difficult time keeping my head absolutely still during my swing, but because I'm having a difficult time imagining her grim-faced in a fierce duel, her hazel eyes icy, staring in putts and staring down opponents. She doesn't have that desperate competitive edge evident in so many great champions. Her manner is gentle and placid. And because of this I ask her how she approached competitive golf.

"Were the major competitions enjoyable?"

"The championships were not enjoyable."

"But your incredible record . . ."

"Oh," she says with a modest smile, "I loved to play golf right. Once on the course, I never looked back but played in the moment."

That's it. Her secret, apparently as simple as slipping on a golf glove but as difficult to achieve as trying to keep the left arm straight during the backswing. Play in the moment.

A slight drizzle is falling, and I ask to see her garden. Then I must leave. Being a dedicated gardener, Lady Heathcoat-Amory is delighted it is raining, delighted that I want to see her garden, and, I feel, since she is a modest, retiring person, delighted I'm leaving. We walk past the thirty-foot-high trimmed hedges of the formal garden, the walk through acres and acres of the informal garden. She points here and there to an incredible variety of plants and flowers she planted last year or ten years ago and tells me their names, which I've long since forgotten. At the car, she gives me clear directions to the motorway that will take me to Surrey. I ask, "Did your late husband, Sir John Heathcoat-Amory, ever beat you playing golf?" I realize full well that he was not a golfer of her stature.

"Oh, yes," she replies. "I remember the first time he did. We were driving home from the club, and he somewhat absent-mindedly said, 'I didn't play very well today.' And then he looked at me and realized what he had said. It was a very odd moment for both of us."

# The Lopez Phenomenon

## Grace Lichtenstein

The New York *Times* Magazine                    July 2, 1978

Nancy Lopez, the amazing rookie pro golfer, hit a spectator in the head recently when teeing off on the 10th hole of the Bankers' Trust Classic at the Locust Hill Country Club in Pittsford, New York. As she rushed up to him, gripping the gold cross around her neck, tears welling up in her walnut-brown eyes, the injured man mumbled to a friend kneeling beside him, "At least I'll get to meet her now."

By her own account, the 21-year-old Miss Lopez was so "shook-up" by the accident that she couldn't concentrate and double-bogeyed the hole. Still crying, she teed off on the next hole . . . and birdied it.

It was only after she resolved to dedicate the tournament, should she win it, to the hard-headed spectator that she truly steadied herself. In the next two days, with pressure on her shoulders that even some World Series veterans would bow under, Nancy sent her huge galleries into spasms of ecstasy on her way to winning her fifth tournament in a row. It was a new record for the women's tour. At the same time, she also broke the prize-money record for both the men's and women's tours for a rookie, an especially impressive feat since there is considerably more prize money in the pot on the men's tour. As of June 18, she had won $153,336. She could break many more records this year, such as becoming the first golfer to be voted both Rookie of the Year and Player of the Year, let alone the first woman to win $200,000 in a single season.

Although her remarkable winning streak ended in Hershey, Pennsylvania, last week, Nancy Lopez has come along faster since turning pro than any woman golfer in modern athletic history. In less than a year as a pro, she has already won more prize money than any other sister competitor, captured seven tournaments (including the prestigious Ladies' Professional Golf Association championship), attracted a following now dubbed Nancy's Navy (a take-off on Arnold Palmer's Arnie's Army), earned the ungrudging admiration of her sister pros, dazzled the press, given Roswell, New Mexico, recognition as the home-town of more than just a singer named John Denver, thrilled Mexican-Americans all over the country, and finally brought women's golf the charismatic headliner it has desperately needed to catapult it into the front ranks of sports.

In person, on and off the fairway, she is a complete charmer, with teeth made for toothpaste ads in a smile that stretches the width of the fairway. Her newly trimmed figure and Vidal Sassoon haircut have won the hearts, minds, and libidos of males from ten to sixty who line up for her autograph. Girls and women as well are won over by her poise, especially when she knocks in 25-foot putts and rips her tee-shots two hundred and fifty yards down the fairway. The bigger and louder the gallery, the happier and more confident she is. She adores her father, who taught her to play; buys her older sister fur coats; cracks jokes when she's angry; and frankly acknowledges the advantages of having handsome young men among her fans. Other than that, she's a pretty ordinary kid. In fact, the other pros call her "The Kid", which also happens to be the nickname of another young phenomenon, 18-year-old Steve Cauthen.

As Carol Mann, an articulate spokesman for the women pros, re-marks, "Comparisons are odious." Yet golf followers are already com-paring the impact of Miss Lopez on the women's game with the dyna-mism Palmer brought to the men's game two decades ago. And the comparisons go even further. Jane Blalock, among the most candid of the pros, calls her "a Nicklaus in golf ability" in a reference to the man generally regarded as the finest modern golfer. "There hasn't been a Nancy Lopez before. No one even close," Miss Blalock adds. "She has the sex appeal of Palmer and the charisma of Trevino," marvels Ray Volpe, commissioner of the Ladies' Professional Golf Association. "They've got the wrong 'Wonder Woman' on TV," says Judy Rankin, the tour's leading money winner last year. Not even the late Babe Didrik-son Zaharias was able to propel the tour into orbit the way Lopez has.

What all this seeming hyperbole means is that in less than a year Nancy Lopez has gone from nobody to a superstar, joining the ranks of Billie Jean King, Chris Evert, Nadia Comaneci, and Dorothy Hamill. Every sport seems to need at least one in the scramble for television and sponsor dollars. For women's golf, Nancy Lopez is that star, and she could not have come at a better time. Athletics are no longer a passing fad for American women but a genuine avocation and, in some cases, a veritable passion. Female players in sports such as tennis, college bas-ketball, and gymnastics are followed as seriously as their male coun-terparts. However, pro golf, which was among the first sports to attract

*Nancy Lopez brought drama to women's golf.*

women in large numbers, has always lagged behind. Now with Ray Volpe as its aggressive commissioner and with Colgate leading the way toward the big prize-money now considered proof of major-league status, women's golf is basking in the sunlight of recognition. Colgate is sponsoring four major events this year, including the biggest purse— $240,000—at the Dinah Shore Winners' Circle.

Like Chris Evert when she first won Wimbledon at nineteen, there is no question about Nancy Lopez's credentials despite her youth. More than that, she has as much warmth, vivacity, and graciousness as athletic talent. It is a rare combination. But what can you say when the brightest new female sports sensation tells you that the celebrity she'd most like to meet is John Travolta, and you notice that in a corner of her suitcase she carries a book titled "Who Is This Man Jesus?"

Miss Lopez showed her class in Pittsford, a posh suburb of Rochester, when she endured the most difficult time of her brief career. She had come in riding a wave of publicity following her victory the week before in the L.P.G.A. championship. That Monday, June 12, she played golf with former President Ford. Tuesday she was in New York for an appearance on "Good Morning America". "When I was in New York, I was walking down the street with my manager, and people were yelling from cars!" she said, wonder in her voice, while relaxing in her motel room a few days later. "One man walked across the street and said, 'I hope you make it five!' "

In Pittsford, she turned on the television set her first day there to see clips of herself hitting shots with Carly Simon singing "Nobody Does It Better" in the background. She was so excited she called her boyfriend, Ron Benedetti, in Houston, to tell him about it.

On Thursday, a practice day during which there are hardly any spectators, Nancy's Navy—some two hundred strong—was already in attendance, cheering every shot. She couldn't walk from the locker-room to the practice tee without a swarm of fans demanding autographs. After nine holes, Nancy, Jo Ann Washam, and their two caddies sneaked off to have a picnic. In the delicatessen where they bought the food, Nancy slipped on sunglasses, but people in that golf-conscious upstate area recognized her, and there was another pause for autographs. When they finally settled down to picnicking, according to Jo Ann, they simply let go, spitting cherry pits at one another. "I can't believe it. I never thought it would be like this," Nancy said, changing her nail polish the evening before the Bankers' Trust Classic began. "A lot of people recognize me! I was always on the other side."

The other side was the obscurity of Roswell, a dusty Southwest town of some 35,000 people in a region called Little Texas because of its proximity and similarity to the western part of the Lone Star State. The Lopez family moved there shortly after Nancy was born in Torrance, California, on January 6, 1957. Although it is unusual for a Mexican-American to star in a country-club sport like golf, it is not unheard of. Lee Trevino is the most famous example. Nancy's father, Domingo, a gentle, gregarious man, loved the game, and he had his second daughter trailing him on the nine-hole municipal course when she was seven. (Delma, Nancy's older sister by eleven years, is married and lives in Southern California.)

"I remember the day my dad gave me a 4-wood and told me to hit along with him," Nancy recalls. "He gave me a ball and said, 'Stay up with us because there are people behind.' I remember taking a peg and teeing the ball up all the way down the fairway because I couldn't hit it off the ground." She pauses a moment. "On the old course I used to hit a driver on the first hole. Now I can hit a wedge," she says with a grin.

The tale of how Nancy practiced with sawed-off 3-woods, how her father gave her the only lessons she's ever had, how both parents saved their pennies and struggled so the apple of Daddy's eye could progress with her game is fast becoming golfing legend. Her brother-in-law, Bernie Guevara, says Nancy wasn't allowed to wash the dishes because her hands had to be protected. Nancy herself says her mother later gave up the chance to buy an electric dishwasher so that her daughter could afford the necessary road trips on the amateur circuit.

Nevertheless, it was not a poverty-to-riches story as much as an all-American one. Domingo Lopez came from a family of nine that lived on a cotton farm in Valentine, in west Texas. Although he never got past the third grade, he learned the trade of auto mechanic. He eventually moved to Roswell because there was better opportunity there.

A good enough baseball pitcher and center fielder to be offered a tryout with a minor-league team, Mr. Lopez turned it down because the money wasn't good enough to support his wife. At the age of forty, he discovered golf through a friend. Within a year, he had become a skillful golfer who played to a handicap of 3. In the evening, his tiny daughter trailed him over the golf course. In time she started to play. She had a natural talent for it.

In high school, Nancy was, in her own words, "just a normal little person", active in swimming, basketball, track, gymnastics, Girl Scouts, and a sorority called "Chums". She played on the school golf team. She managed to tear the ligaments in her left knee playing high-school flag football, which accounts for the athletic-looking scar that still shows. Her best friend was a Mexican-American, but most of her friends were Anglos. In her early teens, Nancy had started to make a name for herself in amateur golf. "I had heard all about her when she was fourteen," Jane Blalock says. "She could outhit me then." Nancy's father managed to keep her going without a sponsor. He was ready to offer to mortgage his house or sell his business if it were necessary. After winning almost every amateur event imaginable, Nancy accepted an athletic scholarship to the University of Tulsa, where she met Ron

Benedetti. At the end of two years, they were engaged. Ron was graduating. After much soul-searching, she quit college to turn professional.

Nancy had already played in her first U.S. Women's Open as an
amateur at sixteen. "I felt like I had no other place to go," she later
explained about her decision to become a professional. Her experience
gained as an amateur began paying dividends immediately. Her first
event as a pro was the 1977 U.S. Women's championship. She was the
runner-up. She came in second in her next two tournaments before
leaving the tour for a while because of a minor hand injury suffered
when a club got stuck on a hidden stump during a swing.

Last summer Nancy's mother died of complications after an appendix
operation. Nancy left the tour for several weeks. She vowed to win her
first tournament as a tribute to her mother. "I was more ready to win
after she passed away," she says quietly. (The comment suggested a
singular characteristic of winning athletes—the ability to turn personal tragedy into a reason for trying harder.) Her first victory came in
Florida this February. Her father thinks it actually might have happened sooner. "Nancy tried too hard for Momma," he suggests. "As long
as you try too hard in any sport, you aren't going to win. As soon as she
won the first one, she relaxed." The Lopez phenomenon had begun.

On the course the phenomenon consists of several parts: an unorthodox swing; a deadly putting game; an aggressive "go-for-it" attitude;
and a composure in tight spots that belies a basically emotional nature.

At the Pittsford tournament, all those elements were present. Friday,
after a breakfast of one egg, bacon, and a muffin—she has lost twenty
pounds since January but is still not as svelte as she would like to
be—Nancy Lopez arrived at the Locust Hill Country Club before noon
for the first round, stepping jauntily out of her butterscotch-colored
Thunderbird in a rust velour sweater and dark blue slacks. At the
practice tee, there was a low rumble of excitement as she approached
with her caddie, 26-year-old Kim (Roscoe) Jones, lugging a red bag of
Ram clubs decorated with a somewhat wilted bouquet, a gift from the
coach of her Tulsa University golf team. "You can tell by the walk," said
one man, knowingly. "Now comes the jockeying for position." And
jockey they did, all but ignoring the blond woman nearby, Judy Rankin,
the tour's leading player last year. As always when competing, Nancy
was wearing a favorite gold cross.

The unorthodox structure of the Lopez swing has probably been over-
emphasized, but her variations on the standard movements of the modern swing are fascinating to explore. Nancy brings her driver back
almost in slow motion; her wrists unusually thrust forward, but some-

where on the downswing the club becomes properly aligned; she follows through in a sweeping arc that leaves the club hanging behind her back. At 5 feet 7 inches and 135 pounds, she is far from the largest woman pro, yet she clobbers the ball between 235 to 250 yards off the tee, decidedly longer than most of the women professionals.

Judy Rankin was all business at the practice tee. Nancy, too, watched her drives carefully as they arched toward the 200-yard mark. Still, when Jo Ann Washam, practicing nearby, accidentally sprayed some turf in her direction, Nancy smiled and yelled, "Jo Ann, you're hitting us with your dirt." Miss Washam's caddie, who once dated Nancy and introduced her last year to Roscoe, came over, and the three of them chatted as if they were still at their picnic. (Roscoe is an employee, adviser, and platonic friend. Nancy fired him for a few hours some weeks ago because she thought he was trying to boss her around, but they kid about that now.)

Next, on to the practice green. Someone mentioned that her name had been listed as a joke that morning on the scoreboard of the men's United States Open in Denver, and that big smile reappeared. At length, wishing Jo Ann Washam good luck, she walked across the lawn to the first tee.

Fast greens and a shifting wind kept most scores high on the first round. Miss Lopez's undoubtedly would have been lower than 72, one-under-par and one behind the leader, had it not been for hitting Jerry Mesolella on the head on the 10th hole. "I really wasn't concentrating very well on the back nine," she admitted after the round. She had never hit anyone before. How rattled was she? I asked Roscoe, who was calmly smoking outside the press room. "She's still rattled," he said.

That night, after dinner with Dick Schaap, the writer who is already lined up to do her biography, Nancy tried to unwind by spending some time at the discotheque across from the motel. All it did was get her to bed later than usual. The next day she was tired, the air was humid, and both took their toll. On the 18th green, she three-putted for a double bogey, a sin of major proportions. Her eyes narrowed under the brown visor that matched her brown pants as she strode into the score-keeper's tent, still one under par but three strokes behind the leader, Jane Blalock.

"If I weren't here, I'd be cussin'," she said with a rather fierce smile as she walked into the pressroom. "I'm mad, I'm hot." She had worked on her putting for three years. In the estimation of Miss Blalock and others, Nancy Lopez is "the best putter, male or female, in the game today". As it turned out, that three-putt double-bogey may have won her the tournament.

Relaxing with friends in the bar, Jane Blalock, a $102,000 winner the previous year, was enjoying leading the tournament. She admitted it was a bit "scary" to have a streaking player like Nancy behind her, but she had resolved not to think about it.

"We've all said, 'Let's win one. Let's one of us knock her off this week,' because it's a challenge," Jane Blalock said of Nancy. "But it's amazed me. There hasn't been any overt jealousy. I think maybe the girls are smart enough to realize how much she's doing for all of us."

Jane Blalock's feelings were seconded by every player I spoke with. Even before the rash of publicity, Nancy Lopez was well-liked by the other golfers on the tour. She tends to keep to herself except for occasional outings with friends, such as Jo Ann Washam. However, she is considered a good partner on the course, and her fellow pros are impressed by her maturity. Kathy Whitworth, at 38 the all-time money winner on the tour—about three-quarters of a million dollars—but just then in the midst of a bad slump, said she was more concerned about her own game than Nancy's. Nevertheless, she added, "She's like on a tidal wave, and I'm excited for her." To Carol Mann, Nancy Lopez had brought the tour an incredible amount of attention. "She's a charming girl, and her personality really comes across. But first, she won tournaments."

That night, Nancy stayed out of the disco. In her motel room, she called her father to wish him an "early" Father's Day. The week before, she had been so confident in Ohio that she had promised him the L.P.G.A. championship as his present. Now, she was thinking about a pool table as his "official" gift.

Sunday, the day of the final round, was a little less humid, but the tension was palpable. Much as Jane Blalock is respected, there was not a writer between Buffalo and Syracuse who didn't want Nancy Lopez to catch up and break the existing records. Nancy wore a green-and-white striped skirt instead of the pants of the previous days. As she walked to the practice green, someone gave her a five-leaf shamrock for good luck. There were girls wearing T-shirts imprinted with the New Mexico sun symbol.

Stepping up on the first tee before a crowd about twice the size of the one the year before, Nancy displayed a cool that might be the envy of Julius Irving as she smiled broadly, tossed a little gloved wave to the swarming gallery, tipped her vizor, and then belted a drive over 250 yards down the fairway. She missed the lengthy putt she had for an eagle and settled for a birdie. On the front nine she narrowed the gap that separated her from Jane Blalock. Birdies on the fourth hole and the eighth hole put her four under par. On the ninth she got down a

25-footer for still another birdie. She moved on to the back nine with a spring in her stride.

Roscoe had told me that at times Nancy can be ruthless. When I had confronted her with this, Nancy didn't shrink from the adjective. She recalled that several tournaments back, JoAnne Carner, the player she most admired as a youngster, jokingly announced that she was ready to leave Nancy "in her dust". All this did was to make Nancy, in her own words, "ready to charge". She went on to say, "It pumped me up. I wanted to feel like I was mad. I birdied the first two holes."

On this day, Nancy and Jane remained tied for the lead after ten holes. "I just looked at Roscoe and laughed because I *loved* it," Nancy said. "He knows that when I get really psyched up like that, I can do anything." On one hole she predicted that she would sink her chip shot. There were few shots that Nancy was unable to summon from her repertoire that day. It was evident that she had risen to the occasion as only a true champion can. In the earlier rounds the back nine had not been kind to her. Now, at each hole she previously had trouble with, she muttered, "You owe me one."

On the eighteenth, Nancy's tee shot flew straight down the eighteenth fairway but her approach ended up in a bunker protecting the green. Her recovery shot left her a dangerous 35-foot putt. One of the golfers in her threesome, who was out of contention, sank a putt that was a shade longer and on the same line as Nancy's. After taking a deep breath, Nancy got set over her ball and rolled in the most important putt of her life.

Nancy was sitting on her golf bag not far from the eighteenth green when Jane Blalock's third shot—the one she had to hole to earn a tie—finished well wide of the flag. Nancy jumped up, her grin running from ear to ear, tears in her eyes. She hugged Roscoe. Regaining some of her composure, she made a fine acceptance speech on the home green. Inside the press room, she went directly to the phone, dialed New Mexico, and shouted, "Dad, I won!" Her nose twitched and the tears came. "I really played well today," she told him, "Happy Father's Day."

# Women Golfers Pay Tribute to a Champion of the Past

## John S. Radosta

The New York Times                                    April 17, 1977

HILTON HEAD ISLAND, S.C., April 16—During the last four days, many of the country's best women golf professionals have been diffidently approaching a white-haired stranger to ask her to pose for a snapshot, either with them or alone. Others ask for an autograph. Some simply introduce themselves for the privilege of shaking hands with her. They are enchanted by her aristocratic bearing, her manner, her English accent, her shy smile. Although she is 75 years old, she is taller than most of them and, of course, she is old enough to be their grandmother.

As it happens, Lady Heathcoat-Amory is as interested in these young women as they are in her: She is utterly bug-eyed at the way they play golf. "And they're all so nice," she adds. "I've been moved so by their kindness."

The occasion for her visit is the second Women's International golf tournament, a Masters-like invitation event for 58 professionals and 12 amateurs that is being played on the Devil's Elbow course of Moss Creek Plantation near here. In the program Lady Heathcoat-Amory, who has come to America for only the second time in her life, is listed as a "distinguished guest." Her present name means little in the world of golf. But her maiden name, Joyce Wethered, means a lot.

Joyce Wethered is considered by the authoritative Encyclopedia of Golf as "the supreme woman golfer of her age, perhaps of all time." After she played a match with Bobby Jones in 1935, he called her the best golfer, man or woman, he had ever seen.

Joyce Wethered won the English Ladies Championship five times in a row, from 1920 through 1924, winning 33 consecutive matches. She won the British Ladies in four of those years, and she won many lesser titles. In 1929 she came out of her first retirement to win the British Ladies at St. Andrews. To do that she had to beat the American cham-

333

pion, Glenna Collett, in one of the greatest matches in the history of women's golf, 3 and 1, in 35 holes.

Counting two retirements, Miss Wethered's competitive career lasted only nine years. Why had she cut it so short?

"I wanted to do other things, and golf takes so much of your time, doesn't it?" Lady Amory said in a quiet chat away from the action of the Women's International. "I was keen on tennis and fishing, and I wanted to stay in touch with my friends."

In the early 1930's she came out of retirement the second time and turned professional in an offhand manner. Although she was prosperous and did not need the money, she accepted a job as manager of the golf department of Fortnum and Mason, the famous London department store. She also gave some instruction there.

She never competed as a professional, but in 1935 she ranged across the United States in a whirlwind tour of 30 exhibitions. Her partners and opponents included Bobby Jones, Gene Sarazen, Horton Smith and Babe Didrikson, who had not then reached the peak of her game.

Through some strange intercession by friends that "I still don't know anything about," she recovered her amateur status after World War II. But that was academic because she had stopped competing in 1929.

Lady Amory has not just been sitting around the clubhouse of Devil's Elbow. She tours the course, sometimes in a golf cart but more often on foot.

In her day she hit a long ball, but she is impressed by the way today's players hit irons into the greens instead of fairway woods.

"I was always using the spoon and brassie," she said. She explained that the spoon and brassie, the old names for today's 3-wood and 2-wood, were the most valuable clubs in a woman's bag.

"I knew I'd be impressed by these girls because I've seen them on the telly," she continued. "But in person they are even more impressive. They're frightfully good, and there are so many of them!

"We used to have a longer backswing than today's women use, but then your girls have a lovely swing and a great follow-through. We did not follow through as much."

Lady Amory grew up with hickory shafts and, although she changed to steel shafts, she never liked them much. She found she was getting greater distance but at the cost of control.

"With wooden shafts you could stay on the ball longer," she explained. "The club face stayed with the ball longer—that is, the ball did not leave it so quickly. You retained the feel longer. The ball didn't spring away from you."

Lady Amory was shown some clippings—"cuttings," the English call

*Lady Heathcoat-Amory, left, the former Joyce Wethered,
at Hilton Head Island, South Caroline, with Hollis
Stacy from nearby Moss Creek Plantation.*

them—and she was amused by the clothes she and her contemporaries
wore. "We had to wear long skirts, of course, and they were rather a
nuisance," she recalled. "You took care they were not wider than they
needed to be or they would swirl in the wind. And we didn't want them
narrower than necessary because they would be constricting. The result
was that our clothes looked alike, like uniforms.

"A Continental woman once showed up in black trousers—they were
not called slacks then. We were shocked," Lady Amory recalled. Then
she corrected herself: "I guess we were surprised more than scandal-
ized."

Admittedly, the skull-fitting hats of those days were "funny." But
they were necessary: "The wind blew so! We had to have those tight
hats to keep the hair out of our faces.

"I see so many of your players wearing their hair long, down their
backs. Some wear pigtails. But if the wind should come up, they'd have
to do something, wouldn't they?"

# More Bad News for Male Supremacists

## Peter Dobereiner

Golf Journal                                    September, 1978

If the weight of scholarly opinion is to be taken seriously, the England of P. G. Wodehouse never actually existed. Wodehouse, earnest students of social affairs tell us, invented the whole thing. He created an improbable land of perpetual summer, populated by vapid young men of independent means who survived from day to day largely through the benevolently despotic machinations of deferential butlers; by an assortment of dyspeptic retired colonels, oafish policemen, and absent-minded aristocrats; and by a race of women who were either absolute dragons (if over 50) or impossibly beautiful creatures in cloche hats (if under 25).

It is true that Wodehouse drew his vision of England with a caricaturist's eye. Granted, too, that he took an occasional liberty with matters of fact. But for all of that, he got the tune right. There really was such a place as Wodehouse's England once, and it endured right up to the Second World War, when most of those vapid young men were killed flying Spitfires or leading platoons of Grenadiers.

After the war, the great proletarian revolution swept away all but the last remnants of the Wodehouse world. Only in one sphere did the malady linger on—in the game of golf, or "goff," as its adherents had it. The dyspeptic colonels became club secretaries; the dragonly aunts took over the Ladies' Golf Union; and the eccentric aristocrats sank deep in the sanctuary of their leather armchairs at the club and defied the forces of bolshevism to root them out. There was also a fierce rearguard action fought, in the goff clubs, in defense of another favorite Wodehouse theme, the comfortable assumption of male supremacy. In 1951, the year of which I write, it was commonplace for golf clubs to display signs reading: "No dogs, no women."

At about the same time in America, where women were becoming assertive in the cause of equality, Fred Corcoran, of affectionate memory, had recently helped form the Ladies Professional Golf Association.

He had signed up a sponsor by the name of Alvin Handmacher, the manufacturer of the Weathervane range of sportswear. As a result of that liaison, the women played a series of Weathervane tournaments across America, and, as a bonus, the six leading scorers were promised a trip to England.

That is how Corcoran came to visit England—to set up a tour for his lady players. And that is how he chanced to meet Leonard Crawley.

Crawley, a large, aggressive, powerful man, was a British golf writer. He was also a Walker Cup player. Actually, come to think of it, he was considerably more than that: Crawley was one of the last of a long line of outstanding amateur sportsmen in the Corinthian tradition, a first-class cricketer who had to choose between playing golf with the Walker Cup team or touring Australia with the English cricket team. By 1951 Crawley had fallen into an eminently sensible routine. He would play goff until the Amateur championship in May, then switch to cricket for the summer. The later months were devoted to shootin'. Between whiles he wrote newspaper articles, including one collectors' item describing an epic golf final between two players, neither of whom happened to be playing in that particular event. Or so legend has it.

In his book, "Unplayable Lies", Corcoran describes their meeting.

*"Just how good are these girl professionals of yours?" asked Crawley.*
*"Good enough to beat any team of British male amateurs," I said without hesitation.*
*Crawley cocked an eye.*
*"Oh, come on!" he exploded.*
*I shrugged. "We'll challenge any team you can put together."*
*Crawley's mouth tightened. "You have a match," he said coldly.*

Thus was set in motion a chain of events which was to change the destiny of golf in Britain, to emblazon the banner of women with their noblest battle honor in the war between the sexes, and to erase for all time the last vestiges of Wodehouse's England.

The West Course of Wentworth was selected as the site of the encounter. July 15, 1951, was the appointed day.

Brigadier-General A. C. Critchley led the team of British male amateurs, each of whom was destined to become an illustrious name in golf (and two, indeed, to achieve the highest distinction as Captains of the Royal and Ancient Club). Four were already Walker Cup players. In addition to Critchley and Crawley, there were John Beck, Sam McCready, Gerald Micklem, and Edward Bromley-Davenport.

Corcoran's squad consisted of Babe Zaharias, Betty Jameson, Peggy Kirk, Betty Bush, Patty Berg and Betsy Rawls. Enshrine their names in glory, for the deeds they performed that day shall never perish!

The Babe, in particular, was inspired. This forthright and courageous woman had been more than slightly miffed by the contemptuous way British golf clubs sought to ignore the existence of women. And she was specially riled by Crawley's snooty attitude. "Save that one for me, son," she instructed Corcoran.

Like many famous battles, this one was preceded by a war of nerves. On her way to the first tee the Babe caught sight of a bicycle with a tiny motor, of half a horsepower, mounted to the front wheel. She was intrigued by this machine, and she got on it immediately and went puttering off through the Wentworth estate for a joyride, holding up the match for twenty minutes.

When she did make it to the first tee, Crawley pointed condescendingly down the fairway and informed her, "There's the ladies' tee down there."

"I'm playing with you, son," she replied jauntily.

Actually, this is getting ahead of the story. And since what was to happen now was surely influenced by what had gone before, I must relate that the teams played foursomes in the morning and the men emerged decisive winners, taking two matches and halving the third. In retrospect, they should have been warned by that one halved match.

As it was, they allowed themselves to be seduced by the twin temptresses of British amateur golf, complacency and kummel. Just why amateurs should have adopted this fiery liqueur as the game's traditional aperitif is uncertain, but for years kummel has been credited with magical properties for quieting nerves, and no match is complete without a few good slugs at midday.

Then it was back to the first tee for the singles. Both Crawley and Zaharias had left their drivers out of their bags, so no invidious comparisons could be made between the lengths of their drives. In any case, the course was baked so hard that the driver was no club for serious golf that day. The ball ran forever.

Crawley could make no sense of his clubbing. At the best of times, he had a tendency to launch his thunderbolts with rather more power than accuracy. (On one famous occasion he misjudged an approach so badly that his ball flew the green and put a dent in the Walker Cup as it sat on a table awaiting the presentation.) Today he was strong on nearly every hole, and Wentworth, with its fairways bordered by silver birch and heather, is no course for the wayward.

The Babe, elegant in her Weathervane sportswear, was ruthlessly accurate, even though she had never seen the course before. Crawley, fuming and sweating, marched along in his Fair Isle jumper and tweed plus-fours. Here I am conscious of that old crack about the Americans and the British being separated by a common language. What are plus-fours? Well, they used to be standard uniform for golfers, and they are what some Americans call knickers. (In Britain, knickers mean something else, a female garment whose nature may be divined from the expression describing a certain type of girl as being not noted for the strength of her knicker elastic.)

After eight holes Zaharias was five up. The crowd was absorbed by the match. On the 16th green the Babe rolled in a six-footer to win by 3 and 2. She was round in an approximate score of two under 4s.

Out in the country, the other men were faring even worse. Berg killed Beck by 7 and 6, Rawls had McCready by 2 and 1, Jameson finished off Micklem by 5 and 4, Kirk took Bromley-Davenport by 2 and 1, and Bush beat Critchley by 3 and 2. It was sensational! Or so it would have been if anyone had realized what had happened. The full impact of the results did not become apparent until everyone returned to the clubhouse.

Even the British reputation for being good losers took a pounding that day. Enid Wilson, the former British women's champion who was covering the match for the *Daily Telegraph*—ironically, that was also Crawley's paper—recalls happily that the men took their beatings very badly. "They stomped off and left their opponents to find their way back as best they could," she remembers with malicious glee. Miss Wilson found the American women back in the club quietly having tea, quite unconscious of the enormity of what they had done. Next day the women played their own tournament and Zaharias won by two strokes, scoring 74-69 over the two Wentworth courses. The men, puce with embarrassment under a barrage of ribbing from their friends, slunk off to nurse their bruised egos.

Today, nearly thirty years later, Crawley can look back on that black day with a semblance of stoicism and rational judgment. "Of course, it was a most fearful embarrassment and we got terribly ragged about it, but really it was not all that much of a surprise, for two reasons. It was out of season for us; I don't think I had touched a club for six weeks or so. And with the course in that state we had absolutely no advantage in length."

Golf in England was never the same after that. The "No dogs, no women" notices began to disappear, and women began to infiltrate ever deeper into the male domain. Some committees put up token resistance, issuing fatuous edicts that women were forbidden to wear slacks, or that they were restricted to certain purdah areas of the clubhouse, or could play only at specified times. But the barriers were down.

The golf establishment, too, tried to carry on as if nothing had happened. They continued to select teams on breeding and background, preferring a good school to a good swing, but the tide of egalitarianism was engulfing them. Pretty soon, youngsters whose fathers were in trade were forcing their way onto the Walker Cup team. Even the sons of artisans began to emerge as leading amateurs. Goff was turning into golf. The world of Wodehouse was gone once and for all.

Let us leave the final word for Crawley, possibly the last survivor from that golden era of true amateurism when men played golf purely for the enjoyment of the game. "The Babe did me a good turn by beating me that time at Wentworth. I made a lot of money out of it. You see, so many people pulled my leg about it that I arranged a challenge match at Pinehurst No. 2 against Louise Suggs, giving her a third and playing off the back tees. I won. And, of course, after Wentworth I got terrifically good odds. I think it might have been 50 to 1."

# Pat Bradley Has Come a Long Way Since She Used To Beat Us Guys in the Hatreds

## Mike Lupica

Golf Digest                                        September, 1979

The last time I played golf with Pat Bradley, she'd moved up to No. 2 in the Hatreds, and she was taking a lot of my money.

"I learned a lot about playing under pressure with you guys in those Hatreds," Pat Bradley says. "I owe you a lot."

It's the only thing I can remember her owing.

Pat Bradley was the first woman Hatred player in the history of the Nashua Country Club in New Hampshire, a distinction much more notable than some twerpy little girl getting onto a boys' Little League baseball team. She's just about the second best woman golfer in the world now, and we like to think it started in the Hatreds.

We called them Hatreds because there was a lot of hate out there. We convened about 4 o'clock Sunday afternoon, by which time our hangovers had gone into remission and most of the old ladies and truly handicapped had stopped cluttering up the golf course. What we had were twenty-four or twenty-five of the best players in the club, plus some real thieves.

It was one fivesome against the others; careening golf cars all over the place; ten million side bets; wonderful tantrums; some club breaking. It was terrific golf, terrific color.

There was T. Whitcomb (Soil) Stanley. Soil was my best pal, and I still don't have any idea what his nickname meant. There was Bones Moriarty, nicknamed Evil, and his brother, Rat. There was Tight Collar Flanagan, who couldn't putt, and Junky Crosby, whose father, Muffin, owned a bakery. There was Winnie the Poo, who'd been rich, and The Pope, who was not religious at all, hating short hitters and slow players. We also had The Blond Spade, Big Kenny, and the Dichard Twins.

We had our own language. Slices were "Cubans," which we somehow derived from bananas; Soil called them "Cubanos" and often would break a club after hitting one. A ball hit into the woods, or some such terrible place, had gone to "DC"—Dead City. A guy who could hit it far had "top arms," an expression I used but never understood. Our swearing was more conventional.

To these Hatreds we reluctantly added this girl, Pat Bradley. The pro, John Wirbal, made us do it. Wirbal said he could probably find a club regulation that forbade Hatreds, so we took her in. By the way, John Wirbal is still Pat Bradley's personal pro.

Actually, we'd heard she was all right—for a girl. She skied, for instance. She'd been to Montana, which seemed important at the time. And we heard she'd once climbed a fence, with her crutches, to sneak into a Red Sox World Series game at Fenway Park. Even Soil Stanley had never done that.

She was always a jock. Her father, Dick, owns a sporting goods store in Westford, Massachusetts, near the New Hampshire border and about half an hour from Boston. Pat played field hockey, and she became an accomplished skier—downhill, slalom, giant slalom. With five brothers, she never had trouble finding a game in just about any sport.

It was in this way that Pat Bradley cracked the Hatreds.

"I'll tell you what," said John Wirbal. "When Pat plays in the Hatreds, she can be on my team, since you guys are so anti-female." Each team had numbered players, one through five. "And just so no one will get offended," Wirbal continued, "Pat will be my No. 5."

Right around this time, John Wirbal's team started taking a lot of our money in the Hatreds. It was really annoying to all of us, but Pat Bradley could flat play. She could hit it far, which particularly bothered me. Pat Bradley also could putt. She took our money. Very annoying.

She never threw clubs, like Soil did, or got bothered by all the dirty talk or crazy betting. We tried to insult her in a nice way, briefly nicknaming her "Beater." She just kept smiling sweetly and hitting greens. She was sixteen years old.

"I had to play well," she says now. "I was the only player in the Hatreds who needed a sponsor. If it wasn't for the pro, you guys would never have let a *girl* play."

She was asked if she remembered the nickname "Beater"?

"Sure," she said. "Even now, I'll be playing a tournament in Florida someplace, and I'll see Soil Stanley on the other side of the ropes, and he'll say, 'How you hitting 'em, Beater?' "

Pat Bradley laughed. She could always manage to laugh about golf. "I'll never forget those Hatreds," she said. "But lemme tell you, I began to see improvement out there. I was always proud of the fact that by the time I left the Hatreds, I'd moved up to the No. 2 position from No. 5. I thought No. 2 was pretty hot stuff."

We tried to keep track of Pat Bradley after she left our Sunday afternoons. We knew she went to a few colleges—Miami-Dade JC and Arizona State and finally Florida International, playing all the time and getting better all the time. When she finally turned pro in 1974, all the Hatreds patted themselves on the backs for being such remarkable judges of talent. John Wirbal, the pro, just smiled a lot.

It's much easier to keep track of her now. Pat Bradley has moved up near the top again. And this time she isn't playing behind Evil Moriarty or Tight Collar or The Pope. She's out there on the LPGA Tour, and that's even bigger than the Hatreds.

Outside of Nancy Lopez, Pat Bradley is probably as good as any of the players on the tour—right in there with Janie Blalock, Sandra Post, Donna Caponi Young, JoAnne Carner, and maybe another one or two. But she would like very much, she says, to be No. 1 some day soon.

"I wouldn't be out here if I didn't think I could be the best player," Bradley was saying one evening this summer after another second-place finish to Lopez. "I know I have the physical ability to be No. 1 on the tour. I have to keep striving for that position, I know that. Maybe it's a minor thing that's going to make the difference for me. But maybe that's going to be the toughest ingredient to find, the thing that's most obvious. I'm just hoping to find it, correct it, and be No. 1."

She has come a long way in six years on the tour, but now she's reached this tremendous roadblock. It's Lopez. Being just behind Lopez isn't too shabby, mind you, but it's aggravating for Pat Bradley.

"There are questions all the time, every week, whether people know me or not," she says. "It's not just annoying. It hurts. I'm not trying to make errors, to miss a shot, but it happens. Every ounce of me is out there trying to be the best. I'm out there spilling my guts.

"Take Atlanta this year. I finish second behind Sandra Post. When the tournament is over, a woman comes over to me—walks right up to me—and says, 'What is *wrong* with you?' What's wrong with me? I wanted to deck her right there."

In 1978 Pat Bradley won $118,000. She won the J. C. Penney Classic, a mixed-doubles thing, with Lon Hinkle, and three women's tournaments: the Lady Keystone, the Hoosier Classic, and the Rail Charity Classic. She finished second in the Borden Classic and the National Jewish Hospital Open. It could very easily have been Pat Bradley's year in her sport, but there was a slight problem.

Nancy Lopez was out there becoming the professional athlete of the year, standing head and shoulders above her sport, winning, it seemed, six or seven tournaments a month. Bradley and her $118,000 and her four tournament wins and her great swing might as well have gone to the beach.

"Playing second fiddle to Nancy didn't hurt me at all," she says.

It hurt.

Through the first six months of 1979, things did not really change, even though Bradley had won nearly $90,000 by then. Through the LPGA championship in June, she had a stroke average of 71.75—and she had already finished second four times. Lopez had won a bunch of tournaments, and had a stroke average a full stroke better. The year 1979 was turning out not much different than 1978 for Lopez and Pat Bradley. Lopez was winning tournaments, and Pat Bradley was winning money, and raves for her terrific swing, and friends for a winning personality that hasn't changed one whit since those Sunday afternoons in New Hampshire.

"I've been out here six years now," she says, "and that's not a great amount of time. Certainly not enough time to panic. But I feel I can't make the excuse anymore that I'm still young."

There are a couple of ways to look at Pat Bradley's current station in life. For one thing, she *has* emerged from the pack as a consistent challenger to Lopez. There were some Carners and Posts and Blalocks out there picking up wins early in '79, but Bradley, in the long run, may be the most solid player.

She won her first tour event in 1975, the Colgate Far East Open. It was an unofficial tournament at that time, but that didn't matter. She had won a tournament. In 1976, she won the Girl Talk Classic and $84,000, and she was named the Most Improved Player on the women's tour by *Golf Digest*.

Bradley's career seemed to be jeopardized in 1977 when she was afflicted by a mysterious thumb ailment. Her left thumb throbbed with pain, and she had a difficult time holding onto the golf club. "I don't know how the thumb kept from falling off," she says.

Various doctors diagnosed the injury in various ways. She checked in and out of clinics, but she still managed to win $78,000 during the year. Finally she entered a Boston hospital for extensive tests, and was delighted when a doctor reassured her that the trouble was merely a chronic sprain. Pat still tapes the thumb carefully before each round, and she is reconciled to the fact that it is bothersome and painful.

Pat Bradley's current situation is similar to the one a fellow named Tom Watson was in a couple of years ago, before he became No. 1 on the men's tour. The questions Bradley is asked these days are the same questions the great Watson was being asked when he was finishing second all the time. Why don't you win more? Why don't you win more?

"I don't mind comparisons with Tom Watson, let me tell you," Bradley says, brightening at that thought. "I know I've been compared to Tom a little bit. A couple of years ago he was a bridesmaid and never a bride.

"It's funny how things change. When I first started out on the tour, I just thought about making the cut. I mean, that was *all* I thought about. Make the cut. Pick up a couple of hundred dollars. But then, as I went along, I came to expect more of myself, a lot more of myself. When I'm not producing, I'm really hard on myself. I used to be happy just to hit a green. Now, that's not enough. I want to be ten feet, or eight feet. I have very high expectations for myself now. I'll never be able to accept mediocre."

She is not mediocre; she is not the best. She thinks a golfer peaks at the age of 31; she is 28. That's why she isn't hitting any panic buttons. She can still win this little Hatred, because she has a terrific golf game from tee to green. Not the longest driver, but one of the longest. A fine long-iron player, always a test of a really solid swing. You can't lie to a 2-iron. A short game that keeps getting better. All she has to do, she says, is putt better.

Lopez is a brilliant putter. Right now, she putts the same bold, laughing way Arnold Palmer did back in the late '50s and early '60s, when he was turning golf into a television show. Pat Bradley doesn't putt that way. Too often, she putts like Arnie does *now*.

"Nancy is a fabulous putter," says Pat. "She looks at 20-footers the way the rest of us look at one-footers.

"I think I have a real good stroke, I really do, but, I swear, I'm the queen of the lip-out and the rim-out. The ball comes out and looks up at me and grins, as if to say, 'Too bad, you missed again.' I just don't know how to die the ball into the cup."

She dies a little and finishes in second and third and fourth place. In 1978, she was out of the top 10 only eight times in thirty tournaments. Through the first six months of 1979, she was in the top 10 on twelve occasions—more than any other golfer.

But she hasn't won any tournaments in 1979.

"I know I can win, though," says Pat Bradley.

She always did before.

# Amy Alcott Kept the Heat On

## Barry McDermott

Sports Illustrated                                              July 21, 1980

While the rest of the players were stumbling around in the fiendish heat of Nashville, Tennessee, muttering imprecations at the weather and the bad bounces they were getting on the sneaky Richland Country Club course, Amy Alcott gulped potassium pills, tied a "bandido" kerchief around her neck, pulled down her painter's cap and demolished the field in the U.S. Women's Open.

Alcott seemed to be staging her own private Grand Ole Opry in Music City, U.S.A. Certainly she was calling all the tunes out at Richland. Her 72-hole total of 280 was a record for the championship, shattering the mark of 284 set by Jerilyn Britz last year. And it was a whopping nine strokes ahead of runner-up Hollis Stacy. Alcott also became the ninth player to lead an Open from start to finish. Tied for first with Barbara Moxness after an opening-round 70, she pulled away with another 70 on Friday, and left everyone in the dust with a 68 on Saturday that gave her an eight-shot bulge over Stacy. On Sunday, after she had clinched her first Open with a safe and sane 72, she was presented with the $20,000 winner's check.

The temperature during play last week hovered around 100° in the shade. A thermometer placed in a sand trap registered about 20° higher. Under these conditions, strong people did uncharacteristic things. At one point, two-time Open champion JoAnne Carner found herself absentmindedly trying to puff on her pencil instead of a cigarette. Nancy Lopez-Melton took a *nine* on the par-5 13th hole the first day and knocked herself into a permanent deficit. Beth Daniel, one of the most consistent players on the circuit, got upset at a photographer during the opening round and made a triple bogey and two bogeys before she cooled down three holes later. On Saturday, with the thermometer at 101° and not a cloud in the sky, Stacy poured water down the back of her neck on every tee.

346

Throughout all this, Alcott remained unruffled. Moxness stayed with her for a time. Then her putter began misfiring, earning itself the nickname "the Mox-Ness Monster." She even four-putted one green. One by one the challengers fell away. On Saturday Lopez-Melton threatened—until she went four over par on a three-hole stretch. The tour's leading money-winner, Donna Caponi Young, was within two strokes early the same day before ballooning to six over par on the next ten holes. After that, everyone was playing for second place.

Alcott, 24, thus fulfilled the promise she showed as a precocious Californian who had learned the game by hitting balls into a backyard practice net and putting into soup cans set into her parents' lawn. After her first lesson, the pro told her mother, "You're a blessed woman." Alcott took the United States Junior Girls title in 1973, turned pro at eighteen, and won the third tournament in which she played. Since then she has won at least one title each season, and last year she blossomed with four victories and finished third on the LPGA money list with a total of $144,839.61.

Other players say that one reason Alcott is raking in so much loot is that she uses her head, especially when she's on the course. The rational approach worked for her in the blast furnace last week. When adversity threatened, she just stared it in the eye and went to her short game, which ranks with the best. On the 16th hole on Thursday, her approach flew forty yards over the green, but she salvaged a thinking-player's bogey. And after a poor first shot on the 17th on Saturday, she was tempted to try to hit her second shot over some trees to the green. She thought better of it, chipped out, wedged on, and sank a ten-foot par putt. Routine.

But smarts isn't Alcott's only notable quality. She seems to have had the good fortune to be born with a killer instinct. She putts so well that she makes the game a whole lot simpler for herself. In the Open, Alcott had only one three-putt green, and that came on the first day.

Because it was the Open and the weather was hotter than hot, even Alcott had troubles. The heat caused her hands to become swollen, and she had to keep putting ice on them. That morning, Alcott had walked into the locker room wearing a kerchief tied around her neck, and when the other players began hooting about it, she had a ready answer. "I'm going to rob a bank today," she said. Actually, the robbery took four days, but it was easier than most.

The new Open champion doesn't play golf as it is taught by your standard pro. However, her unorthodox three-quarter swing is effective, and she has a delicate touch with a wedge. She also carries a seven-wood, an unusual club she has had since she was fourteen.

*"I guess I should be out trying to meet a doctor or a lawyer, but I'm having too much fun."*

"When that baby goes and I have to put it to sleep, it'll be a sad day," she says.

The narrow Richland course and its par of 36-35-71 obviously suited Alcott. "I like bowling-alley fairways," she says. "I like tight courses where you can't wander." Richland was all uphill, downhill and side-hill, with trees guarding not only the greens but also the fairways. Whenever Alcott was faced with a difficult lie in the rough, she escaped with her seven-wood, bent an iron shot, or finessed a chip with one of her three wedges. The heat had one beneficial side effect for her and the other players. To prevent the greens from turning to dust, the USGA had to keep them damp, and iron shots could be aimed right at the pin. That is Alcott's style.

Alcott claims to have made two important decisions in her life. The first came when she was nine and was vacillating between tennis and golf. She chose golf because it was on TV. "I thought everybody was named Labron and Byron, talked with a Texas accent and said, 'Nice shot, pardnah.' " The other decision came after she had graduated from high school and won more than 150 junior tournaments. "Amy, you've found your niche," she said to herself. "You don't want to go to college. You want to go out and knock sticks down."

Alcott has a wry sense of humor and tells a story about what it is like to be young, single, Jewish, and rosy-cheeked on the tour. "These Jewish parents keep calling me up and telling me they want me to meet their sons," she says. "They say, 'You'll like him. He'll walk the course with you.' I guess I should be out trying to meet a doctor or a lawyer, but I'm having too much fun."

# A Brief Vacation From Practice

## Patrick Leahy

Golf Journal                                        November/December, 1980

Thirty-one years ago, in 1949, Dorothy Germain Porter won the United States Women's Amateur championship at the Merion Golf Club, in Ardmore, Pennsylvania, not too far from her home club in Llanerch, which like Ardmore, is a suburb of Philadelphia. This was the major achievement of her career. She had won most of the prestige competitions, including the Women's Western and the Eastern Amateur; she had an array of local and state titles to her credit; and in 1950 she would distinguish herself as a member of the United States Curtis Cup team. When the United States won the match, defeating Great Britain and Ireland 7½-1½, Mrs. Porter had accomplished about everything worth doing in women's amateur golf.

Nearly three decades later, senior women's golf opened another world of competition to her, and when she became eligible for the Senior Women's Amateur in 1974, she was immediately cast as a player who could dominate the championship.

It did not happen that way. She was third in 1974 and 1975, and in 1976 she skipped the tournament to take a vacation with her husband. Then, in 1977, at the Dunes Golf and Beach Club, in Myrtle Beach, South Carolina, she won it. She finished one stroke ahead of Mrs. Alice Dye and became the first golfer ever to win both the Women's Amateur and Senior Women's Amateur championships. After her victory, she sat back in her chair, kicked off her shoes, clapped her hands and in a moment of ecstasy cried, "Thank God! Now, I'll never have to practice again."

It was a short-lived resolution. After she won her second championship, she smiled and said, "I guess I'll have to start practicing again."

Mrs. Porter won her second Senior Women's by finishing one stroke ahead of another former champion, Cecile Maclaurin, at the Sea Island Golf Club, in St. Simons, Georgia. Mrs. Porter had rounds of 81, 80, and 75 for 236 over a course that measures 6,053 yards, almost comparable to a Women's Open course but with a par of 77. Mrs. Maclaurin, of Savannah, Georgia, the 1976 champion, was the runner-up for the third consecutive year.

Mrs. Porter will have to begin practicing if she wants to win this title again. What this championship proved—other than that Sea Island is one of the most beautiful and pleasurable spots on this planet—is that there are many women golfers, fifty and over, who really can play this game and who are quite serious about it.

In its own quiet way, senior women's golf is flourishing. Several major senior women's competitions are now conducted, and they draw the best players from the United States and Canada. The competition becomes more intense each year, the scores and handicaps are significantly lower, and the number of quality players has increased dramatically. Many of these women have been in the vanguard of the development of women's golf in this country, beginning at the junior level. Mrs. Porter, for one, has been a member of the USGA Women's Committee since 1969.

The 1980 Senior Women's Amateur drew a record 186 entries from golfers with handicaps of 14 or lower. The starting field is limited to those 120 golfers with the lowest handicaps, so only players with a 10 or lower actually made it in September. In fact, two former champions, Miss Maureen Orcutt (1962, 1966) and Mrs. Allison Choate (1963), were among the 66 alternates waiting for a spot to open in the starting field.

Mrs. Carolyn Cudone's magnificent record of five consecutive Senior Women's Amateur championships (1968-72) will be extremely difficult to match. The competition is just too keen.

In the championship itself, Mrs. Maclaurin scored a birdie 4 at the 18th hole on the first day, giving her a 78, one stroke ahead of Mrs. Lois Hodge, of San Jose, California, Mrs. Nancy Black, of Greenbush, Massachusetts, and Mrs. Kathryn Salley, of Columbia, South Carolina. Alone at 80 was Mrs. Bea Bower, of Pelham, New York, the 1975 champion, who finished three over par despite losing four strokes to par on the par-4 fourth hole. Mrs. Porter was grouped with seven other players at 81.

On the second day of play, Mrs. Betty Probasco, of Lookout Mountain, Tennessee, playing in her first Senior Women's, posted the first even-par round of the week, a 77, and therewith had a 36-hole total of 158, one stroke ahead of Mrs. Phyllis Germain, of Houston, Texas. Mrs. Porter was three strokes back.

Only a moment before beginning the final round, Mrs. Porter remarked, "I feel fine today. Now all I need is some confidence." Apparently she found it. Her final round of 75, two under par, was the lowest round in relation to par in the history of this championship.

By the turn, Mrs. Porter had taken the lead by a stroke over Mrs. Probasco. Mrs. Maclaurin, Mrs. Bower, Mrs. Germain, Mrs. Hodge, and Mrs. Louise Wilson, of Louisville were two strokes behind the leader. Mrs. Porter retained the lead to the end, although she had some anxious moments on the final hole where Mrs. Maclaurin nearly holed a pitch shot for an eagle 3 that would have tied her. Mrs. Maclaurin's shot slid over the edge of the hole and stopped ten feet past. Mrs. Bower finished third with her 76, the only other sub-par round of the week.

The Senior Women's Amateur championship is unique among USGA competitions because it conducts age-group competitions as subplots to the championship. The four age-group winners were: Group A (age 50-54), Mrs. Maclaurin, 237; Group B (55-59), Mrs. Porter, 236; Group C (60-64), Ruth Miller, of Long Beach, California, 253; and Group D (65 and over), Ann Gregory, of Gary, Indiana, 245, who not only won by 19 strokes in her group but also finished in a tie for ninth place in the overall championship.

*Dorothy Germain Porter*

# Beth Daniel Conquers Her Temper and Climbs to No. 1

## John P. May

Golf Digest                                    January, 1981

Beth Daniel's brown eyes jumped with anger as she strode into the clubhouse. She'd just finished the fourth round of the 1980 U.S. Women's Open with a bogey. Her lips clenched, she headed toward the twin swinging doors leading into the locker rooms. Only sturdy construction kept the doors on their hinges as Daniel forcefully applied the heels of her hands to them.

It wasn't that the scorned bogey had cost Daniel so much. She'd had no chance to catch the winner, Amy Alcott, and despite the bogey, Daniel creditably tied for 10th. But this is not a golfer who suffers bogeys easily. Every setback hurts, every defeat stings.

Since she appeared on the LPGA Tour in February, 1979, Daniel has shown a determination to succeed that may be unmatched by any other current competitor.

"I'm a perfectionist," she admits. "I have to win. If I can't be the best at anything I try, I'd just quit."

Daniel, of course, has never quit, though she has not been perfect—no one in golf is. But for one three-week stretch in 1980 she came awfully close when she led the way in three consecutive tournaments. After winning the Patty Berg Classic in St. Paul, Minnesota, and the Columbia Savings Classic in Denver, Colorado, she took the Women's World Series of Golf in Pepper Pike, Ohio. The last was a $150,000 competition with only twelve contestants. A week later she became the first woman in history to bank more than $200,000 in a single year, and she eventually was 1980's leading money-winner. Earlier in the year she had played well but had won only once, in the Golden Lights championship in New Rochelle, New York.

It was at the Golden Lights, incidentally, that this fiery competitor's intensity reached a zenith of sorts. Tour rules call for an automatic fine for a player who throws a club, and at New Rochelle Daniel pitched not one but two sticks. This Southerner with the baby face is as facile with

*Beth Daniel—her temper shows her fire.*

her tongue as she is with her golf clubs. She was able to convince the officials that her second toss was not done in anger.

Just over three months earlier, she'd been fined for heaving a club at the Bent Tree Classic in Sarasota, Florida. If a player is fined for club-throwing three times within ninety days, she can be suspended. Daniel is the only one who came close to this kind of penalty.

All of this palaver about her short fuse is rather boring to Daniel by now. She's heard about it all her golfing life. "I feel my composure is a hundred per cent better now than, say, a year ago," she maintains, her expression stoutly innocent. On the other hand, she adds: "I think our galleries enjoy seeing some emotion from the players. I don't think there's anything wrong with showing your temper as long as you don't damage the course or do something to disturb another player. Too many of our players are like robots."

Daniel's calmer demeanor in recent times stems from her caddie, Dee Darden, a former Air Force pilot who has caddied for women professionals since he retired four years ago. Darden has carried Daniel's bags since early 1980, and his easygoing temperament seems a perfect foil for his golfer's volatile nature.

"It is so important for your caddie to say the right things at the right time, and Dee does," Daniel said not long ago. "He's taught me that golf is not a matter of life and death."

Professional Derek Hardy, Daniel's first serious teacher and still her favorite, is not concerned about her outlook. When he was the professional at Daniel's home club, the Country Club of Charleston in South Carolina, Hardy began instructing her when she was fifteen. "Her temper just shows her fire," Hardy recently said at his present post, the Snee Farm Country Club in Mt. Pleasant, South Carolina, "When your self-criticism is as high as hers, you're going to have to let that fire burn a little when something goes wrong. I think she'd be worse off if she held it in."

Daniel has always been that way. She and her older sister, Tricia, had some fierce matches when they were growing up in Charlestown. "We played hard," Beth says, smiling at the remembrance. "Usually only one of us would finish. The loser would walk off the course."

Hardy helped his protégé develop the full, powerful swing that today zaps the ball farther than anyone else on the women's tour. Her drives average about 250 yards, and she wins most of the long-driving contests she enters. Hardy believes Daniel's uncomplicated swing will keep her winning good money on tour for as many years as she wants to.

After graduating from College Preparatory School in Charleston in 1974, Daniel entered nearby Furman University in Greenville, South Carolina, and began making golf news almost immediately. She won the U.S. Women's Amateur in 1975, paced Furman's team to the AIAW Women's Collegiate championship in 1976, and won the Amateur again in 1977. She also won seven of the eight matches she played in the 1976 and 1978 Curtis Cups.

In her senior year at Furman, Daniel did not play for the women's team. Showing her usual spunk, she did this to protest what she considered the university's lack of proper financial support of the women's golf program. After playing a few matches for the men's team, Daniel graduated from Furman in 1978, ready to make her presence known in the professional ranks. In the February, 1979 tour qualifier, Daniel was the scoring leader by five strokes. Since then she's done just about everything expected of her.

Another spectacular young woman golfer by the name of Nancy Lopez had preceded Daniel onto the tour by about eighteen months. Lopez was simply amazing, with nine tournament victories in her first full tour year, 1970. In the meantime, Lopez secured a husband and a hyphenated last name, and in 1980 finally showed some signs of slowing down a bit. She won "only" three tournaments to Daniel's four. Both went over $200,000 in prize money, with Daniel a shade ahead.

Daniel clearly thinks she can be the best woman golfer in the world, and that would necessitate upending Lopez from that perch. "I don't want to say Nancy is at her peak," Daniel says, "but I think some players peak earlier than others. I don't think I'll reach my peak for two or three more years, maybe more."

A perfectly diplomatic statement—with a perfectly clear intent.

# Remembering the Babe

## Dave Anderson

Golf Journal                                    September, 1981

*The Babe*

In the LPGA's early years, the other golfers would be out on the range hitting ball after ball when the Babe strolled out to join them. With a big smile, she would look around and, loud enough for the others to hear, she would say, "I don't know why you're practicing so hard to finish second."

She was laughing, but she wasn't joking.

In less than eight years as a touring pro, Mildred Didrikson Zaharias won thirty-one tournaments, including three U.S. Women's Open championships. During the four years from 1948 through 1951 when she was the leading money winner, she won eighteen of the thirty-nine events on the tour. Over those last two years, she won thirteen of the twenty-three tournaments. Nobody else—not Mickey Wright, not Kathy Whitworth, not Nancy Lopez—has ever dominated women's golf the way the Babe did during her reign. For all her success, her total prize money for those four big years was only $37,937. In contrast, the winner of next year's Dinah Shore tournament will collect $50,000. But now, twenty-five years after she died of cancer, Babe Zaharias remains the LPGA's patron saint, its Joan of Arc as a golfer, an athlete, and a woman.

To judge how the Babe would do on today's tour is impossible. The winner of two Olympic gold medals in 1932, she was sculpted in a time of economic depression and limited opportunity for women athletes. Her environment can't be duplicated now anymore than some of today's pros could be dropped back into that era. And yet when Patty Berg, her most illustrious contemporary, was asked how the Babe would do today, she didn't hesitate. "Well," she said, "Babe would be what now—in her late 60s? But she might do pretty well."

"No, no, Patty," she was told. "Not if Babe were *alive* today. If she were in her *prime* today."

"Oh, then Babe sure would be great," she said. "Babe would be right up there at the top."

If the Babe had not arrived when she did, women's golf and the LPGA might still be clawing for stature. She not only helped found the LPGA but she changed the manner in which women hit golf balls.

"Until she came along," Berg says, "women were all swing and no hit. Babe swung, but she also *hit*. She put power into the women's game."

She loved to hit it far. Once she claimed that one of her drives had been measured at 346 yards with a following wind and a hard fairway. At clinics, she would hit a long drive and turn to her gallery. "Don't you men wish you could hit a ball like that?", she would say.

She tried to enter the men's U.S. Open in 1948 but the U.S. Golf Association rejected her application. At the time, the Open was restricted to male golfers; today female golfers are eligible for the Open although no woman has ever filed an entry. The Babe accepted her rejection calmly. "If they had let me in," she commented, "I don't think I'd have finished around the top, but I don't think I'd have been at the bottom either."

Babe knew she was somebody. Before a tournament, the sportswriters would surround her. One day she told them she had just shot a 72 in practice. When the sportswriters left, one of the Babe's closest friends, Peggy Kirk Bell, stared at her.

"You didn't shoot 72," Peggy said. "You shot 77."

"I know, but they don't want to hear I shot 77."

Babe was really her own publicity agent. Walking along Fifth Avenue in New York City one day, she noticed an expensive watch in the window of a fashionable shop.

"I've got to get me one of those," she said.

She phoned the watch firm, told them she admired their watch. Soon she received one as a gift. And at her peak, she held out for $1,000 an appearance on TV shows, then a huge sum.

"And she always got it," Bell recalls.

Babe was a competitor even among friends. In her last years, she was close to Betty Dodd, a tall Texan who strummed her guitar to accompany Babe on the harmonica. Dodd could hit a golf ball almost as far as Babe could. On a practice range Babe once tested a new driver and quickly discarded it as too heavy. But after Dodd picked it up and hit a few long tee shots, Babe quickly reclaimed it.

"Babe wasn't going to use it," Dodd recalls with a laugh, "but she didn't want me using it either."

Babe was always competing. Dodd, who often wore shorts, once hopped over a hedge, prompting Babe to lift up the skirt of her long dress and hop the hedge, too. "And she cleared it," Dodd says, "by a foot more than I did."

Babe intimidated her rivals. When she was introduced on the first tee, she often would glance at the gallery and announce, "I'll show you folks how to play golf." She once asked Peggy Kirk Bell, then a rookie pro, to be her partner in a four-ball match. Bell was flattered but nervous, knowing that if their team lost, she would be blamed by the gallery.

"Lose!" the Babe roared. "We won't lose. I can beat any two of 'em."

Babe was an entertainer. On a long putt in an exhibition match, she sometimes would face away from the hole, look back over her shoulder at the line and then hit the ball between her legs. Every once in a while one of those putts would go in the cup. Even if it was close, her gallery shrieked.

Long before Babe was a golfer, she was an athlete, this planet's best woman athlete. Born in Port Arthur, Texas, the sixth of seven children, she grew up in Beaumont, where a museum is dedicated to her now. The year of her birth is uncertain. She always used 1914, which made her 42 when she died; her sister Lillie insisted it was 1911. Whatever her age, her athletic genes were instilled by her mother, Hannah Marie

Olson, once a skier and figure-skater. Her father Ole, a Norwegian sailor who settled in Texas, instilled the dream of the Olympics by reading to her newspaper accounts of the 1928 Games at Amsterdam. "My ambition," Babe acknowledged, "was to be the greatest athlete who ever lived."

When she was voted The Female Athlete of the Half Century in an Associated Press poll in 1950, golf had provided only a small share of her accomplishments. Restricted to entering only three of the five women's track-and-field events in the 1932 Olympics at Los Angeles, she won two gold medals with world records in the javelin and the 80-meter hurdles. She got a silver medal for second place in the high jump when officials ruled that she had illegally dived over the bar at a height that would have earned her a third gold.

In the National AAU women's meet that served as the Olympic Trials that year, she put on a sensational performance. In a span of three hours at Northwestern University's Dyche Stadium, she competed in eight events, winning five (three with world records) and sharing first place in another (also with a world record). In the meet the Babe accumulated 30 points. The Illinois Athletic Club, with 22 athletes, was second with 22 points.

Although she had hit some golf balls in Dallas occasionally, she did not play a formal round until a few days after the 1932 Olympics. Grantland Rice, the famous sportswriter of that era, took her out to the Brentwood Country Club where she crushed several 250-yard drives and reportedly shot 84.

"Actually," she once said, "I think it was around 100."

Whatever the score, Babe had found the game she wanted to play for the rest of her life. Soon she was taking lessons from Stan Kertes, a Los Angeles pro who tutored Hollywood celebrities.

Her picture swing enabled her to win the 1935 Texas Amateur championship. Shortly after that, the USGA declared her a pro for having competed as a pro in other sports, notably as a basketball player and as a pitcher for the barnstorming House of David baseball team.

Instead of sulking, she went on a tour of exhibition matches at $500 each with Gene Sarazen, who taught her the art of sand play. In 1938 she entered the Los Angeles Open—yes, the men's LA Open. In her opening round she was in a threesome with two strangers—a minister, C. Pardee Erdman, and a wrestler, George Zaharias, known on the circuit as The Crying Greek from Cripple Creek. The minister shot 75, the wrestler shot 83, and the Babe shot 84, but during that round she noticed George staring at her.

"What are you doing?" she asked.

*"What I see, I like," said George.*

"What I see, I like," he replied.

"I'm glad you do. I like you, too," she said. Before the year ended, they were married. With a prosperous husband, Babe soon applied for reinstatement as an amateur by the USGA. When the U.S. Amateur championship was resumed in 1946 after the close of the war, the Babe won it.

On a romp through the amateur circuit, she won seventeen consecutive tournaments, including the 1947 British Ladies' Amateur, at Gullane, in Scotland. Now she had all sorts of offers to turn pro, and she did. The next year she won her first U.S. Women's Open.

"Right after that," George Zaharias recalls, "Babe and I decided there should be a women's pro tour."

When the LPGA was formed, the Babe had her stage. Her cancer troubles didn't really begin until 1953 when she had to be hospitalized for a colostomy. While winning two tournaments in the first few months of that year, she had felt weak but had neglected to see a doctor.

"If she had gone for a checkup right away," Betty Dodd says, "she might be alive today."

Less than four months after surgery, the Babe was playing tournament golf. She entered the All-America tournament at Tam O'Shanter, outside Chicago, on one condition—that Betty Dodd be in her threesome each day. After an 82 in the first round and an 85 in the second, she was still struggling early in the third round. Walking to the sixth tee, she suddenly sat down on a seat cane and sobbed.

"Do you want to walk in?" Dodd asked her.

"Hell, no," Babe said. "I'm no quitter."

On the back nine, she shot 34, two under par. Her comeback had begun. The next week, she finished third at Tam O'Shanter in the World tournament. The next year she won five tournaments, including her third U.S. Women's Open by a record twelve strokes. She finished second on the money list with $14,452 and won the Vare Trophy for the lowest scoring average.

For her accomplishments in 1954, Babe was voted the Woman Athlete of the Year by the Associated Press for the *sixth* time. However, she knew that her illness had eroded her skill. Playing in Montreal around this time, she once had a routine chip shot from a few feet off a green. When she flubbed the ball only a few inches, a spectator told her, "The Babe I saw a few years ago wouldn't have done that." In other years, the Babe might have stared in annoyance at the spectator. Instead, she smiled. "That was the Babe of old," she said. "This is the old Babe."

Early in 1955, the Babe, Betty Dodd, and Betty's sister Peggy were driving on the Texas coast when their car got stuck in the sand. Borrowing a shovel from two old men playing checkers on a nearby porch, the Babe began to dig the car out. "One of those old men looked over," Betty Dodd recalls, "and said, 'I ain't never seen a woman shovel sand like that.'"

Perhaps as a result of that shoveling, the Babe developed a spinal-disc ailment that required surgery. Soon she had other back pains. Cancer again, this time in the pelvic area. Late that year Peggy Kirk Bell visited her in Tampa and the Babe insisted that they play golf. "Her golf shoes hurt too much to wear, so she walked around in loafers," Bell recalls. "She couldn't hit the ball very far. I remember her saying, 'How do you break 100 only driving the ball this far?'"

Soon she returned to a Galveston hospital. Once lean and leathery at 5-6 and 148 pounds, she kept losing weight as the cancer ravaged her. She died on Sept. 27, 1956, but in her last few months, she somehow remained alive out of sheer determination. "She was down to 90 pounds, but she still had muscles," Betty Dodd says. "The nurses told me she should've died six months before she did."

Before the Babe was too ill to get out of bed, she often walked in her pajamas to the little beach on the Gulf of Mexico outside the hospital. She would take a wedge and a few golf balls with her and, one by one, she would knock the balls out into the gentle surf. Then she would return to her hospital room.

Those were the last golf shots she ever hit.

# Rancho Mirage and the Nabisco Dinah Shore

## Sarah Ballard

Sports Illustrated                                        April 12, 1982

In the unreal patch of California desert called Rancho Mirage, they name the streets after stand-up comics, clear blue lakes rise out of the hot sands like Old Testament miracles, and the son of a Philadelphia gambler entertains kings and presidents behind a mile-long oleander hedge. One not-so-improbable aspect of Rancho Mirage is the Nabisco (née, Colgate) Dinah Shore Invitational, and Sally Little gave even that event a tinge of unreality on Sunday when she shot an astounding 64, the best round of her life, to beat Hollis Stacy by three strokes.

Little's irons kept her close to the pins all day, and her putter did the rest. Rarely did she have to make a putt longer than ten feet. She was unmistakably in the zone, or "the ozone," as she put it. "To tell you the truth, I didn't know what I was shooting," she said afterward. Indeed, she could do no wrong. Her 76-67-71-64—278 was 10-under on the Mission Hills course.

If Little didn't know what she was shooting, Stacy did. She had carded a 65 on Friday to lead the field by three shots, and she added a 71 on Saturday to increase her lead to four. But on Sunday she couldn't buy a birdie. As she made par after par, she could only watch Little, playing one group ahead, eating away at her lead until finally, at the 12th, Stacy was in second place to stay.

Both players would have been good bets going in. Stacy had already won two tournaments this year and seemed to have a new determination, as if she had decided to make better use of her considerable talent. A friend said of Stacy, "When Lopez was starting to dominate, Hollis won two U.S. Opens back to back but never got any acclaim. She was put out by that. Now I think she realizes that Lopez is just one of the field and that *she* too can be a star."

Little has been improving markedly over the last three years. A month ago she won the Olympia Gold Classic, near Los Angeles, and she had three other finishes in the top ten coming into the Dinah Shore.

She also had a special feeling for the tournament. "I'm so motivated to play here that I want to practice and get ready," she said. "I don't feel that way every week."

The other great round of Sunday belonged to Hall of Famer Sandra Haynie, winner of the 1974 U.S. Open, two LPGA championships, and thirty-seven other tournaments. Haynie's 65 brought her from seven shots back into a tie for second with Stacy at 281. After a four-year retirement, Haynie returned to the tour last year at the age of thirty-seven and had the most lucrative season of her twenty-one-year career. She won $94,124.

The opening day at Rancho Mirage wasn't auspicious. Drenching rains (driven horizontal by cold gusts up to 45 mph) swept across the desert, blowing umbrellas inside-out and scores sky high. Two young survivors, Kyle O'Brien and Lori Garbacz (pronounced *gar*-buh-cee), both twenty-three, shot 71s and lived to tell about it. Theirs were the only sub-par rounds of the day.

Friday was as glorious as Thursday had been rotten. Stacy moved into the lead with her 65, three strokes ahead of Pat Bradley, six ahead of JoAnne Carner, and seven in front of Jan Stephenson. Nancy Lopez-Melton, after an opening 77, returned with a 71, leaving her ten strokes back—too far for most folks but not necessarily for Nancy.

Not much changed on Saturday, except that Bradley faltered and Stephenson had a 68, tying her with Carner, four behind. Stacy birdied the last two holes for a 71. Still lurking six strokes back after a 67 was Lopez-Melton, but the gap looked unbridgeable now. "It's a lot," she said that evening, "but you never know."

The joyful competitive intensity of a Little in her winning trance, or a Lopez-Melton, is typical of the spirit in which the pros approach the Dinah Shore each year. The tournament is without equal on their calendar. The U.S. Women's Open carries greater historic weight and the LPGA Championship is older, but the Dinah Shore is the players' favorite. It is their Masters without portfolio. They wouldn't consider skipping it, and they would kill to win it. They lie awake in the dark thinking about it. Stephenson claims she cried herself sick the year (1974) she had to sit it out. Last week, when Carner was asked what was special about the tournament, she grinned and said, "Money." But Carner would give an eyetooth and her Honda Trail 90 to win it, and not for its $45,000 first prize alone.

The tournament was created in 1972 by Colgate's then chairman, David R. Foster, to convince the sporting press and the public and, coincidentally, the players themselves, that the LPGA really mattered.

Foster put up the then astronomical purse of $100,000, prodded television coverage out of the Hughes network, and each year hosted a lavish week-long party in Palm Springs for the players and his corporate guests. When Foster was unseated in 1979, however, Colgate's commitment withered and died, leaving the fate of the Dinah Shore after 1981 up in the air.

Enter Nabisco Brands, Inc., created last July by the merger of Nabisco, Inc. and Standard Brands. As it happened, F. Ross Johnson and Martin F.C. Emmett of Standard Brands, which agreed to sponsor the event one month before the merger, were both golfers. "We were delighted to get it," says Johnson, who has since become president and chief operating officer of the new company. "It was a unique opportunity to take on an established tournament. We wouldn't have started our own."

"We had ideas about what we wanted to do," says Emmett, now an executive vice-president. "We wanted to do a first-class job, nothing halfway."

In pursuit of excellence Nabisco Brands spent between $5 and $6 million on the tournament and dozens of related activities. It distributed, for instance, 700 million supermarket coupons and bought a Sunday supplement advertising insert that reached 34 million homes, all calling attention to the Nabisco-Dinah Shore Invitational Sweepstakes.

Watching all the commercial activity from the sidelines last week, with a slightly amused look, was Ray Volpe, the LPGA's commissioner for the last seven years. Volpe, who this month is moving on to possibly greener pastures in independent TV programming, took over the LPGA job in 1975 when the organization was on the brink of bankruptcy. He nursed it back to financial health. Combining his own marketing savvy, learned in the National Hockey League, with a fortuitous surge of public interest in women's sports and the long-awaited emergence of a genuine superstar in Nancy Lopez, Volpe was able to increase the tour's total prize money from $1.2 million in 1975 to $6.4 million this year and to raise the average purse from $52,787 to $168,000. He also set up a retirement plan for his players and earlier this year negotiated the first bonus-point pool in golf, the Mazda-LPGA Series, worth $300,000 a year for the next three years. Under the Mazda plan, the leader at the end of the year in points based on performance will win a $125,000 bonus. Second place will receive $60,000, and so on down to 60th place.

Taking over for Volpe will be John Laupheimer, who was previously executive director for administration of the USGA. Laupheimer has an uncommon asset, a source of insight into the women's game that may be helpful in his dealings with the players. His wife, England's Mary Everard, has had a distinguished amateur golf career, playing on four Curtis Cup teams and three Women's World Amateur Cup teams between 1968 and 1978. Laupheimer will oversee the tour from the LPGA's new offices near Houston.

In 1950 eleven women professionals named themselves the Ladies' Professional Golf Association and created a golf tour. That first year there were nine tournaments. Patty Berg won three of them, Babe Zaharias won all the rest. No record remains of the purse total in 1950, but Zaharias, the leading money winner, earned some $14,800.

Last week at Mission Hills, Amy Alcott and Kathy Whitworth, who finished tied for fourth, won $13,500 apiece. Now that's really unreal.

# Kathy Whitworth Just Keeps Rolling Along

## Furman Bisher

Golf Digest                                    August, 1982

Kathrynne Ann Whitworth and Samuel Jackson Snead have little in common. Sam has the perfect swing. Kathy gets a little loose at the top. Sam's a little portly in his autumn years. Kathy was as a juvenile, but now is as trim as a 1-iron. Sam can always be found under a hat. Kathy never, or almost never, wears one.

Sam can be loud, charming, profane, irritable, entertaining, garrulous, tight-lipped, tight-fisted. Kathy can be the almost-perfect lady, varying only now and then to grit her teeth and glower after an unsatisfactory shot.

But those points on which they strike a similarity are memorable in the history of golf, one to covet, one to curse. Sam has won 84 tournaments, the record on the PGA Tour. Through mid-June, Kathy had won 83 on the LPGA Tour, the record for women professionals.

In those two vast collections of victories, though, there isn't one U.S. Open between them. Sam is almost as famous for all the men's Opens that got away as for the British Open and all the Masters and PGA championships he's won. Kathy's case hasn't reached the state of a heralded plague but it's coming close. She'll be trying again to win the Women's Open at Del Paso Country Club in Sacramento, July 22–25. At least *she* has a reasonable chance left of winning it one year. She won't be forty-three until September. Sam was seventy in May.

Three years ago it was looking as if Kathy Whitworth was about to sing her own September song. Her swing had gone sour. She didn't win a tournament, her first barren year after seventeen flushed with victories. The new, young talent was coming on in waves: Nancy Lopez, Amy Alcott, Hollis Stacy, Beth Daniel, Sally Little, Pat Bradley, and the like. And, of course, there was the stern middle guard to contend with: Jane Blalock, Sandra Post, Judy Rankin, JoAnne Carner and Donna Caponi. Whitworth was being written off as a fine but fading

*Snead has won more tournaments than any other man in golf history, and Whitworth has won more tournaments than any other woman.*

player whose time had come to walk off into the sunset. "I thought it was over, too," she says now. "I didn't win for two years. My swing was out of shape, and I didn't know what was wrong."

All around her, players were checking in with $100,000-a-year winnings, and there she was, so far down the line you had to dig to find her name. Kathy's earnings in 1979, $36,000, would have led the LPGA in twenty-one of its first twenty-three years, but it was chicken feed in the new golf economy.

The remarkable twist to the story of Kathy Whitworth is that she made it back. She came on with a charge worthy of Arnold Palmer, and the last two years she has been the center of attention on the women's tour. In May she won the Lady Michelob tournament at Brookfield West, one of those country clubs in a real-estate development near Atlanta. It was victory No. 83. It broke the tie with her old friend and former competitor, Mickey Wright.

For all these years the women's tour has scratched and clawed to make its place in the sun, and here was a grand moment to have the Monday sports pages all for itself. Wouldn't you know that Jack Nicklaus finished with a surge and won the Colonial Invitation, at Fort Worth, breaking a drought of almost two years. Whitworth, if she didn't wind up on page two, at least had to share page one with "The Bear."

Kathy had the headlines to herself, however, for three golden days last summer at the U.S. Women's Open at LaGrange Country Club near Chicago. She entered the tournament approaching another frontier in women's golf: $1,031 more and she'd become the first million-dollar career winner. "Making a million isn't my motivation," she said. "All I want to do is get it over with."

Whitworth led or shared the lead in each of the first three rounds with scores of 69-70-71. She'd make her million for sure, and maybe win her first Open. Going into the last day, Kathy led Bonnie Lauer by a stroke, Beth Daniel by two, and Pat Bradley by three. Bradley and Daniel quickly turned it into a two-way battle, Bradley firing a 66 for a record 279 and Daniel a 68 for 280. Whitworth fell back with bogeys on the third and fourth holes and another on the seventeenth. With still a chance of winning, she hit her tee shot into the water on the eighteenth and took a double-bogey 5 to finish five shots back. It was a bittersweet day for Whitworth, who collected $9,500 and celebrated her first million with champagne supplied by Donna Caponi.

After twenty-three years, Kathy still has no Open victory to show for all the money and the eighty-three tournaments she's won. Does this bug the lady?

"Not often," she says. "Maybe sometimes more than others. I'll be coming on with a good year and have my game at a peak, and there's no reason not to win it. I guess I got too high those years. Everything became magnified and I got totally out of shape about it. I thought the course at LaGrange was perfect for me. It wasn't long, the greens were small, just right. Then it rained Saturday night and softened the greens. That made it easier for everybody else, but it hurt me.

"That's really the only time I've ever come close. I finished second when JoAnne Carner won at Erie (1971), but JoAnne won by a mile. The year Donna Caponi won at Pensacola (1969), I had a chance, but I let that one get away."

Long before she even started thinking about the Open, Whitworth came on the LPGA Tour when the purses for the whole year totaled less than single tournament's pay today. It was a scraggly, disorganized little circle of women run by the players themselves, bouncing around the country two or three to a car, playing any kind of cow pasture they could get on. Galleries were so small they never needed restraining ropes, and when they did, the girls took their hammers out and drove the stakes in the ground themselves.

In Whitworth's second year out, Louise Suggs was queen of the money-winners. Louise collected $16,892. That's about a week's first-place check now. In Whitworth's third year, only seven players won tournaments, not Kathy though. It was out about this time, in 1961, that she began wondering if there was any future for her in golf. She panicked. "I shot an 89 at Hyde Park in Jacksonville and just came unraveled," she remembers. "I ran for home. My family convinced me that I should go on back, that they loved me whether I made it or not, and finally I cashed a check. I finished in a three-way tie for last at Asheville, N.C., and collected $33.33."

In the spring of 1962, three years after her launching, along came the first of Kathy Whitworth's eighty-three winning finishes, in the Kelly Girl Open, in Baltimore, sponsored by a firm that specialized in on-call working girls. But that one had no kick to it. "I backed into it," Kathy recalls. "I won sitting in the clubhouse when Sandra Haynie three-putted the last green." Her second win, the Thunderbird at Phoenix, had the spice of excitement. In a tight race down the back nine, she beat Mickey Wright by a stroke. "Now, that was gratifying!" she says. "I really felt like I knew what it was like to win."

It is remarkable that Whitworth is still carrying on at an age when most athletes are looking for a comfortable chair and a porch with a view. Retirement isn't in her foreseeable future.

She has comfortably invested, mainly through the efforts of a long-standing friend in Odessa, Texas, who has guided her through the jungle of stocks and bonds. She has no business agent but she signed recently with a firm in San Jose, California, called Technical Equities, which deals in investment advice. She would like to become a specialist in athletes' investments.

All this is a long way down the road from Jal, New Mexico, which is as far as you can go in the southeast corner of the state without running into Texas. Jal is a ranch and oil-field town of about 6,000 where Whitworth's father ran a hardware store until his recent retirement. He was then elected mayor.

Tennis was Cathy's game growing up until her girl friends insisted one day that they go out to the golf course, a little nine-hole spread with cottonseed greens. "I went along for no good reason," she says, "and am I glad I did!"

She was a hefty girl at the time, a refrigerator raider who ate anything that didn't bite back and drank enough milk shakes to fill a lake. The summer before high school she weighed in at 215. "I'd probably been up to 250, but I just happened to be 215 at the time. I'd probably be the fat lady in a circus right now if it hadn't been for golf. It kept me on the course and out of the refrigerator."

By the time Whitworth hit the tour, she had boiled down to 170. Three years later she was down to 145, and has hung in there ever since. At five feet-nine, she has the good, clean lines of a buggy whip, the Al Geiberger of the women's tour.

Her early instructor was the local professional, Hardy Loudermilk, now a retired resident of Fort Worth. Once Whitworth had won the New Mexico Women's Amateur championship, Loudermilk unselfishly said he'd taken her as far as he could and that she needed more sophisticated help. He drove her to Austin and put her in the hands of Harvey Penick, who has shaped careers at the University of Texas and the Country Club of Austin. Penick is still her port in a storm. It was to Penick that she ran three years ago when the bottom dropped out of her game.

"Harvey always said, 'Don't come to see me unless you need me,'" Kathy adds. "Well, I needed him. I was spraying the ball. I had no idea why. It was a matter of weight transfer. Once we agreed on that, Harvey told me what I had to do. It was just a matter of doing it."

Penick got her to stand taller at address, which made a fuller shoulder turn possible. Whitworth had allowed her head and upper body to slump at address, and her right shoulder had moved closer than her left shoulder to the target line. "There was no way I could turn my shoulders freely on the backswing until Harvey showed me how," she says. "By holding my upper body straighter over the ball, I was able to make a free takeaway that led to a proper weight shift—right on the backswing, left on the through-swing." She began hitting the ball much crisper and straighter. Kathy had never lost her excellent short game and started returning low scores again. They had been writing Kathy off prematurely—over forty and over the hill. She had played with Suggs and Berg and Rawls, and now she was playing with Lopez and Alcott and Stacy and a crop of crisp new starlets. She'd led the female world in earnings. She'd won eighty tournaments. Only Marlene Hagge, who had come on the tour as one of the Bauer wonder children, had been around longer.

Whitworth had enough awards to open her own private museum. Leading money-winner from 1965 to 1973, except for Carol Mann's year; seven-time Player of the Year and winner of the Vare Trophy for best scoring average; twice Associated Press Woman Athlete of the Year; LPGA Hall of Fame; Texas Hall of Fame for all sports; and certainly with enough credentials to be voted into the World Hall of Fame at Pinehurst. Why keep on hanging around if the party was over?

Then came the comeback, which took the form of an eruption. Last year, seven strokes down with nine holes to play, Whitworth caught and tied Alice Ritzman in the Coca-Cola Classic at Paramus, New Jersey, then beat her on the second hole of a playoff. Victory number 81.

She didn't merely win the Women's International at Moss Creek, South Carolina, in April, 1982, she scorched the area. She finished *nine* strokes ahead of the field. No. 82. Tied with Wright.

One month later she "got it over with." From the start, the Lady Michelob seemed to be "Whitworth's tournament." The field wasn't up to par. Several of the girls had taken off for Japan, but there were enough left—Pat Bradley, Amy Alcott, Hollis Stacy, Donna Caponi, and Janet Coles among them—to make it a contest and not a walkover. Whitworth strolled in four strokes ahead of Barbara Moxness. No. 83.

The cameras ground on. Interviews stretched into the evening. Telephones rang. Telegrams arrived, one from Mickey Wright, who reacted exactly as Whitworth had expected her to: "Thrilled to death for you. Know you're relieved. Keep winning," it read.

"That's what I plan to do," Whitworth says. "Just because I've won 83 doesn't mean I'm where I want to be.

Jal is still where the Whitworth hearth is, but in recent years she moved about, from a suburb of Dallas to Connecticut. She now is looking toward Texas again, perhaps Midland, the airport nearest to Jal and Odessa. Her personality is still as basically Southwestern as it was when she packed the car her father got her and set out on the tour. She's a woman of the 1940s. She seeks no liberation except what she has created for herself.

All the while, Kathy strides the fairway in a ranch-style gait. Her emotional meter rarely varies a degree. If she'd been a teacher, she'd have taught math. In any family, she'd have been everybody's favorite sister. The fact remains that she found her way to the golf tour and became famous and wealthy, neither of which makes her particularly comfortable. She resists glorification. "I'm not trying to become a legend," she says.

Like it or not, she has.

# Meet Brian Inkster: Husband, Caddie, Teacher

## George Eberl

Golf Journal                                                                    October, 1982

Can a club professional find happiness as a caddie for a woman who has won three successive U.S. Women's Amateur championships and who, incidentally, happens to be his prize golf pupil and his wife? Before anyone steels himself for a sponsor's message, it should be pointed out that this is reality, not soap opera.

Meet Juli and Brian Inkster. She is wife, champion, and student. He is husband, club professional at the Los Altos Country Club in California, and her caddie—just occasionally. It isn't uncommon, of course, for a husband to caddie in amateur events. Mrs. Anne Quast Sander's husband, Stephen, and Mrs. Lindy Goggin's husband, Charles, toted their wives' golf bags during the week at the Broadmoor.

The decision to become her caddie for the 1982 Women's Amateur was dictated by the importance of the occasion: Juli would be seeking her third consecutive championship. "I wanted to be with her for this one, and she agreed." But would it work out? They used the U.S. Women's Open, in July, at the Del Paso Country Club, in Sacramento, California, as their testing ground.

It didn't take Brian long to learn that there is more to caddying than meets the eye. "We blew it a couple of times—I blew it," Brian says. "Juli had a 75 the first day—that wasn't bad, because the scores were high—but on the second day, she was even par through seven holes. The eighth is a par-5, and she hit two good wood shots and was just a flip from the green. When I play, I look at the flag and say, 'That's an 8-iron, or that's a wedge.' Juli wants to know exact yardage. So she asked me how far it was. I paced it off from a sprinkler head that I thought we'd used earlier for measuring. I said it was 94 yards. She hit the ball over the green and wound up taking a 6. As it turned out, I had used the wrong sprinkler head. I had blown it."

At that, it worked out well enough to persuade the Inksters to team up in the Women's Amateur. It may have been just as well for Brian. By

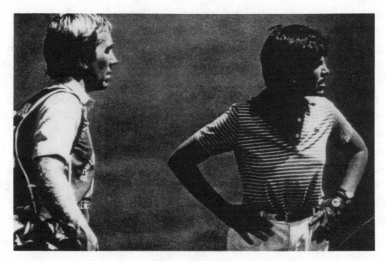

*Brian and Juli*

his own admission, he is nervous enough for both of them, so caddying kept him busy.

Does it work in Juli's favor that he is a professional? "Not at all," says Brian. "She swings the club, and there isn't much I can tell her now." And yes, she does decide which club to use. She may ask what he thinks about the distance to the green or how a putt is likely to break, but Juli is the ultimate arbiter.

In 1976, Brian was an assistant professional at the Pasatiempo Golf Club, in Santa Cruz, California, and Juli Simpson, then sixteen, was one of his students. In 1978, she went off to San Jose State, in San Jose, California, about thirty-five miles away. By that time, Brian was head professional at Pasatiempo. In 1979, he shifted to Los Altos, twenty-five miles north of San Jose, thus shortening what had become a romantic road. They were married in 1980, shortly before the Women's Amateur championship at Prairie Dunes, in Hutchinson, Kansas. He recalls that she considered withdrawing from the championship—they were on their honeymoon—but he held her to her commitment and she responded by winning.

Perhaps their most important golf talks occur in the evening. Juli will get down on herself if her game isn't going well. For example, during the second qualifying round, she strung together bogeys on the fifth, sixth, and seventh holes at Broadmoor. By the time she reached the eighth tee, she was kicking at the grass. She parred the eighth, bogeyed the ninth, then recovered her poise on the homeward nine with a 35, one under par. "We had one of our fireside chats that evening," Brian recalls.

Brian is happy in his own career. He shrugged off any whimsical suggestion that he might caddie for Juli if she qualifies in January for the LPGA Tour. He doesn't see her prospects of extensive travel as a major problem. "I'll try to join her on Sundays and Mondays during the Tour. We've talked about this, and I'd guess that she'll only play for three or four years. We want to have a family."

His admiration of the champion is widely shared. Yet Mrs. Inkster shows no sign, at twenty-two, of arrogance or conceit. She seems to take her remarkable achievements in stride. At the presentation ceremonies, her first words of thanks were for Brian, her husband, caddie, teacher, and best friend.

# Big Momma's Big Money Swing

## Sam Snead

Golf Digest                                       November, 1983


I believe that JoAnne Carner is the best women player I've ever seen. Patty Berg may have been better around the greens, but JoAnne is the best overall player. At age 44, she's having another spectacular year: a first in the Nestle World championship at the Shaker Heights in Ohio, seven seconds, and more than $250,000 in money winnings, tops on the LPGA Tour.

JoAnne is the easiest person I've ever worked with—and I've worked with quite a few golfers in my day. The reason she's such a consistently good player and is so easy to teach is that she has a very simple swing and an uncomplicated approach to the game. She doesn't worry a whole lot about swing mechanics. She just gets up and figures out the best way to get the ball from A to B with the odds in her favor. That's a pretty good approach to the game for all golfers.

She trusts what I tell her and, in a way, I serve as an extra set of eyes for her. Since she can't really see what she's doing, she makes adjustments in her swing by feel. Sometimes she gets in funny positions for that reason, and her game suffers. Fortunately for both of us, she's such a great natural athlete that I can tell her what she's doing wrong and she makes the change very quickly. I'll give you an example.

Earlier this year, about the time of the Corning Classic, JoAnne was having real problems with her swing, so I told her to come to Virginia and I'd take a look. Well, she and her husband Don hopped in the car and made the eight-hour drive. Fifteen minutes later her swing was back on track, we had a little lunch, and they drove home. It was just a case where she had let her stance get too wide and too open.

When I got her stance back where it should be, she said, "Sam, this just feels funny to me," but I told her that anytime you do something that's different from what you've become used to, it will feel strange for a while. You just have to stay with it.

The point of this story is that every player—whether you're a JoAnne

377

Carner or a 36-handicapper—should have a professional that he or she has confidence in. Trust what the pro tells you and stay with it.

There is a lot that most golfers can learn from JoAnne's swing, whether they're male or female, big or small.

As I said, she has a very simple swing. She doesn't have a lot of lost or wasted motion. I can't count the number of times I've had people come for a lesson and found that in trying to correct one problem in their swing they'd caused another. In the golf swing every action causes a reaction, but, like the fella says, two wrongs don't make a right. JoAnne doesn't manipulate her swing. She doesn't force herself into any unnatural positions. In a way, she swings like a kid. She just does what comes naturally.

The other strength in her swing is her balance. Over the years a lot of people have talked about the rhythm of my swing being so natural, but I'll let you in on a little secret. Old Sam figured out a long time ago that you could make this game a whole lot easier for yourself if you could just make solid contact with the ball. I played enough sports as a kid to know that you can't do that very often if you're swinging out of control and falling all over yourself. A good rhythm results in good balance, and balance makes all the difference in the world. Show me a player who swings out of his shoes and I'll show you a player who isn't going to win enough to keep himself in a decent pair of shoes for very long. That's a problem JoAnne Carner will never have.

*Looking at these pictures of JoAnne—or is it Jack Nicklaus?—hitting a 5-iron, you can see that she has a perfect "turn inside the barrel" swing. She has a beautiful weight shift but she doesn't sway laterally. If you put a stake on either side of her (shown by lines), she would stay within the stakes. JoAnne has excellent balance, and that's a result of good tempo and legwork. Notice that her legs are flexed the same amount from picture 1 through impact. You can prove this by noting the position of the line drawn over her head. Her head doesn't move up or down. JoAnne has a powerful swing but it's a "quiet" swing. There are no unnecessary movements.*

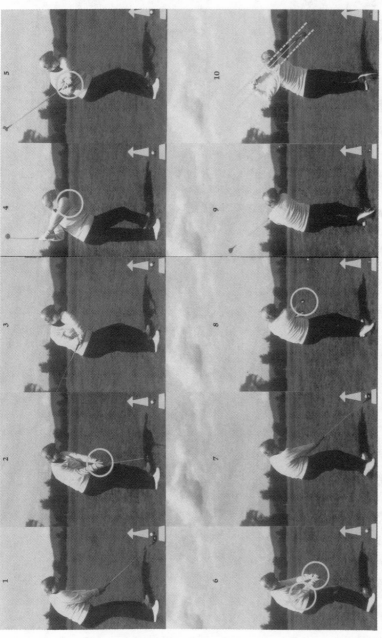

*JoAnne has a very uncomplicated but effective swing, as you can see in this driver sequence. In photo 2 you'll notice there isn't much wrist cock. Usually, when people cock their wrists early they have a tendency to throw the club from the top, which leads to an outside-in swing path and either a slice or pull. In photo 4, JoAnne has made a good turn on her backswing, and her high left shoulder shows that she's turned—not dipped. In photos 5 and 6 JoAnne has maintained her late wrist cock, and her right elbow (6) is close to her body, showing that the club is coming at the ball from the inside. In photo 8 the clubface is perpendicular to the ground, showing that JoAnne has released the club through the ball. The final picture—JoAnne's follow-through—shows the club and her right arm in line. That tells me there hasn't been any manipulation or divergent moves in her swing.*

# Reflections on a Life in Golf

## Anne Quast Sander

Golf Journal                                                    May/June 1984

*Mrs. Anne Quast Sander, whose distinguished amateur career covers more than thirty years, was named in January to the 1984 United States Curtis Cup team, which will play Great Britain and Ireland June 8 and 9 at the Honourable Company of Edinburgh Golfers, at Muirfield, in Gullane, Scotland. It is the seventh time she has been chosen to play for the American side; no one else has played as often for the United States. She was selected previously in 1958, 1960, 1962, 1966, 1968, and 1974. Mrs. Sander won the U.S. Women's Amateur championship three times—in 1958, 1961, and 1963—and she won the Ladies' British Amateur championship in 1980. She was also a member of the victorious United States teams of 1966 and 1968 in the Women's World Amateur Team championships. Mrs. Sander was asked to examine her feelings about being chosen for the seventh time to represent the United States in the Curtis Cup Match. This is her response.*

I can still remember, as if it were yesterday, playing in my first USGA competitions—the Girls' Junior at the Monterey Peninsula Country Club, in Pebble Beach, California, and, the following week, in the U.S. Women's Amateur, at the Waverley Country Club, in Portland, Oregon. The year was 1952, and I was fourteen years old.

From that summer on, competitive golf has held a special place in my life and in my heart. It became my dream during that summer long ago to become a member of a Curtis Cup team one day, and, pipe dream though it seemed at the time, to win the Women's Amateur. Both dreams came true in 1958. Today I'm often asked what keeps me going. Why am I even more elated and excited about being named to this year's United States Curtis Cup Team than I was the very first time, twenty-six years ago? Why do I still try to compete on a national level and work so hard to make another Curtis Cup team? The answers lie in an intertwining of altruistic and personal goals.

*Anne Quast Sander*

I am reminded of something that Joseph C. Dey wrote to me after I had won my first Women's Amateur: "There are two sides to the championship coin—privilege and responsibility."

I have been blessed with privileges through golf, and during the years that Joe Dey was Executive Director of the USGA (1934–1969)—years coinciding, in part, with my best competitive years—he imbued in me a sense of what I could or should do in return.

I developed the belief that the most significant way I could contribute was to demonstrate that it was possible to remain an amateur, live a complete and normal life, compete only on a limited basis, yet remain competitive at the highest level. I haven't been able to achieve this consistently throughout this entire period, but I have tried.

On the personal side, there have been additional influences. One is rooted in my relationship with JoAnne Gunderson Carner. Gundy and I, growing up thirty miles apart in our little corner of the United States, the Seattle area, became both friends and arch rivals. Gundy ultimately went far beyond me, both as an amateur and then as a professional.

I probably could not have kept up with her even if I had tried, but I have wanted very much to do something a bit unique in golf on my own level, on my own terms. JoAnne's achievements provide me with continuing inspiration.

My sons are motivating forces. David, who is nineteen years old, used to tease me, saying that he had been a bad omen because I had not won since he was born. He caddied for me for the first time in 1980, when he was fifteen and I finally won the British Ladies' Amateur. This had been a dream of mine since I first visited Great Britain with the 1960 Curtis Cup team.

Ned, 11, and Mark, 7, also help to keep me going. Ned was only a year-and-a-half in 1974, the last time I was on a Curtis Cup team. I have so wanted them to share with me something of what I have experienced, to understand "what makes mommy practice." They are special reasons why I am thrilled to be playing in another Curtis Cup match. They will be at Muirfield, just as David was at the San Francisco Golf Club for the 1974 Curtis Cup Match, when he was 9.

Steve, my husband, has played an important role, too. In 1973 he encouraged me to return to competitive golf after I had been away from it for three years, and, after a difficult period of struggling to regain my old form, he encouraged me to go to the 1980 British Amateur.

This difficult period occurred when we lived in Great Britain, between 1974 and 1979. That experience gave me a much greater appreciation of the difficulties the British face in trying to be competitive in both the Curtis and Walker Cup matches. There is the basic fact of numbers. There are simply many fewer girl and women golfers in Great Britain and Ireland than in the much, much larger United States. Of at least equal significance is their cold and windy climate. Weather like that is not conducive to the development and maintenance of a consistent golf game.

Despite my continuing devotion to practice while we were living in Great Britain, my game deteriorated to a point where I was incapable of competing in the United States. I was literally down and out as a competitive factor. In the fall of 1979, after an embarrassingly painful 83 in the then single qualifying round of the Women's Amateur—now 36 holes rather than 18 holes—I went to Billy Derickson, a Seattle golf professional, who told me that I must make some major changes in my swing. Marvin E. (Bud) Ward, to whom I credit my early successes, had died in 1969. Since then, I had tried on my own to keep the game he had helped me to build. Whether it was because I was just unable to manage it alone or because different methods are needed at different ages, whatever I was doing no longer worked.

I made the changes, and 1980 marked the beginning of a long, tough road back. A detour came in April, 1981, when I sustained a spiral fracture of my right arm. I competed in a total of eight tournaments in 1982 and 1983, twice my annual average over the years since 1963.

Being named to this year's Curtis Cup Team has made all the effort worthwhile despite disappointments and failures, notably in the Women's Amateur. This hurts especially because it is the tournament that has always meant the most to me. Yet, sometimes the new swing has worked, and I have played as well as I ever have. Those rounds help me keep going with the faith that anything is still possible.

Golf can be a very social game, but competitive golf is extremely lonely. There are times of inner agony for anyone who has ever played tournament golf, but there is also the indescribably rewarding feeling that comes when one hits a crucial shot just the way one dreams of doing or holes an important putt. That feeling is magnified when one is playing not just for one's self but for a team representing the United States. I think that anyone who has ever been on a Curtis Cup, Walker Cup, or World Cup team has felt a lump in the throat at an opening or closing ceremony when the American flag is raised and the band plays our national anthem. It adds a dimension to one's experience that cannot be measured, and it saddens me that many young people turn professional before they have that opportunity. They will never know that feeling of being part of something bigger and beyond themselves as individuals.

I believe the Curtis Cup is even more meaningful for our team when it is played in Great Britain. First, one feels the sense of being in the home of golf. Second, amateur golf—and especially matches with the United States—holds such great meaning for the British people.

Sadly, amateur golf in this country has suffered in public esteem with the ever-increasing dominance of professionalism. In Great Britain, one definitely has a heightened feeling that what one is doing really matters. Although the statistical outcome is important, the friendships formed are even more significant. The spirit envisioned by the Curtis sisters is sustained and furthered.

I am especially thrilled to be on this team because it is going to Muirfield. We lived just across the Firth of Forth from Muirfield for two years, and Steve and I had traditional foursomes matches there with our friends Dr. David Greenhough and Jean Donald Anderson. Muirfield is one of the special places in the world of golf because of its setting, the course, and the aura of tradition.

On many mornings since the telephone call from the USGA inviting me to again be a member of the Curtis Cup team, I awake and pinch myself to make certain that it is not just a lovely dream.

# Baseball, Motherhood, Apple Pie, and Nancy Lopez

## Peter Andrews

Golf Digest                                    August, 1984

And baby makes three. . . . A common enough equation in marriage. But not in a marriage between two popular sports stars, especially when the mother is Nancy Lopez, the most famous, most admired woman golfer in America. Babies need to be loved and looked after and cared for. But there are also a hundred or so practice balls to hit every day, a tour grind to follow, and an elusive putting stroke to regain. There are only so many hours in the day, and Nancy doesn't have enough of them to go around.

As golf fans with even the shortest memories know, Nancy Lopez burst on the scene like a star shell. In her first full season, 1978, she won nine tournaments—five of them in a row—collected a record-breaking $189,813 in prize money, and won the Vare Trophy with a 71.76 stroke average, the best in the history of women's golf until the next year when she lowered it to 71.2. Her bright personality and sunshine smile took hold of the golfing public's imagination as no woman had ever done.

While she was at it, Nancy helped to change the LPGA Tour from a sideshow of sport and made it a center-ring attraction. In 1979 there was a highly publicized marriage followed three years later by an even more highly publicized divorce and accompanied by what by Nancy's standards would be called a prolonged slump during which her scoring average shot up to 72.1.

Now happily re-married to Ray Knight, the star third-baseman for the Houston Astros, the mother of baby, Ashley Marie, and stepmother of 4-year-old Brooks Knight, Nancy Lopez is attempting to regain her pre-eminence in golf. The statistics indicate that her quest is likely to be a difficult one. The list of mothers on the LPGA Tour is not a long one—perhaps ten. Since the beginning of the tour, only two mothers, Kathy Cornelius, who won the U.S. Women's Open in 1956, and Susie Berning, who won the Open in 1968, 1972 and 1973, have won a major

*Nancy and Ray with their daughter Ashley Marie, and Nancy cheering Ray at the Astrodome, while Brooks, Ray's four-year-old son from a first marriage, naps.*

tournament. Nancy needs only one more major or seven lesser events to insure her entry into the LPGA Hall of Fame. That would be a stern enough challenge for any golfer, but Nancy has often set her sights higher than most of the ladies on the tour.

"I think my problem is that I want too much," she explains. "I don't just want to have a family and win tournaments. I want to be a *great* mother and a *great* wife and a *great* golfer." Her face screws up into a rare frown.

"I don't know if I'm good enough to be all three."

For someone who gives the impression of having the sunny, uncomplicated disposition of the girl on the old raisin boxes, Nancy has often been at odds with herself. When she was a little girl growing up in Roswell, New Mexico, she was a very determined young woman who more than anything wanted a pair of golf shoes because she liked the scraping sound they made when her father, Domingo, walked through the parking lot on his way to play at the local public course. She got them. When Domingo gave her a bicycle for Christmas, 6-year-old Nancy borrowed his pliers and unscrewed the training wheels herself. It was this kind of starch that led Nancy at the age of nine to win her first golf tournament by 110 strokes. Now that Nancy is a millionaire superstar, she is still a little kid who, whenever she gets a bogey, draws a little fence around the offending number on her scorecard so it will not spread throughout the round. And when she makes a birdie, she gives herself a little star just like she used to get for being one of the neatest kids in kindergarten.

Sometimes it seems Nancy can't make up her mind how she wants to play golf. She professes to be a devotee of JoAnne Carner's take-no-prisoners approach to the game. "I love the way JoAnne plays," Nancy says. "The way she hits the ball, goes and finds it, and then hits it again. As long as she has a golf club in her hand, JoAnne feels she can win."

Although Nancy says that she, too, would rather come in fifth trying to win than play safe for second place, her conservative nature makes her try to manage a course rather than attack it. "I'll try to hit a long second shot on a par 5 if I think I have a good chance to reach the green, but I don't want to try anything crazy." She wants to humble a course with bold play, but she also wants to win the Vare Trophy for lowest stroke average per round at least one more time. She wants to slash at the ball, but she also wants to save strokes. It's hard to do both.

A certain amount of inner confusion is not unusual for Nancy. With a new marriage and a new baby, the stakes and the pressures are immeasurably higher. Her conflicting desires to have a family and play big-time golf are more sharply drawn than ever. "When a tournament begins on Thursday," Nancy explains, "I want to win as much as anybody. But I haven't yet made that commitment to work on my game on Tuesday when I need the practice. I should be practicing right now. That's what I used to do. I'd hit balls, play an 18-hole practice round, hit more balls and then work on my putting for two hours. I would sometimes practice until I almost fell out of my shoes. Tomorrow I'm going to start practicing again."

She pauses for a moment.

"That's beginning to be the story of my life: I'm going to start practicing tomorrow."

Mr. and Mrs. Knight—Nancy plays golf as Nancy Lopez, but in everything else she likes to be known as Mrs. Ray Knight—pursue the affluent, comfortable life in Sugar Creek, Texas, a development of six-figures-and-then-some homes adjacent to the mandatory club golf course. Cooled by air conditioning and force-fed by abundant water, Sugar Creek is a manicured gesture of defiance against the flat and barren countryside south of Houston. Beyond the guard house that marks the entrance to Sugar Creek, hardscrabble land turns green and well ordered. Their house, a handsome, brick-faced structure, reflects the Knights careful sense of neatness—and economy. (Nancy once used the same golf glove for eight years). Everything is immaculate and polished to a high gloss. The house is still sparsely furnished, however, because Ray and Nancy still haven't had time to get the place fixed up. There is a couch and a few comfortable chairs in the living room. Two of Nancy's golf trophies are on the mantelpiece. Nancy has been meaning to hang some pictures on the wall, but that will have to wait for a while. "When I finally quit," Nancy says, "for the first time in my life I am going to unpack everything, get all of my clothes pressed, and put them on hangers. I used to love the tour when I first started because I didn't have to make my own bed. Now I hate living in motels. I want to come home."

Ray has the intensity of a highly skilled athlete, but he is an affable young man, as you might expect of someone who hits around .300, can play first or third base with equal facility, and has a five-year contract for $2.6 million in his pocket. Both are quietly religious and devote themselves to the Christian life. It is not true, however, as has often been reported, that neither Ray nor Nancy drink. Nancy confesses that as frequently as twice a year they will go to one of the local Mexican restaurants and split an entire margarita. They are palpably in love with each other and seem like the sort of couple who will still be acting like newlyweds when they are in the old-folks home.

The union of two stars from different sports has required some adjustments. "One night I got on the team bus," Nancy recalls. "The Astros had lost, but Ray had gone 4-for-4. I started to congratulate him, but Ray hushed me up. I have to remember that baseball is a team sport, and if the team loses you can't look too happy no matter how well you've done individually."

Nancy is an all-round athlete who still carries a small scar on her left knee from a football injury. She knows enough about baseball to know when Ray is pulling off the ball, but she refrains from making too many suggestions. She has, however, done wonders for his golf game. Ray gets to play only about eighteen times a year, but his handicap has dropped from 11 to 7 since their marriage. "I'm much more thoughtful about my game now," Ray says. "I used to be the typical jock golfer trying to muscle the ball around the course. Nancy has taught me five or six new shots, especially those knockdown and low punch shots."

Ray understands that right now little Ashley is the principal preoccupation in Nancy's life. The very helplessness of a baby cries out for its mother to stay home. But, as a blue-chip athlete, Ray also knows a talent that is not being tested is a talent that will atrophy. If Nancy does finally decide to go back on the tour with her old intensity, it will largely be because of Ray's urging. "Talent fades," he explains. "The key to being known as a great athlete comes in being able to exhibit consistent excellence over a long period of time. I think that as long as

Nancy has the chance to be great, she should take it. If Nancy were struggling every week to make the cut, then I'd say stay home and raise babies because I'm a family man. Nancy is still in the infancy of her career. I don't want her to look back at the age of forty-five and say, 'I could have been the greatest woman golfer who ever lived, but I gave it up to be with my family.' It's funny. A man with the same talent Nancy has wouldn't think about it for five minutes. He'd be out on the course every day."

"I'm not a man," Nancy says. Ray reaches out and holds Nancy in his arms.

"Nancy loves so hard," he continues. "She's afraid of being selfish. Well, I'm here to tell you that selfishness is part of being a champion. I think Nancy sometimes senses that selfishness in herself, and she pulls back because she wants to be a perfect mother. The night Ashley first rolled over by herself on the bed I called Nancy to tell her, and she started crying because she wasn't there to see it. The important thing is for Nancy to understand we will always be here for her."

Ray and Nancy have employed a full-time nursemaid, Fe, to help look after Ashley. As a result, Nancy is frequently able to take Ashley on tour, sometimes even out on the course in a stroller. It is pleasant to have a sweet-natured baby who just gurgles along with you when you're trying to play golf. When Ashley gets to be a 2-year-old who likes to run around and ask Mommy a lot of questions, the situation may change. But Nancy will play that one by ear.

Nancy's first season back on the tour after Ashley's birth has hardly been a disaster. In her first three tournaments she finished two under par, one over, and two under—scores that might have been winners in 1979 but did not get her into the top 10 in 1984. She won the Uniden Invitational in a breeze, setting a record-breaking 66 for the Mesa Verda Country Club. In mid-June she stood eighth on the money list. All in all, it was rather like George Brett hitting .304 at the All Star break. A good, solid, professional showing, but not quite what is expected from a star of such high luster.

Nancy has never been much interested in analyzing her golf swing, which Carol Mann describes as "a collection of corrected mistakes". It's a crude amalgam with an exaggerated forward press followed by a takeaway that eventually brings the club in on the wrong line, but she manages to scramble forward just in time to hit the ball squarely. Nancy attributes the idiosyncratic nature of her swing to "bone structure." She explains: "My swing is no uglier than Arnold Palmer's, and it's the same ugly swing every time."

This doesn't apply to her putting, which was once the strongest part of her game. "I have been putting badly for the past two years," Nancy believes. "Since Ashley was born, I think I'm actually hitting the ball longer than before. I've been hitting sixteen of eighteen greens every round and then taking 38 putts. It's really psyching me out because I depend on my putting so much."

Somehow—and don't ask Nancy because she doesn't know why either—she started changing her matchless putting stroke, and what used to be a short, compact touch with a long follow-through has become an unreliable affair. In a word, Nancy Lopez, even as you and I, is having trouble on the greens.

"I just have to work on it," Nancy says, which is all you can say when your putting stroke turns gray.

Nancy has learned the hard lesson that professional women's golf is a solitary sport where there are only a few friends and no teammates.

At the Astrodome she is one of the most vocal fans in the park. "C'mon, darling," she says to Ashley. "We've got to help our guy. Cross your fingers, cross your toes, cross anything." In the on-deck circle, Ray looks up into the stands and flashes Nancy a surreptitious wave in a minor violation of the baseball code against players communicating with spectators.

Being Nancy Lopez now also means being Ashley Marie's mother and Ray Knight's wife. She is delighted with all her roles. One afternoon she was leaving the Astrodome with Ashley in tow when a teenage boy wearing a Houston Astro sweat shirt and baseball cap approached her. He had no idea who Nancy was, but he had seen her sitting in the wives' section cheering for Ray every time he came to bat.

"Are you Ray Knight's wife?" he asked.

"Yes I am."

"He's a terrific ball player."

Nancy gave him the full 3,000-kilowatt smile. "Isn't he?" she said.

# Recalling the Formative Years of the LPGA Tour

## Betsy Rawls

"Gettin' to the Dance Floor", by Al Barkow        Atheneum, 1986

My father was the only one in my family who played golf, and he taught me the basics. Then I started taking lessons from Harvey Penick at the Austin Country Club when I was in college at the University of Texas. For my first lesson Harvey charged me $3. Even then that wasn't a lot, but Harvey never charged much. Anyway, I stayed out there with him for about an hour and a half. The next time I went to see him, when I got ready to pay he said, "No, I'm just telling you things I told you last week," and he never let me pay him again. I got a lot of mileage out of that first $3. I took lessons from Harvey for twenty years. He's the only teacher I've ever had, and I owe a great deal of my success to him, just as Ben Crenshaw, Tom Kite, and a lot of others do.

It didn't take me too long to become a good player, and one reason, I think, is because I started a little later than most—at seventeen. I think you can do it easier at that age than at twelve or thirteen, because you're more mature and stronger. Also, I always thought well on the course. I was a good student. Phi Beta Kappa. I studied a lot, and that helped my concentration. Maybe it helps to have a very controlled, logical sort of mind to play golf. I studied physics in college, and my father was an engineer. Maybe there's something to that. Of course, you also have to play a lot when you're young. You have to pay your dues. When I was in college it was hard to play much, because I had a lot of math. In summer, though, I played just about every day.

There is always the problem of women athletes being taken as too masculine. But when I started out I can't remember there being any kind of stigma attached to women athletes in Texas, at least not to women golfers. Most of the ones I ran into were at country clubs and from the upper classes, so to speak, and they knew how to behave. Eventually I was given a membership at the Austin Country Club. At the start I played with the boys except in tournaments, carried my own bag, did a little gambling—skin games—and held my own. It was fun.

Maybe we weren't socially conscious back then. Of course, women golfers are different in that they wear skirts—*we* did, anyhow—and golf is not that physical a game where you have to be very muscular or big. If you watched women's basketball, you'd get a much different impression of women athletes. A lot of women golfers are small and feminine-looking. So we never really fought that battle. We were always conscious of needing to dress properly and to look and act like ladies, and we always did.

The feminist movement never really touched the women's tour, we were all totally unaware of it. I think that's because we were so involved in playing golf and winning tournaments. We weren't interested in furthering women's rights. We felt we had everything, and nothing to prove. We had a golden opportunity to go out there and make money if we played well. We had nothing to gain from the women's movement, so consequently we pretty much ignored it.

I didn't pattern my swing after anyone in particular because, for quite some time after I started, I never saw a real good player, man or woman. The first good player I saw was Byron Nelson, in an exhibition match in Fort Worth. I was absolutely amazed. I had no idea people could hit the ball so far. At the first tournament I entered, the Women's Texas Open, at the Colonial Country Club—imagine playing your first tournament at Colonial!—I didn't know anything. I didn't know people had shag bags and warmed up before they played. I came from Arlington, a little town in Texas not far from Fort Worth. I had never even *seen* a golf tournament before. I just went out and played, and that was it.

Anyway, I qualified for the championship flight and won my first match. But I lost my second match, to Dot Kielty. She was runner-up once in the U.S. Women's Amateur. Then I lost in the first round of the consolation matches. I did pretty well for my first tournament ever, but I was *so* mad that I lost. I just hated losing. After that I really started working on my game. I gathered together some practice balls and went at it. Once you play in a tournament, you get hooked on practice.

I played amateur golf for about two and a half years before I turned pro in 1950. Wilson Sporting Goods asked me to join their staff. They had Patty Berg and Babe Zaharias and needed someone else to do clinics and play exhibitions. I considered the offer carefully and decided that golf would be more interesting than physics. I played professional golf for almost twenty-five years and was in on the beginnings of the Ladies Professional Golf Association. The LPGA got started in 1950, and Wilson hired Fred Corcoran to be the tournament director. Wilson needed places for Patty and Babe to play. Eventually, MacGregor and Spalding, the other two major equipment manufacturers at the time, joined with Wilson to pay Freddie's salary. Fred booked tournaments, but that's all he really did; he never came up with the promotional stunts he was known for when he ran the men's tour. We handled the day-to-day operation of our tour. One of us kept the books and wrote out the checks, and someone else handled the correspondence. I remember making rulings on other players in a tournament I was competing in. In this day and age, you'd probably get sued for something like that.

We didn't have any staff because we couldn't afford to hire people. That was the situation for a long time. I mean, the average purse in our tournaments was $3,000, perhaps $4,000. Five thousand was considered a rather big tournament in the early 1950s. We didn't mind that the touring men pros were getting so much more.

How do I account for that feeling? I guess the men are more spectacular to watch. They hit the ball farther, score better. They're just better players because of their strength. I think that's the only way they differ. Then again, we had our moments. One year six of us were in England. We played a team of the country's best men amateurs and beat them. We played four-ball matches in the morning and were behind by one point, but in the afternoon singles every woman won her match: Babe, Patty, myself, Betty Jameson, Peggy Kirk, and Betty Bush. We played at Wentworth, the "Burma Road" course, from the same tees as the men—about in the middle of the men's tees. The press made a big thing about it.

On our circuit at home in the early days, we drove almost everyplace. We didn't have as many tournaments as they have now, so we didn't play every week. I got my own car my second year on the tour, a Cadillac which everyone drove because of its weight and room for clubs and baggage. We would travel two in a car and caravan. Caravaning was following each other on the road, usually two cars. It was fun. I got to see the country. We drove across the United States at least twice a year and did a lot of sightseeing. Driving through the Rockies, we'd stop and have picnics. I know that if I were starting out now I would never see the country. I would fly everyplace. I would see the golf course, the hotel, the airport, and that's it.

In the beginning a woman could get on the tour by just showing up. She would apply to join the LPGA and come out and play. She was either good enough to stay on tour or she wasn't. Money was the only limiting factor. People didn't turn pro then unless they were good players. Nowadays there are other things that appeal to players—the life,

*This group in the 1954 Triangle Round Robin played at the Cascades course in*
*Hot Springs, Virginia, was the earliest regular group of LPGA tour players.*
*From left to right, top row: Betty Jameson, Jackie Pung, Betty McKinnon,*
*Betty Hicks, Marilynn Smith; middle row: Patty Berg, Beverly Hanson,*
*Louise Suggs, Babe Zaharias, Betty Dodd; bottom row: Fay Crocker,*
*Marlene Hagge, Mary Lena Faulk, Betty Bush, Alice Bauer,*
*Marlene Stewart Streit, Betsy Rawls.*

the exposure, the endorsements, being on television. In the early days
you just made out from the purse money, and the only reason you did it
was because you loved to play golf.

When I first turned pro, there were only fifteen people playing our
tour regularly. Then it went to about twenty and gradually built up.
Now, almost every good amateur turns pro. In the old days, we thought
of the tour as more of a competition than a show. The first prize would
usually be around $1,000. We decided at one of our meetings how much
the winner would get and then break down the remaining money
places. There was no particular formula for that. I must have made up
a hundred formulas over the years. We just figured what percentage of
the total purse we wanted to allot to first place—it was usually fifteen
percent—and then go from there.

We had some tournament sponsors in the first years who were kind
of patrons and saw us through. The first was Alvin Handmacher, who

made Weathervane suits for women. The next big one was Sears, Roebuck. But most of the other tournaments were sponsored by local organizations, the Lions Club or Chamber of Commerce. They could afford to put one on, because the prize money was low and the tournament was nice for the community.

We had some sponsors who reneged on the prize money. There was one in Oklahoma City, I remember, but it wasn't Waco Turner. He had plenty of money, and we never had anything to worry about with Waco. He put on two or three tournaments for us. He built his own course in Burneyville, Oklahoma, out in the wilderness. The course was so new when we played there the first time, and so badly built! I remember Bob Hagge and some other guy who was on tour with us went out to cut the cups, and the greens were so hard they couldn't do it. They had to hammer them out. So they didn't change the cups for the rest of the week. That was when Waco was paying so much for every birdie and eagle you made. I remember having a good week. I won the tournament and made two or three eagles, which were worth $500 apiece. I walked away with all kinds of money.

Then there was Tam O'Shanter in Chicago, George S. May's tournament. That was the biggest event on our tour, the largest purse we played for. It was very exciting, because you got to see everybody in the whole world, the whole golf world at least. There were tournaments for men and women pros and for men and women amateurs. It's hard to find an assembly of golfers to compare with Tam O'Shanter in excitement. Everybody in the game was there, the money was terrific, the clubhouse facilities were special, and there were the biggest crowds. People came out and had picnics in the rough. First time I ever saw that. I watched Sam Snead and Ben Hogan and other great men players. But I didn't get much of lasting value from their swings that I could use in mine.

The strength of my game was the short game. I could really scramble well, manufacture shots, play out of difficult situations. Driving was the weakest part of my game. Whenever I did drive well, I won tournaments. But nobody is ever going to be better than Mickey Wright.

Mickey was much better than Babe Zaharias. No comparison. Babe was stronger and maybe a better athlete—she was so well coordinated—but Mickey had a better golf swing, hit the ball better, and could play rings around Babe. I think Babe got started in golf too late. She didn't really take it up until she was past thirty. If she had started as a kid, the way Mickey did, maybe nobody would ever have beaten her. She was just that good an athlete. Babe loved to win. She hated to lose is the better way to put it. She was absolutely the worst loser I ever saw. She wasn't a bad sport, but if things didn't go her way, she could show her displeasure.

The sponsors made all the decisions about running their tournaments in the early days, and I must say they were greatly influenced by Babe Zaharias. Babe was not above saying she would drop out of a tournament if this or that wasn't done. She knew how much they really needed her, and they did. She was the draw. For instance, back in '51 we were playing someplace and Babe was leading the tournament. Patty Berg was second. They were paired together for the last round, in the last group, and Babe started out horrendously. So Patty caught her and passed her. Then it started raining. They were near the clubhouse at the time, and Babe marched in there and told the sponsors it was raining and she wanted the round canceled. And they did it. They rescheduled for the next day. It wasn't even close to being rained out. Patty was absolutely furious. But Patty beat Babe the next day anyway. Played rings around her.

But I loved Babe. She was good to play with, fun to be around. She was witty and kept the gallery laughing all the time. Very uninhibited. Some things she said shocked me a little, because I was just the opposite, but the gallery loved her.

In those early years the local course superintendent or pro would set the cups and tee markers, and as a result we played tough courses. We would never play the ladies' tees. Generally we hit from the middle or the back of the men's tees. The local greenkeepers and pros just couldn't stand for the women to score well on their courses. We played some monstrous ones, much longer than they play now. And pin placements were tough. But nobody ever thought of complaining. There was nothing wrong with long courses; everybody had to play them. It was when we got worried about our public image and the scores in the newspapers that we became concerned with long courses. But back then it didn't matter if you shot a 75 as long as you won the tournament.

But I remember Patty Berg shooting 64 at the Richmond Country Club, in California—a tough course. I was partnered with her, and to this day it may be the best round of golf I've ever seen played. Now the players come close to shooting 64, but on courses that are nothing like those we played in the early years. Those courses averaged 6,400 yards. Mickey and Babe had an advantage on them, and so did I. Mickey would have won on any golf course, any length.

In the early days there was not much of a future for women pros in golf except on the tour. There were very few club jobs available. But I don't think the really good players ever thought that far ahead. Patty-Berg, Louise Suggs, myself, we had contracts with Wilson and Mac-

Gregor. We had clubs made with our names on them, so we didn't have to worry too much. When you got past the first five, it was a problem. I don't know whether any of them were prepared for living without tournament golf. When you're playing the circuit you think you'll always play and there will never come a time when you will have to quit and go to work. People become addicted to it. It's a protected kind of existence. You don't have the responsibilities people have in the real world. You go from place to place, and, nowadays, sponsors take care of all your needs. They meet you at airports. You don't have to make beds, do wash, and the other mundane things. People hate to give that up. Even players who aren't having a lot of success don't prepare for life after tournament golf.

It was a shock for me to quit the tour. I had withdrawal symptoms. It was traumatic. But that was mainly in making the decision to quit. Once I did it, I got so involved in my job as the LPGA's Tournament Director that it never bothered me at all.

Today it's much easier for women to get club-professional jobs. They are in great demand. More women golfers want to take lessons from women pros. Women pros are admired now.

I won fifty-five tournaments as a professional. I won ten of them in 1959, and won a little over $26,000. But I don't feel any resentment at the amount of money the girls are playing for now. That's not why I played, for the money. If it was money I was after, I probably would have done something else. I thoroughly enjoyed playing and got a lot of satisfaction from it. I take pride in being a pioneer who helped make today's tour possible.

*Betsy Rawls is a member of the LPGA Hall of Fame. She won a total of fifty-five tournaments, her last one in 1972. After serving six years as the LPGA's Tournament Director, she left the position to become executive director for the McDonald's Championship, an LPGA event played annually at the White Meadow Country Club in Malvern, Pennsylvania. Betsy lives in the neighborhood, which is just outside Philadelphia.*

# The Main Things My Father Taught Me About Golf

## Patty Sheehan, with Robert Carney

Golf Digest                                                    June, 1986

In more ways than I sometimes like to admit, I'm a chip off the old block—my dad, Bobo Sheehan. My father introduced me to golf and, though I competed mostly against my three brothers, I think I've inherited his timing. I've certainly got his strong hands through the ball.

But it's more than that. My dad exposed me to golf so that I could excel at it and still enjoy it. From the time I followed him and Mom around the course at Middlebury, Vermont, when I was four, he never pushed me. But he did encourage me. He encouraged me to be good.

Some of my fellow LPGA players have said that I'm a tenacious competitor, that I'm tough under pressure. I learned patience from my mother, but I got that toughness from Dad. He is one of the most competitive people I've ever met. He was a superb athlete, an especially great skier; he coached the U.S. Olympic men's Alpine team in 1956. He coached football, baseball, golf, and skiing at Middlebury College, that extremely fine center of learning and sports in central Vermont. Although I didn't have a chance to see him compete, I know how competitive he was by how he taught me to approach sports.

One day in particular comes to mind, an incident I remember often on the golf course. I was eleven and had won my first national ski title the previous year. I was racing in a downhill event at Alpine Meadows, and as I came out of the gate, I caught the tip of my ski and spun around. I started to cry because I thought the race was over. But as I did I caught sight of my dad at the side of the run. "Get going!!" he yelled. And I took off as fast as I could because I knew I was in trouble. Despite that horrible start, I finished fourth in the race. And I learned the lesson he most wanted me to learn: never give up. Some of the caddies call me "Sunday Patty" because I am apt to shoot a very low score on Sunday. They never count me out. Chalk that up to Bobo.

*Patty Sheehan's characteristic follow-through*

Dad always said, "There's no use competing if you're not going to win," but in skiing, as in golf, the *choice* to compete was always mine.

When I was thirteen I decided to give up competitive skiing because I was burned out. I knew that Dad had dreamed of one of us becoming an Olympic skier, and I was sure when I told him of my decision he would be disappointed and angry. I agonized over how to tell him. Finally I called and said, "I don't want to do this anymore." Dad said, "Fine. I've frozen enough of my life. Why should you have to?"

All sports appealed to Dad. At home, sports took place around the house. We had a sand pit for the pole vault. We had a ski jump in the backyard. We had a miniature golf course in the backyard—the putting green was in the garage—and our house was just off a real golf course so we could play whenever we wanted. Dad never confused us with a lot of mechanics when he coached. In skiing we weren't pretty, but we could get down the hill fast. In golf, he just said, "Keep your eye on the ball." To this day, I don't get bogged down in swing analysis.

That's my dad. As tough as he is, as competitive as he is, he always made sports fun for me. If it looks like I'm having a good time on the golf course, that comes from him. He's a good player himself, at age 63 a 6-handicapper at Hidden Valley Country Club in Reno. And he likes to win. He played (and lost to) my brother Butch for the club championship there. But when Dad hits a bad shot, or if he has a bad day, he just laughs. He has always told us to have fun. As a coach he was, and is, the life of the party. Now, no matter where I go around the country, people come up to me and ask me how Dad is.

# The Curtis Cup: American Dominance Comes to an End

## Robert Sommers

Golf Journal                                    September, 1986


In 1982, the trophy case off the lobby of Golf House, the USGA Museum and Library, in Far Hills, New Jersey, was crammed with emblems of American golf supremacy—the Eisenhower Trophy, the symbol of the World Amateur Team championship; the Espirito Santo Trophy, for the Women's World Amateur Team championship; the Walker Cup; and the Curtis Cup. Now only the Walker Cup and the Espirito Santo Trophy remain.

Where once the United States could be practically assured of winning every international competition, now it has trouble winning anything. Japan won the World Amateur Team championship in 1984, Europe won the Ryder Cup last year, and in the latest indication that the end of American dominance is near if not upon us already, Great Britain and Ireland won the Curtis Cup early last month by defeating the United States by the startling score of 13-5 at the Prairie Dunes Country Club, in Hutchinson, Kansas.

Furthermore, not only has no American won the British Open since 1983, none has even threatened to win it the last two years, and this July only two finished among the low 10. No American has won the British Amateur since 1979. In 1983, Philip Parkin, of Wales, ended an extraordinary run of American successes by defeating Jim Holtgrieve, an American Walker Cupper, in the final at Turnberry, Scotland. Members of the visiting American Walker Cup teams had won all but one British Amateur since 1926. (Michael Lunt, an Englishman, won in 1963.) To cap this surprising trend, last year a Japanese teenager won our Women's Amateur.

Today the United States' long domination of both the Espirito Santo Trophy and the Walker Cup seems to be in danger. In October, some of the women who won the Curtis Cup will represent Great Britain and Ireland in the Women's World Amateur Team championship, in Venezuela, and the British and Irish men can hardly wait for the upcoming Walker Cup Match, which will be played at the Sunningdale Golf Club, near London, next spring.

Looking back at what happened at Prairie Dunes, William J. Williams, Jr., the president of the USGA, believes the result was good for the future of the Curtis Cup as a competition, and he wonders whether the recent defeats suffered by our teams in international competition might not happen again: "I would not assume this is an aberration. The Americans will have to pick up their socks if they expect to win next time." That match, is scheduled for the Royal St. George's Golf Club, in Sandwich, England, next year.

The fact that golfers from the rest of the world have become better players was emphasized dramatically at Prairie Dunes. The victory by the British and Irish ladies was no fluke. They clearly outplayed the Americans, and, for two days at least, they were the better golfers. This was their third victory—the United States has won nineteen team matches, and two have been halved. This was the first time an American team has lost at home in the Curtis Cup, the Walker Cup, or the Ryder Cup competitions.

We are still left with the question of what has happened to American golf. Why can't a nation of more than 200 million turn out better golfers than much smaller countries?

Mark McCormack, who handles the financial affairs of a number of the leading golfers, has a theory: "Arnold Palmer, I think, put his finger on why American golf has declined. The American professional tour, he says, makes it too easy for golfers to earn a living. No longer do they play to win; they play to get a good paycheck. Nowadays when you ask golfers, 'How did you do last week?', they answer, 'I finished fifth,' as if that was something to be proud of. After all, a fifth-place payday might be worth $15,000 or $20,000. The great champions, like Palmer and Nicklaus, cared more about winning and treated the prize money as secondary. I think the Europeans have that same championship mentality.

"I have a hunch that one reason for this complacency is the departure of match play from college golf. In match play (which was replaced by stroke play about ten years ago) you either win or you lose, and it's that win-lose mindset that makes golf champions. When you've lost in match play, all you can say is, 'The other guy beat me.' That's a very definite statement, and to a true competitor it's a very painful one."

What effect the recent success of foreign golfers has had on foreign attitudes is impossible to assess, but Frank Hannigan, the Senior Executive Director of the United States Golf Association believes that if European men had not won both of the last two British Opens and the Ryder Cup, the European women wouldn't have dared win the Curtis Cup.

Over the two days of the Match, the women play three alternate-shot foursomes matches each morning and six singles each afternoon—eighteen matches in all. The British and Irish won all three foursomes the first morning, which they had never done before, and they then followed up by winning three singles matches and halving another. At the end of the day they led, 6½ to 2½. To hold onto the Cup, the Americans had to win all three of the second day's foursomes and four of the singles. When they salvaged only half a point in the foursomes, the team match was over.

During the two days the Americans won just three matches, and only two when it mattered. Both Kandi Kessler and Cindy Schreyer won their singles the first day when the Cup could have been saved, but only Kim Gardner won the following afternoon, and by then it was far too late.

Even though the British and Irish frequently play foursomes matches at home, they have always been weak at that form of play in both the Curtis and Walker Cup Matches. Not this time. At Prairie Dunes, for the first time since the Curtis Cup began in 1932, the United States did not win one foursomes match. The British and Irish won five and they halved the last, the only one the Americans might have won. Miss Gardner and Kathleen McCarthy were leading by one hole, but Miss McCarthy overshot the 18th green, and the hole went to Belle Robertson and Mary McKenna.

"We learned to play foursomes from the Americans," said John Bailey, the husband of Diane Bailey, the British and Irish Captain. "For years and years, every time we had a shot to play, we would always confer with our partner. It was sort of a cop-out, really, sharing the responsibility. The Americans never did that. Each played her own game and took the responsibility for the shot."

This visiting team was not what everyone had come to think of as a typical British team. From the start they played like the Americans had in the past—forceful, attacking golf, going for the flagsticks, looking for birdies. Mrs. Robertson pitched in for an eagle on the 11th, Jill Thornhill chipped in to birdie the ninth, Patricia Johnson holed from off the back of the 18th green, and Mrs. Robertson holed from across the 18th. On the other hand, the Americans played tentative, cautious golf. They seemed always to be short, not only of the hole but often of the green. Polly Riley, a Curtis Cupper of the 1940s and 1950s, seemed distressed at the Americans lack of aggressiveness. Furthermore, the British and Irish out-putted the Americans, another reversal of form. Jill Thornhill, the English Women's champion, gave the impression she holed everything she looked at.

Mrs. Thornhill played in four matches and won 3½ points, but while this was outstanding golf, she was outdone by 20-year-old Miss Johnson, the youngest member of the team, who won all four of her points. A tall, strong, tousle-haired blonde who held both the English match and stroke play championships last year, she was clearly the best golfer on either team. Over 33 holes of singles play, she was even par in defeating Leslie Shannon by one hole the first day, and she then played Prairie Dunes in three strokes under par the next afternoon in defeating Miss McCarthy 5 and 3 and winning the point that actually won the Curtis Cup.

The United States had no one to match her. Mrs. Shannon was only two over par in losing to Miss Johnson the first day, and she was four over in halving her match with Mrs. Thornhill the second afternoon. Even though she played the best golf of the Americans, she came away with only half a point. Both Miss Kessler and Miss Gardner won 1½ points.

The British and Irish came into the match convinced they could win, and while they had said that in the past, this time they meant it. They had gained great confidence when they lost by only one point at Muirfield, in Scotland, two years ago, and last fall they won a match against the continent of Europe for the Vagliano Trophy.

With the exception of Karen Davies, a student at the University of Florida, the team that won the Curtis Cup was the same team that won the Vagliano Trophy, and so they came to Prairie Dunes with the experience of having played together in international competition. On the other hand, this was the first American team since the original match that did not include at least one former Curtis Cupper.

Not only was the British and Irish team composed of first-class golfers, it also made serious preparations for the Curtis Cup. After the players were chosen by a committee of four selectors, they got together for a weekend of golf in July. At Walton Heath they played a group of men golfers that included Michael Lunt, a former Walker Cupper. While no one would say precisely how the match came out, the women claimed they won.

Based on their records, the British and Irish team had an exceedingly strong group of players. In addition to Miss Johnson and Mrs. Thornhill, it included Lillian Behan, the 1985 British champion; Claire Hourihane, the Irish champion from 1983 through 1985; Belle Robertson, the current Scottish champion (at 50 she is the oldest player ever to have played in the Curtis Cup); Vicki Thomas, the Welsh champion; and Mary McKenna, of Ireland, who has now played in a record nine Curtis Cup matches, the most anyone ever has.

# Pat Bradley: All Alone at the Top

## Jim Moriarity

Golf Digest                                    December, 1986

I had known Pat Bradley for a couple of years before she won the U.S. Open at La Grange (Illinois) Country Club in 1981. She called me "Jimmy" then, as she does now. She's the only person in the world who calls me that. Not that I take offense. She calls her eldest brother "Ricky" and he lands fighter planes on an aircraft carrier. With Pat Bradley, you're either "sir" or you're her brother. There's not much in between.

There are a couple of reasons why La Grange is so fresh in my mind. First of all, it was one of the greatest U.S. Open Sundays ever, male or female. Kathy Whitworth was the sentimental favorite, trying to shake the dubious distinction she shares with Sam Snead as the greatest player never to win a U.S. Open. But that day evolved into a punch and counterpunch battle between Beth Daniel and Pat. The standard of play was glorious. One would pick up a birdie, then the other would answer. The *coup de grace* came on the 15th when Pat rolled in a birdie putt that was so long it had to change buses on the way to the hole.

Rather than wait in the scoring tent for the last twosome to finish, Pat vanished into the basement of the clubhouse. In all the confusion, we ended up standing there alone. She was bent over at the waist, hyperventilating as she peeled off the white adhesive tape that supports her weakened left thumb. Her hands were shaking. I remember thinking she looked like someone who had just set a world record in the 440. She said, "Thank you, Lord, oh thank you," to the floor. Then, with tears in her eyes, she said, "Jimmy, I just can't believe it." She threw her arms around me and kissed me on the cheek. It remains to this day the only time I've ever been kissed by a United States Open champion.

Pat Bradley doesn't smile like Nancy Lopez. She doesn't swing like Amy Alcott. She's not theatrical like JoAnne Carner, acrobatic like Patty Sheehan, pretty like Laura Baugh, or sexy like Jan Stephenson. All she is is the best woman golfer in the world.

In 1986 Pat won five tournaments including three of the LPGA's designated majors—the Dinah Shore, the LPGA, and the Du Maurier. In addition, she posted six seconds, finished in the top ten 70 percent of the time, and missed completing an incredible slam of the women's majors in the U.S. Open by three shots. She passed the $2 million mark in career earnings and became the first player to win each of the LP-GA's four modern major tournaments. As impressive as that accomplishment is, it should be pointed out that both Mickey Wright and Louise Suggs won the LPGA's four designated majors when the Title-holders and Western Open were not among them. That fact in no way dulls the shine of Bradley's brilliant year or remarkable career. In 363 tournaments spanning 13 years, Bradley has 21 firsts (including six majors) and 42 seconds. As Val Skinner has said, there are but three certainties in this life: Death, taxes, and Bradley on the leader board.

So what makes Pat Bradley the Rodney Dangerfield of golf? She just gets no respect. Even in those years when she has lapped the field in nearly every statistical category, the naysayers were muttering under their breath, "Well, Sheehan is bored. Lopez is pregnant. Carner is sick." The Bradley's-all-that's-left implication was all too clear. And unfair.

It's not precisely clear when the rap on Bradley began or what started it. Somewhere along the line, the phrase "lacks aggressiveness" became part of her permanent record. "Subject is female Caucasian, 35 years of age, 5-8, weight classified, salt-and-pepper hair (more salt than pepper these days), no visible marks or tattoos, lacks aggressiveness."

Curiously, Pat's ability to win was never in doubt. Sure, she could win—her detractors would say—but only coming from behind. The bizarre logic went something like this: Bradley can win by shooting the lowest score ever posted in the final round of the U.S. Open (a 66 in 1981), but she collapses as a front-runner.

Big Momma Carner puts it like this: "Pat was always very happy with second. She would play great but never seemed to want to take charge and win the tournament." A big year has its public-relations advantages. All those seconds and thirds are magically transformed into the mark of consistency rather than a badge of failure. Bradley's 1986 season has turned that corner for her.

The perception of her among her peers has changed. "I think she's a smart player," says three-time Open champion Hollis Stacy. "She is aggressive when she has to be and conservative when it counts."

The tournaments in which Bradley made her epic collapses were the Nabisco Dinah Shore in 1984 and the Women's Kemper Open in 1985. Bradley was leading with four holes to play in the Dinah Shore when NBC, concerned that the pros were playing so fast the tournament would end before the telecast was over, ordered a 10-minute delay. Bradley then scrambled for pars on 15 and 17, took a bogey on 16, and missed a 12-foot birdie putt on 18. She also messed up the playoff hole, allowing Juli Inkster to win with a par. In the Women's Kemper, she played even worse. She took a 7 on the final hole when she hit a wedge shot into the water to lose the tournament by a stroke.

Pat's critics clearly struck a nerve. "I think I'm an extremely smart player out there," she says. "I know when to be aggressive and I know when to say, hey, I think we'll try a different route. True, I've had a tremendous amount of seconds. People have said that's because I'm not aggressive enough, but I think they're wrong. A lot of my seconds have come from being 13th and then shooting 68 or 69 in the final round. True, I've made mistakes and lost tournaments. A number of other players have done that. I'm not out here to defend my way of playing. If Joe Blow doesn't like it, tough. I play the way that's best for me."

Statistically, her record supports her contention, all the way from that closing 66 in the U.S. Open to her Sunday 66 at the Du Maurier this past year. Pat Bradley is, and always has been, a great finisher. At the Nestle World championship in August, she fired a closing-round 63 to win by two strokes over Nancy Lopez and Betsy King. Ironically, this lady who theoretically lacks aggressiveness turns out to be one of the true "chargers" in women's golf. And as for coming in second, the golfer with that record salted away is somebody named Jack Nicklaus, who has managed to do it 58 times, 19 of them in majors.

There are two ways to learn the golf swing. The first is an end in itself, as if it were a work of art. The second is as a means to an end. In the latter, the golf swing is like a shillelagh—it doesn't have to be pretty as long as you can beat people with it.

You should probably know that Pat will never win Miss Congeniality on the LPGA Tour. In fact, she has a tendency to keep a distance between herself and the people she competes against.

"I played with Pat at the LPGA Championship," Carner says, "and she said more to me in the two rounds there than she has in all the years she's been on the tour. Pat's just one of those people who has to be serious all the time."

She is no-nonsense on the golf course, on the driving range, on the putting green, and in the clubhouse. No chitchat with the girls.

"Nothing has come easy to me," she says. "I have worked my butt off and I continue to. I do not take this game lightly."

Nor does she take any competition lightly. Ask Clint Eastwood after Pat beat him in a downhill skiing race, despite his head start. Or ask Ara Parseghian, who played some friendly games with Pat and Gene

*Pat with her mother and father, Kathleen and Dick Bradley.*

Sarazen a decade ago down on Marco Island. "I used to kid her a lot, you know, a little gamesmanship," says Ara. "But she gave no quarter."

To those previously unfamiliar with Pat Bradley, "discovering" her at this stage in her career can be curiously satisfying. It's like stumbling across a prolific novelist late in the writer's life. There's no need to wait around a couple of years for new titles, the shelves are already stocked with past masterpieces.

Pat grew up in Westford, Massachusetts, wedged among five brothers. She learned to play from club pro John Wirbal at the Nashua (New Hampshire) Country Club, but she learned to fight at home. "All my brothers are extremely competitive, and I was always a participant," she says. "My brothers were the quarterbacks and wide receivers, and I always got the unglamorous jobs like blocking. It was fun, but I mean it was tough. I had to hold my own."

Pat's father, Dick, owns and operates the R.J. Bradley's Ski and Tennis Shop in Westford. Pat still works the counter there during the busy Christmas season. Her mother, Kathleen, is notorious locally for ringing cowbells to announce another Pat Bradley victory. When Pat won her first professional tournament, the '75 Colgate Far East, she immediately called from Japan with the good news. Unfortunately, it was the middle of the night stateside. That didn't deter Kathleen, however. She grabbed the first object she could find that would make noise—an old cowbell—charged out on the porch and started clanging it for all she was worth. In retrospect, the townsfolk are probably thankful she didn't come across a shotgun.

Pat's parents have had more than just an audible impact on her career. "I was pushed a little bit," Pat admits. "I needed to be pushed. As a youngster I didn't recognize my true ability or talents. And, yes, I had a little bit of rebellion in me. I wanted to be with the gang. Sure, I said I was going to the golf course, but when I got my driver's license, man, as soon as I got out of sight, I took the next left."

Some people say Pat Bradley is more aggressive today. Some say more confident. Some more relaxed.

For the last two years Pat has worked with a sports psychologist, Bob Rotella. With or without Rotella, Pat would have improved and become a better player. What Rotella has done more than anything is help get Pat Bradley out of her own way.

"Through Bob I've been able to be a little more patient, to take a tough shot or a tough round a little more in stride. I still get disappointed but I don't dwell on it. I've learned to give myself a break.

"No one out here really cares except you. If you have a not-so-good day, nobody gives a rip. They've got their own problems. I had to learn how to be a friend to myself."

Rotella has worked with top-flight athletes like Tom Kite, but he'll confide that Pat Bradley is the most determined athlete he has ever known. "We constantly praise the work ethic and dedication, commitment and all that stuff," Rotella says. "Then we turn around and give praise of the highest kind to the people who are born precocious. With Pat the thing that stands out is the self-discipline, the mental toughness it takes to be so successful year after year. And after all those years of playing that well, to be able to go out there and still raise your confidence to another level. That impresses the hell out of me. The thing I love about a Larry Bird or a Pat Bradley is that they were born with a lot of talent, but it didn't all come together at a very early age. You see them, through unbelievable self-discipline and willpower, make a commitment to become the best they can be—in their cases the best in the world. Most people would have given up long before they got there. They'd just say, hey, I don't have that much talent. It takes a special kind of willpower to want it so badly that even when you aren't dominating the world, you know you're going to some day."

# A Lively Legend: Glenna Collett Vare at Eighty-Three

## James Dodson

Golf Journal                                                    August, 1987

The sunny morning I called on Mrs. Glenna Vare, I found a lanky young man mysteriously thumping a tennis racket against the outside wall of her house.

It was a lovely old mansion with big windows and a rambling porch and a breathless view of the sea, set back from the road among century-old trees on a gentle dorsal of land just outside the old summer spa of Narragansett, Rhode Island.

The reason I had come to visit had entirely to do with time and fantasy. A few days before, I'd happened to read in the Providence *Journal* that Glenna Collett Vare was about to participate in her 62nd straight Point Judith Invitational golf tournament. The story mentioned that Glenna Vare was 83 years old and still played golf with a 15 handicap.

That was remarkable in its own right: she could almost shoot her age. But, in truth, I had not driven all the way from Boston just to meet another spry octogenarian who stalked after a golf ball. For lack of a more fitting way of putting it, I'd come—a combination graduate student and sports groupie—to lay eyes on living golf history.

Glenna Collett Vare is a name of great significance in the ledger of American golf. She belongs to a separate—if remoter—latitude of golfing fame, a time when the game was played not for money or rank but rather for the simple, exhilarating pleasure of the game itself. Between the years 1922 and 1935, Glenna Collett Vare won the U.S. Women's Open six times, something no other golfer has accomplished. In her competitive years, she dominated women's golf here with a patrician good cheer that was as beguiling as it was revolutionary. In the 1930s, she helped orchestrate the biennial Curtis Cup matches between the top women amateur golfers of the United States and Great Britain & Ireland. Not surprisingly, the award given annually by the LPGA to

410

the woman professional with the lowest scoring average bears Glenna's name—the Vare Trophy.

"Is Mrs. Vare here?" I asked the lanky youth armed with the tennis racket.

"Yup," he replied and nonchalantly gave the wall another solid whack. "Check inside. Follow the noise."

I reluctantly let myself into a cool foyer. Positioned loosely in a brass umbrella stand by the front door was a cluster of ancient clubs: spoons and cleeks and a well-worn brassie. These clubs were gorgeous relics, totems from another age. I touched one of the clubs, wanting to feel its talismatic spell. I felt like a child taking a peek at Christmas toys hidden beneath the bedskirts.

On a table beside the umbrella stand stood a magnificent brass statue of a woman smashing a golf ball—the famous compact swing, a model of power and grace, of the youthful Glenna Collett frozen in time.

A young fair-haired woman appeared in the hallway, frowning slightly and clutching a broomstick. She was dewy from wall-banging.

"Are you Mrs. Vare's daughter?" I asked.

"No," she replied courteously. "I just work for her in the summer. Mrs. Vare is in back. Go back, if you like."

At that moment a comfortably upholstered version of the splendid statue strolled into the foyer, a no-nonsense amble that had accompanied her from the fairways of youth to the hallway of old age. She had on a bright green skirt and a yellow knit shirt, open on her tanned leathery neck. Grass-stained tennis shoes completed the ensemble. She was carrying an old golf club, a trusty spoon.

"You're probably the one who called," she began without preamble, in a smoky, bossy contralto.

"Yes, ma'am," I replied.

She fixed me with her alert gray eyes.

"Have you ever had raccoon piddle in your rafters?" she demanded, though not unkindly.

I admitted that I hadn't.

"Well, it's a nuisance. I can tell you that," she went ahead firmly. Then she gave the wall of the foyer a solid whack.

"Look up there," she said, scowling at a corner of the ceiling.

Naturally, I did what I was told. The ceiling, in the spot where she aimed her club, had been discolored by brown hieroglyphics.

"That's raccoon piddle," she informed me briskly. "Every spring,

*Glenna Collett Vare with Jimmy, her constant companion.*

when I come up from Florida, I find that raccoons have spent the winter having a party in my house. It's a real annoyance. We think there's a mother and her babies in there now. This man's supposed to come out and do something. I don't know where he is. Anyway, you see, if we could find the hole they use, chase them out, and seal the hole up, the problem would be solved."

I agreed it sounded like a solid theory.

"But I don't want the creatures hurt," she injected.

She nodded at the wall, as if her game plan for evacuating the unwanted houseguests was irrevocably set. Then she turned her handsome face on me again.

"Now what can I do for you?" she said, clearing her throat.

"I just wanted to ask you a couple questions about golf." I proposed somewhat weakly. "Do you remember the first golf shot you ever hit?" It was a serious tactical mistake.

She waved an irritated hand. "Heavens, *no*. Of course I don't. Do you? Listen here, I don't like to talk about golf," she grumped with irritation. "I have a terrible memory. Everything I did was so long ago, you know. If you want to learn something about me, there are history books that can tell you what you need to know. Don't waste your time and mine, young man."

I thought I was about to be permanently dismissed—or forced to thump the walls with the hired help. Instead, she put her club down and said, "You'd better come with me to the porch."

She led me through the grand old house onto a beautiful sun porch. Potted geraniums blazed in pink and red splendor, and the surface of Narragansett Bay shimmered like a billion jewels beyond the salt-marsh that began at the edge of the yard.

She fixed me a hearty gin and tonic and sat down facing me with a glass of tomato juice.

"My game," she said with a sigh, "is really very bad. I'm sorry to say that. Very bad. You probably wanted to know about Bobby Jones or something, didn't you? That's what reporters usually want to know. It's like I'm some living monument. . . ."

A patch of silence fell between us, a requiem for a game she once loved for the thrill of playing it so very well. A sailboat, I noticed, crossed on the horizon behind her.

Finally, she leaned forward in her wicker chair and, in a surprisingly quiet voice, inquired, "Did you say *you* play golf?"

It sounded, I thought, a little like an accusation.

"Yes, I do," I told her. "Anywhere from a 10 to 15 handicap."

For the first time she smiled. Something amused her. She picked at a leaf of a geranium. "That's funny," she allowed a little wistfully. "Mine's about a 15 now, too."

"That's what I read," I told her. "To tell you the truth, that's one of the reasons I came. I had it in my mind that it would be fun to play a round together. A head-to-head match."

I smiled; she frowned.

"What do you say?" I asked.

"You must be dreaming," she replied, sipping her drink.

Glenna Collett Vare's start in golf was the stuff of sporting legends. One summer day in 1917, at the Metacomet Country Club, in Providence, Rhode Island, an insurance man and retired cycling champion named George Collett invited two of his cronies to watch his precocious daughter Glenna hit her first shot on a regulation course.

Glenna was 14. She may have weighed 70 pounds. The ball she hammered flew well over 100 yards and split the fairway.

George Collett's cronies were astonished and deeply impressed. The willowy child could hit a golf ball as competently as most men. This display was hardly a surprise to George Collett. At 9, Glenna had been an accomplished diver and swimmer; at 10, she drove the family car. For a while she played baseball and could throw the ball farther and more accurately than any boy in her neighborhood. At 12 she was winning tennis matches left and right.

About that time she happened to attend an exhibition golf match with her father. The match featured three of the brightest young names in the game—Alexa Stirling, Perry Adair, and Bobby Jones. "I was so thrilled by what I saw them do," she said, "that the next day I went out and broke 50 for nine holes."

She was a year younger than Bobby Jones. The next spring, George Collett took his daughter to see Alex Smith, a Scottish teaching pro who had won the U.S. Open twice. The chemistry was right. "He, Alex, was a go-getter. He insisted I practice all the time," Glenna recalled. "Without him, I might never have gone very far."

In 1922, just 19 years old, Glenna won the U.S. Women's Amateur championship at White Sulphur Springs, West Virginia, and suddenly a nation of sports fans hungered to know more about the politely restrained and attractive schoolgirl who was so superstitious she often wore the same hat and clothes ensemble, the same color of red fingernail polish, throughout a five-day tournament. In 1924 she played sixty golf matches and won fifty-nine of them. The next year she won the Women's Amateur for a second time, in St. Louis. Over the next five years she nailed down three more national championships and gained an international following. Her matches against Britain's Joyce Wethered became headline news in sports pages around the world.

In 1931 she married a wealthy Philadelphian, Edwin H. Vare, Jr. They had two children. Glenna played less competitive golf, took up bridge, needlepoint, and trapshooting, and continued in her role as advocate for women's sports.

Glenna, however, was not through with golf. In 1935, the female Bobby Jones, as the press called her, began an historic comeback. At Interlachen, in Minneapolis, where Jones had won the 1930 Open, the third leg of his Grand Slam, Glenna was matched in the final against a popular hometown girl named Patricia Jane Berg. Glenna was old guard; Patty Berg was part of a newly emerging breed—young women who, like their male counterparts, were destined to become professionals and play the game for something more than its uncommercial rewards. The press and 6,500 spectators swarmed after the two when they met in the final. On the 34th hole, Glenna rolled in a slippery putt for her par and won the championship for a record sixth time.

Glenna Vare had been sitting perfectly still on her porch for several minutes. The sun lay on her square brown face. She looked very peaceful with her tanned hands folded—a czarina at rest. Her eyes fluttered open and she glared at her wristwatch with annoyance. "Oh," she fretted, "it's almost noon. I have to go get Jimmy."

She asked me to ride with her. A few minutes later we got into her blue Fleetwood Cadillac and she revved up the engine. A golf ball rolled out from under the seat, and I picked it up. The word *dammit* was written on it.

It didn't occur to me to ask who Jimmy was, and Glenna's mind was elsewhere, focused on the annoying green sportscar that buzzed in front of her as we rolled along in sluggish U.S. 1 traffic. She braked abruptly and puffed her cheeks in dismay. Every spring since the death of her husband ten years ago, she explained, she and Jimmy drove north from Delray Beach, Florida, Glenna's winter home, and every year just lately her daughter Glenny, who lives in Venezuela, has insisted that she no longer make the drive. "She thinks I'm getting too old, though I don't agree with her," said Glenna. "She worries, I suppose, about people getting in my way. Hah. Listen, I love driving. I'd hate flying. And so would Jimmy. He just wouldn't stand for it."

Jimmy, it turned out, was her constant companion—a small beige Norwich terrier.

A few minutes later, he was delivered into her sturdy arms from a local pet grooming establishment. His hair was clipped and he looked embarrassed by the light blue bow that someone had tied around his neck.

"Oh, Jimmy," Glenna said with sympathy as she deposited him on the seat between us, "they really did a number on you, didn't they?" She untied the ridiculous bow and patted his head. Jimmy sat down loyally beside her on the front seat, sniffed at me, then looked out over the vast hood, ready for action.

As we passed back through thick Narragansett traffic, the street became snarled with traffic wedged around a mammoth condominium construction project that was visible from Glenna's yard.

She closed her eyes, disgusted. "It's really awful, what's happened to Narragansett," she complained. And then she told me the story of how she and Edwin had bought the Narragansett house in the late summer

of 1938—just a few weeks before the hurricane of the century struck
New England. "That night," she explained in the voice of a storyteller,
"Edwin was playing backgammon down at the Dunes Club. He left
there just before the storm hit and everything got demolished. You
know, hundreds of people were killed. . . ."

Her voice trailed off into private thoughts for the rest of the ride
home.

On the porch, we settled into the comfortable chairs again, while
Jimmy looked the place over for changes.

"Do you like tomato soup?" asked Glenna politely. "It's homemade."
I said I did.

"Good," said she. "I made it. But I'm not so sure it's any good."

The young fair-headed girl who had been thumping walls with the
broomstick brought us each a bowl of Glenna's homemade soup. The
house had grown peaceful and silent. I imagined the raccoons were
getting some sleep at last.

"How's the soup?" she asked seriously.

"Excellent," I told her.

"I don't know," she said.

As we'd informally agreed, for the moment at least, there was little or
no discussion of golf. The subject, it seemed, was all too familiar, like an
overgrown yard in which a beautiful flower bed had once blazed in the
sun but now had gone rank.

Her own handsome yard was green and a bit overgrown. We talked
about gardening for a while, about the 12-meter sailing races she can
see from her porch; about children and bridge. When I casually mentioned I was engaged to be married, she took a genuine interest in the
date and the details about the wife-to-be. Inevitably, we wound our way
back to tomato soup.

"At the Gulfstream Golf Club, where I belong in Florida," she said,
"everyone's become too old to play good golf, so a lot of people have quit
playing and taken up gourmet cooking. That's where the real competition is now." She laughed. "I had to either join them or be left alone on
the golf course."

Do you have many friends left in Narragansett?" I quietly asked her.

She thought a moment. "Not too many," she conceded. "People still
come to see me. Reporters discover I'm still alive and call up. I don't
enjoy reporters because I can't remember everything properly. They
want to know what Bobby Jones was really like, or what the golden age
of amateur golf was like. I wish I could tell them, but I can't. . . . But
there are all these stories still floating around."

She wagged a finger at the air, chasing away history like an intruder.

Since she had raised the subject, I mentioned a story I'd recently read in *Golf Magazine*. It went thus: Years ago Glenna was competing in an important championship in Philadelphia. Halfway through the final round of play, it became clear to the tournament's sponsors that Glenna was going to be the runaway winner. But there was a big problem. The Philadelphia jewelry company had not delivered the tournament trophy. Thinking quickly, an official raced home to get a temporary replacement trophy from his own book shelf. He was a champion dog breeder. When the victory was hers, as the press looked on, Glenna was handed the substitute trophy. The inscription read: "Best Bitch in Show." Glenna supposedly flung it down and stomped away in disgust.

"You know," she said with surprising pleasantness, "I've heard that story for *years*. It's followed me everywhere. They keep printing it. But it's absolutely not true. Not one word. Once, I thought I might threaten to sue them for perpetuating that myth. Then I thought, 'Oh, no, let it go. . . .' "

She gave me a look that reminded me I was skating on thin ice.

Then she calmly sipped her drink again. "So the soup is good?" she asked, eyeing me.

"Great," I replied.

"Well, soup's easy," she said skeptically.

I said, "Sort of like golf—at least for you."

Her face darkened quickly. "Oh, the heck it was," she fired at me defensively. "Golf's hard. Anybody who thinks golf is easy is nuts."

I apologized and explained that I meant that her compact swing and courageous putting had been a role model for countless thousands of young female golfers. And men, too.

"In fact," I said, "I'd love to see you play. If you won't play with me, perhaps I can come watch you play in the Point Judith Invitational."

American's greatest woman golfer, the woman who seemed to have outlived history, turned and looked out to sea. "Oh, no," she said in a firm but distant voice, "I just couldn't allow that."

Then she transferred her gaze to me again. It was a withering look. "Do you want some more soup?" she asked, the soul of politeness. "Now listen, tell me something more about that young woman you plan to marry. . . ."

Two weeks later, on a morning wreathed in sea mist, I ignored Glenna's objections and snuck out onto the Point Judith Country Club to watch the living legend set yet another record: she appeared in her 62d straight club championship.

I loitered around a yew hedge and Glenna never saw me, but if she did, she chose not to speak. She was teamed with three women who were perhaps a third her age. She was dressed in bright yellow, looking like a daffodil in the ocean's gloom.

She strolled to the tee and placed her ball on a wooden peg without a fuss. The other women ceased taking their practice swings and watched respectfully. There was an instant of stillness. Glenna's driver met the ball squarely, and the ball flew well over 100 yards, dead straight. One by one, the other women in her foursome hit their opening drives. Glenna outdrove them.

"She always could pound the cover off it," remarked a man who was suddenly standing beside me. We began to chat about Glenna Vare and I discovered, to my delight, that my fellow voyeur-spectator, a pharmaceutical salesman from St. Louis named Ed, had once been Glenna Vare's caddie "years and years ago." He added, "I'm sure she's forgotten me, but I could never forget her."

"I haven't heard about her in twenty-five years," he reflected. "Geez. She's so old. I wonder what she does now."

I told him someone said she made soup.

Glenna appeared ahead in the distance—a yellow dot burning far down the fairway, headed resolutely for her ball.

# Laura Davies: A New Force in the Game

## Jaime Diaz

Sports Illustrated                                    August 10, 1987

A safe par was all Laura Davies needed when she came to the 493-yard, par-5 17th hole at the Plainfield (New Jersey) Country Club in last week's playoff for the U.S. Women's Open. The 23-year-old Englishwoman led Japan's Ayako Okamoto by two shots and JoAnne Carner of the U.S. by three. Davies choked up on her driver and punched a low, controlled draw 250 yards down the heart of the fairway. Then she smashed a three-wood 237 yards to the front of the green. Three putts produced a safe par, the Laura Davies way.

Moments later she holed a four-footer on 18 to become the first British player to win the event which, because of rain delays and the first three-way tie in Open history, seemed to go on and on. The victory also made Davies, who won last year's Ladies' British Open, the only woman to triumph in both Opens.

At 5'10" and nearly 200 pounds, Davies is the longest hitter ever in women's golf. In contests in England she has driven nearly 300 yards, and at Plainfield she recorded a drive of 276 yards. She averaged 250.3 yards on her drives for the week, whereas the field averaged 218.7. It's fair to say that if Davies played on the men's tour, she wouldn't be its shortest hitter.

But she didn't have much time to think about that at Plainfield. The Tuesday playoff created havoc in her tight schedule. After politely thanking everyone, she packed up her trophy and high-tailed it back to England to defend her British Open title, starting Thursday. She arrived at Heathrow on Wednesday morning with just enough time to stop at home in Ottershaw, in Surrey, before making the 4½-hour drive to St. Mellion in Cornwall. Upon her arrival, she was lured into the pressroom on the pretense that she was needed at a press conference and was surprised by all her pals with a champagne celebration.

Then, without so much as a peek at the course before teeing off, Davies shot 73-72 to lead the field by two strokes after 36 holes. No one

*Laura Davies—the longest hitter ever in women's golf.*

was more surprised by those rounds than Davies, who admitted, "For me, making the cut was the big thing." She finished tied for second, one stroke behind her close friend, Alison Nicholas. "I didn't feel mentally tired," she said, "but my legs got tired walking up all those steep hills."

All in all, Laura Davies had a remarkable two weeks. "When Nancy Lopez turned pro and won everything, she was just exceptional," commented JoAnne Carner, whose powerful game was dwarfed by Davies's at Plainfield. "Everything about Laura's game is impressive."

Davies has been a star on the women's tour in Europe since turning pro in 1985, several months after representing Great Britain and Ireland in the Curtis Cup. She was the leading money winner ($35,000) and Rookie of the Year in 1985. Last year she won four tournaments and repeated as the top money winner.

Plainfield was only Davies's fourth tournament in the States. She finished 11th, six strokes back, in last year's U.S. Open, outside Dayton, Ohio. She missed the cut by one stroke at the '86 Dinah Shore. At this year's Dinah Shore she shot 66 in the first round to take the lead but ballooned to an 83 in the second, and finished tied for 33rd. Since then, Davies has harnessed her power, choking up on her clubs and not going for every pin with her irons.

In the enervating heat and humidity at Plainfield, Davies made intelligent use of her tremendous strength. On a wet, hilly course, which played backbreakingly long for the majority of the golfers, Davies could hit smooth, controlled tee shots with three- and five-woods and still hit less club on her approaches than players who used drivers off the tee. She did hit her driver on the four par 5s, and she reached two of them in two shots. No one else reached any of the par 5s in two. Moreover, Davies needed only 120 putts for the 72 holes, third-best in the field.

Okamoto was direct in her praise. "I do not feel I am even on the same plane with her," she said. "Laura might be the most impressive player I have ever met. She is thrilling to watch." Such accolades embarrass Davies. During the fourth round at Plainfield, when she was tied for the lead, she turned to her brother, Tony, 26, who caddied for her, and said, "This is ridiculous. We could win the U.S. Open."

At the same time, she takes pride in proving that she isn't merely a long hitter. "Nothing annoys me more than my reputation of being wild," she says. "I may miss a fairway, but I don't miss it by much. I'd rather be called a straight hitter than a long hitter any day."

That's about as contentious as Davies gets. Although she is physically imposing, she is a gentle soul, eager to please and easy to approach. Such an attitude is in keeping with Davies's humble golf beginnings. She started when her father, Dave, a mechanical engineer, draped a blanket over a rope between two trees in the backyard and had Laura and Tony hit balls into it. Her parents were divorced when Laura was eight, and she and Tony grew up with their mother and stepfather.

At thirteen, Laura got serious about golf. She played mostly with Tony and his friends, and the sibling rivalry produced some sparks. "I used to sling the old golf club quite a distance," she says. "Tony and I used to be dreadful. We would spend twenty minutes or longer trying to retrieve a club one of us had thrown into a tree."

"Laura is first and foremost a girl who plays games," says her stepfather. "Be it golf, snooker, soccer, or whatever, the game is the thing. She loves competing."

As for talent, her father says, "Laura is a natural. I have home movies of her hitting the ball when she was eight, then at twelve and later at sixteen. It's the same swing as today—short, compact and powerful." It's a swing fashioned mainly through play on the course rather than on the practice tee.

Recently, Davies bought a house next to her mother's in Ottershaw, where she may be seen walking her dog, Dominique, a greyhound who has won five of eleven races at the local track.

# Enid Wilson and the Curtis Cup

## Robert Sommers

Golf Journal                                                  August, 1988

Enid Wilson is now seventy-eight years old, one of the few survivors of the first Curtis Cup match fifty-six years ago. Among the two or three finest golfers of her time, she won three consecutive British Ladies' championships in the early 1930s, a couple of English Women's championships, and, for many years afterwards, held her position in the game by writing about golf for London's *Daily Telegraph* and a variety of magazines.

Her shoulders are stooped with age but, in early June, wearing a tan suede jacket, dark blue trousers, and mannish black shoes, with her short, straight gray hair under a dark blue pork-pie hat and her hands stuffed into gray woolen gloves with the fingers cut off at the first knuckle, she plodded along in the galleries of the younger heroines of British golf, those who defeated the United States, 11-7, at Royal St. George's Golf Club, in Sandwich, on the coast of the English Channel.

Victory by the United States was a foregone conclusion in Enid's day and afterward. From 1932 through 1984 the Americans won nineteen of the first twenty-three matches, Great Britain and Ireland won two, and two matches were halved. The assumption of American victory had become so embedded that as the teams assembled for the 1986 match, one of the American golfers said to Judy Bell, the captain, "We always win this, don't we?" But the British and Irish won that 1986 match decisively, beating the United States, 13-5, at the Prairie Dunes Country Club, in Hutchinson, Kansas, becoming the first foreign team ever to win in the United States. Now they have won twice in succession.

Because of the strong golf played by the host team during those cold, windlashed days at Royal St. George's, some have asked if the level of women's golf in Britain and Ireland has advanced that far or if the level of women's golf in the United States has fallen below our expectations.

Her face creased with the wrinkles of her many years but her eyes still ablaze with her zest for competition, Enid said, "If you look back at what I was writing in the '30s, you'll see I was after our people to adopt the big ball and to really learn how to putt. I've always felt that in all those matches over the years, we lost them within two or three yards of the hole."

Enid walked only in the morning, watching the foursomes on both of the two days. She found the ground at Royal St. George's too lumpy to stay afield longer than that, and she was afraid she would be knocked over by the surprisingly large crowds. Dressed against the cold, they came by the busload and raced after the individual matches, adding a feeling of excitement and urgency in their eagerness to witness the turning tide of golf fortunes. What Enid was able to see, despite the galleries clustered tightly about the greens, was enough to convince her she had been right those many years ago.

"Now our girls have learned to putt," she said.

# Golf and the American Woman

## Sarah Ballard

"The First One Hundred Years,
  Golf in America"                    Harry N. Abrams, Inc., 1988

When Robert Lockhart returned from a business trip to Britain in 1887 carrying three woods, two irons, a putter, and two dozen gutta-percha balls for his friend John Reid, it was Mrs. John Reid who made room for them. And when Reid and his friends gathered to formalize their friendly association on a November evening in 1888, it was over dinner at Reid's home in Yonkers, New York, a dinner undoubtedly overseen by the mistress of the house. Furthermore, the dinner was a success. Afterward, Mr. Reid, a Scottish immigrant, was induced to entertain his guests by singing "Scots Wa Hae," with encores. But the one thing the pioneering Mrs. Reid was *not* was America's first golf widow. On March 30, 1889, she teamed with John B. Upham in the first mixed-foursome played on the St. Andrews six-hole course, and beat her husband and a Miss Carrie Law.

The three new sports that preceded golf in post-Civil War America were baseball, bicycling, and lawn tennis. Baseball, the spectator sport, was a man's game; but bicycling and tennis were pastimes at which women were more than decorative adjuncts. The bicycle-built-for-two moved women out of the Victorian parlor and into the sunshine, and tennis kept them there. By the time golf took hold in America in the 1890s, women were ready to play. For precedent they could point to the Ladies' Green at St. Andrew's, Scotland, a course that was little more than a glorified putting green but which had existed at least as early as 1875.

The Shinnecock Hills Golf Club in Southampton, New York, opened in 1891. By 1893, the wives of the members had convinced their husbands to create a separate nine-hole course for them. Where the men could not be persuaded to share, women created their own courses. In Morristown, New Jersey, a group of female golfers organized a club, built a seven-hole course, and opened it for play in the spring of 1894. In October that year, they held their first tournament, won by Annie

*Beatrix Hoyt was the first great American woman golfer. Her club, the Shinnecock Hills Golf Club in Southampton, New York, built the first golf course for women in the United States in 1893.*

Howland Ford, who shot 48-46-94 to win by fourteen strokes. That first tournament at Morris County was a social if not an athletic milestone. The *New York Sun* reported, "As soon as the game was over, all hands adjourned to the clubhouse for tea and gossip and to discuss in particular the popular new creation—the golfing cloak. The next day the men were permitted to hold a tournament, and they bettered substantially the remarkable low scores made by the women golfers."

Meanwhile, in Boston, Florence Boit had returned from France to spend the summer of 1892 with her aunt and uncle, Mr. and Mrs. Arthur Hunnewell of Wellesley. While visiting Pau in the south of France, site of the first golf course on the Continent, Boit had learned the rudiments of the game. She returned to America with her golf clubs in tow. Boit's description of the game and her demonstrations of the clubs' use interested her uncle sufficiently that, with his brother-in-law whose property adjoined his own, he laid out a seven-hole course. In the fall of that year, Hunnewell invited several of his friends to try the game. Among them was Lawrence Curtis, like Hunnewell a member of

The Country Club in Brookline, Massachusetts. The Country Club had been established ten years earlier to provide "a comfortable clubhouse for the use of members with their families, a simple restaurant, bedrooms, bowling alley, lawn tennis, a racing track, etc., also to have race meetings occasionally and music in the afternoon." After little more than a month's exposure to Florence Boit's new game, Curtis saw to it that The Country Club added golf to its roster of activities.

Had enthusiasm for golf grown less rapidly among clubmen of the nineties than it did, women might have remained fairly represented on the early courses. But crowding set in early, and the women were frequently the ones forced to make room. In 1899, The Country Club course was expanded to eighteen holes, but at the same time the club forbade women the use of the course on Saturdays, holidays, and before 2:00 p.m. on weekdays. Earlier, in 1895, the men who had financed the establishment of Morris County, the first women's golf club, and had been given membership and voting rights in return, took the club back. They voted in an all-male slate of officers, but when they offered Annie Howland Ford an "honorary presidency" she declined, which makes it clear the coup was not bloodless.

Shinnecock Hills abandoned the ladies' course; the first women's course west of the Alleghenies, King's Daughters in Evanston, Illinois, was swallowed up; and Saegkill, a women's club founded by Mrs. Reid and her friends when St. Andrew's barred women altogether, was taken over by male golfers. Only the Women's National in Glen Cove, New York, created in 1924, escaped confiscation until 1941, when it merged with the Creek Club.

If American women golfers were handicapped in their early efforts to master the game by the territorial imperatives of their male counterparts, they were further hampered by the fashions to which they were slaves. Wide-brimmed straw hats, starched leg-of-mutton sleeves, corseted waistlines, and graceful ankle-length skirts that drifted charmingly in the slightest breeze were enchanting subjects for the illustrators of the day, but they must have been infuriating to their victims. Joyce Wethered, England's greatest woman player, once described a device called a "Miss Higgins," "a band of some elastic material intended to slip over the knees as a preliminary to putting." Wethered also pointed out that the game's cardinal rule, "Keep your eye on the ball," was irritating advice "when any glimpse of the ball, quite apart from swinging, was a matter of extreme uncertainty."

In spite of adversity, the hardiest of the women golfers persevered. In 1895, they held the Women's Amateur championship at the Meadow Brook Club in Hempstead, New York. It was a one-day, eighteen-hole affair, with lunch between the nines. Thirteen women competed for a silver pitcher, but the occasion was of greater significance than their scores. Mrs. C. S. Brown of Shinnecock Hills won with a 132. Annie Howland Ford finished tied for eighth with 161.

The next year, the Women's Amateur was held again. By this time the scoring and the event were much improved. A visiting Scot, Robert Cox of Edinburgh, who had helped lay out the Morris County course in 1894, donated a graceful, thistle-topped, silver loving cup, the trophy that is still in competition, on the condition that the tournament be held at Morris County. The United States Golf Association (USGA), which was a year old at the time, agreed. A notice was put out to member clubs announcing a "Women's Championship Golf Competition for the championship of the United States, open to all women golfers belonging to the clubs which are members of the United States Golf Association."

Mrs. C. S. Brown chose not to defend her title, which was just as well, since, in the medal round, Beatrix Hoyt, also of Shinnecock Hills, shot a 95, lowering Mrs. Brown's eighteen-hole score by thirty-seven strokes. In the final, Hoyt, who was sixteen, beat Mrs. Arthur Turnure, 2 and 1, for the first of her three consecutive titles. Possibly even more amazing than Hoyt's score were the number and enthusiasm of the spectators for the final match. They required restraint behind a rope.

In 1899, the championship was played in Philadelphia for the first time, at the Bala course of the Philadelphia Country Club. The runner-up that year was the pride of the Huntingdon Valley Club, Mrs. Caleb Fox, who had reared a family before she took up golf. Margaret Fox was already thirty-nine in 1899, yet she continued to compete for the next twenty-six years. She retired in 1925 after her twenty-second Women's Amateur, never having won but having been medalist, co-medalist, and three times semifinalist.

Women's golf grew and prospered in Philadelphia as nowhere else. A Women's Golf Association was formed as early as 1897, and Women's Interclub matches have been held from that day forward. The Merion Cricket Club in Haverford, later the Merion Golf Club in Ardmore, produced some of the great players of the early years of the American game. One was Frances Canby ("Pansy") Griscom, who had played in the 1896 championship at Morris County and won the 1900 title at Shinnecock Hills. She played for Merion in the first Philadelphia Interclub matches and in every subsequent series through 1924. She also drove a Red Cross ambulance in World War I, and is thought to have been the first woman in Philadelphia to own and drive an automobile. In 1965, at the hundredth birthday celebration of the Merion Cricket

*Glenna Collett Vare had an uncanny ability to find four-leaf clovers and to win national championships. Here she shows a four-leaf clover to her husband, Edwin Vare. In 1935, after their two children were born, Glenna came back and won her sixth and last championship.*

Club, Pansy Griscom returned to the club the silver cup its officers had given her when she became Merion's first amateur champion in 1900.

In 1909, the Women's Amateur was held at Merion a second time. The winner was Dorothy Iona Campbell, a native of North Berwick, Scotland, who was that year's British Ladies' champion. The next year Campbell, now living in Canada, acquired the Canadian title in addition to the British and American titles, making her not only the first double winner in women's golf but its first triple winner. She was a slip of a girl when she appeared on the American scene in a wide-brimmed boater and a high, stiff collar, but she looked at the camera then just as she did for the rest of her life—directly, eye-to-lens, as if to say she was interested and ready, at any moment, to be amused. She became a Merion institution, and when her record was totted up, she was said to have won 750 tournaments, among them three American titles, two British titles, and three Canadian titles.

World War I and the immediate postwar years were dominated by Alexa Stirling, a childhood golfing companion of Bobby Jones in Atlanta. Both were pupils of Stewart Maiden, a celebrated Scottish-born teaching professional. Alexa was a fragile-looking girl of seventeen with long curls when she played in her first Women's Amateur in 1914 at the Nassau Country Club in Glen Cove, New York. That year she lost in the first round of match play, but the next year she survived to the semifinals, and, in 1916, she won the first of her three consecutive titles.

During the war, when all USGA championships were suspended, Alexa and Bobby Jones played in an exhibition match for the benefit of the Red Cross at the Wannamoisett Club in Rhode Island, where one of the spectators was a tall, athletic fifteen-year-old girl from Providence who before long was to blossom into America's first great female player. Until she was introduced to golf by her father, Glenna Collett had been a swimmer, a diver, and a baseball player on her brother's team. Watching Alexa Stirling on a summer afternoon in 1918 inspired Collett to become a golfer, which she did with the encouragement of her athletic father and the guidance of a transplanted Scot, Alex Smith. Smith then was the pro at Shennecossett in New London, Connecticut, in the summer and Belleair, on the west coast of Florida, in the winter. Collett was a promising golfer from the start, but it was 1922 before she won the first of her six Amateur championships. Throughout the twenties, however, she was the preeminent American woman player. Predictably, newspaper writers called her "the female Bobby Jones." Like Jones, Collett traveled to Britain to compete, but she never was able to add the British Ladies' to her collection of titles, although she tried four times between 1925 and 1930. Twice she was eliminated by England's greatest player, Joyce Wethered.

With her marriage in 1931, Collett, now Mrs. Edwin H. Vare, Jr., competed less frequently, but in 1935, having borne two children, she returned to win the last of her six championships.

Glenna Collett Vare threw a long shadow over women's golf through the twenties, but her triumphal progress was by no means unopposed. An expanding corps of fine female players had come to the game in a new, postwar mood of liberation, their swings unfettered by restrictive clothing and their competitive spirits freed, to an unprecedented degree, of societal restraints. Mary Kimball Browne, who upset Collett in the semifinals of the 1924 championship, was a prewar tennis champion, who two weeks earlier had made it to the semifinals of the national tennis championships. A few years later, Browne accompanied France's incomparable Suzanne Lenglen on her professional tennis tour of the United States.

In 1925, when the championship moved west of the Mississippi for the first time, to the St. Louis Country Club, Collett beat the former Alexa Stirling, now Mrs. W. G. Frazer of Toronto, 9 and 8 in the final,

*Glenna Collett Vare's principal rival during the 1920s
and 1930s was Virginia Van Wie, on the left. During an
eight-year stretch (1928–1935) Glenna won four and
Virginia three national championships.*

but only after her opponent had set a new scoring record of 77 in the
medal round.

In the late twenties, Glenna's principal rival was Virginia ("Gino")
Van Wie, a delicate young woman from the Beverly Golf Club, near
Chicago, who had taken up golf for the sake of her health. In their first
meeting in the Amateur, Collett routed Van Wie 13 and 12 in the
thirty-six-hole final. Later, with Collett married and playing less, Van
Wie took the upper hand, winning the title in 1932, 1933, and 1934.

Glenna Collett Vare's sixth and last victory in our ladies' championship in 1935 actually marked the beginning of a new era. Her opponent
in the final at the Interlachen Country Club, in Minneapolis, was Patty
Berg, a freckle-faced, seventeen-year-old local golfer. Three years later,
Berg won the title; two years after that, she turned professional, going
to work promoting the products of Wilson Sporting Goods Company.
Berg was not the only American woman champion to turn professional— Helen Hicks, who won in 1931, also went to work for Wilson—

*The LPGA tour began in 1949. It survived and*
*flourished largely because of Patty Berg and Babe*
*Didrikson Zaharias.*

but Berg is the surviving link between the pre-World War I of the amateur and the postwar rise of the professional. It was she who, along with later Women's Amateur champions Betty Jameson (1939 and 1940), Babe Zaharias (1946), Louise Suggs (1947), and seven other women professionals met in Wichita, Kansas, in 1949 to charter the Ladies Professional Golf Association (LPGA), with 1950 as its official founding date. The Wichita meeting set in motion an organization that has grown by fits, starts, and, finally, million dollar leaps, into the vehicle that provides frequent competition for women golfers at the highest level.

Open competitions, in which professionals could compete for prize money alongside amateurs, were virtually nonexistent in the 1930s. The few that did exist, such as the Women's Western Open, which started in 1930, offered prize money that would hardly have covered the winner's train fare. In 1939, when Helen Dettweiler, who eventually became a celebrated teacher, won the Western, she received no cash prize at all, only a silver bowl. In 1941, the total purse available to women professionals in American golf was five hundred dollars.

Forming a professional organization for female golfers, even in 1949, was a shot in the dark. An earlier effort, the Women's Professional Golfers Association (WPGA), had struggled along for a few years and had staged three Open Championships, but its failure to attract either financial backing or an affiliation with the men's professional tour spelled an early doom.

What the fledgling LPGA had that the WPGA did not was Mildred Didrikson Zaharias. Babe, as she was always known, had been a national celebrity since the 1932 Olympic Games in Los Angeles, when, as a raw-boned twenty-one-year-old from Beaumont, Texas, she had won two gold medals and a silver in track and field events. There was nothing Babe could not do and do well. After the Olympics, having been declared a professional by the Amateur Athletic Union, Babe earned her living in a variety of bizarre ways—barnstorming with the bearded House of David baseball team or with her own basketball team, the All-Americans, or appearing on vaudeville stages running on a treadmill and playing her harmonica. (She was good at that, too.)

Meanwhile, with encouragement from sportswriter Grantland Rice, Babe was becoming a golfer, hitting a thousand balls a day whenever her schedule allowed. Her first important tournament was the 1935 Texas Women's Amateur at the River Oaks Country Club in Houston, which she won, only to be barred from all further amateur competition on the grounds that if she was a professional in the eyes of the AAU, she was a professional golfer as well.

From 1935 until 1940, when she requested reinstatement as an amateur, Babe played the two or three tournaments open to professionals each year, endorsed Wilson golf equipment, and, one summer, toured with Gene Sarazen playing exhibitions. After a three-year purification period, during which she mastered tennis and bowling, Babe was reinstated as an amateur by the USGA. She celebrated by shooting 70-67 in a thirty-six-hole charity match against Clara Callender, the California champion. In 1944 and 1945, in spite of the difficulty of civilian travel in wartime, she got herself to Indianapolis for the Women's Western Open and won that too. In 1946, with golf's tournament schedule returning to postwar normality, Babe was playing the best golf of her life. She won seventeen straight tournaments in one year, including the U.S. Women's Amateur and the British Ladies'.

In 1947 Babe turned pro again. She acquired the services of Fred Corcoran, a well-known agent who also handled Sam Snead and Ted Williams, and she signed with Wilson for $100,000 a year. She was making money, but what she needed even more was competition and an audience. It was primarily to meet and exploit those needs that Corcoran and Wilson agreed to assist at the birth of the LPGA. At a meeting in 1949 at the Venetian Hotel in Miami with Patty Berg and Babe and George Zaharias, Corcoran agreed to stage manage the tour, and Wilson to pay the bills.

Babe Zaharias was not the greatest female golfer who ever lived. Her swing was not a model, and she gave something away on the tees because she so much liked to astonish the galleries with the enormous distance of her drives. She played to her audiences, and she hated to lose, both traits leading her to excesses that made enemies of some of her colleagues, but she was a personality made to order for a professional sport in its infancy. Patty Berg once said, "Sometimes I find myself leaning back in a chair thinking about Babe, and I have to smile. With Babe there was never a dull moment. Her tremendous enthusiasm for golf and life was contagious. Even the galleries felt good when Babe was around."

Betsy Rawls, who played the tour from 1951 to 1975, then served the LPGA as its tournament director for six years, said of Babe, "She was the most physically talented woman I've ever seen, and if she had started golf at an earlier age she would have been sensational."

Through the 1950s and well into the 1960s, women's professional golf remained a hand-to-mouth business. Players supplemented their prize money with clinics and exhibitions, those of them who could, and as the scattered tournaments that made up the schedule grew into a tour, they traveled from place to place by car, sharing expenses and living out of their trunks. They set up their own courses, distributed their own prize money, and, when the tournament was over, they got on the phone and publicized their own accomplishments. Their real rewards were independence and a career in golf.

Seven of the first twelve U.S. Women's Open champions were former Amateur champions who had turned professional—Patty Berg (one), Betty Jameson (one), Babe Zaharias (three), and Louise Suggs (two). The logical inference from these figures is that the best golf was now being played among the professionals. But the professional life was not for everyone. Some excellent players continued to compete in the amateur ranks. Foremost among them for more than a decade were JoAnne Gunderson Carner and Anne Quast Sander. Between 1956 and 1968, those two Seattle area champions batted the Women's Amateur back and forth like a shuttlecock. Carner won in 1957, 1960, 1962, 1966, and 1968 and was runner-up in 1956 and 1964. Sander won in 1958, 1961, 1963 and was runner-up in 1965 and 1968. Their long

*JoAnne Gunderson Carner, the greatest amateur
since Glenna Collett Vare.*

rivalry was especially interesting because it was a match-up of oppo-
sites. Carner was a strong, long-hitting athlete in the mold of Zaharias,
a fun-loving competitor who was at ease with galleries. Sander was an
intense, high-strung golfer whose nerves sometimes got the better of
her, but whose will and finesse more than made up for what she lacked
in power. Sander has remained an amateur; in 1980, while living
abroad, she won the British Ladies. Carner turned professional in 1970,
when she was thirty, and since then has won two Women's Opens,
forty-two tournaments, and more than $2 million.

An early milestone on the LPGA's road to respectability occurred in
1953 when the USGA took over conduct of the Women's Open. As
keeper of the flame lit by Mrs. C. S. Brown with her 132 in 1895, the
USGA could do no less. With the change in stewardship, however, Open
courses became tougher. The year before the USGA took over, Louise
Suggs won a second Open title at the Bala Golf Club in Philadelphia
with a 70-69-70-75—284, the lowest seventy-two-hole score ever recorded by a woman in a major tournament. But the Bala course was

*Flawless Mickey Wright*

only 5,460 yards long, and par was sixty-nine. Under the auspices of the USGA, the first competition was held at The Country Club of Rochester (New York)—6,417 yards with a par of seventy-four. Betsy Rawls and Jackie Pung of Hawaii tied at 302, and Rawls won in an eighteen-hole playoff. The event still attracted more amateurs than it did professionals, but the low amateur's score that year was thirteen strokes off the pace. In fact, only once since 1946 has an amateur won the Women's Open, that being Catherine Lacoste of France in 1967. Lacoste was the daughter of France's famous tennis player of the twenties, René Lacoste, and of Thion de la Chaume, the British Ladies' golf champion of 1927. Catherine Lacoste also won the Women's Amateur two years later.

With the death of Babe Zaharias of cancer in 1956, the era of the pioneers ended, although the hardships attendant to establishing a place in the sun and in the public imagination for female professional athletes continued. The emergence of Mary Kathryn ("Mickey") Wright in the late 1950s made life a little easier for all. As one of her contemporaries said, "Mickey got the outside world to take a second look at women golfers, and when they looked they discovered the rest of us."

Mickey Wright was reared in San Diego and attended Stanford for one year. She was a tall woman with an engaging manner who combined a beautiful swing with great distance from the tees. She had started playing golf when she was eleven, and at seventeen she won the USGA Girls' Junior championship. In 1954 she was low amateur in the Women's Open. In the same year, Wright left college, and a year later joined the LPGA Tour. In 1958, when she was twenty-three, she won the first of four Women's Opens.

It is a personal tribute to Mickey Wright that her colleagues thought so highly of her, since she was taking bread from their mouths every time she entered a tournament. In 1963, she won thirteen of the tour's thirty-two events (40.6 percent) and earned $31,269, which at 1988 levels would be just under $1 million. Between 1959 and 1968, she averaged almost eight victories a year, and for five straight seasons (1960-1964), she won the Vare Trophy for low scoring average. Single-handedly she overcame the reluctance of the sporting press to cover women's golf, and, as the press was won over, so was the public. Ten thousand golf fans showed up at Baltusrol in Springfield, New Jersey, to watch her win the 1961 Open. Her 72-80-69-72—293 on Baltusrol's par-72 lower course beat Betsy Rawls by six strokes. Her final round has been called "nearly flawless." On Baltusrol's four par-five holes, she was seven under par for the tournament.

After 1969, Wright played only occasionally, but in 1973 she returned to take the Colgate-Dinah Shore tournament. The winner's purse alone was worth more than she had made in all but her four best years.

International golf for women had its origin in a group, organized by Pansy Griscom of Philadelphia in 1905, which traveled to England to championship play in the British Ladies' championship. Eight prominent American players of the day made the trip, among them Harriot and Margaret Curtis, sisters from Boston, who later won four United States championships between them. In 1927, the Curtis sisters donated a trophy "to stimulate friendly rivalry among the women golfers of many lands," and in 1932 the first biennial Curtis Cup matches between amateur teams from Great Britain and the United States were played in Wentworth, England. Since then, the Curtis Cup has been the crown jewel of women's international amateur competition, at least from the colonial perspective. Although British teams won in 1952 and 1956, United States amateurs held a thirteen-match winning streak until they were defeated in 1986.

The LPGA's purses increased from $600,000 in 1970 to $4 million in 1979. The reasons, simply stated, were corporate sponsorship, television, Title IX, and Nancy Lopez, not necessarily in that order. The first major corporation to see advertising potential in women's golf was Sears, Roebuck & Company, which sponsored a $100,000 event in Port St. Lucie, Florida, for a few years. However, it was David R. Foster, chairman of the giant Colgate-Palmolive empire, who was the first visionary. Foster threw his weight and his budget behind golf and later half a dozen other women's sports on the theory that they gave better value for his promotional dollar than did the higher-priced men's sports. As a manufacturer of dozens of household products, Foster figured that endorsements by women for women would be useful.

Eventually, Foster's beneficence toward the LPGA extended far beyond practical considerations. He fully intended to give women's golf credibility equal to men's. For a start, he created the Dinah Shore-Colgate Palmolive Winners Circle tournament in the desert near Palm Springs, California, and turned it into a lavish, week-long party which attracted to its pro-am the same mix of CEOs and Hollywood celebrities who regularly showed up for the Bing Crosby and Bob Hope events on the men's tour. As long as Foster remained the head of Colgate, the LPGA had a godfather. By the time he was replaced, and Colgate withdrew from sports sponsorship, the LPGA had Nancy Lopez, its first bona fide charismatic champion of the television era.

Nancy Marie Lopez was born January 6, 1957, a little over three months after Babe Zaharias died. She grew up in Roswell, New Mexico, the daughter of Mexican-American parents who played golf on Roswell's municipal course. Her father, Domingo Lopez, known in Roswell as Sunday, owned a small auto body repair shop. When Domingo shook a stranger's hand, he would apologize for his own, which was callused and hardened by the chemicals he used in his work. Her mother, Marina, was, well, motherly. Nancy was their adored youngest child, the others being grown and gone. Domingo was the only teacher Nancy ever had, and what he knew of swing techniques he learned from reading instruction articles in golf magazines.

Once it became clear that Nancy had the knack and the interest, Domingo devoted his life and all his limited resources to giving her what she needed to become a golfer. When her youthful interest flagged, he would invent games and offer her small daily rewards. What Domingo could not give his daughter was access to Roswell's country club course, out of bounds to Roswellians of Mexican descent. Nancy earned her way onto that and other country club courses by winning everything in sight, starting at twelve with the New Mexico Women's Amateur. Afterward, though, she always returned to the flat, arid terrain of the municipal course. In spite of a swing that the experts said was suspect, Nancy won the U.S. Girls' Junior championship when she was fifteen, the same year she won the New Mexico Women's Amateur for the third time and the Western Junior for the first of three times.

By the mid-seventies, the effects of Title IX legislation, enacted in 1972, were being felt in colleges and universities. Under threat of federal funds being withheld from institutions that discriminated against women in any area, women's athletic teams were springing up where none had existed before, and athletic departments began to compete for the services of talented female athletes. Thanks to Title IX, Lopez went to the University of Tulsa on a full golf scholarship. Although she left

*Nancy Lopez: She's got the whole world in her hands.*

school at the end of her sophomore year to turn professional, she did gain two extra years of seasoning in amateur tournaments. During that period, she won the Women's Collegiate championship, finished tied for second in the Women's Open, and played on the winning 1976 Curtis Cup and Women's World Amateur teams.

When Lopez began playing the tour in the waning months of 1977, she was well-known in golf circles and unknown elsewhere. Within a year, she had played golf with a president of the United States, and her face had been on the cover of the *New York Times Magazine*. Lopez's rookie year was phenomenal. She won two tournaments early on the schedule, and then, beginning in May, she won the next five events she entered, including the LPGA championship. That tournament was played at the Jack Nicklaus Golf Center in Cincinnati, at 6,312 yards one of the longest the women play, yet rookie Lopez shot a thirteen-under-par 275 to beat her old junior rival, Amy Alcott, by six strokes. Before the year was over, Lopez had won nine tournaments, lowered the LPGA record for a year's scoring average, and earned more prize money than any rookie golfer ever had, male or female.

Lopez is now married to baseball player Ray Knight and has two young children. In her ten years as a pro, she has bettered every record she set that first year except winning five tournaments in a row. She has not been able to repeat that feat, but neither has anyone else. The only prize that has eluded Lopez so far is the U.S. Women's Open.

A gauge of the growth of the LPGA in the 1980s is that in 1981 Kathy Whitworth became the first woman to reach $1 million in career prize money, and in 1986 Pat Bradley was the first to win $2 million. Whitworth, a Texan who joined the tour in 1958, had to wait four years to win her first tournament, but in the ensuing twenty years she passed Mickey Wright's record of eighty-two victories and has since added six more. Bradley, who once considered a career as a ski instructor, is not so much a late bloomer as a hardy perennial. She has played in nearly four hundred LPGA tournaments and finished in the top ten in more than half of them.

A century has passed since Mrs. John Reid made space in a Yonkers closet for Mr. Reid's new toys. Making space for women in a game with masculine traditions already centuries old has been more difficult. Where opportunity has been denied, women golfers have created their own, with the result that today nearly half of all golfers entering the game are women. In its hundredth year, American golf is close to being a truly *All*-American game.

# Ayako Okomoto: Japan's First Lady of the Links

## James Dodson

Golf Magazine                                    November, 1988

Few players can know what it takes to play constantly in the eye of a typhoon, but that is exactly what Ayako Okamato faces every time she picks up a golf club in public almost anywhere in the world.

In this country, where she plays nine months of the year, Okamoto's stunning achievements—Player of the Year and leading money winner last year; three victories this year, fourteen lifetime—have merely informed many Americans that there is a new star on the LPGA scene, an attractive star rising from the Far East. But in her native Japan, where golf is a status game played with the fervor of a secular religion, Okamoto's accomplishments have had the effect of turning an already popular sports figure into something along the lines of a prime-time Shinto god. Wherever Okamoto goes now, so goes an entourage of admirers and at least two dozen Japanese newsmen and photographers, a watchful horde that seeks deeper meaning in Okamoto's every move, every gesture, every single waggle of her Mizuno pitching wedge.

It's a national idolatry no other golfer in the world can appreciate. Paparazzi regularly camp outside Okamoto's house in Tokyo, the way they would, say, for an American rock star. Fans constantly shower her with expensive gifts, rare family heirlooms, even marriage proposals. Her weekly half-hour television show, *NEC Supergolf*—a skins game that showcases American LPGA players and features a much more animated Okamoto than we see here—is the highest rated of several golf programs in Japan: eighteen million viewers per show. On those same screens, Japan's first lady of the links is regularly seen endorsing everything from pens to patio doors.

The results of Okamotomania are not always pleasant. "Last year I was playing in Japan with Ayako in the Takara Tournament," says her close friend and fellow LPGA pro Jane Geddes, "and the number of people following her was simply staggering. It was the size of a stadium

441

*Ayako Okomoto*

crowd and as boisterous—and a little frightening to some of us who are used to a very different golf scene in the States."

It's been widely publicized that minor riots have broken out at tournament sites in Japan as giddy fans wrestled to get near Okamoto. Many feel that she has replaced Tatsunori Hara, the colorful third baseman of the Tokyo Giants, as the country's reigning sports figure. That's a remarkable accomplishment—and no small burden—for a woman in a country that traditionally reveres the male ethos in matters of business and sport.

"For better or worse," says Okamoto's agent, Margie Kato, "this places Ayako in a world of her own. She is charting new ground. As such, it's sad to say, home is not an easy place for her to be now." After having her coat torn off by adoring fans, Kato points out, Okamoto stopped riding the Tokyo subway. To visit her family in Hiroshima, where she grew up and where her father still farms rice and potatoes, Okamoto is often forced to don disguises and hide in anonymous speeding cars.

Quite logically, Americans might ask what all the fuss is about. In this country, the polite, surprisingly soft-spoken farmer's daughter has, in a little over seven full years on tour, compiled one of the most impressive records of anyone. But she has yet to capture a major championship, LPGA observers point out, and that's what finally separates the Lopezes and Bradleys from the rest.

The pressure to live up to the huge expectations of a nation began to intensify in July of 1987 when Okamoto finished second to Jody Rosenthal in the du Maurier Classic after shooting a final-round of 74. She lost the U.S. Women's Open two weeks later in an 18-hole playoff with JoAnne Carner and England's Laura Davies, the eventual winner. There was talk, and even some statistical evidence to support it, that Okamoto played her best opposite the *men's* major tournaments—when the massive Japanese press corps veered off to see what Greg Norman and Jack Nicklaus were up to.

Entering the final round of this year's Mazda-LPGA championship at King's Island, Ohio, Okamoto looked to be about to grasp her first major. For a while she shared the lead with Amy Alcott, then faltered and finished with a humbling 73. "I felt something heavy," she told the Cincinnati *Enquirer*, smoking a cigarette and drinking a beer afterward. "It was not that I was not feeling well. Maybe you could call it pressure."

That same pressure manifested itself in the size of the Japanese gallery and press contingent that gathered in hazy summer heat at the Baltimore Country Club's Five Farms layout for this year's U.S. Women's Open. By the fourth day, however, the pride of Japan was miles out of contention, eleven strokes off the lead. Yet as a matter of national honor, and perhaps as a measure of Japanese hunger for recognition on the world sporting scene, Ayako's Army was dutifully at the ready, anxious to march her home to victory.

Aided by straight drives and a fairway game that seems to function by radar, Okamoto calmly knocked in three birdies before the turn. As usual, she exhibited only the faintest emotion, but her entourage became jubilant. One could sense earthly happiness breaking out in the broadcast booth. When Okamoto is in the hunt in a championship, televised sports ratings in Japan leap to their highest levels. "There has never been anyone from Japan like Okamoto," a reporter for the JiJi news service said as he hurried along after her. "Once in America you had Arnold Palmer. Now in Japan we have Ayako Okamoto. When she wins, she brings honor to the Japanese people. When she does not win, the Japanese people want to know why."

The day after Okamoto had failed to win at Five Farms, several newspapers in Tokyo sharply questioned why. A few even offered their own creative explanations. One prominent daily said her ailing back had been responsible (In 1985 she took time off to recuperate from a herniated disc). Another stated that she was too old (she's 37) to play successfully with traditional clubs and that she should probably ditch them and switch to sponsor Mizuno's high-tech equipment. A third paper reported that, bitter at having failed to win the Open, Okamoto had decided to retire.

None of these assertions was true. But a fourth report was perhaps the most disturbing of all. An ESPN field director was quoted in the New York *Times* as saying that the American press found Okamoto "too boring to cover," which explained why fans in the United States didn't know much about her. Americans supposedly believed Okamoto was aloof and mechanical—a human Mazda sedan.

Among her LPGA peers, Okamoto's nickname is "Funya"—a Japanese word that, strictly interpreted, means "wishy-washy." It really means, as Patti Rizzo, another of Okamoto's close friends on tour explains it, "Fun-loving, easy going, and confident in the middle of a storm. She has a great sense of humor and a pace that seems to shut out the distractions of the outside world."

When you are Ayako Okamoto, that kind of psychological armor is sorely needed. In the past, inaccurate news stories have reported that Okamoto, who is single, was engaged or secretly married or planning to emigrate to the United States. One columnist criticized her habit of chewing gum during a major championship, implying that she lacked a serious desire to win. A reporter friend once invited Okamoto to dinner, then plied her with sake. The conversation was supposed to remain between friends, but the tape recorder was secretly running. The resulting story, which featured some highly critical comments about the Japanese LPGA, caused Okamoto extreme embarrassment and got her into hot water with some of her sponsors.

The knocks Okamoto took in the Tokyo press the week after this year's Open were finally too much for even a fun-loving Funya to shrug aside. On the eve of the first round of the Greater Washington Open at Bethesda, Maryland, the week after the Open, Okamoto toyed with the idea of pulling out of the tournament to protest the harsh liberties taken by the Japanese media. Then, in typical Funya fashion, she decided to sleep on it.

In the morning, the sun was beaming brightly on the Bethesda Country Club, and Okamoto decided that playing well would be her best revenge. That turned out to be fortunate for the fledgling tournament, which almost had been canceled due to sponsors' concerns that the big-name players would not show. It was good for the LPGA, too, which has been plagued by sponsor woes of late—Okamoto is considered a major lure for Japanese corporations that underwrite 10 of the 37

LPGA events. And best of all, it was a wise decision for Okamoto. On the final day, she calmly shot a 67 to edge out Connie Chillemi and Beth Daniel and win the tournament by a stroke. It was her third victory of the year.

Back home, newspapers reported that, despite bruised feelings toward certain of her countrymen, their national treasure was back on top of her game.

It remains to be seen if Ayako Okamoto, child of Hiroshima, becomes anything close to a tabloid celebrity in America. In a nation that invented the rags-to-riches concept, Okamoto's biography is the stuff of a publicist's dream. Growing up in her father's rice fields outside Hiroshima, Okamoto played baseball and softball with two older brothers and became such a terror on the mound in high school that the Daiwabo Textile company invited her to play in the Japanese corporate softball leagues—the equivalent of a sports scholarship. Within five years, she was the best known female softball pitcher in Japan, with a left-handed fastball that cruised at 150 kilometers. "I was fast," she says, smiling, "but I had no control."

Not entirely so. On the playing field, she displayed a composure well beyond her years. With friends and family, however, she exhibited an earthy sense of humor, developed a softball warrior's taste for cold beer, and liked to smoke cigarettes and go fishing alone or with chums—just your basic Asian girl-next-door. "I was very ordinary," she says. But being herself in a country hungry for sports heroes was the beginning of her public relations problem. On public occasions Okamoto was painfully shy, especially when confronted by the press. "I specialized in 'yes' and 'no' answers because I never knew what to say to them."

Okamoto was twenty before she saw her first golf course. While playing in a softball tournament in Hawaii, she and a few teammates looked out a hotel window and saw a golf green below. Not realizing what it was, they decided to go sit on it. They were chased off and severely warned not to come back.

Three years later, Okamoto did come back, When her softball career ended, her coach suggested she take up either bowling or golf. The farmer's daughter chose golf, learned to play with men's right-handed clubs, and worked as a caddie in Osaka. She practiced at sunrise and sundown when members weren't around. She shot 47 on her first nine holes and taught herself to play from reading books by American players, watching instruction videos, and following Japan's best players, especially Chako Higuchi, who won the LPGA championship in 1977.

In three years, Okamoto was good enough to turn pro. Between 1975 and 1980 she won twelve times on the Japanese LPGA Tour. In 1981 she set a record by winning eight titles and earning $130,000—and became a sensation. She had her own TV show. She also set off for America. "Everyone has a dream" she told the Boston *Globe* in 1984. "Mine was America, where everything seems to be number one. In Japan, I started to be a superstar, but I didn't want to be famous. Back home a star has no privacy. If you have a hole in your jeans, everyone wants to know why. Here in America, nobody cares."

Ironically, the freedom she felt playing in this country was aided by the buffer of a language difference. One of her first deep connections was with Rizzo, a rookie on the Tour in 1982, who roomed with Okamoto, helped make her travel plans, and taught her the rudiments of English. Okamoto won five times through 1985. Then she hurt her back and spent time recovering at Rizzo's parents' house in Fort Pierce, Florida. Okamoto later bought a condominium nearby. "The injury turned out to be a blessing in disguise," Okamoto says. "It made me slow down and evaluate everything—my life as well as my game."

After a full recovery, Okamoto took it upon herself to become a bit more independent off the course. She made her own travel arrangements and often drove to tournament sites in a rental car. She believes that the peace of mind she regained may have set the stage for 1987 when she became the LPGA's fifteenth millionaire.

"I think Ayako *thought* her way to Player of the Year," Jane Geddes has said. "She became a lot calmer about the incredible pressure she has to deal with on an international scale. I believe that she just told herself that she was going to win for herself, not for her country."

As another successful season closes, most observers agree that the majors will come to Okamoto. In the meantime, she savors the fact that she is not a household name in the United States—yet. Not long ago, Margie Kato says, she and her superstar client stepped into a discount golf shop near Okamoto's home in Florida. When the young clerk observed the beautiful way Okamoto swung a club and realized she was Japanese, he couldn't resist asking her if she knew "that really good Japanese golfer, you know, *what's-her-name* . . ."

"Do you mean Ayako Okamoto?" asked Ayako Okamoto.

"Yeah," the clerk shot back enthusiastically. "I hear she's, like, *awesome*."

"Is that so?" replied Ayako, smiling like just another what's-her-name.

# Juli Inkster: Six Major Championships and Counting

## Dwayne Netland

Golf Digest                                          September, 1989

In the bright sunshine of a California morning, Juli Inkster and her husband, Brian, are battling one-on-one in the driveway of their hillside home forty miles south of San Francisco. Tension is high—the next basket means the other does last night's dishes. With a cold stare, Juli takes the ball and quickly administers a shake-and-bake move she picked up from her customary courtside seat at Golden State Warrior NBA games. Swish. "Snuffed again," grumbles Brian, heading for the kitchen. "I've done a lot of dishes this year."

Juli Inkster loves sports and particularly their winning moments. In fact, in the sport she plays for a living, winning moments are her specialty. If the true measure of a golfer's stature is determined by major championship victories, Inkster already has an honored place in the game's history. She's won six majors, a total surpassed by only eleven men and women of the modern era.

These numbers may come as a surprise to all but the game's most diligent statisticians, but the facts are indisputable: Inkster won successive U.S. Women's Amateurs in 1980, 1981 and 1982, the du Maurier Classic in 1984 and the Nabisco Dinah Shore in 1984 and 1989.

If you're going to count Jack Nicklaus' two U.S. Amateur titles as part of his unassailable record of 20 majors, and Bob Jones' five Amateurs as part of his total of 13, then you've got to give Juli her total of six. The only modern-era players who have won more, in addition to Nicklaus and Jones, are Walter Hagen with 11; Ben Hogan and Gary Player, 9; Arnold Palmer, Mickey Wright, and Tom Watson, 8; and Gene Sarazen, Sam Snead, and Jo-Anne Carner, 7. Carner's total includes five Women's Amateurs.

Inkster has achieved another remarkable number. In the crucible of LPGA Tour playoffs, where one mistake is usually fatal, Juli is 4 and 0. She defeated Pat Bradley in the 1984 Dinah Shore; Debbie Massey and Cindy Hill in the 1986 Lady Keystone; Rosie Jones, Betsy King and

*Juli Inkster, like JoAnne Carner, was remarkably good as an amateur and is remarkably good as a professional.*

Nancy Lopez in the 1988 Crestar Classic; and Beth Daniel in the 1988 Atlantic City Classic.

"I've always been a streaky player," says Juli, whose extremely upright swing is difficult to keep fine-tuned. "I had hot weeks during that du Maurier and the two Dinahs. I still can't explain those three Amateurs in a row. I look back now and I don't see how I could have done it. In the playoffs I've gotten some good breaks. They're as important as hitting the right shot."

What the future holds for Inkster would now seem to depend upon her ability to adjust to a new lifestyle. Earlier this summer Juli announced that she and Brian would become first-time parents in January.

Inkster plans a busy fall schedule, and then hopes to return full-time by next spring to defend her Nabisco Dinah Shore title. "I haven't worked out the details yet," Juli says. "We'll either hire someone to travel with me, or my mom will do it. Just because you've had a baby doesn't mean you can't win tournaments. Nancy Lopez proved that."

This will indeed be a new role for the buoyant Californian whose entire adult life has been wrapped up in marriage, tournament golf, and a consuming interest in professional athletics. Juli is equally at home in backyard games or sitting in the stands rooting for the baseball Giants, the football 49ers, and the basketball Warriors. "I'm having a hard time picturing Juli cooing a baby to sleep," says Hollis Stacy. "I see her shooting baskets or working on her curve ball."

Inkster cheerfully acknowledges her reputation among the women pros as the tour's ranking sports nut. "She can tell you the batting average of every player on the Giants," says Bonnie Lauer, "or how many touchdown passes Joe Montana has thrown. Whenever we want to know something about pro sports, we ask Juli."

It's been that way since Juli's childhood. She grew up with two older brothers, Danny and Mike, in Santa Cruz, California. Her father, Jack Simpson, a retired captain on the local fire department, was a minor league ballplayer in the Cincinnati Reds farm system. Juli played basketball and softball through her high school years and took up golf as a fifteen-year old sophomore. She got a part-time job at the Pasatiempo Golf Club shagging range balls and washing down carts. It was there, a year later, that she first met Brian Inkster, then the 25-year-old head pro, who began giving lessons to the spirited teenager.

"I could see right away that Juli had some real athletic ability with a great attitude for golf," says Brian, now head professional at the Los Altos Golf and Country Club. "She was never a great junior golfer, but she had a terrific desire to improve. At that time we had strictly a teacher-student relationship. You don't, or at least I didn't, think of romance when you're looking at a 16-year-old girl."

Juli went on to become an All-American golfer at San Jose State, and in her freshman year she started dating Brian. They were married the summer between her sophomore and junior years, three weeks before the 1980 Women's Amateur.

The site was Prairie Dunes, a sprawling linksland course in Hutchinson, Kansas, that was totally foreign to anything Juli had ever seen in northern California. Early in the week, Juli lost the wedding ring. It had been hanging on a gold chain around her neck. Her caddie found it in the parking lot. Considering that a good omen, Juli sailed through her first five matches and then survived a tough 2-up final against Patti Rizzo.

In 1981, at the Waverley Country Club in Portland, Oregon, Inkster, using clubs borrowed from Patty Sheehan, became the first back-to-back Women's Amateur champion in forty-one years. The pressure was stifling at the 1982 Amateur, played at the Broadmoor Golf Club in Colorado Springs. This time Brian was taking no chances. He left his golf shop to caddy for his wife. "It was brutal," he recalls. "I was nervous and Juli was up tight. I couldn't sleep. Then we nearly got knocked out in the first round."

That was when Inkster had to make a 15-foot putt for par on the 18th to stay alive against Caroline Gowan and then won on the first extra hole. In the final she beat Cathy Hanlon, 4 and 3, her eighteenth straight winning match in that championship, to become the first woman since Virginia Van Wie in 1932–34 to win three successive Women's Amateurs.

With those credentials, most people considered it a foregone conclusion that Inkster would cruise through the LPGA Qualifying School, held early in 1983 at the Bent Tree Golf Club in Sarasota, Florida, and become an instant star on the women's tour. Fate had other plans. On the eighth green of the second round of qualifying, Juli lost a contact lens. Brian turned her bag over to a volunteer in the gallery and raced back to their hotel to retrieve a spare. En route, he be picked up a speeding ticket. Juli never recovered, and missed the cut. "That was the low point of my life," Juli acknowledges. "I just sat around for six months and moped." The LPGA held three qualifying schools that year, however, and in August she got her card as co-medalist. She finished fifth in her first pro tournament, the Henredon Classic, in North Carolina, and broke through in her fifth tournament, the Safeco Classic, in Seattle.

Through the next six years the victories have continued to mount. At last count, she had thirteen. "She's a feisty bulldog, a tough one to take the lead away from," observes Amy Alcott. Her putting stroke is a source of envy among her peers. "When Juli gets the ball rolling," Hollis Stacy says, "you'll never see a better putter."

At twenty-nine, Inkster has reached the top level of her profession. She has lucrative contracts with several companies. Brian gets out to watch her play eight or nine times each year, and she has found the ideal caddie in Worth Blackwelder, whose wife, Myra, plays the tour.

"I'm happy with my life," Juli says. "I love playing golf, and I really enjoy my time at home with Brian. And now we've got a new addition to think about."

# Vicki Goetze versus Brandie Burton

## Ron Coffman

Golf Journal                                                    October, 1989

Vicki Goetze, a slender 16-year-old high school girl from the little town of Hull, Georgia, appears to be smaller than her five feet four inches and 110 pounds. Her forearms seem to be only a little bigger than the black shafts of her golf clubs; her blonde hair is pulled back into a ponytail; and her penchant for pastels runs mostly to pinks and roses, matching the tape on her putter grip. She looks as fragile as a ceramic doll.

But in her own small way, Vicki is an intimidator, especially at match play—or perhaps only at match play (although she was the only amateur to play all 72 holes in the 1989 United States Women's Open). Nearly always outdriven by her opponents, often by as much as fifty yards, Miss Goetze turns that disadvantage into a plus with a bagful of incredibly accurate wooden clubs, a sand wedge that performs magic, and a putting stroke equal to anyone's.

At the Pinehurst Country Club's No. 2 Course, in Pinehurst, North Carolina, during the first week of August, Vicki put together all her special talents and became the fourth youngest player ever to win the U.S. Women's Amateur championship. She defeated Brandie Burton 4 and 3 in the 36-hole final a week after Miss Burton had defeated her by one hole in the semi-finals of the U.S. Girls' Junior championship at the Pine Needles Lodge and Country Club, about five miles down the double-lane road that connects Pinehurst with Southern Pines. Miss Burton, who comes from Rialto, California, adjacent to San Bernardino, was trying to join JoAnne Gunderson Carner and Pat Lesser Harbottle as the only winners of both championships, and, furthermore, to become the first player to do so in the same year. Instead, Miss Goetze joined Michiko Hattori, who won in 1985, Laura Baugh, the 1971 champion, and Beatrix Hoyt, who won in 1986—all sixteen-year-old champions. Vicki turns seventeen this month.

With two years of high school remaining, Vicki hasn't thought about her choice of colleges, but she can be described as a hardened tournament competitor. She is the younger sister of Nicky Goetze, runner-up to Brian Montgomery in the 1986 United States Junior Amateur. When she was five, she played in her first tournament, a four-hole affair, and won it.

Vicki came to the front in USGA competition in 1986, reaching the final of the Women's Amateur Public Links championship when she was just thirteen, and lost 3 and 2 to Cindy Schreyer. She had been a semi-finalist in the previous two Girls' Junior championships, and she had also reached the semi-final round of this year's North and South Women's Amateur, her only previous visit to Pinehurst. After a few rounds over Pinehurst No. 2, a Donald Ross course, Miss Goetze described this grand old golfing ground as "a nice course." While she is too young to know of Ross and his work, she does know that Pinehurst suits her game. Contrary to modern design, which often demands a pronounced carry to the greens, the putting surfaces at No. 2 are open in front and accommodate run-up shots. "It's definitely an advantage for me," Miss Goetze said. "I've never played a course quite like this one."

If golf had a six-club limit, Vicki would be the best player in the world. Give her four woods, a sand iron, and a putter, and she's comfortable. She doesn't hit her driver much more than 200 yards, but plays fairway woods with the accuracy of medium irons. Her work around the greens is uncanny.

Those talents became obvious in the final. With her caddie/father, Gregg, a high-school psychologist, giving her moral support ("He basically just carries the clubs," Vicki said. "I do my own thing."), Miss Goetze ignored the length of Miss Burton's drives.

Early in the match, Brandie's length—or Vicki's lack of it—looked as if it would be too great a factor to overcome. Vicki could not reach the 392-yard second hole with her second shot, and she lost it to Brandie's par 4. She then dropped the next two holes to birdies. After four holes, Miss Goetze was 3 down, and she looked as if she might lose the par-5 fifth as well when her second shot dived into a deep bunker yards short of the green. She played a marvelous sand shot to twenty feet, however, and holed the putt for a birdie 4. Miss Burton meanwhile took three strokes to get down from just off the green. Brandie later claimed that this swing, where she lost a hole she figured to win, wasn't important because it happened so early in the round, but Miss Goetze knew better. "It was definitely a key to the match," she said. "Things were not going well for me at that point. When I won that hole, it changed my frame of mind."

Indeed, Miss Burton won only one more hole during the morning

*Brandie Burton and Vicki Goetze, the two most certain future LPGA stars, doing battle in the 1989 U.S. Women's Amateur.*

round, and she went to lunch 2 down. Miss Goetze controlled the match throughout the afternoon. With a bogey-free outward nine, she increased her lead to three holes, and she recovered coolly from her only lapses, bogeys at the 10th and 11th, which allowed Miss Burton to close to within one hole. Miss Goetze won the 12th when one of her opponent's enormous drives darted off-line. She applied the *coup de grace* two holes later with one of her precision 5-wood shots. It came to rest no more than three feet from the cup, and moments later the match ended, 4 and 3, when Vicki holed a 30-footer for a birdie 2 after a 5-wood to the 165-yard 15th hole.

While she was disappointed, Brandie Burton was hardly disconsolate. "Today was the best I've played in two weeks," she said. "I didn't lose with bogeys. I lost to birdies, and that's the way you should lose." As for Miss Goetze, she had earned a measure of revenge for her loss to Miss Burton a week earlier in the USGA Girls' Junior.

# Using the Left Side

## Kathy Whitworth, with Rhonda Glenn

"Golf for Women"                                   St. Martin's Press, 1990

The golfer's left side must be the dominant part of the swing. This is the only way to get the maximum power and accuracy. If the right side takes over, there is no golf swing.

This is not to say that you do not use the right side for some power, but the left side cannot collapse. Even on the backswing the left side must be in control; it swings the club.

Some top players minimize the role of the left side, but they may not realize what they are actually *doing* during the swing. Study the golf swing of any top player and you will see that the left side moves through the hitting area first and is the side that controls the clubhead.

I stress fundamentals, or things that must occur in a good golf swing, because they are things I have been taught. Now, after years of playing and competing, I know why these things must happen to maximize a golf swing. Golfers can swing the club many different ways. No two people have identical swings, but, as I've said, they do certain fundamental things the same way.

Some players and teachers today have a theory of hitting from the right side, hitting with the right hand, or feeling that they are pitching the ball with the right side. To some degree, that's okay, but if the left side does not come through the shot and remain strong throughout the swing, this theory will not work because the player has no control of the clubhead.

In starting the club back, the left hand and the left side of the body swing the club to the top of the backswing. The great teacher Ernest Jones demonstrated this by swinging a string with a rock tied to the end of the string. My teacher Harvey Penick, who has so successfully taught many great players like Ben Crenshaw, Betsy Rawls, and Tom Kite, demonstrated the start of the backswing by saying it's like swinging a bucket of water.

Harvey wanted a one-piece move away from the ball and he would

*On the backswing, I'm staying level, moving neither up nor down, and there is no lateral movement. At the top of the backswing, I'm square, with the left arm and left side strong and in control. On the downswing, my weight shifts back to the left. There's a lateral move with the legs. The left side (left hand and shoulder) still leads throughout the swing. My hands are moving past my body, and my weight continues to move to the left side.*

actually demonstrate, with the bucket of water, the forward press to initiate the swing.

You wouldn't swing a bucket of water from a total standstill because that would be a very jerky motion. Harvey showed me that in the backswing as well as in swinging a bucket of water, you move a little forward first, then you move back. That creates a one-piece takeaway. That's why most great players have some type of move to initiate the swing, like a waggle or perhaps a slight press with the right knee. Mickey Wright did that, and Patty Berg had a bit of that. Lee Trevino has what golf announcers refer to as his little dance step. That's Lee's forward press and his way of initiating the swing, but each individual player has to develop his or her own.

I was taught these principles by Harvey Penick and Hardy Loudermilk at an early age. Since I've become a better player and more of a student of the game, I've discovered why they taught those principles.

Each golf student needs to be told, and have it periodically reaffirmed, that the left side must be the dominant side in the swing. That's why a correct grip is so important and why the left hand must be put on the club correctly so that the left side will be strong. If the left side is strong, the right side will pretty much take care of itself. I know that sounds almost too easy, but it's one of the great fundamentals of golf. Also, with a correct grip, the right elbow will fold in almost automatically on the backswing.

# Beginnings

## Kathy Whitworth, with Rhonda Glenn

"Golf for Women"                                          St. Martin's Press, 1990

I was fifteen when I played my first round of golf. I was so terrible that I played by myself for an entire year before I became brave enough to play with anyone else.

We lived in Jal, New Mexico, a little community that had sprung up in the cattle country near the western border of Texas.

Since my folks weren't members of the country club, I paid green fees. Like many golf courses in that part of the West, Jal Country Club was first built with sand greens. By the time I started to play, in about 1955, we had cottonseed greens, and a short time later the greens were converted to bent grass.

Junior players were only allowed to play on weekends. During the week, I'd gather up a few golf balls and hit practice shots in a cow pasture.

I practiced and played for about a year before Mother and Dad decided golf wasn't a passing fancy. They joined the country club so that I could play all the time, and I began to play with my aunt and uncle, Nell and George Addison. George was a wonderful athlete, a scratch golfer with a beautiful touch around the greens, and he won almost everything in our area. Nell was a good player, too, and won the club championship and a lot of local tournaments.

My father, Morris Whitworth, played basketball in school, but I don't think he was a serious player and I never really thought of Dad as an athlete.

My mother, Dama Robinson Whitworth, was athletic. She was terribly competitive and still is, for that matter. She played high school basketball. Mother's team used to travel from one little town to another, playing against local teams, and I'm sure she was a pretty good player.

I was born September 27, 1939, in Monahans, Texas, where Dad was working for a lumber company. I was the youngest of three daughters.

457

*My mother, Dama Whitworth, has been a staunch
supporter through good times and bad. This was one
of the good times, when I was inducted into the Texas
Golf Hall of Fame.*

Carlynne was the eldest, then Evelynne, then me. Shortly after I was
born, we moved back to Jal and I lived there until I went on the LPGA
Tour in 1959.

My mother's family homesteaded that part of the country. Her father
opened a grocery store in Jal, and they did some farming. They had
cows and pigs, and I remember playing in the barn when I was growing
up. My sisters and I used to try to ride calves and horses. We watched
my grandfather butcher a hog, and we'd swim in the big tanks where
they watered the livestock in the pasture.

Local lore says that Jal was named for the J-A-L ranch brand. It
eventually became an oil and gas town, and the story was that all
pipelines led to Jal. Because of our refineries, almost all of the natural
gas in the Southwest came through Jal, so we had a prosperous little

town, in that respect. Jal never got very big and at its peak had about 5,000 residents.

My father's father, "Whit," opened a lumber company in town and Dad worked for him for a while and, later, for several gas companies. My grandmother, Jessie Whitworth, bought a hardware store. Mother worked in the store and Dad kept Jessie's books at night, as he did for several businesses around town.

My folks were productive working people, and very active in the community. Mother had a big family, eight brothers and sisters. At one time, my cousins and aunts and uncles made up about half the population of Jal. You could hardly talk to us about anybody in town—they were probably our relatives.

Mother and Dad eventually bought Whitworth Hardware, which they ran for years. Dad was very involved in local politics. He was on the city council for years and was elected Mayor three times.

Dad has written a humor column for *The Jal Record,* our weekly newspaper, for many years. Mother is very active in the church, in community and charity organizations, and in Democratic politics.

I played all sports as I was growing up, but mostly in sandlot games. I hated physical education because we never really got to do anything but run around the basketball court, which didn't appeal to me at all, so I joined the band. I played the bass drum. My sister Carlynne was a drummer and she was sort of my idol; anything she did, I had to do. I don't know whether I could have played another instrument. I was always the biggest girl in school so I could carry the drum.

I was on the Jal High School tennis team and I was fairly proficient at tennis, depending upon the competition. In fact, that's how I started playing golf. Some of my tennis friends insisted one day that we play golf. I used my grandfather's clubs. Whit had been a pretty good golfer who shot in the 80s.

I'll never forget that first round. I was *terrible,* but that made golf a real challenge. Because other sports had come to me so naturally, I was fascinated with this game I couldn't master. Golf also appealed to me because I didn't have to rely on another person in order to play. It was just me against the golf course, and I played against myself. How well I played didn't depend on anyone else because I had par to shoot at.

In those days, the Jal Women's Golf Association traveled to quite a few little tournaments, and the members were nice enough to take me with them. My family wasn't poor, but with two other children there wasn't a lot of extra money lying around for golf. I paid my own expenses, and the members of the women's golf association saw to it that

I went to tournaments by letting me ride with them. I'm sure I wasn't as grateful then as I am now. As the years go by, I look back and think about how great it was that I had nice people like that in my life.

After playing for about a year, I took lessons from Dode Forrester at Hobbs Country Club, about forty miles from home. He taught me things that I use today, including a strong hip move on the downswing.

My first real mentor was Hardy Loudermilk, our pro at Jal Country Club. Hardy taught me a lot, then did something that showed unusual generosity and humility and caused me to take what was probably the most important step of my career. When I was seventeen, Hardy said, "I don't know enough to take you where you need to be."

Hardy had met Harvey Penick, the golf professional in Austin, Texas, who was one of the world's best and most respected teachers. Hardy said that I had advanced to a point where I needed more instruction if I was going to be a really good player, so he called Harvey and set up an appointment for me.

Mother and I drove the 450 miles to Austin and, on this trip, I spent four days taking lessons from Harvey. I hit practice balls from sunup to sundown. Harvey would keep an eye on me, even while he was giving someone else a lesson, and Mother sat behind me on the practice tee taking notes. At night, we would go to a driving range and I would practice until the lights were turned off. Harvey would also telephone Hardy back in Jal, tell him what I was working on, and when I returned home, Hardy would watch me to make sure I followed Harvey's instructions. Most of what I know about the golf swing, I learned from Harvey Penick.

In 1957, I won the New Mexico State Women's championship in Farmington, New Mexico. The tournament committee had planned to present a beautiful turquoise necklace to the winner. Typically, like a seventeen-year-old, I wanted a trophy. The committee kept the necklace and sent a trophy to me, which I thought was just outstanding. Of course, today I wish I had taken the necklace!

In 1958, I won the state championship again and began to meet some of the women golf professionals.

Wilson Sporting Goods often sent Betsy Rawls and Mickey Wright to small towns to play exhibitions. This was thirty years ago. A young player who showed promise was big stuff back then, especially in our part of the West, so I was invited to play in these exhibitions. In our general neighborhood, from Amarillo to Pecos, it was nothing to jump in the car and drive 400 miles to play golf, especially if you could play with the real stars of the game.

In Hobbs, New Mexico, I played with Betsy. I played with Mickey in Hobbs and then in Pecos. It became like a regular tour. Every time Mickey came to that area, there I'd be.

After we played an exhibition in Amarillo, I asked Mickey if I could talk to her. We went into the pro's office and I told her I was very seriously thinking of turning pro. Mickey thought, however, that at nineteen, I was still too young for the tour. She advised me to wait a year and to continue to work with Harvey on my swing. I followed her advice. If Mickey said it, that was the way to go.

However, I had financial backers if and when I turned pro, which was unusual for that day. Dad, Hardy, George Blocker, who owned a gas company, and George Kendrick, who worked for El Paso Natural Gas, had agreed to put up $5,000 a year for three years. The only stipulation was that I was to give them 50 percent of my winnings during that time, which turned out to be nothing. When we discussed my career at home, Mother and Dad said, "Well, let's just do it." I agreed. And that was it.

I sent my application to the LPGA in January, 1959. Mother and I hit the highways in my little green Plymouth. My first professional tournament was the Mayfair Open in Sanford, Florida. We believed all the propaganda about how warm Florida was in the winter and almost froze to death. It was so cold that Mother and I would hurry back to the motel after I played, jump into our beds, and pull the covers over our heads to get warm.

Two other players turned pro that year: Mary Ann Reynolds and Barbara Romack. Their amateur records were much better than mine. Barbara, a former U.S. Women's Amateur champion, was a great player, and Mary Ann had won some big tournaments. You band together when you're the new kids on tour, so Mary Ann and I became friends and that helped me because I was quite shy. Eventually I got to know some of the other girls and some of the nice people in our tournament towns.

Those were great times. Our purses were meager by today's standards, but you could make a living, and the top players made a very good living. Of necessity, because we were always on the road and there were only a few dozen players, we were closer, too. After a tournament, we'd always sit around together and have a party. Usually the winner would buy the drinks because she was the only one who had any money!

We ran all the tournaments ourselves. We had a pairings committee, a rules committee, and a course set-up committee. We even did our own publicity. In fact, all of us were very public-relations conscious. We really believed in the association and its potential, but we felt that the only way we could really sell it was to capture the good will of our galleries and sponsors. We worked hard to be friendly, cooperated with the press, and attended all of the Pro-Am cocktail parties. It worked. We got a lot of grass roots support from golf fans, and we were able to keep our tour going. I believe very firmly that this approach still works, and I try to foster that sort of spirit today.

We went to great lengths to keep up our public image. We knew we had to look sharp, neat, and well-ironed, with our shoes polished. We even had fines for temperamental outbursts. If you threw a club, you'd get tabbed for $50. One of our players, JoAnne Prentice, better known as Fry, had a terrible temper. We had a rule that if you tossed a club, it couldn't touch the ground or you'd be fined. One day Fry missed an iron shot and heaved a club into the air. Just about the time the club reached the peak of its arc, Fry remembered the $50 fine, frantically circled under the falling club, and made a diving catch worthy of Willie Mays.

In off-hours, we often split into two groups, the bridge players and the poker players. I wasn't real good at either, but it was a nice way to pass the time between tournament rounds. Betty Jameson, the Hall-of-Famer and former U.S. Open champion, was a fanatical hearts player. She even wore a green eyeshade when she played. She may have worn the eyeshade because she had great peripheral vision. For that reason, it was difficult to play golf with Betty. She could see so many things going on around her that she was easily distracted by other players. I have great peripheral vision, too. I can see a lot of movement to the side even when I'm looking straight ahead, and it can be very distracting. Betty had a reputation for moving her playing partners around. She'd be standing over a putt, head anchored, eyes looking straight at the ball, and, without moving, she'd gesture frantically for some player thirty yards away to move! For that reason, tournament golf, with its galleries and other distractions, was difficult for her.

Years later, Betty remarked, "Too bad I never played with you."

"Yes, you did," I said. "I just stayed in the trees on every hole so I wouldn't bother you."

Betty had a very solid swing, very compact. She was built very solidly and looked like she was going to hit the ball well when she stood up to it. Good grip, good address position. The only thing that hurt her was her timing, which would sometimes get a little fast. But I enjoyed watching her play.

Mary Lena Faulk was another of our good players. Mary Lena hit her shots with a little draw, and that ball just ran like a little bunny. She was a great fairway-wood player and had a really impressive short

*Betsy Rawls and her mother celebrate on Betsy Rawls day in Spartanburg, South Carolina, 1959. Betsy was honored for her achievements in golf, including four U.S. Women's Open championships. In 1959, she won the Vare trophy, named after Glenna Collett Vare.*

game, better than most players. She's a wonderful lady and never had a bad word to say about anybody. Under the most trying circumstances, she'd find something good in just about everything. You could depend on Mary Lena.

I loved watching these great women golfers play, and I learned a lot by studying them carefully. I'd watch Suggs and wonder, "Why is she so consistent? Why is she always able to hit her shots the same way? Why does she have the same routine putting, chipping, and hitting full shots?"

Louise's routine never varied. All good players have that routine because it helps build their confidence. Timing and feel change from day to day, and if you go through the same routine, you have a better chance of hitting the ball the same way each time.

I have a great deal of respect for Louise. Her execution was so great, she was like a machine. She wasn't a flashy player or one who comes crashing out of the trees all the time. She executed her shots so well that she was seldom in trouble. Louise and I have sort of the same temperament; we don't talk a lot on the golf course. She was very pleasant to play with.

Betsy Rawls was another player I've always admired. Her record speaks for itself. She's a four-time U.S. Women's Open champion, a member of the LPGA Hall of Fame, and she remains a key administrator in women's golf.

Betsy had one of the best short games I've ever seen. She had a very soft touch around the green and a wonderful approach to putting. Long ago I read of her putting philosophy in a magazine article, and I've followed it ever since. Betsy always tried to putt the ball to the hole, rather than stroking a putt past the hole, because she felt that this helped her to get all of the corners. Betsy has a terrific mind. She was Phi Beta Kappa at the University of Texas and a great thinker on the golf course. Although I never talked to her about her course strategy, I just assumed that she played the percentages. She never gave up. You never knew if she was shooting 60 or 90 because she tried so hard on every shot. I believe her great reasoning ability helped her develop that attitude.

Another thing that made Betsy a great player was her ability to be unemotional on the golf course. I hardly ever saw her show any temper or any elation, which is a valuable attitude because it's hard to play well when you're going through a lot of emotional highs and lows.

Her short game was exceptional. She could get the ball up and down from almost anywhere. I'll never forget seeing her do this from the side of a mountain. We were playing the Esmerelda golf course in Spokane, Washington. On a short par 4, a dogleg right around a mountain, Betsy cut the corner a bit too close on her drive and the ball bounded up the side of the hill. We weren't even sure we could find the ball. When we did find it, Betsy analyzed the situation and proceeded to create a special technique for the situation. She managed to hit the ball close to the green. Then she chipped it close to the hole and made her putt for a par. You could almost hear her mind clicking away.

When Betsy retired, she became the LPGA's first Tournament Director. She was just the person for it—good with people and good at making policies and judgments. She would never allow her personal feelings to interfere with her decisions as to what was fair and right.

I have a great deal of respect and admiration for Betsy, and today I consider her a good friend. I feel very close to her, in the sense that I shared her career with her and watched her put her imprint on LPGA policies that we still use today.

What I most admire about these women—Betsy, Louise, and others—is that, had it not been for their desire to play professional golf, we would not have a tour today. They started from zero. To be sure, they had a lot of help— from the sporting goods companies, for example. This brings me to Patty Berg. Patty worked for Wilson Sporting Goods before a women's pro tour existed. Patty got Wilson to support the tour through her personal dedication, the respect that the Wilson people had for her remarkable golfing ability, and their personal fondness for her. For these women to start from scratch in 1950 and establish a tour that is still going strong today, is a marvelous achievement. I can't think of many of us who would have that much gumption and fortitude today.

Anyway, at nineteen, I was a rookie on the LPGA Tour and thrilled to be there. I was a pro! I hadn't signed with an equipment company, but Wilson was giving golf equipment to me. I had a big new golf bag and a shag bag of practice balls. My game, however, didn't match my enthusiasm, and, as the season progressed, I became very discouraged. I almost quit during my first year. I was playing terribly and not making any money, so I drove home to discuss the future with Mother and Dad. They convinced me to give it a little more time, to keep trying. I returned to the tour feeling a little better about my career. The next week, in Asheville, North Carolina, I tied with two other players for the last prize check. We split $100. I had won $33. I called home, feeling as good as if I'd won the tournament.

# Pine Valley: Par Excellence

## Pamela Emory

Philadelphia                                              June, 1991

Lots of people know about Pine Valley. Soap opera buffs recognize it as the setting for the popular show, *All My Children*. New Jersey politicians know it as a political subdivision—that little borough between Pine Hill and Clementon in Camden County. There's a cocktail called a Pine Valley: a refreshing mixture of gin, lime juice and fresh mint. To all eighteen full-time residents, Pine Valley is home. To environmentalists, it's a sanctuary for a wide variety of native flora and fauna, but especially for the endangered swamp pink flower and mud turtle. Above all, it's known to golfers. To them, Pine Valley is legendary as the greatest golf course in the world.

Yes, millions of people know *about* Pine Valley. Last year 21,263 had the privilege of playing golf there. (Among them were Mike Schmidt, Tip O'Neill, Phil Simms, Yogi Berra, Michael Jordan and Senator Sam Nunn.) But only 1,007 men really can say they *know* the club. They're the members. These men know and love Pine Valley for what it is: an unpretentious clubhouse filled with warmth and camaraderie, surrounded by 6,656 yards of abject terror.

In no way should Pine Valley be confused with a country club. There aren't any kids splashing in or nannies lying around the club swimming pool; there isn't a pool. Don't bother looking around the club's 623 acres for tennis, squash or paddle tennis courts, or any other amenities associated with country clubs; they're not here either. Nor will you find its members doing the fox-trot in front of a bored dance band on Saturday nights. This is an exclusive club, all right, but it is about golf and only golf.

Back in 1926, a newspaper article observed that Pine Valley "will still remain first, last and all the time what it started out to be—a golf club. They have their own way of doing things at Pine Valley, their own manners and customs." Sixty-five years later, they're still doing it *their* way.

Never mind that the name sounds like a computer-generated moniker for a suburban housing development. Golf at Pine Valley is like Mount Everest to mountain climbers. This is the place where the two standing bets are: 1) that an average player won't break 100 or a good player 90 the first time he plays the course; and 2) that on at least one hole the player will be more than four shots above par.

Pine Valley is such a hallowed place in the world of golf that the opportunity to play a round there is treated with reverence.

A *New York Times* sportswriter once suggested there were three ways to deal with an invitation to play Pine Valley: "Say, 'Yes, I'll be down tomorrow,' and leave for Europe that same night. Say, 'I've got something easier to do,' and make good on it by going over Niagara Falls on a bicycle. Or, you can bid your family and friends farewell, fasten a package of emergency rations to your belt, and go down and play."

What makes Pine Valley so difficult is that the course was carved into the Pine Barrens, so scrub pines vie with sand for dominance. One bunker is affectionately called "Hell's Half-Acre," but it really covers three times that much sandy-scrubby area. Some say the course has more sand than most beaches, but it's the proportion and arrangement of sand and "grungle"—a combination of scrubby, knotty, twisting Scotch broom and honeysuckle, cacti, and imported heather—that gives the course the look of a testing ground for a ballistics company.

In addition to the volume of sand, it's the condition in which it's kept—or, more accurately, not kept—that is alarming to most who play there for the first time. Pine Valley is one of the few places where a caddy doesn't bother raking a bunker after his player extricates himself. Sand occupies such a large area of the course that it would be a full-time job and increase playing time considerably, if a caddy were expected to clean up after his player successfully returned to the terra firma of the fairway.

For the par shooter—that rare bird—Pine Valley is a relatively short course. From the back tees, it measures 6,656 yards. (From the forward tees, it's only 214 yards shorter.) As a reference, many of the courses being built today use 7,000 yards as a *minimum* length. The course has other characteristics which make it seem enticing: wide fairways, no out-of-bounds and huge greens. To the top-caliber player, the typical Pine Valley drive from the tee is an unalarming airborne shot which must carry some 140 to 184 yards in order to reach the desired fairway. That's all. However, to most golfers—us mortal types who are not par shooters—the lay of the land is as twisted as a Stephen King novel.

The physical motion in golf is simple: Hit a little ball that sits still for you. But beyond this physical game, golf is a test of a player's psychological control and patience. Nowhere is the mind-game of golf put to the test more than at the Valley. Just by knowing that the results of the first slightly mis-hit shot will ruin his score, the player becomes partially paralyzed, waiting for disaster to happen.

Not that this is an impossible course; it just requires perfect shots. Nearly perfect ones won't do; they're the ones that cause double-digit scores on one hole. They're the ones that lend themselves to the club's fascinating history and lore. Pine Valley is the course where Babe Ruth took a *12* on the 15th hole and yelled to his friend, "Hell, I don't need to know where the green is. Where is the *golf course?*" It's the place where, legend has it, "only God can make a 3" on the long and demanding par-3 fifth hole. But it's also where Arnold Palmer shot a 2-under-par 68 and won enough money in bets to buy his wife's engagement ring. It's where newlywed Jack Nicklaus played the course while his bride sat in the car in the club parking lot.

There has always been a benevolent dictator in charge of Pine Valley, not numerous committees, as at most country clubs. Only four men have been president in the club's 79-year history, and one of them—John Arthur Brown—served almost 50 years.

It was during Brown's lengthy tenure, from 1929 to 1977, that Pine Valley's worldwide reputation grew. He was a first-rate golfer, and still holds the club record for the best "ringer" score (adding up the lowest score ever made on each hole), a remarkable 45.

It must have been the dictatorial side of John Arthur, as he is often referred to, which greatly reduced the playing time for women at Pine Valley. In the early years, women could play anytime. Then came the first restriction: They could play there any day after 3 p.m. and Sundays after 1 p.m. Some forty years ago, Brown's new policy concerning women's play was announced. According to club chairman Ernie Ransome, Brown's successor, "It happened in the fall of the year, when the days were perceptibly shorter, which made playing a complete round of golf before dark difficult when started after 3 p.m. The wife of a club member suggested to John Arthur that he 'do something' about women's playing time at Pine Valley. He replied, 'I will.' His solution was announced the next day, in a memorandum: 'Women will be allowed to play *only* after noon on Sundays.' "

Normally women are not allowed into the clubhouse; they are, however, when the annual Crump Cup trophy is presented. They can dine in an enclosed porch area (one of the six additions to the clubhouse), or, if weather permits, in a new outdoor dining area. They now have their own small changing room (another addition), which is a lot nicer, and closer, than their former facility—up the hill in one of the dormitories.

Some of the club's oldest photographs, circa 1915, show women golfers in action at the Valley, and several of the photos are included in Shelly's *Chronicle*. Pine Valley has used females as employees in the past, most often during wartime, to work on the ground crew—weeding the course by hand—and as caddies.

When the right cause comes along, all rules can be held in abeyance. Even the strict "Women Only Sunday After Noon" policy has been known to be relaxed. Last July, *on a Monday,* the club hosted a group of about thirty-five British and American women amateur golfers, sixteen of whom were members of the 1990 U.S. and Great Britain and Ireland Curtis Cup teams. The rest were officials of the USGA and the Ladies Golf Union.

Great strides were made for women at Pine Valley that hot, humid day. In fact, July 30, 1990, will long be remembered at the Valley because it was on that day an unofficial female club champion, Carol Semple Thompson, of Sewickley, Pennsylvania, was crowned. With the greatest of informal pomp and circumstance, Ransome presented Thompson—*inside* the clubhouse—with not only a "trophy" (two aluminum funnels welded together at the skinny parts, with iced-tea spoons as handles and "engraved" with plastic tape) but also with a poster-board "plaque" with Thompson's name and winning score—a 75—etched onto it in felt pen.

Thompson is a former U.S. Women's Amateur champion (1973) and has played Pine Valley three or four times, never shooting a score in the 80s—or worse. Before she played there the first time, her father bet her she wouldn't break 90. She won the bet when she shot a 78—her worst score at Pine Valley. The eleven-time winner of the Pennsylvania State Women's championship will have plenty of time to practice for her Pine Valley title defense. The next scheduled unofficial female club championship, according to her "plaque", will be in the year 2000, with another set for 2010.

# A Putting Primer

## Vicki Goetze, with Cliff Shrock

Golf Digest                                                    September, 1991

Although I've tried my best to convince people that my tee-to-green game isn't too bad, they find it hard to believe that someone 5-foot-4, 110 pounds, and 18 years old can even *scare* the ball 100 yards. I admit I could use some extra distance, but 220-yard drives haven't stopped me from reaching the winner's circle. Having said that, when some women can hit it forty yards past me and I still get the best of them, I can see how the focus shifts to my short game and putting. My putting has bailed me out quite often, as it did in my third-round match in the 1989 U.S. Women's Amateur against Terri Thompson. I was two down with three holes to play, and then made three straight birdie putts of fifteen, four, and thirty feet to win.

That sort of success, combined with extensive practice, gives me a lot of confidence in my putting. It makes me feel like I'm always going to putt well, whether on a downhill five-footer or a double-breaker from fifteen yards away. I think these drills, done regularly, can give you that confidence, too.

Here are two putting aids in one. This drill teaches you how to swing the putter on line and align the face square to the hole every time.

It makes sense to use a straight line if you want to swing the putter on a straight path. Using a chalk-line tool that you can find at a hardware store, locate a straight putt of about five feet on your practice green and mark a line to the hole.

The sweet spot on my putter is marked with a white line on top. Mark your putter with a piece of tape if it isn't already marked. Then make sure the white line on the putter runs into the chalk line at address. When it does, you know the clubface is square. Then all you have to do is swing the putter back and forward.

I've also got two rows of four tees set up about half an inch wider than the putterhead at address. I use them to keep the putter moving on

track. There's no way I can get lazy and let the putter stray from the chalk line or I'll hit into the tees.

I do this drill until I make 100 putts in a row. That number may sound extreme, but I see the repetition as helpful mentally. I don't want to practice missing putts from longer distances. The more I see the ball go in, the better my composure and confidence will be the next time I'm under pressure to hole a crucial putt on the course.

Bad habits can appear so quickly in your putting stroke that it's dangerous to take it for granted. Faults such as stopping your stroke too soon after impact, or letting the putter-head pull to the left after striking the ball can easily creep into your stroke if you're not constantly

*Practice full forward stroke.*

checking your technique. Whenever I'm in a putting slump—leaving the ball short or missing to the left a lot—those faults are the first things I look for.

Here's a drill I do to counteract both. First, I find a relatively flat three-foot putt. Then, from my normal address position, I simply push the putter forward, extend my follow-through, and hold it for a couple of seconds. That encourages a full and straight-down-the-line finish to my stroke.

By now you've probably noticed that it's better to be creative when you practice. Except on short putts, don't just hit ball after ball from the same spot to the same target. This "ball-progression drill" for long, uphill, and downhill putts is a good example of how some imagination can help your putting average. Take a handful of balls—sometimes I'll use up to twenty—and pick a spot about 10 feet away. Putt the first ball to that spot. Then hit the next one a foot beyond the first, the third another foot farther, and so on. You can't help but gain a better feel for distance and the speed of the green.

For the ultimate in feel, use a blindfold. I don't think I'm *that* good that I can make putts blindfolded, but you really test your sense of feel with this drill. Hit the ball toward a hole, guessing whether it will finish short or long, right or left, or in the hole. You'll concentrate better than you ever have before.

Almost everyone I've seen on the practice green putts with a few balls toward one hole. The first putt is usually a poor one, but the others end

*Two ways to gain feel for sloping and long putts.*

up around the hole. I don't like that method by itself because it gives you the illusion that you have a good feel for the pace of the greens. What I like to do—when the practice green isn't crowded—is place tees around a section of the green at various distances and slopes, and putt one ball to each tee. That makes you think more about the speed of the green and simulates tournament conditions. After all, you get only one chance to make each putt out on the course.

## Additional tips:

**Setup:** Play the ball off the left heel. Hold your hands high, away from your body, and use a forward press as your swing trigger. During the stroke keep your left wrist firm in order to maintain the same angle.

**Reading greens/pace of play:** Get locked in on what you want to do and go with it. If there is any doubt in your mind, you'll miss the putt. Concentrate on the target, which can be the edge of the cup, a spot two inches to the left, or whatever amount of break you expect the ball to take. When it's your time to putt, don't delay. Think "target, ball, go." Everyone has a different speed. Putt as quickly as you can without rushing.

**Fast greens:** I putt better on fast greens because I putt by feel. Good feel is a must if you're trying to die the ball into the cup. Pick "higher" targets to allow for the extra break that occurs when the ball loses speed around the cup.

**Slow greens:** Although I don't change my basic stroke, I like to make a longer backswing and concentrate on hitting the ball firmly on the sweet spot of the putter.

**Breaking putts:** Play the ball forward in your stance for left-to-right breaking putts. That makes aiming left more comfortable and insures that the ball starts on the high side of the hole. I position the ball in my usual setup for right-to-left putts, but you should experiment with moving it back slightly in your stance, just the opposite of left-to-right putts.

# Help for Senior Golfers

## Peggy Kirk Bell and Dr. Jim Suttie

Golf for Women                    November/December, 1991

As senior women golfers reach the age where they have more time to play, they usually have new challenges to face—some physical, some mechanical, and some psychological.

Through our golf schools for women at Pine Needles over the years, we have identified several swing-related problems prominent among senior women golfers. Essentially, these problems arise from two areas: incorrect concepts of the swing; and specific physical problems which limit the correct golf swing motion and encourage compensatory movements during the swing.

### Misconceptions of the Swing

In order to swing a golf club properly, we must understand what a good golf swing involves. In brief, a good swing fulfills four important objectives:

• clubhead speed at impact, which translates into distance;

• a square clubface at impact, which translates into accuracy;

• an inside-to-straight swing path on the downswing, which translates into more clubhead velocity;

• repeatability, which translates into consistency.

If one of these objectives is not met, we can't call the swing efficient. If you view the concept of the swing as an inclined, circular motion of the clubhead, you will realize that turning the shoulders and hips is the easiest way to achieve this motion. Also, the big muscle movement of the feet, knees, and hips on the downswing can produce more clubhead speed. The arms-only swing never allows you to achieve your full golfing potential.

Many senior golfers have misconceptions about the golf swing. They'll do anything in their power to achieve distance. Unfortunately, when trying to get this distance, they often commit serious swing flaws which actually limit their distance potential.

For example, many players simply swing their arms without turning their bodies. As a result, the small muscles of the hands and arms dominate both the backswing and downswing. But the big muscles of the shoulders, hips, and legs should dominate the swing, and this can only be achieved by emphasizing the body turn or coil.

The arms-only downswing is a sure way to lose distance. If you rotate the shoulders and hips and just allow the arms to follow during your backswing and downswing, you will indeed discover the golfer's source of power.

Another common misconception concerns the use of the feet, knees, and hips during the swing. Senior golfers tend to do too much with their feet, knees, and hips on the backswing and too little with them on the downswing. One major problem we have observed often is incorrect hip movement.

Well-meaning senior players try to turn their hips on the backswing. Rather than turning, however, they lift and sway their hips to the right (right-handers), a movement that makes it impossible to start the downswing with the legs. Instead, the arms initiate the downward move, and a weak hit usually results. Try to control the hips and the center of gravity during the backswing, and you will get better results.

Another incorrect concept many golfers have is related to the psychology of hitting the ball. Some players think they must help the ball up in the air with the right hand. This scooping action always causes poor results.

We will study three major swing problems as personified by the arms-and-body lifter, the sitter (poor posture), and the hip swayer.

Ultimately, only you know your physical limitations. Try to build as sound a golf swing as possible around your own set of strengths and weaknesses. Listed below are a handful of specific problems with which most senior players eventually must contend:

*Lack of Strength:* As we age, our overall body strength decreases, especially in the hands. Some of us compensate during our swing in an effort to generate more clubhead speed. Our advice is to keep your body as fit as you can.

Do some walking, swimming, or biking on a daily basis to build up your legs and help your endurance and strength. Also, consider doing some light strength-building exercises. This is especially important for the hands, wrists, and forearms. Squeezing a rubber ball is a good exercise for everyone.

*Control of the Hips:* Whether we like it or not, most of our weight is located in the hip areas—our center of gravity. At least 90 percent of the seniors we teach move their hips too much to the right in the backswing (for right-handers). This sway and lift of the hips makes it all but impossible to lead the downswing with the legs. As a result, the downswing is arms-dominated, which causes the club to come down steeply from the outside-in.

Try to control your hips by turning them only 45 degrees, by keeping your left foot closer to the ground in the backswing, and by holding the right leg post in its original address position throughout the backswing.

*Arthritis or Bursitis:* Golfers who suffer from one or both of these problems must inevitably put up with a little pain when swinging a golf club. You must find the most pain-free movement you can make while still trying to perform a fundamentally sound swing. Lighter graphite-shafted clubs, which act as shock absorbers when the club hits the ground, may help.

*Flexibility:* Generally speaking, women are not as strong as men but they have more flexibility, and we should use it to maximum advantage by achieving a long swing arc and a good body turn. Most of us don't use our flexibility because we tend to wrap our arms around our head but fail to rotate our body while doing so. Remember, the swing is a combination of body turn and arm swing. Use your flexibility wisely and turn your body.

*Lack of Balance:* Some of us lose balance during our swing. Some of us don't complete our follow through and are not balanced over the left leg at the finish. Often, coming up on the toes through the impact area is a characteristic of the off-balance golfer. The root cause of imbalance can be traced to posture in the address position.

Golfers who begin with most of their weight on their heels will always lose balance toward the toes during the swing. Also, we must not sway or lift our hips during the backswing. This causes an imbalance on the downswing. To avoid coming up on the toes through impact, try to start the downswing with the feet, knees, and hips—not the hands and arms.

*Tension and Tightness:* Some of us tend to hold the club too tightly at address, which always causes tension in the hands, arms, shoulders, and neck, and makes it all but impossible to turn and coil the body on the backswing. The result is a fast, jerky arm swing with little or no rhythm. Our advice here is to hold the club very lightly, which allows your arms to swing as your body turns on the backswing.

*The Overweight Player:* The overweight golfer must bend forward more from the hips in order to make room for the arms through the impact area. Be careful not to lift your body up.

*Coordination and Timing:* Some of us complain that we don't have coordination. Essentially, this is not true. But body coordination is difficult to attain when there is too much movement in the swing.

*The one-piece takeaway.*

Remember, don't sway the hips to the right or lift the hips and torso on the backswing. These movements create poor coordination on the down-swing.

Coordination and timing mean the same thing: moving the parts of your body in the correct sequential order. The correct backswing se-quence calls for the clubhead, hands, arms, shoulders, and torso to move together to initiate the swing; then the hips, knees, and feet are pulled around by the upper body to complete the backswing.

The process is reversed on the downswing: the feet, knees, and hips move first; the torso, arms, hands, and clubhead follow. Your timing and coordination will improve if your backswing is dominated by your shoulder turn and your downswing is dominated by your legs and hips.

*Incorrect Body Turn*                    *Correct Body Turn*

*Chicken Wing Left Arm*                    *Correct Arm Extension*

**Misconception One: The Arms-and-Body Lifter**

*The golfer at top left has lifted her hands too high, causing the hips and torso to raise out of their original posture. At top right, Peggy Kirk Bell demonstrates the correct body turn. In her swing, the arms are in the correct swing plane and she has stayed down in her original posture.*

*The arms-and-body lifter has an incorrect concept of distance. She thinks it is directly related to swinging the club high above her head. This misconception causes the following results in the backswing: • lifting the hips and torso from their original posture; • stiff legs at the top of the swing; • lifting the left foot too far off the ground at the top of the swing; • usually, very stiff wrists at the top of the swing; • and an exaggerated upright swing plane.*

*The lifter swings the club so high that she must start down with the arms and hands from the top of her swing, which always causes a steep approach angle and an outside-in swing path through the impact area. This steep outside-in approach to the*

ball causes topped shots, slices, and pulled shots. In addition, the left arm collapses in toward the body just after impact—the chicken wing *left arm. This is a result of trying not to dig down into the ground when coming from a steep approach angle to the ball.*

**Corrections for the Arms-and-Body Lifter:** • *Make sure your weight doesn't start on your front leg as this will encourage a high, vertical swing.* • *A low-extended, one-piece takeaway will help your shoulders turn. Don't just pick the club up with your hands and arms. Don't break your wrists until waist-high in the backswing. Just turn your shoulders and extend your arms.* • *Turn the shoulders and hips to the right; don't lift them.* • *Keep the legs flexed all the way back; don't straighten the knees at the top.* • *Stay in your original posture once you get to the top of the swing.* • *Keep your arms down in a lower swing plane at the top; the arms should feel as if they are connected and close to the body at the top.* • *Allow your wrists to cock on the backswing; if the wrists don't cock, the arms and body will lift up.* • *Following these suggestions will enable you to start the down-swing with your hips and legs instead of your arms. This, in turn, will allow you to hit from inside the target line and also create more clubhead velocity.*

*The sitter.*                    *Correct setup posture.*

**Misconception Two: The Sitter**   *The sitter is the player who sits back on her heels at address with overflexed knees. This causes her to get in a very poor posture with the hips tucked under too much.*

*The sitter displays overflexed knees, weight back on heels, a rounded back, and arms too close to her body. This posture makes it virtually impossible to turn and rotate the body correctly on the backswing and downswing. Instead, the golfer will tend to sway the hips on both the backswing and forward swing. Also, this poor posture makes it difficult for the golfer to keep her balance and to get her arms past the body in the hitting area.*

**Guidelines for Correct Posture:**   • *Bend forward from your hips about 25 degrees while keeping both your upper (neck area) and lower spine straight.* • *Get your fanny up and out.* • *Flex your knees only slightly to distribute your weight on the balls of your feet—not on your heels.* • *Allow your arms to hang vertically beneath your shoulder sockets. There should be absolutely no tension in your arms and hands at address.* • *If you follow these guidelines, good things will develop. You will create a better hip and shoulder turn. You will eliminate most of your swaying. Your arms will stay more connected to your body in a lower position at the top of the swing. You will be able to get your arms by your body in the hitting area without coming up on your toes. Your balance will improve dramatically.*

*Hip Swayer's Set-up*

*The Hip Swayer: When the hips sway to the right, the spine is thrown to the left, causing an incorrect weight movement called the reverse pivot*

**Misconception Three: The Hip Swayer** *About 90 percent of all seniors we teach sway their hips to the right on the backswing. Once the hips sway to the right, the shoulders will not be able to turn. They will usually dip or tilt once the hips sway. When the shoulders quit turning, the correct weight movement is affected.*

*Hip swayers usually have the following in common: Too much weight on the left leg in the set-up. • The right leg straightens and sways as the club is taken back. • The hips slide to the right causing the shoulders to dip downward on the backswing. This retards the correct shoulder turn and the correct weight movement to the right leg. • The downswing is an arms-dominated motion because the weight has swayed so far outside the right foot on the backswing. This doesn't allow the legs to work first on the downswing, which leaves the majority of the weight on the back leg at impact.*

**Corrections for the Hip Swayer:** • *Assume the correct posture in your set-up.* • *Make sure your weight is not on the front leg at address. Get your head behind the ball and your shoulders tilted with a little more weight on the right leg.* • *Maintain the right leg post on the backswing as the hips and shoulders feel as though they are rotating level with the ground. The right leg must stay in its original position all the way into the backswing. This is called* keeping the post. *The weight should go to the inside of the right heel on the backswing. You are actually turning around the post.*

*Correct Turn of the Shoulders and Hips*

• *Don't keep your head so still that it limits the motion of your shoulder turn. Allow your head to rotate with your upper spine. This makes the correct shoulder turn possible.* • *Start your downswing with your lower body. Push off your back foot. Get your weight to the left side and then open up your hips.*

# Prejudice and Pride

## John Hopkins

*Financial Times*                    December 7, 1991

The name Joanne Morley probably does not strike a chord unless you follow women's amateur golf closely, in which case you will know that Morley was one of the outstanding players of the past season.

She won the English and British stroke-play titles; and her haul of three points out of four in the match between Great Britain and Ireland against the Continent for the Vagliano Trophy was the best by a player from either side. In recognition of this success, Morley was named amateur woman golfer of the year last week.

Morley is a purposeful, assured 24-year-old who spends her winters working in Woolworths to earn enough money to pay for the competitive golf she plays all summer. She says she will turn professional at the end of next year but, for the moment, her sights are levelled at the Curtis Cup at Hoylake next June. And therein lies a story.

The Royal Liverpool Golf Club, at Hoylake on the tip of the Wirral peninsula, is among the oldest and most distinguished in the world. It was founded in Hoylake in 1864 and, twenty years later, started the Amateur championship, the oldest event of its kind. It was at Hoylake in 1902 that Alex Herd won the Open with a rubber-core ball, thus killing off the gutty ball that had hitherto been used so successfully.

It was at Hoylake in 1921 that a match between the men amateurs of Britain and the US was played, an event for which the Walker Cup was presented the following year. And it was at Hoylake not long ago that women were told they could walk through the men's lounge to the dining room instead of, as previously, having to go outside the clubhouse. At the time of this historic pronouncement, it was made clear to the women that this concession was available only "so long as they look straight ahead."

If this chauvinism sounds remarkable in 1991, be assured it is not— or, rather, was not. Golf as a game, and the clubs which its participants had to join in order to play, traditionally have remained the homes of racists and chauvinists.

Prejudice against Jews, for example, was such that they had great difficulty in joining golf clubs which operated a Jewish quota—and most of them did. This led to Jews founding their own clubs, of which Moor Allerton outside Leeds, Bonnyton in Glasgow and Hartsbourne, Potters Bar and Abridge near London are all good examples. Jews and gentiles now mix harmoniously at most London clubs. The new outcasts in golf are the Japanese.

The Japanese ambassador to Britain has playing facilities at Sunningdale, Berkshire, but many of his countrymen have to make-do with sessions at driving ranges and occasional outings at accommodating courses, of which there aren't many. This unwelcoming attitude has made the Japanese buy their own golf clubs. Recent acquisitions include Camberley Heath in Surrey, Old Thorns near Liphook, Hampshire, and the Turnberry hotel and course in south-west Scotland, the site of the 1986 Open.

Women, when faced with obvious discrimination, had no choice but to grin and bear it. When a man said: "Women don't play golf, they play *at* it," women had to like it or lump it. They had to do likewise until recently when they came across such indignities as a sign at the entrance to one golf club that read (and note the order of the nouns): "No dogs or women."

There are still clubs in Britain where the reaction of the men members is reminiscent of Robert Morley's in the film *Round the World in Eighty Days* when he saw a woman in the Reform Club. "A woman in the club!" exploded Morley. "It is the end."

That has had to change. It took the Equal Opportunities Commission to bring about change. In 1988, and prompted by an average of one complaint a day for 13 years, the EOC proposed an amendment to the 1981 Sex Discrimination Act. The EOC wanted to bring into line those clubs that purported to offer membership to both sexes but, in reality, offered women limited rights.

"This absence of choice is particularly disadvantageous to women because of the restricted privileges attached to associate membership which may lead, for example, to prohibitions on the use of sporting facilities at weekends and on weekday evenings."

This definition fits many of the 200 golf clubs in the UK where women have limited rights, little representation and pay a subscription not significantly lower than the men.

Although the government has so far declined to implement the recommendation of the EOC, the Ladies' Golf Union recently took it upon itself to become more militant. It announced in mid-summer that it was boycotting the all-male clubs even if they had staged events for women in the past. This ruled out Royal St. George's, Sandwich, site of the 1988 Curtis Cup match, and Muirfield, where the Curtis Cup was held in 1984. Both remain bastions of male chauvinism.

Mary Anderson, the chairman of the LGU and a woman of considerable charm and forcefulness, asked: "Why do men have the right to feel superior? I think women are far superior to men or, at any rate, we're all equal. I don't see why I can't have the same rights as a man."

To its credit, Hoylake is acceptable to the LGU. Next June when the Curtis Cup is held there, Joanne Morley, who will assuredly be playing for GB and Ireland, will be able to experience the historic links and the equally historic and imposing clubhouse. As she does so, I hope she does not have to look straight ahead.

# Pat Bradley and the Hall of Fame

## Rhonda Glenn

Golf                                                    February, 1992

Old Leo Durocher would sit by his telephone each April and wait. The combative Durocher, who once terrorized baseball as the manager of the Dodgers, Giants, and Cubs and who coined such delicate phrases as "Show me a good loser and I'll show you an idiot" and "Nice guys finish last," was hoping for a call that would confirm his election to baseball's Hall of Fame either by baseball writers' vote or by the nod of a special committee. When he died last autumn at the age of 86, he'd waited all that time in vain. The telephone call never came.

Pat Bradley didn't have to wait for any telephone call. Last September she became the twelfth player selected for induction in the LPGA Hall of Fame. She made it by playing her way in. Over a period of sixteen years, Bradley recorded thirty tournament victories, including two different major championships.

Reflecting on Durocher's situation, Bradley said recently, "He may have stepped on a few toes during his career and, as a result, never got that telephone call, even though many people considered him Hall-of-Fame material. In my case, I didn't have to deal with that kind of subjectivity. I was Pat Bradley, Hall-of-Famer, the moment I won my 30th."

The LPGA Hall of Fame's prerequisites are like those of no other sports organization. A player must be an LPGA member for at least ten years and must have at least thirty official victories, including two different major championships; or thirty-five victories with one major; or forty victories if there are no majors in her portfolio.

Many members of the press and several players, including Bradley, have criticized the criteria as being too difficult. But the formula has identified only the true greats over the years and has remained unchanged since the Hall was conceived in 1967.

That Hall originated with the first Women's Golf Hall of Fame, which was founded at the Augusta Country Club in Augusta, Georgia, in

*Pat Bradley is one of the select few inducted in the LPGA Hall of Fame.*

1950, by the organizers of the old Titleholders event. Professional women's golf was a new entity at that time—the LPGA had just been chartered—and the Titleholders field included more amateurs than professionals. Sportswriters cast ballots, and it wasn't surprising that the first members of the Hall of Fame were all amateurs: Joyce Wethered (Lady Heathcote-Amory), Margaret Curtis, Beatrix Hoyt, Dorothy Campbell Hurd (Howe), Alexa Stirling Fraser, Glenna Collett Vare, and Virginia Van Wie.

Four professionals were inducted the following year: Patty Berg, Betty Jameson, Louise Suggs, and Babe Zaharias. Betsy Rawls was inducted in 1960, and Mickey Wright followed in 1964.

In 1967, LPGA players voted to establish their own Hall of Fame and to limit it to LPGA members. The six LPGA players who were existing members of the Women's Golf Hall of Fame were inducted automatically. New inductees, it was decided, would have to meet a new criterion of multiple wins. Three players made it in the 1970s: Kathy Whitworth in 1975, and Carol Mann and Sandra Haynie in 1977. But the dearth of inductees in the 1980s—only JoAnne Carner in 1982 and Nancy Lopez in 1987—prompted renewed discussion of changing the standards or even instituting an election process.

As the 1991 season began, however, critics quieted down. Five players seemed to be on the verge of induction: Amy Alcott (28 wins), Beth Daniel (25), Patty Sheehan (25), Betsy King (23), and Pat Bradley (26).

Daniel and Sheehan picked up early victories. In April, Alcott won the Nabisco Dinah Shore and, only one win short, appeared to have the best chance. Bradley, meanwhile, had pushed aside all thoughts of the Hall. "In May I won the Centel Classic, which was a tremendous boost," she recalls, "but I got nipped twice—in the LPGA championship and the U.S. Women's Open. That was tough, because I'd played well enough to win."

Bradley eventually began to think about one more victory in 1991 and perhaps induction in 1992, but rebounded for a spectacular September, winning the Rail Charity Golf Classic and the Safeco Classic three weeks later. She now lay one victory away from the LPGA's highest plateau.

At the MBS LPGA Classic in Buena Park, California, the following week, Bradley didn't think of the Hall, even though she was leading on the final day. "I kept my eyes away from the leaderboard," she says. "I thought my competition was in the final pairing of Meg Mallon and Lisa Walters. I bogeyed the last hole and thought maybe I could get into a playoff." As it turned out, Bradley's closest competitor was Michelle Estill, who already had returned a higher score. When Bradley realized she was "in," it was time to celebrate. Back home in Westford, Massachusetts, her mother rang a cowbell on the back porch, just as she had to celebrate every Bradley victory since 1976. "I think that bell will be ringing all night long," an ecstatic Bradley predicted.

Bradley's new status hasn't stopped her from questioning the the criteria for entry into the Hall of Fame. "A Player-of-the-Year title or Vare Trophy winner perhaps should have some validity," she says, "and maybe our major championships should be more equal. As it is now, only two different majors count towards the Hall of Fame. But what if someone wins three U.S. Women's Opens?"

Overall, however, Bradley believes that the LPGA's policy of keeping politics out of the Hall of Fame race is sound.

One of the best things the LPGA rules do, Bradley feels, is preclude some distaff Durocher from having to sit in sad futility, waiting for a telephone call. "Getting into our Hall of Fame isn't the result of a popularity contest," she says. "I greatly admire my foremothers for their perception in setting standards."

### As It Stands
Here is the current roster of LPGA Hall-of-Fame inductees

| Player | Year Inducted |
|---|---|
| Louise Suggs | 1951 |
| Patty Berg | 1951 |
| Betty Jameson | 1951 |
| Babe Zaharias | 1951 |
| Betsy Rawls | 1960 |
| Mickey Wright | 1964 |
| Kathy Whitworth | 1975 |
| Sandra Haynie | 1977 |
| Carol Mann | 1977 |
| JoAnne Carner | 1982 |
| Nancy Lopez | 1987 |
| Pat Bradley | 1991 |

### Who's Next for the Hall?

The LPGA Hall of Fame inducts LPGA members of at least 10 years' standing who have won 30 tournaments including two different major championships, 35 tournaments with one major or 40 tournaments without any majors. Here's who's in the running for induction, as of the start of 1992.

| PLAYER | Victories | Different Majors | Needs |
|---|---|---|---|
| Amy Alcott | 29 | 3 | 1 win |
| Beth Daniel | 27 | 1 | 8 wins or 3 wins inc. 1 major |
| Patty Sheehan* | 26 | 1 | 9 wins or 4 wins inc. 1 major |
| Betsy King | 25 | 2 | 5 wins |
| Hollis Stacy | 18 | 2 | 12 wins |
| Jan Stephenson | 16 | 3 | 14 wins |

*Has since been inducted.

# Betsy King's Finest Championship—
# So Far

## Jaime Diaz

The New York *Times*                                          May 17, 1992

Few golfers have ever stayed in a flawless groove longer in a major championship than Betsy King did in the 1992 L.P.G.A championship at the Bethesda Country Club in Bethesda, Maryland. Her four rounds of 67, 66, 68, and 66 over a narrow and demanding course gave her a total of 267, 17-under-par and eleven strokes ahead of the second-place finishers: Karen Noble, a rookie who closed with the tournament low round of 65, Liselotte Neumann, and JoAnne Carner, a seemingly age-less challenger in the big tournaments. King hit all but 11 of the 72 greens in regulation, and in four days play posted only two bogies.

Asked if she had ever seen a more impressive performance, the ven-erable Carner, whose own remarkable play at age 53 was almost com-pletely overshadowed by King's brilliance, answered, "No. Betsy lapped us."

All the superlatives used to describe King's play will be supported by the record book:

• Her four-round total was the lowest in Ladies Professional Golf Association history, a stroke lower than Nancy Lopez's 20-under 268 on a par-72 course at the 1985 Henredon Classic.

• Her 17-under total was the lowest under-par figure in a women's major championship.

• With a high round of 68, King became the first woman to win a major championship with four rounds in the 60s.

• Her 11-stroke margin of victory also exceeded by one Patty Shee-han's 10-stroke victory at the 1984 championship. The only greater margins of victory by women occurred at the 1949 United States Women's Open, where Louise Suggs won by 14 shots, and the 1954 Women's Open, where Babe Didrickson Zaharias won by 12.

The victory today gave King five major championships. She has won both the United States Women's Open and the Nabisco Dinah Shore twice. It was also the 26th victory of King's 16-year career, leaving her

*Betsy King's rounds of 68, 66, 67, and 66 in the 1992 LPGA championship set a host of records for women's major championship golf.*

only four victories short of automatic induction into the L.P.G.A. Hall of Fame. The $150,000 first prize pushed King into second place behind Pat Bradley on the career money-winning list with more than $3.5 million.

More important, the victory represented a dramatic change in the recent fortunes of King, who had not won a tournament since last July. For several months, she had been in one of the worst slumps of her career, having shot in the 60s only three times in eight tournaments.

King's problems began with her decision last summer to break with her long-time teacher, Ed Oldfield, and seek other instructors with the goal of flattening her decidedly upright swing plane. But after missing the cut at a tournament in Atlanta four weeks ago, King decided to scrap the experiment and renew her work with Oldfield.

"I had so many changes going on that I had to go back to someone that knew me a little," King explained.

In playing the best tournament of her life, King swung the golf club with "absolute, total confidence," as Carner put it. Her upright swing gave her the ability to carry the ball long distances off the tee and to land the ball softly with high-flighted approaches, which was the ideal mode of attack at Bethesda. But King, who has been a streaky putter most of her career, felt her play on the greens was the key.

"As good as I hit it, I think it was the putter more than anything," said King. "I just didn't miss one crucial putt."

She played so well today, she didn't have one.

# Some Advice to Male Players

## John Hopkins

*Financial Times*                    May 30, 1992

A few years ago Laura Davies was playing in a pro-am in Palm Springs, California. The members of her team were all men, and she worked hard to help them judge distances, select clubs and read putts. There was a lot of laughter and lively conversation from the group who were nearly all English.

The main aim of Davies's team was to combine well and win one of the handsome prizes that were on offer. It soon became clear, however, that there was another competition going on. It was the battle of the sexes. The aim in this competition was to outdrive Laura.

It was hopelessly one-sided. Davies, the biggest hitter ever in women's golf, once drove a ball 340 yards, and she regularly drives 260 yards. Few men can compete with her in this department, and, frankly, it is pointless to try.

But that is not to say there is nothing to be gained from watching women's professional golf. The opposite is the case. Most men amateurs can learn far more from watching a women professional golfer than from her male equivalent, because the game of the average player has much more in common with that of women professionals than with that of Seve Ballesteros. So the text for this morning is this: why can't a man be more like a woman?

Women professional golfers are prey to the same self-doubts that plague men. You do not like fast downhill putts? Neither do they. You find long bunker shots hard? So do they. Worried about shanking the occasional chip? So are they.

Men are reluctant to admire or learn from anything that is not male. They dress in their Nick Faldo shirts with their Ballesteros rainsuit in their bags. They tee up their two-piece, high-compression ball and stand on the first tee of a monthly medal hoping they won't make a complete hash of things. Faldo does not have the same fears nor does Ian Woosnam. But many women professionals do.

A golfing partner of my father's remarked last week: "I like watching the women play golf because I like to see their figures and look at their legs, but what I really like to watch is the rhythm with which they play golf."

This is the most obvious area in which men can learn from the women. Women have to acquire good rhythm because that is more than half the secret of hitting the ball any distance. This lesson was brought home to me when I played in a pro-am with Katrina Douglas. Bad weather restricted us to nine holes, but this was long enough for her to demonstrate the repetitive rhythm of her swing and her remarkable accuracy. After about six holes of watching this, a funny thing happened to me. I started swinging more slowly. And sure enough, I hit the ball better and further.

Another area where men can improve is in their attention to the short game. Men practice their long game, if they practice at all. Women do not ignore this department, but they do not concentrate on it at the expense of their short game. "When men practice they practice hitting their drives as far as they can" says Davies. "They think they miss a lot of full shots. But if they think about it, I reckon that nine times out of ten if they miss the green, they do not get up and down. They need to work on their short games. All amateurs are let down by their short game."

Helen Wadsworth is in her second season as a professional on the European tour and already she has noticed some characteristics among the men who play with her in pro-ams. The first is their tendency to underclub and to talk about their own game. The second is their inability to accept advice.

Bertie Wooster was once moved to remark: "Women, the way I looked at it, simply couldn't do . . . what a crew! What a crew! I mean to say, what a crew!" I beg to differ. Women are there to be learned from, however hard it is for the male ego to accept this. If you do not believe me, then go to a women's tournament in your area and see for yourself. You will be all the better for it. And your golf will improve, too.

# Deriving Benefit from Defeat

## Robert Sommers

1992 Curtis Cup Programme,                          June 5-6, 1992
Royal Liverpool Golf Club


Nothing is quite so valuable as a jewel lost or, more to the point at hand, a trophy taken away. Two consecutive losses in the Curtis Cup matches—in 1986 and again in 1988—brought home how highly we Americans treasured that old trophy and how sorely we missed it during those four lean years. Despite reclaiming the Cup in 1990 by 14-4 at Somerset Hills in New Jersey, the American players realized that they could no longer count on automatically winning the Curtis Cup.

The truth is that we had grown complacent; we felt the trophy was rightly our own. A day or two before the 1986 match, one of our players swaggered up to Judy Bell, our captain, and said: "We always win this thing, don't we?"

She had the right idea, of course, because except for four occasions in the 23 matches that had been played up to then, our side always did win. Great Britain & Ireland had won twice and two matches had been halved. Our side had held the trophy for twenty-four years. But at Prairie Dunes, your side won rather clearly—13-5. Two years later, at Royal St George's, Sandwich, the margin was down but the result was essentially the same—11-7 GB&I.

While familiarity might not have bred contempt, it had evidently spawned complacency and overconfidence. Our players expected to win, and the public had become so accustomed to our winning that they didn't care.

That unfortunate remark about the Americans always winning emphasized that, for the most part, American golfers have had only a vague idea about the history of the Curtis Cup. The two consecutive losses have changed all that.

When the players gather at Hoylake, you can be sure that every member of the American team will know the state of affairs precisely. They know that if they are to win, every team member must play her best golf.

Periodically during the era of automatic American victories, some critics called for an end to such a one-sided competition, claiming the Curtis Cup no longer served a useful purpose and that it should be abandoned—left to go the way of the dinosaur and the stymie.

It seems to me those were exclusively British critics. No such opinion surfaced on our side of the ocean, certainly not within the walls of the United States Golf Association. From the beginning, the USGA has treasured the match, as well as its relationship with the Ladies' Golf Union and the R&A, and has never considered calling it quits.

Mind you, there was a time during the dark period when our women lost those two matches that we wondered what had happened. Things weren't supposed to go that way, especially in 1986 when the two teams met at the Prairie Dunes Country Club, in Kansas, the heartland of the United States.

The American women played tentative, even timid golf at Prairie Dunes while the British team attacked. Walking with Polly Riley, among the gamest players American amateur golf has known, I gleaned some insights into how the Americans controlled the matches for so long. Polly had played in six consecutive matches, from 1948 through 1958, winning four of her six singles, usually with plenty to spare. She was always a bold competitor, and she couldn't understand why the American players at Prairie Dunes played such hesitant golf. There is little doubt that they had underestimated the opposition, but I believe the eventual outcome turned more on their cautious golf than on anything else.

Of course, the women's golfing scene has changed enormously from Polly Riley's playing days. With the financial attractions of professional golf being as rewarding as they are, we aren't likely to see many women play on more than one or two Curtis Cup teams. Half the players from the last two American sides have become professionals, and four players on the 1992 team, half the side, are new to the match.

We must remember, too, that Vicki Goetze, our best player, will be lost to amateur golf within another year or so. Carole Semple Thompson, however, is back for her seventh match.

Whether this American team will be strong enough to win again and perhaps set off another run of consecutive victories, won't be known for a few days yet, but it seems certain the Curtis Cup will never again turn into the walkover it was from 1960 through 1984. It would certainly be better for the match to remain as well-balanced as it has been lately. Your side is much too good these days, and, to tell you the truth, I wouldn't want it to happen.

# The 1992 Curtis Cup Match at Hoylake

## David Davies

The *Guardian*                    June 7, 1992

In a match that was never mean nor moody but just magnificent, Great Britain and Ireland won the Curtis Cup at the Royal Liverpool Club on Saturday, beating the United States by ten matches to eight.

It was the third time in the last four matches that the women, who unlike the Ryder Cup men have no Continentals to help them, had beaten the might of America. And aspects of Saturday's play, as the home team narrowly managed to compile the points they needed, were only a little less than fantastic.

As with the Ryder Cup at Kiawah, it went to the last hole of the last match, and it involved the youngest and perhaps the best player on both teams: nineteen-year-old Caroline Hall, recent winner of the English Girls' championship, and America's Vicki Goetze, also nineteen, draped with nearly every honor that a young golfer can win.

Knowing that her team needed a half-point for overall victory, and with her match against Vicki Goetze level, Caroline Hall surveyed the shot that would decide the cup's home for the next two years.

She was in the semi-rough to the left of the 18th fairway with about 170 yards to carry the bunkers in front of the green and to avoid the bunkers to the left and right of the green. Fortunately her ball had landed on a lovely smooth patch of fescue grass running towards the green, and she was able to use it as a launching pad for the four-iron shot she decided to play. Goetze had previously played a 5-wood from 180 yards out, and her ball had caught a greenside bunker, but Goetze was always dangerous from the sand.

It wasn't an easy shot at all. A brisk ten to fifteen miles-an-hour wind was directly in her face, everything was at stake, the entrance to the green was perilously narrow, and the course was Hoylake, which had earned a reputation in the numerous Amateur and Open championships held there of having, in Bernard Darwin's words, "Surely the most exhausting finish to be found on any links in the world." From the

*Vicki Goetze needed to sink this bunker shot on the
eighteenth to win her singles match.*

*After Caroline Hall beat Vicki Goetze on the last hole
and Great Britain and Ireland won the Curtis Cup, the
whole team came out to congratulate her.*

moment it was struck, the ball was bound for the heart of the green, and
when it finished, some twenty feet beyond the pin, Hall had pulled off
an historic shot and Great Britain and Ireland had won the Curtis Cup.

Hall's battle with Goetze showed those two prodigious talents at their
best. Both had been deliberately placed at the bottom of the order as
anchor-women, and both had responded by playing superbly. Both were
around in 72, two under par, which, on a perfect links day of bright sun
and a brisk breeze, represented outstanding play.

# Catching Up with Virginia Van Wie (II)

## Reid Hanley

The Chicago Tribune                              June 24, 1992

She is the best woman golfer in Chicago history: Virginia Van Wie. She won the U.S. Women's Amateur championship in 1932, 1933, and 1934. She retired at the age of twenty-five at the height of her career. There was no place else that she could go. There was no LPGA Tour, no TV exposure, no big money endorsements—just more of the same. "I was satisfied," Van Wie recently said at her summer home in Michigan. "I didn't want to turn pro. I still played the game but not in competition. I don't think I missed out on anything."

Miss Van Wie made her mark without the tremendous support provided today's young female golfers. When she started playing, there was no United States Girls championship, no golf team at her high school, and the Chicago District Golf Association had no tournaments for girls. She was fortunate to come from a wealthy family that could support her coast-to-coast tournament play from the time she was forteen until she retired from competition.

Miss Van Wie, who played out of the Beverly Country Club, was a child prodigy. She took up the game at twelve, and two years later she was playing at the top amateur level. She won her first title, the Western Junior, at sixteen. She won the Chicago District title three times the Florida State twice, the Florida East Coast twice, the Mid-South once, and the South Atlantic twice. The Women's Western Amateur was the only title that eluded her.

During the last three years of her competitive career, she was the best woman player in the world. In 1932 she defeated the great Glenna Collett Vare, 10 and 8, at the Salem Country Club in Massachusetts. The next year, at the Exmoor Country Club in Highland Park, on the edge of Chicago, she defeated Helen Hicks, a close friend, 4 and 3. In 1934, she was a 2-and-1 winner over Dorothy Traung at Whitemarsh Valley near Philadelphia.

"It's hard to choose one championship over another," said Miss Van Wie, who still plays occasionally. "The first victory in a national championship is always great, and the last one made it three in a row. In the middle one, I played in front of my family and my friends—the championship was held at Exmoor."

Her first victory was an amazing display of golf for those times. She was 4 under par on her first eighteen holes of the final with a 73 that put her 8-up over Mrs. Vare, who had defeated her twice previously in the final. Van Wie's chipping and putting were flawless.

After her final victory in 1934, Van Wie left the game she loved so much. Over the years she owned an ice-cream parlor in Florida, and then became a market researcher for a Chicago food company. In the mid-1950s, she finally turned professional, teaching the Ernest Jones method of swinging the clubhead, the method with which she became the best in the game. She taught in her studio on East 75th Street until 1975.

*She is not a movie star posing as a golfer. She is Virginia Van Wie, one of the finest amateur golfers of all time.*

# Oakmont Prepares for the 1992 Women's Open

## Pamela Emory

Golf Digest                                                        July, 1992

The city of Pittsburgh and its golfing pride and joy, the Oakmont Country Club, have hosted some of the most important events in men's golf: six U.S. Opens, four U.S. Amateurs, three PGA championships, and two NCAA championships. Now that the club is eighty-nine years old, it will finally test the championship mettle of the best players of the other sex by hosting the U.S. Women's Open this July.

Oakmont isn't the first club of its stature to host both the Open and the Women's Open. Baltusrol, Winged Foot, Atlanta Athletic, and Hazeltine National all have been the site of both championships, although seldom on the identical courses. But Oakmont offers a rare opportunity to compare how the U.S. Golf Association adjusts its course setup for the two Open championships.

By definition, Open courses are long, with narrow fairways, thick rough, and the slickest and firmest of putting greens. "What separates the Open from all the other events is that you know the numbers won't be real low," Meg Mallon, the defending Women's Open champion, said recently. "I love playing the Open courses, and, because I respect them so much, I think I probably focus more than I do during regular tournaments. Of course, I'd hate to try and make a living on them week in and week out."

The responsibility for insuring that Oakmont will play like the USGA wants it to—which is basically the same as Oakmont's architect, founder, and first chairman Henry C. Fownes, intended it to—rests primarily with Judy Bell, Secretary of the USGA. Bell comes by her authority and expertise honestly. She has been a top-notch player and was trained in course preparation by, she says, "the best possible teacher," the late P.J. Boatwright Jr., who was the USGA's longtime executive director of rules and competitions. She has been sharpening her skills for more than ten years, but she became "really focused" after the 1984 Women's Open at the Salem (Massachusetts) Country Club, where several greens were too firm and would not hold a properly struck shot. After Salem, Bell began to assume a more overt role in the preperation of the women's championship courses, assisting Boatright as a member and later the chairman of the USGA's Women's Committee—the group ultimately responsible for running the Women's Open.

Bell's primary responsibility, as she sees it, is to set up the course so that it insures fairness for all the players. "If someone, say Liselotte Neumann, can come along and shoot seven under par in the Women's Open, that's terrific," she says. "The main consideration is not the score the champion shoots, it's whether or not the course provided a fine test of all the skills a top player should possess."

Ann Beard, the current chairman of the Women's Committee, shares Bell's philosophy: "Judy wants, if it's possible, to have all four par 3s call for a different club. On the par 4s, a player ideally should be hitting a different club into each green. All the par 5s should be three-shotters except for one that will give the player the option of getting home in two."

If you consider 630 yards, 4-$\frac{1}{16}$ inches, and the difference between 10.5 and 11.5 on the Stimpmeter (roughly a foot's worth of roll) to be significant, then Oakmont is a different test for the fields in the men's Open and the women's Open. The bulk of the difference—total yardage—breaks down to some 35 yards less per hole for the women, which in most cases means a three-club swing. Most of the rest of the difference—the four and a fraction inches—is in the height of the rough. The USGA requests two inches of primary rough for the women and five for their stronger brethren, with smaller variances in the respective heights of the intermediate rough.

In addition to its renowned Church Pew bunkers, Oakmont is most famous for, and proud of, its putting surfaces. They are immense, averaging about 7,500 to 8,000 square feet, with the mammoth ninth green, which encompasses the club's practice putting green, measuring a whopping 18,000 square feet. But the speed of the greens is the factor members like to brag about most. For everyday play they run at a Stimpmeter reading of 10.6 to 11. Head course superintendent Mark Kuhns says, "We can get them up to 12.6 and higher for 'special events' without really trying." Kuhns recalls, with a chuckle, how once during his first spring at Oakmont he and his assistant were driving up the second hole and were called over by two elderly members. "We were real worried at first, but it turned out they just wanted to shake our hands," he says. "They told us, 'These greens are perfect. We just hit onto No. 1 and rolled over the green. Chipped back and then three-putted. They're perfect!' "

It's a fact that most women do not have the strength . . . which creates the hand action . . . which creates the spin . . . which makes the ball stop on a dime . . . that the men do. Good women players can handle the speed of the Open greens, even at Oakmont, but they cannot deal as effectively as men with extremely fast *and firm* greens. The biggest actual difference at Oakmont for the Women's Open is insuring slightly softer greens than for a Men's Open. To that end, Kuhns will reduce the time his crews spend rolling the greens and will monitor the moisture level to keep them a little softer than normal.

Otherwise, the USGA has requested few alterations in Fownes's masterpiece. The par-4 15th hole, like the par-4 18th, will receive a new, very basic teeing ground. The original tee on the long, par-3 eighth has been enlarged, reshaped, and redirected. The fairway on the 17th, a par 4 of only 285 yards (322 for the men), will be widened about five yards to decrease the severity of the dogleg, and the rough in front of the green will be eliminated to entice players to try driving the green, as such greats as Ben Hogan and Jack Nicklaus have done. Finally, Oakmont, on its own initiative, has begun a bunker restoration project, which is no small undertaking, considering that the course has over 180 bunkers.

It is a testament to the strength and beauty of Oakmont's architectural design that so few changes have been requested. As Judy Bell explains, "What dictates course setup *is* the golf course. You don't go to Oakmont or Colonial or Five Farms and take your little cookie cutter and go to work. You let the course dictate the flavor. "For instance, historically, around the greens we had an intermediate cut and a primary cut of rough. Last year at Colonial, we tried to bring the pitch-and-run shot back into the game and create some variety around the greens. It's subtle, but the players know it. Some of us involved with course set-up believe it takes as much nerve and skill to hit a delicate little pitch-and-run as it does to hit a sand wedge out of long grass—possibly more."

Oakmont is a classic example of how certain holes on a great golf course that is designed for the good male golfer are all wrong for the good female player. The first, 10th and 18th holes, for instance, are fabulous par 4s for men but they severely challenge the length limits for a women's par 4. The 18th is a good example of the great/weak finishing hole, depending on gender. It is listed as 456 yards for a men's Open but will measure 419 yards for the women. The hole plays downhill from the tee, with bunkers guarding both sides of the landing area. This setup presents more of an obstacle off the tee for the women, since men can carry the hazards with ease. The second shot plays uphill, and here is where the 35-yards female-male difference seems more like 60.

On an overcast day last July, Judy Dickinson, Beth Daniel, Pat Bradley, Missie Berteotti and Betsy King played Oakmont. The clubs they used for their second shots on 18 ranged from a 5-wood to a 4-iron for the long-hitting Daniel, which put her relatively in the same league as the men who have won the Open at Oakmont. In 1953 Hogan used a 5-iron for his second shot on the last hole of the last round. Nicklaus hit a 6-iron on his 72nd hole in 1962, and Johnny Miller, the 1973 champ, hit a 7-iron into 18 when he shot his remarkable 63 in the final round. All the other women playing with Daniel hit fairway woods to the 18th green, which is what Larry Nelson did when he won in 1983.

The 18th is one of Bell's major concerns as she completes plans for the setup of Oakmont. She describes the hole as a "really *big* hole that plays as the longest par 4 on the golf course because the second shot is all uphill. The green is well bunkered and it's elevated. There's an abandoned tee slightly forward of the present tee, which we may restore. There's a trade-off here—if we shorten the hole by using this forward tee, then we take the fairway bunkers out of play, but we make the second shot much fairer."

Women may never be as strong as men—in a muscular sense—but the sexes seem equal when it comes to an ability to complain about the difficulty of an Open site. Betsy Rawls, one of only two four-time Women's Open champions, looks forward to a real gripe session this year: "You know the scores will be high. It's kind of fun to have a golf course so tough, the way an Open should be. You know you've got a good test if the pros start complaining. They don't *have* to play in it. It's *fun* to have a tough golf course. I *always* looked forward to it, whether I played well in it or not. I liked the challenge."

Oakmont, ranked seventh in Golf Digest's 1991 ranking of America's 100 Greatest Golf Courses, will give the world's best women golfers plenty to squawk about. But it will also give them a chance to play their most prestigious championship on one of the country's great golf courses under tournament conditions, as the architect intended it to be played.

And just like Women's Opens are supposed to be played.

# Oakmont Produces a
# Memorable Championship

## Jaime Diaz

The New York *Times*                                July 26, 1992

## Part I

Oakmont, Pa., July 26—Reacting to an 11th-hour lightning delay as if electrified with inspiration, Patty Sheehan courageously birdied the final two holes today to tie Juli Inkster after 72 holes of the 47th United States Women's Open.

Sheehan and Inkster, longtime rivals and friends seeking to win the most prestigious championship in women's golf for the first time, will be paired together on a drenched Oakmont Country Club course for the third straight day, Monday, in an 18-hole playoff beginning at 11 A.M.

Today, the two veterans produced one of the most exciting duels in the history of the championship. Each shot two-under-par 69 for a four-round total of four-under-par 280, four strokes better than the third-place finisher, Donna Andrews.

While Inkster's journey around historic Oakmont was almost exclusively limited to the fairways and greens of the 6,312-yard course, Sheehan took a more erratic but decidedly more dramatic route.

Two strokes back after three-putting the par-3, 16th, the 35-year-old Sheehan appeared to be a beaten player when United States Golf Association officials suddenly halted play because of lightning as the two players walked off the 17th tee.

After a deluge further soaked already soggy Oakmont, it took nearly two hours to prepare the course for the final two holes. It also gave Sheehan, who has been runner-up three times in this championship, a chance to marshal her energy for a remarkable finish.

"I just thought that I had lost several Opens and it was about time I showed some guts," said Sheehan, who came closest in 1990 when she led by ten strokes with thirty-three holes to go before losing by one stroke to Betsy King. "I never gave up, I never give up."

*In the 1992 U.S. Women's Open at
Oakmont, Patty Sheehan birdied the last
two holes of regulation play by sinking putts
of ten and eighteen feet to tie Juli Inkster
and force a play off.*

Guts is exactly what Sheehan showed. When play resumed, she hit a
sand wedge from 65 yards within 10 feet of the flag on the par-4 17th.
Inkster, who missed only one fairway and one green on one of the most
difficult courses the women have ever played, followed with a wedge of
her own to 12 feet.

Inkster's putt, which would have wrapped up the championship, hit
the right lip of the hole before spinning out. Sheehan, whose last putt
of any length had been a five-footer she missed for her par on the 16th,
seemed a new player as she drilled her birdie putt into the center of the
cup.

That accomplished, Sheehan drove into the edge of right rough on
the 390-yard par-4 18th, while Inkster again positioned her ball in
the fairway. From 155 yards, Inkster hit a solid 6-iron to twenty feet
below the hole. Because of casual water, Sheehan was allowed to drop
in the fairway, from where she hit a 5-iron just inside of Inkster.

The 32-year-old Inkster, who earlier this year lost the Nabisco Dinah

*Good friends Juli Inkster (left) and Patty Sheehan were paired for 54 holes of Open competition.*

Shore to Dottie Mochrie in a sudden-death playoff, carefully stroked her approach putt to within a foot of the cup for a sure par. With the championship and her greatest golfing ambition on the line, Sheehan boldly stroked her uphill putt directly into the center of the hole.

"My last thought was just to get the damn thing to the hole," said Sheehan.

Until the lightning delay, it looked as if Inkster had met every challenge Oakmont and Sheehan had thrown at her. Her on-target, high-trajectory game had been the perfect answer to Oakmont's extreme length and precariously perched pins. Meanwhile, her steadiness looked as if it would wear down Sheehan, her former San Jose State teammate and former California neighbor.

Let us go back to the start of the round. Inkster took a two-shot lead when Sheehan bogeyed the first two holes after hooking her drives into the rough. Sheehan cut the deficit to one with a tap-in birdie on the par-4 third.

Inkster increased her lead to three with birdies on the fourth and seventh. Sheehan answered with a birdie at the eighth, but Inkster applied what looked like a death blow when she holed a 20-footer for birdie at the par-5 ninth. When Sheehan left her 12-footer short, she once again trailed by three.

Sheehan fought back with a brilliant birdie on the par-4 tenth, the most difficult hole on the course, when she holed a curling, downhill 20-footer. Inkster bogeyed the hole, and now led by only a single stroke. On the 572-yard 12th, Sheehan dropped another stroke to par and fell two strokes behind.

On the 396-yard 15th, Sheehan hit a bold approach to 10 feet, while Inkster, playing for the middle of the green, left herself a 30-footer. She again hit her approach too firmly, leaving herself a difficult four-footer. The putt undoubtedly looked longer after Sheehan holed for birdie, but Inkster, with her lead on the line, once again knocked in her comeback putt.

After Sheehan bogeyed the 16th to trail by two, both players hit good drives on the par-4 17th. But just as they strode off the tee, the U.S.G.A. sounded the siren, terminating play.

"There's nothing I can do about it," Inkster said in a television interview during the postponement. "I think the U.S.G.A. did good pulling us off."

"Funny things can happen, Juli," Sheehan told her rival during the same interview.

Funny and stunning and spectacular.

# Part II

Oakmont, Pa., July 27—The United States Women's Open was the tournament Patty Sheehan would go to each year to get her heart broken. It was where her swing and her nerves failed down the stretch, where other players made the key shots and where she found a way to finish second in the championship she wanted more than any other.

But today, in an 18-hole playoff at historic Oakmont, Sheehan received a cosmic payback as the 35-year-old defeated Juli Inkster by two strokes to win the 47th edition of the biggest title in women's golf.

With inspiration and guts more than flawless shot-making, Sheehan posted a one-over par 72 and finally broke through in the championship in which she had been runner-up three times. Amid the oppressive humidity that rose from Oakmont's soggy fairways, it was Sheehan who seemed comfortable on the fabled greens, while Inkster never found her usually velvet putting touch on her round of 74.

When Inkster seemed poised to mount a charge with a superb tee shot on the par-3 13th, Sheehan knocked her shot just as close and made the birdie to increase her lead to three. And when Sheehan's tee-to-green game began to come apart, she used her short game to stand off Inkster.

It would be impossible to discern Sheehan's domination from raw statistics. Just as she had on Sunday, Inkster outdrove Sheehan on nearly every hole. By the end of the day, Inkster had hit fifteen greens in regulation to Sheehan's nine. But on the greens, where championships at Oakmont are always decided, Sheehan took only 29 putts and Inkster took 36.

"I made some really key putts, or otherwise Juli would be sitting here right now," said Sheehan. "It was just a matter of who got the lucky breaks early on. Fortunately for me, it was my turn."

For Inkster, the defeat was even more painful than her sudden-death playoff loss at another women's major championship—the Nabisco Dinah Shore—to Dottie Mochrie in April. She appeared to be the winner on Sunday until Sheehan recovered from a seemingly fatal three-putt green to birdie the 71st and 72d holes.

"I'm just disappointed because I played so well for five days," said Inkster, who was paired with Sheehan in the third and fourth rounds. "Patty made the putts when she had to. But it seems like my putting let me down when I've needed it most."

It appeared at times that Inkster was fighting against a pre-ordained script. Sheehan was on a roll from the time that lightning in the area stopped play on Sunday with two holes to go and Inkster leading by two strokes. When play resumed, Sheehan made two birdies to get into the playoff.

"I probably played that 18th-hole putt one thousand times in my head last night," said Sheehan of the 18-footer that forced the playoff. "I couldn't get it out of my mind. It was so exciting, I wasn't sure I was going to be able to get enough energy for today."

But when she woke up this morning, Sheehan felt so relaxed that she forgot to bring her golf clubs, leaving them in the private home where she was staying.

"I got back there in twenty minutes, and back here in about seventeen," Sheehan said of a drive that usually takes twenty-five minutes. "I was lucky there were no cops around."

Sheehan began the playoff with a birdie on the 419-yard par-4 first hole, where she hit a 2-iron from 206 yards to ten feet and made the putt. Inkster had two early opportunities to tie, but she missed a four-foot birdie putt on the second hole and a six-footer on the fifth.

Sheehan increased her lead to two when Inkster bogeyed from a bunker on the seventh, and made it three when she made a twenty-foot par putt on the difficult tenth as Inkster was making another bogey. The lead was back to two on the 153-yard thirteenth. Inkster hit a 6-iron to eight feet, but Sheehan responded with a 5-iron to ten feet. Seizing the moment, Sheehan holed her putt. When Inkster missed hers, she seemed beaten, although Sheehan had to protect her lead with three more one-putt greens before it was over.

The victory gives the thirteen-year veteran from Reno two major championships among her twenty-nine career victories. One more tour victory will put her in the L.P.G.A. Hall of Fame. Without another major beside the L.P.G.A. championship, which she won in 1983 and 1984, Sheehan would have needed 35 victories for entry.

# Mickey Wright Makes the Grade with a New Generation

## Steve Ellis

Golfweek                                                    May 8, 1993


As a freshman at Stanford University in the early fifties, Mickey Wright received a grade of "D" in, of all courses, golf. The teacher, Mrs. Brown, obviously was not impressed with Wright's college prep work, which included winning the 1952 U.S. Girls Junior championship.

"I haven't told that story in a while," Wright said, laughing. "I don't blame her. I was a smart-aleck whippersnapper back then."

It was Sunday, and Wright had just completed her final round in the $250,000 Sprint Senior Challenge at Killearn Country Club in Tallahassee. And while she did not win the tournament, she was in good spirits after shooting a one-over par 74, a four-stroke improvement over the previous day's score.

Not bad for someone who had played just nine 18-hole rounds since 1985 and had tackled the course sight unseen without a yardage card, trusting her vision and that of her friend and caddy, Peggy Wilson, a former LPGA Tour player. After failing to make a birdie the first day, Wright made three in succession Sunday on holes fifteen, sixteen, and seventeen, and, in addition, eagled the par-5 fifth when she knocked a 4-iron four feet from the flagstick.

But then, this is Mickey Wright, winner of 82 tournaments, a player considered the greatest woman golfer of all time, a player whose swing elicits awes and ahhs even from the half dozen or so other Hall of Famers in attendance last week who took time out to come over and watch her hit balls.

Wright—tall, trim, and still athletic-looking at the age of 58—could relax. She had passed the test. Apprehensive about playing competitively for the first time since 1985, she came away satisfied, or as satisfied as a noted perfectionist could be. Only her short game appeared rusty, betraying a long game that would make most of today's players envious.

"I played a little better today." she admitted. "At the beginning of the

509

week I would have been happy to break 80 both days". She was using the same Wilson Staff irons and woods she has had since 1963 and wielding the Bulls Eye putter she had used to record each of her 82 victories. "I'll take the few good shots home with me and forget the bad ones."

Although Wright finished fourteen shots behind the eventual winner, Sandra Palmer, the gallery, which included a number of current LPGA players, could have cared less about what she shot. They were there to see in person for the first time a legend they had only heard about.

"I was fortunate enough to have been paired with Mickey a couple of times in the early '80s, but I told as many players as I could that it might be worthwhile to come out and watch her play," said Kathy Postelwait. "One player asked me, 'Who's Mickey Wright.' I felt like slapping her.

"To me, she was my version of Palmer and Hogan growing up," Postelwait added. "She's the best there ever was. For a lot of players, it's like seeing a god."

Australian Jane Crafter galleried both days, watching and learning. "I like the history of the game, and I am anxious to learn more. This is awesome." she said. "When I watch her hit balls, her plane and angles are perfect."

"I can learn more here today than anywhere else," said Missie Berteotti, who taped Wright's final round. "I can't say I'm a golf historian and know the swings of all the great players of the past, but I'm really impressed with Mickey Wright's swing."

Patty Sheehan was up bright and early Saturday morning, sitting in the bleachers behind the driving range to watch Wright hit balls. It was 7:30, and Sheehan did not tee off until five hours later. It was another forty-five minutes before Wright appeared, but Sheehan didn't mind.

"How many times do you get to see a legend?" she explained.

"Is that impressive?" she asked of Wright's swing. "It's so fluid. No hitches. No wasted movement."

Wright was pleasantly overwhelmed by the attention from the players. "This has been a delightful experience, especially meeting all of the young girls. I was sincerely flattered by their interest."

With that, Mickey Wright said a few more goodbyes and then made the trip back to her home in Port St. Lucie, FL.

# Re-Enter Mickey Wright

## Steve Ellis

Golfweek                                              May 8, 1993

Some things about Mickey Wright have not changed in the nearly twenty-five years since she graced the fairways of the LPGA Tour on a regular basis with her classic swing and strong opinions.

Wright exhibited both during a rare public appearance last week at the LPGA's Sprint Classic. The 58-year-old Hall of Famer was there to participate in the Sprint Senior Challenge, her first competition since she and Kathy Whitworth teamed in the 1985 Legends of Golf.

Wright quit playing regularly in 1969 at the age of 34, although she continued to play occasionally through 1980, winning the Colgate Dinah Shore Winner's Circle tournament in 1973 and losing in a playoff to Nancy Lopez in the 1979 Coca Cola Classic.

The player Ben Hogan said had "the finest golf swing I ever saw, man or woman" admitted during a congenial April 29th press conference—which drew a standing-room only crowd of reporters, players, and tournament officials—that she rarely plays golf anymore, opting instead to tend to her garden, go fishing, and follow the stock market.

"When people ask me what do I do," Wright said, "I say, 'I just live.' As you all know, that takes a lot of time."

Wright's well-known aversion to publicity was not apparent during the conference. In a 20-minute give-and-take, she was candid, charming, witty, and self-effacing.

"I'm very flattered that people like Patty Sheehan are interested in seeing me," Wright said of her Hall of Fame colleague who was seated at the back of the room.

She said she was "scared to death" about playing in the tournament. "I'm just two pops off 60 and this golf swing will not be what it was 30 years ago, and I hope no one expects it to.

"Someone told JoAnne Carner I had a bug—I've had a little bronchitis and have been taking some antibiotics—and JoAnne said, 'Bug my foot, she's got a butterfly.' And she might be right."

Wright said she played her first 18-hole round of golf since the Legends four weeks before arriving here. But she added that she practices almost daily.

"I'm fortunate enough to live on a golf course (Sandpiper in Port St. Lucie, FL), and I have a little driving range mat on my back porch where I can hit balls most every day onto the 14th and 15th fairways. I start as soon as the sun comes up, and my house is far enough along that people don't come through until 10 or 10:30, so I'm out there every morning scurrying to pick my balls up."

Wright officially retired because of a growth (metatarsal neuroma) on her foot that made it painful to wear shoes, but she said surgery corrected that. She admitted a bigger reason she stopped playing was the pressure and demands of success.

Wright won 80 of her 82 tournaments over a 12-year span. Her close friend Whitworth, who won 88 tournaments, believes that Wright's total could have been far greater. "I've maintained for years that Mickey could have won another 100 tournaments if she hadn't quit early," Whitworth has said. "The pressure on Mickey was so great. Sponsors would threaten to cancel a tournament if Mickey didn't play. And knowing that if she canceled, the rest of us wouldn't play, Mickey would always play."

Wright said the pressure "exhausted" her.

"I'm not real good as far as wanting to be in front of people, glorying in it and loving it. And I think you have to love that to make that kind of pressure tolerable.

"It finally got to where it wasn't tolerable to me."

Wright did not shy away when asked her opinion on some of the issues facing the LPGA today. When asked if the criteria for the Hall of Fame should be changed, she said no.

"I think it should be exactly the way it is, no easier, no harder. I don't think the criteria is as hard as I've heard people say it is. And I honestly can't think of anybody who should be in there who isn't there already or is certain to be."

Mickey said she admired the play of contemporaries like Donna Caponi, Judy Rankin, and Marlene Hagge, each of whom won over 20 tournaments but is not in the hall. She asked, "Where do you draw the line? The Hall of Fame should be special, and everybody shouldn't be in it.

"People always tell me I won my tournaments when there weren't as many good players as there are today, and that this state of affairs will probably never happen again," Wright added. She averaged 11 wins a year between 1961 and 1964. "I disagree with that. I think that about

*Mickey Wright made a rare public appearance during the Sprint Senior Challenge in Tallahassee, Florida.*

every ten years you are always going to have two or three players coming along who can dominate.

"Someone is going to come along in women's golf—and maybe she's already out there—who can win ten tournaments a year even with a field of 144 good players. All they have to do is think they can."

As for her thoughts on what the LPGA must do to improve, she said: "The only thing I can think of, and Commissioner (Charles) Mechem may not agree, is that you need more good players. Good players need to work harder and do whatever they have to do to get better.

"Fine players make any sport. Publicity and marketing are essential, but until you get fifteen Patty Sheehans every week out there battling, it isn't enough. The more good players, the more great players are bound to come along, and the more golf fans will come out and watch."

Wright said she would welcome the opportunity to work with players. She said she hasn't in the past because none have asked.

"I'm not making any comparison, believe me, but I remember when I lived in Dallas and Hogan practiced every day at Shady Oaks in Fort Worth, I bought a membership so I could go over there every day and watch him practice. It took me about a year and a half before I ever said a word to him.

While it has been suggested her name might be worth millions in endorsements, Wright said she has no interest in pursuring them.

"Golf is just one thing to me—the pure pleasure of the golf swing."

# Illustrations

*Afterword*

*by*

*Peggy Kirk Bell*

*I can't recall ever finding a four-leaf clover, and I've looked for them too. Glenna Collett Vare found them all the time. Everyone knew that she had this special gift: the ability to find four-leaf clovers. Perhaps that's why she was such a great putter—she could read the lines and slopes so clearly. When I played in the 1950 Curtis Cup match in Buffalo, Glenna was the Captain of the U.S. team, and the night before the first day's play she posted my name for the singles competition. I was petrified I would lose, so I went to her that night and pleaded with her to take my name off the list. The Curtis Cup is such an important event—the most important for women amateurs. I remember when JoAnne Carner was inducted into the PGA World Golf Hall of Fame, she said, "The happiest days of my life were my amateur days". What a statement for a professional to make! Anyway, I just didn't think I could handle the pressure of playing for my country. I remember almost begging Glenna: "Please don't play me." Glenna just said: "I call the shots. I'm the captain. You're playing."*

*The next day in my match I was one down with three holes to play. Glenna was watching from the left side of the fairway. She came over and asked me how I stood. I told her I was one down. Glenna walked off and came right back holding a four-leaf clover she had just found. She handed it to me and said: "Go get her". I won on the eighteenth.*

*I'm pleased to find so many articles about Glenna in this book. She was my idol. She managed a golf career and a family. She was wonderful with the young golfers. I was just beginning when her career was winding down. She won her sixth national championship in 1935, I think. I didn't start playing until after that—the summer before I went away to college. I recall thinking it was much too hot on the courts to spend the whole summer playing tennis. I asked the golf professional about playing golf. He loaned me a couple of old clubs, gave me a few balls and showed me how to grip the club. I lost all the balls on the first hole. I walked in and told the pro I wanted to learn how to play, figuring that he would show me then and there. "You'd like to learn how to play*

518

*golf?" he asked. I nodded. "O.K., come over tomorrow at nine o'clock, and I'll give you your first lesson."*

*I played some golf with Glenna. The first time I did I noticed how her left foot came up quickly and was slapped down even faster. She'd just twirl it up and down as fast as a wink, and I said to myself: "So that's her secret. A six-time winner of our national championship, and I've discovered her secret." I had a relatively slow swing, and I started pumping my left foot up and down like Glenna. Helen Sigel Wilson, who was playing with us, noticed my contortions and asked me what on earth I was doing. "I'm trying to copy Glenna's foot-action," I replied. "That's probably the worst part of Glenna's swing," said Helen. "That foot popping up and down". Well, of course, I stopped trying to copy Glenna. But that swivel wasn't all that bad. It showed how much she used her legs and her feet in her swing.*

*Glenna used to stop at the Pine Needles resort on her way to Florida. She had fond memories of the hotel and golf course when the property was owned by George Dunlop, the winner of the 1933 U.S. Amateur championship. Of course, Glenna had been a regular at nearby Pinehurst where the women's North and South championships are held. She won it three years in a row—in 1922, 1923, and 1924. George had asked Glenna to stay at his hotel during the winter and play golf with the guests. She told me: "Peggy, I sold every lot on that golf course that there was to sell, and I got to play golf there most of my winter, and I love that course!"*

*Glenna had a very quick swing, just like her foot-work. She played quickly too, and it all stemmed from her having such a quick mind. I'll always remember what she said at the 1950 Curtis Cup dinner in reply to the British captain, Diana Fishwick Critchley. Diana had beaten Glenna in the final of the 1930 British Ladies' championship at Formby. It was a fluke. Diana couldn't carry Glenna's bag, but she had the gall to get up at the dinner and say: "I hope that my team can do to your team what I did to your captain in 1930 at Formby." Glenna, who hated public speaking, was so angry she jumped to her feet and said: "Let's hope that the best team wins—this time." That's how quickly her mind worked. She wasn't happy unless she could play speedily like the British do. She'd go through people who were playing slowly. She'd just say, "We're going through", and drag the rest of us with her.*

*After Glenna I was closest to Babe Didrikson Zaharias. I loved the Babe. Glenna was shy and modest. She was always saying how Joyce Wethered was the best golfer and how JoAnne Carner would have won more Amateur championships than she had if JoAnne hadn't turned professional. Well, the Babe was the opposite. No one had ever been better at anything. And I mean* anything. *She showed us, for example, how good she was at ironing. She'd be ironing our shirts in my room, and she'd say: "Look at this—I'm the best ironer there is". She probably was, too. She was a marvelous cook, and she could knit and sew like a demon. She included men in her long list of what she did better than anyone else. One night at dinner—it was in Los Angeles, I believe—a gentleman came up to our table and, in the most polite way, said: "Mrs. Zaharias, I hate to bother you at a time like this, but we have made a sizeable bet on how far you threw the javelin in the Olympics." The Babe hardly turned her head and said rather rudely: "Farther than anyone else in the world". The man was most embarrassed. We were shocked and told the Babe she had to go over to his table and apologize. It wasn't like Babe to be rude to people. She had a great sense of humor. She said, "Watch this. I'm going to have some fun." She strolled over, pulled up a chair and sat down with them. "Let's talk about me for a change," she said to them. She spent twenty minutes with them, and they loved her.*

*Then there was the time in New York City after she was named Woman Athlete of the Year. (I forget which year, she won the award so many times). The press asked her what her plans were for the coming year. She said she intended to play in the U.S. Men's Open championship. The press ran out, and the story flashed across the country. The USGA hurriedly called a special meeting to officially ban all women from the men's Open. She never intended to play in the men's Open, but she loved to shock people.*

*The first time I met the Babe was during the 1945 Western Women's Open. Her mother had just died, and I asked her what she was going to do. I assumed she would withdraw. She said: "I'm going to win it for my mother". She did. A few months later, the phone rang and a voice said: "This is the Babe. Are you going to Florida this winter?" I said I was. "Well, I am too, and I need a partner for the Women's International Four-Ball, and you might as well win a tournament." I should mention that this was not an idle boast. At the time she called me, she had won something like seven tournaments in a row, including the national championship. We did, naturally, win the Women's International—that was ten in a row. I was so nervous before that tournament I was literally shaking. "What's the matter with you?" asked the Babe. I told her I was afraid we'd lose because of me and ruin her streak. "I can beat any two of them without you," she replied. "I'll let you know if I need you."*

*We spent a good deal of time with Tommy Armour when we were in Florida. The Babe had improved her golf swing enormously before Tommy worked with her, but he refined her game. Early in her career, she had a big, long, loopy, John Daly-like swing and had no idea where the ball was going. Then she practiced and developed a short, upright, compact, Byron Nelson-type action. She became much straighter and just as long. She loved Tommy, and Tommy loved her. He refused to call her anything but Mildred. Whenever we weren't in a tournament, we'd hurry down to Boca Raton, have lessons in the morning, and tee it up with Tommy in the afternoon. He refused to teach me until I learned how to waggle correctly. "I want your waggle to be this small half-circle: back here, down here, back again, down here. It's the swing in miniature. That's all there is to it. That's the whole deal". To this day I have that little circle waggle of Tommy's.*

*I once asked the Babe how she hit the ball so far. Most people think she was a big woman. She was not. She was 5'6" and not at all heavy, but she had strong legs and arms. "I just keep my elbows together, and I hold the club very softly in my hands." Then she spoke about a muscle in her back, behind her shoulder. She believed this large back muscle had something to do with her distance. She had an extremely simple swing. Sometimes it looked as though she was falling backwards in her finish, but that was because she came through so fast she sort of recoiled like a gun going off. Actually, she was in perfect balance. I remember one time we were playing with Sam Snead, and Snead, remember, was very long. On one of the early holes—we were all playing from the same tees— Snead's drive ended up a few yards behind the Babe's. He couldn't believe it. He accused her of playing with souped-up balls. "Where'd you ever get those balls?" he kept asking. Oh, she could hit it. She was the longest I've ever seen until perhaps Laura Davies. I think she was a little longer than Mickey Wright, who hit the ball like a man with the best swing ever. And could the Babe get it out of the rough! Where I would have to take my sand-wedge and just blast the ball out, she'd take whatever club she needed and just swing right through the grass.*

*The real beauty of her golf was her short game. She was a sensational putter, like Glenna Collett. The Babe putted with her shoulders, her feet close together, and her left elbow pointed directly at the hole, which steadied her wrists. Five and six-footers were "gimmes" to her. Her wedge play was equally superb. How she could hit those little shots in tight to the pin! You could ask Patty Berg or anyone about her wedge play, and all they could do was shake their heads and say, "Whoooo".*

*After she won her seventeenth tournament in a row—her sixteenth was the British Ladies', and she was the first American to win it—she decided that so much money was being offered to her that she had to turn professional. Her husband, George, was making a good living, but the money was too big to turn down. Fred Corcoran, the promotion director of the men's Professional Golf Association, was anxious to set up a wom-*

en's pro tour around the Babe. It certainly does not disparage anyone else
to say that the Babe almost singlehandedly put the women's tour on the
map. She had a famous name and personality; she was a born showperson; she could talk almost anyone with money into sponsoring a tournament; and she could handle the press. Not many could do that.

Whenever I played a practice round with the Babe before a tournament, I tried to beat her because she was the best. She played casually on
her practice rounds and sometimes hit a few extra balls. The press was
always waiting for her. One time I heard her tell them she'd had a 70.
"You didn't have a 70", I said to her later. "Well, I should have," she
replied. "I tell them what they want to hear. They don't care about a 75.
They're not going to print that." In this case, Louise Suggs had shot a
great 72 in her practice round, but the story was all about the Babe's 70.

Of course, the Babe was far from being only a showperson. She had
character and a burning desire to improve herself. She came from an
immigrant Norwegian family and, through golf, she felt she could rise to
the top. She had plenty of brains, too. She tied for first in the high jump
in the Olympics by going over the bar head-first. They took the medal
away from her because you weren't supposed to dive over the bar. Her
method was really a version of the "western-roll," which today is a standard method.

I don't think many people realize how much she did after she got
cancer—how much she helped other cancer patients—or how much she
and George loved each other. She loved people. She loved life more than
anyone else I can think of. "If I could just play golf again," she said at the
end. "If I could just watch it. You know, I love to paint. If I could just live,
I could paint".

Babe was fortunate to be so close to George, and, of course, for Glenna
Collett Vare, her family was paramount. It's relatively easy for golf to
become an obsession excluding everything else. I see it happening to some
of the young women players. They get caught up with the idea of being
the best—along with all the money that can be made these days—and,
suddenly, it's the only goal in their lives. They sacrifice everything for it.
Then they turn forty and look around and wonder where all the cute-
looking guys went. They don't have a husband. They don't have a family.
I'm involved with many young players, especially those promising
youngsters who are at college on scholarships. I sound like a broken
record with them: Golf is giving you your education, and some of you will
be good enough to go on and be professional golfers. Just don't miss the
chance to have a full life. Golf, believe it or not, isn't everything. When
you are playing and competing, you can't imagine a future without golf.
But that day will come. I feel so fortunate that I had a husband, have

*children and grandchildren, and golf. Golf is important to me. I love the game. I love what it can do for your character, and I love the wonderful people you get to know, like Glenna Collett Vare and Babe Didrikson Zaharias, but golf can't compare with my family.*

*Peggy Kirk Bell*